30

Usher Parsons in middle life. Loaned by Professor George Erikson of Brown University. Copy in Brown University Archives.

Yankee Surgeon

The Life and Times of
Usher Parsons

(1788–1868)

Seebert J. Goldowsky, M.D.

Published by
The Francis A. Countway Library of Medicine, Boston
In Cooperation with
The Rhode Island Publications Society
1988

Sole distributor:
Science History Publications/USA
a division of
Watson Publishing International
P.O. Box 493
Canton, Massachusetts 02021

ISBN 0-88135-088-5

Frontispiece: Usher Parsons in middle life. Photograph supplied by Professor George Erikson, Brown University. Copy in the Brown University Archives.

Yankee Surgeon is a publication of the Boston Medical Library and was supported in part by the Library's Jean Alonzo Curran-James F. Ballard Publication Fund.

Contents

List of Illustrations

Preface

There are a number of criteria by which a man may be evaluated:
the esteem of his contemporaries and his contributions to the life
and thought of his times, or in terms of his place in the long stream
of history and his contributions to intellectual and philosophical
advancement. In the latter perspective, Usher Parsons was not a
major figure, although his participation in the events of his day was
much more significant than has generally been realized.

The *Memoir of Usher Parsons*, published by his son Charles two
years after his father's death, sketched the essential facts of Usher
Parsons's life, but left him a somewhat colorless figure. Although
this slender volume and a rather limited body of available docu-
mentation served as the original basis for this study, several biblio-
graphical breakthroughs were later accomplished which led to an
almost embarrassing riches of source material. These showed that
Parsons was a man of wide interests and broad contacts, who participated personally in events of historical importance. His observations of these events have permanent value. He was a well-educated doctor for his day and a surgeon of proven competence. He
contributed to the medical literature of his time many well-written
essays that were equal to the best of his contemporaries, even if he
made no important basic contributions to the science of medicine.
His historical, biographical, and genealogical studies were solid,
although at times parochial.

I have aspired in undertaking this portrait to correct the deficiency of his earlier biography by presenting Usher Parsons as a live
being of flesh and blood, able, humane and intelligent, possessing
a native shrewdness and a keen sense of humor. His abundant letters
and diaries, discovered in the course of researching this work, reveal

that Usher was motivated by desires, loves, ambitions, and dislikes which are both human and eternal. Through them we gain a picture of the colorful times and the teeming scenes in which he lived and acted out his life. More importantly, they open a window upon the social and intellectual life of contemporary America in general and of Providence in particular, his place of abode for the greater part of his life. There can be no doubt that Usher Parsons lived a full and productive life in a significant period of American history. To document what he accomplished is adequate justification for this effort.

The capricious spelling in letters and diaries has occasionally been preserved. Punctuation has generally been modernized for ease of reading.

Acknowledgments

Many hands have touched this project since its genesis more than a quarter of a century ago. Librarians too numerous to mention from as far away as the British Museum in London and the Huntington Library in Pasadena, California have lent their invaluable skills. More especially I will mention my long-time friend, Helen Moffitt De Jong, Librarian Emerita of the Rhode Island Medical Society, who, first among many, started me on my way. I should also like to acknowledge the assistance of Paul Campbell of the Rhode Island Historical Society and Martha Mitchell of the Brown University Archives for many of the materials that illustrate this work.

I recall that the late George W. Potter, editorial writer of *The Providence Journal*, first acquainted me with Parsons lore when he showed me a copy of Charles W. Parsons's *The Medical School Formerly Existing in Brown University*. Soon thereafter the late Doctor Peter Pineo Chace, surgeon, authority on Doctor Samuel Johnson, and Editor of the *Rhode Island Medical Journal*, encouraged me to write my first piece on Rhode Island medical history.

Others have contributed significantly to this work. The late Theodore Woolsey Dwight of Albany, New York and Kennebunkport, Maine, great grandnephew of Usher Parsons, donated to Brown University the invaluable carefully preserved papers of Usher Parsons, while Hugh Upham Clark of Arlington, Virginia, a descendant of Ann Holmes Upham, Usher Parsons's sister-in-law, made available the abundant letters relating to Mary Holmes Parsons and the Holmes family. The late Georgia Stearns of Alfred, Maine; Joseph W. P. Frost of Eliot, Maine; and Doctor Lawrence D. Longo of Loma Linda, California have all been generous in providing access to their private collections of letters.

I am greatly indebted to Professor Patrick T. Conley of Providence College, historian, scholar, attorney, and friend, for understanding the significance of this project. He made available through the Rhode Island Publications Society and the Providence Heritage Commission grants to provide editorial assistance. I am also greatly appreciative of the financial support provided by Dr. and Mrs. Thomas Perry, Jr. of Providence. Richard Alan Dow of Hope, Rhode Island, through astute and perceptive editing, separated the wheat from the chaff, while Professor Philip Cash of Emmanuel College in Boston, Massachusetts, chairman of the history department and an authority on medicine in colonial America, provided scholarly editing and historical perspective.

I wish further to express my gratitude to my medical school classmate, Dr. Mark D. Altschule, clinician, scientist, editor, medical historian, and Honorary Curator of Prints and Photographic Collections in The Francis A. Countway Library of Medicine of the Harvard Medical School, and to Richard J. Wolfe, Curator of Rare Books and Manuscripts at the Countway, for their sympathetic understanding and sponsorship which have brought this project to fruition.

Finally, two other persons warrant special mention. The first is my former long-time secretary, the late Marie T. Clair, schoolteacher by profession and a war-time lieutenant in the Army Counterintelligence Corps, who labored by my side through many early rewritings and whose canny insight was a source of strength. The other is my devoted wife Bonnie, who helped in the typing of the first definitive draft and labored valiantly in transcribing to typescript the difficult Parsons diary and manuscripts, but, much more importantly, meticulously proofread the final version and encouraged and supported me throughout.

Major Sources Employed in Compiling This Work

Information for this biography of the Yankee surgeon Usher Parsons derives from a great variety of sources, both printed and unpublished. The *Memoir of Usher Parsons*, which his son, Charles, compiled and published a few years after his father's death, has served as the main outline for this work. In addition to preserving the direct impressions of his son, the *Memoir* provided source materials which Charles obtained from diaries and manuscripts, some of which have since disappeared or perished.

Charles wrote in the Preface of the *Memoir:*

> My father left a large amount of manuscript material illustrating different portions of his life. He had gathered together, probably during his visits to his native town, many fragments relating to the period of his boyhood and youth, which he had marked "juvenile." The documents pertaining to his naval career are particularly abundant, consisting of letters, diaries, hospital records, official accounts, requisitions and other papers, many of them of so little permanent importance as to make me wonder at their preservation, when I found them after his death. For many years he kept a diary. He also filled a series of note-books with more extended records of incidents in his life, reflections and reminiscences, containing many passages which throw great light on his personal history, and his modes of thinking.

Charles donated the naval diaries and the "Day Book of Practice" to the Rhode Island Historical Society, of which both he and his father were devoted members. Charles returned many letters to the senders, which probably accounts for a number of them appearing in the collection of papers cited below as the "Hugh Upham Clark Collection." Very few letters between Usher Parsons and his brother-in-law, Oliver Wendell Holmes, have survived. This results from the reckless destruction of many books and manuscripts found in the apartment of Justice Oliver Wendell Holmes after his death. There is only a scattering of letters in the Rhode Island Historical Society and the Rhode Island Medical Society. A bibliograhy of Parsons's writings in Charles's *Memoir* lists 58 items compiled, according to Charles, "from memoranda in his handwriting."

The main body of Parsons papers, which the author has titled the "Dwight-Parsons Collection," were apparently transmitted for safe-keeping to one of Charles's cousins (i.e. one of Usher's nephews), possibly George Parsons (Dwight's antecedent) or Henry Parsons. Charles died in 1893 without issue, his wife Mary Hallowell Boylston Parsons having predeceased him. The "Dwight-Parsons Collection" is the most important manuscript resource employed. This is a mass of Usher Parsons's papers, correspondence, and manuscripts which the late Theodore Woolsey Dwight of Albany, New York and Kennebunkport, Maine, great grandnephew of Usher Parsons, donated to Brown University and which are now preserved in the Brown University Library in Providence. Also at Brown are other materials relating to the subject of this biography, including scattered letters and the records of the Brown University Medical School, the Brown University Medical Association, and the Brown Corporation, all of which have reference to Usher's brief association with the university.

The manuscript collection of the Rhode Island Historical Society contains many manuscripts relating to Usher Parsons. In addition to the Society's own "Minutes," which record Doctor Parsons's Society activities, its Parsons holdings comprise the important diaries kept during the Lake Erie Campaign, the diaries which Doctor Parsons maintained during cruises on the naval vessels *Gurrière* and *Java*, his "Day Book of Practice" during his various naval cruises, notes he assembled for a contemplated (but never completed) life of Oliver Hazard Perry, and some letters. The diaries and many of the other items, it has been noted, were given to the Society by his son Charles. The Archives of the Rhode Island Medical Society and of the Providence Medical Association, which formerly were in the possession of the Rhode Island Medical Society, were in 1987 transferred to the Rhode Island Historical Society, and, at the same time, the Society's medical library was transferred to Brown University.

Another major source for this work is the mass of family papers constituting the "Hugh Upham Clark Collection." These are a portion of an extensive private collection of family papers, owned by Hugh Upham Clark of Arlington, Virginia, a direct descendent of Ann Holmes Upham, the sister of Usher's wife, Mary Jackson Holmes Parsons. These materials, which record the doings of the Holmes family, into which Usher married, are available on microfilm and in Xerox copies at The Francis A. Countway Library of Medicine of the Harvard Medical School. Most are also available in Xerox copies at the Rhode Island Historical Society. The service records of Usher Parsons while in the Navy in the 1812–1823 period are maintained in the War Records Division, Navy Branch, in the National Archives in Washington, D.C. Also preserved there is the official log of the U.S. frigate *Guerrière* kept during his service on that vessel and his invalid file, which details his petitions for a pension arising from a service-connected injury.

Usher's native state of Maine harbors several collections containing letters and manuscripts, either written by him or touching on his life. The Parsons Memorial Library in Alfred, Usher's birthplace, preserves letters he wrote to family and friends there, including, for example, his letters to his sister Frances Leighton. The Maine Historical Society in Portland has several of Usher's letters written to his friend and adviser John Holmes, as well as the diary of his brother-in-law, General Samuel Leighton. (A mimeographed copy of General Leighton's diary is also on deposit in the Parsons Memorial Library in Alfred.) Finally, there are pertinent materials in two private collections in Maine which are listed below.

Many of Doctor Parsons's letters to correspondents are scattered in libraries on the east coast, in the midwest, as far west as California, and in England—in the following institutions: the American Antiquarian Society, the Boston Public Library, the British Museum, the Buffalo Historical Society, Dartmouth College Library, the Henry E. Huntington Library, the Historical Society of Pennsylvania, the Houghton Library of Harvard University, the Massachusetts Historical Society, the New York Public Library, and the Ohio Historical Society.

Finally, three private collectors or holders, the late Georgia Stearns of Alfred, Joseph W. P. Frost of Eliot, Maine, and Doctor

Lawrence D. Longo of Loma Linda, California, have all been generous in providing access to their own collections of Parsons's letters.

A great many printed sources have been employed throughout this work, so many, in fact, that it would be useless to list them all individually. These are noted in the endnotes—with full citations initially and with abbreviated titles thereafter.

Abbreviations of Frequently Quoted Sources and Repositories
(Described in the foregoing explanation of sources)

C. W. Parsons *Memoir*	Charles W. Parsons, *Memoir of Usher Parsons, M.D., of Providence, R.I.* (Providence, Hammond, Angell & Co., 1870)
DPC	Dwight-Parsons Collection, Brown University Library
HUCC	Hugh Upham Clark Collection, Arlington, Virginia
RIHS	Rhode Island Historical Society
WRDNA	War Records Division, Navy Branch, National Archives, Washington, D.C.

CHAPTER ONE

Medical Apprentice

On a summer day in Alfred, Maine, in the early years of the new Republic, a male-child was born whose eventful and productive life was destined to span the first eighty years of the new nation. Usher Parsons, the last of nine children born to William and Abigail Parsons, came into this turbulent world on August 18, 1788.

William Parsons was the son of a Congregationalist minister and a fifth generation descendant of one Joseph Parsons, cornet of horse, who had emigrated from England in 1635.[1] In 1769 William had married Abigail Frost Blunt of New Castle, New Hampshire, the great-niece of Sir William Pepperrell, hero of the Battle of Louisbourg. Usher's peculiar first name came from his paternal grandmother, the daughter of New Hampshire lieutenant governor John Usher.[2]

William Parsons brought his wife and family to Alfred, then a part of Sanford in York County, during the eventful year of 1775. The chaste and graceful white farmhouse he built, and in which Usher was born, still stands on a shady road not far from the center of the village. Its present appearance, like that of the nearby village, probably has changed little since the days of Usher's boyhood.[3]

Besides managing a small farm, Parsons at various times manufactured lumber and potash, surveyed land, kept a retail store, for many years served as town clerk and selectman, and was the first justice of the peace in Alfred. He was associated at one time with the building of a grist mill. A "General List" of taxpayers (122 in all) dated March 28, 1799 is signed "Wm. Parsons, Principal Assessor." In 1806 he was appointed to a committee to draw plans and select a "proper site" for a courthouse. A plot was selected "on the southwest side of the road leading from Alfred meeting house to

1

Kennebunk ... and partly on the land of William Parsons." This beautiful building, a stone's throw from the Parsons homestead, still survives. In spite of his many interests, William Parsons, with a family of nine children to raise and educate, was never more than marginally prosperous.[4]

Maine, not yet separated from Massachusetts at this time, was considered a part of the frontier country. For the most part the economy of Alfred was self-contained. Grains grown for home consumption were ground at Parsons's or one of his neighbor's grist mills. Most of the villagers kept a cow, and livestock of all kinds grazed on the local hay and grass, providing an adequate supply of essential fertilizer for gardens. Farm implements were made within the town, the iron parts of the ox-drawn wooden plows forged by the village blacksmith. The family clothes were made of homespun from the wool of sheep grown on the farm. The artisans of this town of four hundred souls included a tanner, a weaver, a blacksmith, a shoemaker, a bowl and mortar turner, a potter, brickmakers, saw and grist mill operators, and the necessary millwrights.[5]

Usher grew up in this healthful, rural environment, attending classes during the winter in the old frame schoolhouse and working on his father's farm in the summer. He later recalled to his son, Charles, how on the last night of 1799 he had learned of George Washington's death, and had afterward walked in a solemn memorial procession with other school children, wearing crepe.[6]

Raised in the Congregationalist faith of his Puritan ancestors, Usher attended the local parish church where the Reverend Moses Sweat of Sanford, who in later years was his classics tutor, frequently preached.

A leading citizen of Alfred and a prominent figure in Maine politics was the eminent John Holmes, for many years a friend and adviser to Usher. Holmes entered Brown University in 1792, was admitted to the bar in 1798, and, looking around for a place to settle, tried his luck in Alfred, then a promising and prosperous young community. The first person he called upon was William Parsons, the only justice of the peace in town. In 1818, as congressman from Massachusetts, Holmes was a leader in the successful movement to confer statehood on Maine. He was immediately chosen as United States senator from the new state. His lovely home, built in 1802 and crowned by a balustrade decorated with a unique motif of bows and arrows, stands prominently in the village green today.[7]

In May of 1800, in his twelfth year, Usher was sent to nearby Berwick Academy, where he studied for about a year. The oldest preparatory school in Maine, founded in 1791, Berwick holds a charter signed by Governor John Hancock of Massachusetts. Little is known of this period in Usher's life, however, and there is no record of his stay at the school.[8]

During the next few years he served as a clerk in retail stores in Portland and Kennebunk, then a part of Wells. David Little, one of his employers, called Usher "a capable lad, possest of steady habits, and well calculated for bookkeeping." (Little was the father of Charles C. Little, co-founder of Little, Brown and Co., Boston publishers.)[9] During the summer of 1806 Usher sought employment in Boston. He was offered an apprenticeship but, because of his need for hard cash, declined.[10]

He left Wells on March 29, 1807, and on May 6 he entered the office of Doctor Abiel Hall (Senior) of Alfred to begin the study of medicine. Here he saw a little of medical practice, studied human bones, and read some medicine, including Cullen's *First Lines* and the works of Erasmus Darwin and Robert Brown. His medical apprenticeship was often interrupted while he worked on his father's farm or picked up a little money teaching school in Alfred, Berwick, Kittery, or other nearby towns. Doctor Hall, apparently an adequate country practitioner according to prevailing standards, probably had had no formal medical education of his own beyond the customary apprenticeship.[11]

Most physicians in New England acquired their medical knowledge through apprenticeship to older practitioners. Medical care in the smaller towns was provided almost exclusively by men trained in this way. The apprenticeship system was absolutely essential at the time, given the limited resources of the nation and the great demands on available capital. The economic returns provided little motivation for the establishment of medical schools, which under the circumstances were deemed to be a luxury. As a result there were few in existence. The sole medical schools in New England at the time were at Harvard and Dartmouth, and these were beyond Usher's meager resources. Only the sons of wealthy parents, ambitious to obtain the best in medical education, could afford to travel to Europe, and the schools in Philadelphia and New York seemed far away.[12] There were both advantages and disadvantages in training by apprenticeship. The more salient benefits were the opportunity provided by clinical training, the exposure to professional attitudes, and the avoidance of excessive theorizing. The narrowly based nature of the training and the lack of controls as to duration and quality of the education were, however, obvious liabilities.

Doctor Abiel Hall, Junior, who succeeded his father in practice in 1809, was a longtime friend and confidant of Usher's. In the late summer and fall of 1808, young Abiel attended a series of lectures on anatomy given in Fryeburg, Maine by the eminent Scottish anatomist Alexander Ramsay. The two young medical students carried on an active correspondence. Hall was impressed with Ramsay's knowledge, but judged him a better anatomist than physician. He admired Ramsay's excellent museum and library and sent Usher detailed summaries of the lectures. Hall's enthusiastic recommendation doubtless influenced his friend.[13]

By the summer of 1809 Usher was finally able to scrape together enough funds to attend a course of lectures with Ramsay at Fryeburg. That this world-renowned, if somewhat eccentric anatomist should have chosen to teach in the frontier wilderness was one of the peculiarities of the American scene. Of his talents there seems little doubt; that he was irascible eventually became evident to all. It was this educated, if somewhat odd, Scotsman who first inspired in Usher Parsons an ambition for the further pursuit of the discipline of anatomy.[14]

Usher had hoped to attend another course of lectures with Ramsay in the fall of 1809, but fate ruled otherwise. Many years later, Usher described how he charted his course for the future:[15]

> Being disappointed of a remittance from my father of some money to enable me to attend a second course of lectures in Portland by Dr. Ramsay, I walked fifteen miles in the night, nearly to Saco, slept a few hours on some hay in a barn, and reached Kennebunk the following noon, and Alfred in the evening. During my moonlight walk, I meditated on the past and the future course of my life. I thought of the misspent time of my past years, of my low aims in the medical profession until within the last weeks, and asked if it would be possible, at this my twenty-first year, to begin a new course that should redeem the time and

elevate me to a respectable rank in the medical profession. I was now wanting in preparatory education, unable to parse the most simple sentence in Latin, and hardly able to write a common letter in English grammatically. I had no means of educating myself but by school-keeping. How many years am I willing, I asked, to devote to this and to hard study for the attainment of a rank in the profession that, with my present ambitious views, I shall be satisfied with? I concluded that ten years would be required, and determined that all my energies should be employed for that length of time, and to be satisfied could I arrive at eminence in respect to knowledge, although the tenth year should find me as penniless as at this hour.

There is a tradition in Alfred that William Parsons wanted Usher to stay on the farm and had little enthusiasm for his eldest son's ambition to be a doctor. Although a somewhat prosperous trader, miller, farmer, manufacturer of potash and lumber (he had earlier supplied masts for British ships), land-holder, and town officer, he begrudged financial assistance to Usher that might have eased his struggle. Usher's story continues:

My resolution was now fixed and my plans matured this night, and in the main were not deviated from during that length of time. I determined to obtain the degree of A.M. and M.D. and to become a teacher of anatomy. On arriving at Alfred I packed up my Latin books and went to Sanford, four miles off, and placed myself in the family of Parson Sweat. I began with the Latin grammar, and by the last of November had gone over it several times and read two books of Virgil, and was able to read the Greek Testament a little.[16]

In his later years Usher recalled with gratitude and affection his debt to this bucolic scholar, who first introduced him to the splendors of the classics. The Reverend Sweat, who was fond of books and ardently interested in the study of oriental and dead languages, could read Greek and Hebrew fluently, and had "made some progress in the study of Syriac, Arabic, and Chaldaic!"[17]

In December 1809 Usher inquired of his kinsman, Doctor William Frost (who had established a medical practice in, of all places, Havana, Cuba) regarding the opportunities there for an American physican. Because of the uncertainty of transportation in those days, he did not hear from Frost until late in May of 1810. The prospects for a practice in romantic Havana, he learned, were most discouraging.[18]

Usher taught school intermittently in Berwick, Eliot, and Alfred, but also returned briefly to both Parson Sweat's home and Berwick Academy. Evenings he laboriously read Cicero and Virgil in Latin and the New Testament in Greek. To get through "college" in this tedious way, he concluded, would consume ten years. He determined, therefore, to return to medicine, to read with Doctor Abiel Hall in Alfred for a few months, study with an eminent physician for six months, and finally attend a course of lectures. He would then enter practice whenever a vacancy appeared, meanwhile continuing his "college" studies. He sought out Doctor Thomas Kittredge of Andover, son of a prominent medical family and a surgeon at Bunker Hill, but found him away from home. He decided, thereupon, to enter the office of Doctor John Warren of Boston.[19]

Early in the summer of 1811 Usher set out on a small sloop for Boston. Upon his arrival he boarded with his brother-in-law, Samuel Leighton, husband of his sister Frances, at Market Tavern. Leighton, a brigadier general in the militia, was in Boston attending the General Court (the legislature) of Massachusetts as representative from Eliot, Maine, a part of the Bay State at that time.[20]

Usher's preceptor would be the eminent John Warren, younger brother of General Joseph Warren, who was tragically killed at Bunker Hill while fighting in the line. John Warren was the founder of the Medical Institution of Harvard College (as the Harvard Medical School was then called) and its first Professor of Anatomy and Surgery. He was also busily engaged with private medical pupils in his home, as was customary. The Massachusetts General Hospital, with clinical cases convenient for teaching, was still ten years in the future.[21]

John Warren, born of Puritan stock, was in his 59th year when Usher joined his household. Warren had not had a formal academic medical education, but in accordance with the times had served his medical apprenticeship with his eminent elder brother, Joseph. Although, like his brother, he had wanted to be a regular combat soldier, he had been persuaded to take care of the wounded. Appointed senior surgeon at the age of twenty-two, he was badly needed, as there was an acute shortage of physicians, many of the established doctors of Boston having been Tories. After the ending of the seige of Boston, John Warren was transferred to general hospitals at Long Island and Philadelphia, and eventually back to Boston. In 1777, although practically penniless, he married seventeen year old Abigail Collins, daughter of a prosperous Quaker family of Newport, Rhode Island. Her father would later become governor of his state.

Warren's large experience in military medicine and his extensive exposure to surgery and anatomy led to his preeminence among Boston's medical preceptors. He was a handsome figure, and, although he suffered from periodic depressions, he generally radiated grace and vivacity. He was adroit, highly intelligent, and greatly respected in the Boston medical community, although he was disliked by many former Tories. He benefited greatly from the Revolution politically, professionally, and in medical experience. He was an enthusiastic teacher and extremely popular with his students.[22]

On August 7 Usher wrote to a young friend, Isaac Day of Kittery, to ask his advice about moving in with Doctor Warren and extending his stay from three months, as planned, to six months. Although not a physician, Day showed good sense in calculating the costs and balancing the advantages against them, advising Usher that he should do it if he could obtain a credit for $50. By the time Usher received this sound advice in early September, he had already moved to Doctor Warren's establishment. He eventually obtained the necessary credit.

Warren's house, on School Street in what is now downtown Boston, was surrounded by trees and gardens, to which Warren devoted as much time as his busy practice would allow. Doctor Edward Warren, son and biographer of Doctor John, has left a vivid description of the house in which he grew up and in which Usher received his first indoctrination in medical practice:

> The house itself was a large building with an ell two stories high, covered with a flat roof, tarred and gravelled. At the end of this ell were out-buildings, and a wood-house extending to the barn . . . On the western side of the house, towards Tremont Street, inclosed from the street by a high gate, was the medicine room . . . and back of this [was Doctor Warren's] study, separated by a narrow entry which led . . . to the garden. At an early period, when there was no Medical College or lecture room, the back windows of the house were occupied with drying preparations of

legs and arms and other anatomical and morbid specimens, prepared by Dr. Warren, and forming the basis of the Warren Museum
afterwards in the Medical College.[23]

The "medicine room" was an apothecary's shop in miniature, and
here Usher and the other students sat and put up medicines. Patients were ushered through the medicine room (also serving as a
surgery), and then through a narrow entry into the doctor's study.
As the students admitted the patients, they undertook treatment
of minor problems or actually to prescribe in the doctor's absence.
They dressed small wounds and assisted at operations when
needed.[24]

As virtual apprentices, the students performed all sorts of chores,
bordering on drudgery at times, but also valuable as a teaching
device, such as spreading plasters, making pills, putting up "recipes," and cleaning and wiring skeletons. Each night one student
slept in the house to take care of night patients. There were special
irritations and discomforts, particularly in the winter, such as
smoky stoves and skylights which leaked when the snow thawed.
Despite the hard work and the lack of hospital instruction, the
training was not without merit. The young men had an intimate
association with Doctor Warren and received personal instruction
from him. He was a kind, earnest, and conscientious teacher, and
fostered frequent contacts between his students and his patients.
Usher, however, incurred financial obligations with Doctor Warren
which remained troublesome. "It was with much difficulty that I
got through with the expense of lectures and board, although assisted to fifty dollars by my father," he later wrote.[25]

While Usher was studying with Warren, a controversy arose in
which Warren was deeply involved. In 1810 the Medical School had
been moved from Cambridge to Boston and was in the process of
reorganization. Motivated by personal jealousies and some real, as
well as fancied grievances, a group of prominent physicians petitioned the legislature to charter a rival "Massachusetts College of
Physicians." "Experience has proved," they said, "that two literary
and scientific bodies produce more than double the advantage of
one." They requested "such powers, privileges and immunities as
other medical associations of the like nature and views enjoy." This
was in reality a struggle between men on the make, largely Jeffersonians, and those who had it made, largely Federalists.

The Massachusetts Medical Society contended in a statement signed by president John Warren that the new organization "would be so far from promoting a laudable and useful emulation, that candidates rejected by one society would resort to another." Hearings were held before the legislature, and the issue became a political football. Irascible Benjamin Waterhouse, already at odds with other members of the Harvard medical faculty and soon to be separated therefrom, alienated himself further by appearing for the insurgent group. Even Governor Elbridge Gerry (after whom the gerrymander was named) took sides, favoring, as he termed it, "competition." Gerry and most of the new group of petitioners were Jeffersonians.[26]

Even as he was busily engaged with medical tasks, Usher found in these tumultuous events inspiration for his second experiment in literary composition. (His first had been a satirical discourse in the classical mode, titled "A Pettifogger's Soliloquy" and published in the February 17, 1810 issue of *Freeman's Friend*, a Portland newspaper.) The new idea came from family friend, Henry Holmes of Alfred, who wrote to Usher on October 18, suggesting that he try his hand at dissecting a certain local politician.[27]

Contrived in the Biblical manner and titled "Book of Chronicles," the unsigned contribution in three installments (probably only the first two of which were composed by Usher) appeared in the *Scourge*,[28] a short-lived, scurrilous Boston newspaper, during November 1811. Much of the obscure political satire is now incomprehensible, but the writing marks the beginning of Usher's strong and long-maintained interest in political matters. On the medical controversy he wrote caustically:

> 14. And he spoke unto them on this wise, that Waterhead the physician should write unto their brethren which were afar off by the Chronicle.
> 15. So Waterhead did as he was commanded, and he wrote an Epistle concerning the College of Physicians.
> 16. And his words were like apples of mud in pictures of filth.

Following completion of his course with Warren, Usher applied for membership in the Masssachusetts Medical Society, which was responsible for licensing and for the quality of medical care in the state. "Licensing" did not as in modern usage grant legal permission to practice, but involved rather examination of a candidate and certification that he had the skill and fitness to practice appropriately. While denial of a license did not bar the right to practice, it precluded fellowship in the Society, which was an important privilege. (Medical licensure in the modern sense did not generally become a responsibility of state government until the latter part of the nineteenth century.) As a "candidate for the practice of Physick and Surgery," Usher was examined by the censors of the society. Having been found qualified, he was "approved and licensed" on February 7, 1812 as a "Practitioner of medicine." His license was signed by the Censors, Doctors Lemuel Hayward, Thomas Welsh, Aaron Dexter, Josiah Bartlett, and William Spooner, as well as by President John Warren, his friend and teacher, and by John C. Warren, recording secretary.[29]

While still in Boston, Usher received a letter from his sister-in-law Charlotte, reporting an opening for a doctor in the Ellsworth-Sullivan area, halfway up the Maine coast on Frenchman's Bay, and advising him to consider it. Usher, however, was not interested in this remote area, about which Charlotte, who corresponded with him regularly, complained, "It is the same lonesome place. I sometimes feel sick almost for want of society."[30]

During his stay in Boston, Usher was commissioned by a friend, Doctor Richard Hazeltine of Berwick, to procure a good skeleton at a good price. There was much correspondence back and forth until a satisfactory transaction was consummated. In a letter of February 21, Hazeltine congratulated Usher on his receiving his license and the expectation of becoming a fellow of the Medical Society in three years. As for the skeleton, he had commissioned a merchant, one Samuel Lord of Portsmouth, New Hampshire, to arrange for its shipment by a coastal vessel. He advised that it be labeled "merchandise" and cautioned: "Be sure that you procure a substantial box & that it be well nailed."[31] Lord was apprehensive that customs officers might discover the contents, but agreed to cooperate.[32] There were no legal provisions for the obtaining of anatomical specimens in those days, and body snatching and other unauthorized methods of procurement were frowned upon, to say the least.

While Usher was preoccupied with these matters, the clouds of war were gathering rapidly. England and Napoleon were struggling for world hegemony, and neither belligerent respected the rights of the United States as a neutral. The British Orders in Council, preventing all commerce with ports held by France or her allies, regardless of nationality, closed virtually the whole coast of Europe from Copenhagen to Trieste, and laid a heavy hand on American commerce.

The arrogant and often brutal impressment of American seaman by the British continued despite protests. In reprisal, Congress enacted the Embargo and Non-Intercourse Acts. While extremely oppressive to American business interests, they affected the course of the war very little, if at all, although they did have a delayed effect in making the British more amenable to negotiation after the War of 1812. While the commercial Northeast strongly resisted involvement in the hostilities, the country at large was clamoring for war. The drift toward conflict was virtually irresistible, fired by the appetite of the West for dominance over Canada and annexation of the Floridas.

Despite Britain's provocative behavior, she had no stomach for war with her erstwhile colonies; on the contrary, she felt strongly the necessity of avoiding conflict at all costs to permit maximum concentration of resources on the continent. In a final belated effort to appease the United States, the Orders in Council were rescinded on June 16, 1812. But slow communications had an ironic impact on both the beginning and the end of the War of 1812 (the Battle of New Orleans was fought *after* peace had been declared). Before word of Britain's most important concession could reach the United States, President Madison had already read his war message to Congress, and war with England was declared on June 18, 1812.

With war pending, prospects for young physicians in the military service seemed promising. Upon completing his medical studies and licensure in Boston in February 1812, Usher went home to Alfred to take stock of himself. He tried unsuccessfully to get a job teaching school "to repair my wardrobe," then traveled to Exeter, New Hampshire seeking a place as a physician "but was soon discouraged." Moving on to Dover, he "commenced the practice of Physick" there, but fared badly. "There was now a prospect of war," he wrote, "and I tried hard for a place of surgeon's mate in the Army, but failed."[33]

That Usher saw an attractive opportunity in military service is not surprising. Medical service in the armed forces was a valuable form of auxiliary medical education. Some forty per cent of doctors practicing in 1775, in fact, saw some medical service during the Revolution. It provided the participants with the likelihood of encountering a wide range of disorders and surgical problems, and broadened their social, intellectual, and medical outlook. Massachusetts contributed more to the current war effort than any other state except New York. The navy was manned and officered largely by New Englanders, including a significant contingent from Rhode Island, a circumstance which would have an important influence on Usher's later life.[34]

From Dover Usher carried on a running correspondence with his student friends in Boston. To Pliny Hayes, Jr. he expressed the hope of returning to Boston soon.[35] With something less than true candor, he wrote to George W. May about his successful practice, prompting May to congratulate him on the success of his "professional engagements."[36] Both May and Amos Farnsworth were concerned about the condition of Usher's anatomical preparations, but May later assured him that they were now varnished and were almost dry, though threatened by an invasion of insects.

That Usher was obviously downcast and despondent at this time is evidenced by a letter to him from his wise young friend, Isaac Day, who offered advice as well as sympathy.[37] He also wrote about his problems and uncertainties to his sister-in-law, Charlotte. She again suggested that he try his luck in eastern Maine.[38] To Usher, however, the prospect of the Maine frontier was no more attractive than before. While awaiting a new turn of events, having failed to obtain a surgeoncy in the army, Usher joined the New Hampshire militia.[39] The build-up of these units was part of the general mobilization then going on.

His efforts to obtain a commission in the Navy nevertheless continued. On May 22 he wrote to Doctor Josiah Bartlett, Congressman from New Hampshire: "Finding Dover a place in which I cannot succeed in the practice of physick without encroaching upon the interest of the other physicians; and knowing of a no better opening, I am very desireous to persevere in trying for an appointment in the navy, concluding the *Chesapeake* and other ships of war which are preparing for service will offer some vacancies for officers."[40] Bartlett replied with encouragement and sent a strong recommendation to the Secretary of the Navy.[41]

Despite his discouragements, Usher was able on June 6 to report to Abiel Hall, Jr. that he had booked his "first obstetrick case" in Dover, which prompted Abiel to wish him success and hope he would have "a good subject."[42]

In a gossipy letter to G. W. May[43] Usher admitted, with more candor than before, that he had "but little business," which gave him leisure for "good society," reading, and gardening. "Many of the inhabitants of the town," he wrote, "are Quakers, and in order to gain business I outwardly embrace Quakerism; that is, attend their meeting twice a week—borrow their religious books—visit them and adopt their dialect." He then thanked May for having taken good care of his anatomical preparations and gave him instructions for forwarding them to Dover.

As May was aware, Usher was anxiously awaiting a federal appointment, but was informed regularly by Headquarters in Boston that there were more applications for officer appointments than vacancies. Yet, recent assurances from Congressman Bartlett encouraged him to hope that he would soon receive an appointment as naval surgeon or surgeon's mate—on which ship he could not say. He might after all soon be strutting about with an eagle big as life and a cockade "large as a wagon wheel."

May and others continued to work actively in his behalf. The presence in Boston harbor since June 1 of the U.S. frigate *John Adams*,[44] which happened to be in need of a surgeon's mate, appeared to offer him an opportunity. On June 29 May, alerted by news of Usher's interest in a Navy commission, sent him an urgent message:[45]

Dr. McReynolds of the U.S. Ship *John Adams* is without a mate, and expects to sail for New York in five days. If you will be in town (Boston) within that time you may have the appointment if you are still desirous of an appointment in the Navy. I think you will do wisely in accepting it in this Ship, and an appointment now in the Navy may ensure you the Birth [sic] of full *surgeon* & $900 per annum in six or eight months, so says Dr. McR., as doubtless it will be very much increased at that time. The pay is about the same in the army, $48.00 per month, and when at sea expences nothing, if you are lucky in captures more lucrative. In fine: I will give my opinion unasked for. If you wish an appointment in the U.S. service the Navy is preferable to the Army. Do not infer from what I have written that I wish to persuade you into the service; no, you are the proper judge on that point. . . .

P.S. If you are in Town by Wednesday or Thursday you will receive your appointment from Commodore Bainbridge (who has the command of the northern station & lives in Charlestown), which will agreeably to usage be confirmed by secretary of the

Navy—at any rate if you accept you will start immediately for Boston. If otherwise, send me a line addressed to me by the returning mail.

Your preparations wait only for an opportunity to be sent to you. I shall detain them till I see or hear from you, which *must be* as soon as possible after receiving this. For the Utmost hurry!

By the time the letter arrived, Usher had a bare sixty hours to reach the ship. "I made all dispatch, but did not reach there till sixty-four hours and then found the ship sailed," he later wrote.[46]

This was on the Fourth of July. His discouragement was abysmal, and furthermore he was broke, down to his last dollar. He succeeded in borrowing another forthwith and set out for Dover. He stopped off at Salem, trying unsuccessfully for a berth on a privateer. He reached Dover depressed and "not a little mortified." Despairing of ever obtaining a navy commission, he still hoped he might be offered a chance on a privateer.[47]

Despite his frustration, Usher's prospects for a Navy commission were much brighter than he realized. In fact, he already had been appointed a Surgeon's Mate by the Navy Department on July 10; but due to delay compounded of military red tape and slow transportation, it was almost two weeks before he received the exciting good news. He returned to Dover around the 19th, and on the 23rd he was told of a package waiting for him at the post office. He hastened to pick it up, finding to his great delight that it contained his commission:

Your nomination by the President to the Senate of the U.S. as a Surgeon's Mate in the Navy of the U.S. having been confirmed, I have the pleasure to hand you herewith your commission as a Surgeon's Mate in the Navy. I enclose a copy of the Navy rules, regulations, a copy of the uniform, & the requisite oath, which you will take, and return to me. This appointment must be accepted by letter, from the date of which letter your pay will commence.[48]

He wrote later, "No one can imagine my great joy; it was ecstatic, frantic."[49] He immediately dispatched the following reply to the Navy Department:[50]

Your letter of the 10th inst. accompanying my commission as Surgeon's Mate with other papers having been directed to Dover in Delaware instead of New Hampshire I had not the honor of

receiving before this day.—In obedience to your order I have taken
the oath and enclose it. [Sworn before a justice of the peace in
Dover on July 24]—I likewise affirm my acceptance of the commission and shall hold myself in readiness in this town to obey
your further commands.

The U.S.F. *John Adams*, in the meantime, had arrived in New
York on July 8. Unaware that a commission had already been
granted, McReynolds had apparently continued his activities in
behalf of Usher's candidacy. On July 19, May[51] wrote to Usher that
he had just received a letter from McReynolds in New York informing him that he was still in need of a surgeon's mate, that he
depended upon Usher to fill the spot, had recommended his appointment to the Navy Department, and assumed he would be
appointed. Since McReynolds urged that Usher report without delay, May advised him immediately to take the New York stage and
"ride *night and day for 50 hours*" so as to be there in time. Since
this letter did not clear the Boston post office until the 20th, it
probably did not arrive in Dover before the 21st or 22nd. There is
no record of Usher's reaction to this new admonition for a wild
jaunt. Perhaps he considered it patently impractical, or the letter
may have arrived after he had learned of his commission on the
23rd. At any rate, he never made the trip. Instead, he proceeded to
New York much more leisurely by stagecoach.

During a stopover in Boston, news arrived of the capture on
August 19 of the *Guerrière* by Captain Isaac Hull of the *Constitution*. Usher was in the crowd of citizens which greeted Hull on
State Street. The morning he left Boston for New York he heard of
General William Hull's capture at Detroit on August 16, the first
of a series of American disasters along the Canadian frontier. These
events brought home the war in earnest.

Usher reached New York about September 1 and for the first ten
days there boarded on shore. Then, having been assigned quarters
in steerage aboard the *John Adams*, he had his first taste of navy
life.[52]

NOTES

1. [Henry Parsons]. *The House of Cornet Joseph Parsons, Together with
   the Houses of a Line of His Descendants and Their Allied Families,*

1655–1941. [Kennebunk, Me., 1941]. A copy of this can be found in the American Antiquarian Society.

2. Charles W. Parsons, *Memoir of Usher Parsons, M.D., of Providence, R.I.* (Providence, Hammond, Angell & Co., 1870), pp. 1–2. This work, compiled by Usher Parsons's only child, has remained the major biographical source on him until the present time. It is cited hereafter as C. W. Parsons *Memoir*.

3. C. W. Parsons *Memoir*, pp. 1–2.

4. Usher Parsons, *A Centennial History of Alfred, York County, Maine. With a Supplement by Samuel M. Came, Esq.* (Philadelphia, Sanford Everts & Co., 1872). Much information on the town in which Usher Parsons was born and raised derives from this work. Additional information comes from a privately printed account entitled *A Review of Alfred*, which can be found in the Brick Store Museum in Kennebunk, Maine. This was compiled by George Frost Blunt Leighton when in his eighty-sixth year. Leighton was a nephew of Usher Parsons, born in Alfred in 1816.

5. Usher Parsons, *A Centennial History of Alfred*; G. F. B. Leighton, "A Review of Alfred."

6. C. W. Parsons *Memoir*, p. 2.

7. Usher Parsons, *A Centennial History of Alfred*; G. F. B. Leighton, "A Review of Alfred."

8. C. W. Parsons *Memoir*, p. 2.

9. *Ibid.*, pp. 2–3.

10. Thomas Furber to Usher Parsons, August 29, 1806, DPC.

11. Usher Parsons, *A Centennial History of Alfred*; C. W. Parsons *Memoir*.

12. *Medicine in Colonial America, 1620–1820*. A Conference Held 25 & 26 May, 1978 by the Colonial Society of Massachusetts (Boston, Colonial Society of Massachusetts, 1980), p. 107, 170.

13. Abiel Hall, Jr. to Usher Parsons, August 7, August 27, September 3, September 11 and September 25, 1808, DPC. Alexander Ramsay remains one of the curiosities of early American medicine. Less than five feet tall, with a crooked back and a short neck, large head, limbs clumsy and misshapen, the elements of his mind were said to be as strange as his somewhat grotesque body. By all accounts, he was vain, egotistical, ill-tempered and quarrelsome, but a superb anatomist despite it all. Trained initially at Edinburgh under the third Alexander Monroe, and afterwards at London under the Hunters, he came to America about 1801 with the intention of founding an institute of anatomy in the wilderness. He eventually settled at Fryeburg, Maine, where he gave anatomical lectures and demonstrations. He also taught at Dartmouth and in neighboring states. At times he made lecture tours on anatomy and physiology up and down the eastern seaboard. As an anatomist, he was one of the best in the United States in his time. He died in 1824 at Fryeburg, and his achievements were deemed important enough to

earn him nearly a page in the *Dictionary of American Biography* (New York, Charles Scribner's Sons, v. 15, p. 337). The most extensive biographical treatment of him to date is G. P. Bradley's "Biographical Sketch of Alexander Ramsay, M.D., of Parsonsfield," published in the *Transactions of the Maine Medical Association*, 8:161–182, 1885.

14. C. W. Parsons *Memoir*, p. 3.

15. *Ibid.*

16. *Ibid.*, pp. 3–4.

17. *Ibid.*, pp. 59–61.

18. William Frost to Usher Parsons, March 2, 1810, DPC.

19. C. W. Parsons *Memoir*, p. 4.

20. *Ibid.*, p. 5.

21. Thomas Francis Harrington, *The Harvard Medical School: A History, Narrative and Documentary* (N.Y., Chicago, Lewis Publishing Co., 1903, 3 vols.). The Harvard Medical School was founded in 1782, and the Massachusetts General Hospital was opened in 1821. See Vol. 1, pp. 251–262 for the role of John Warren in the founding of the Medical School and p. 368 for the role of his son, John Collins Warren, in the founding of the hospital.

22. Rhoda Truax, *The Doctors Warren of Boston, First Family of Surgery* (Boston, Houghton Mifflin Co., 1968), pp. 69–75, 91, 106–111; William Frederick Norwood, *Medical Education in the United States Before the Civil War* (Philadelphia, University of Pennsylvania Press, 1944), pp. 169–171.

23. Edward Warren, *The Life of John Warren, M.D.* (Boston, Noyes, Holmes and Co., 1874), pp. 305, 308, 313–314.

24. *Ibid.*

25. C. W. Parsons *Memoir*, p. 4.

26. Thomas Francis Harrington, *The Harvard Medical School*, pp. 222–227.

27. Henry Holmes to Usher Parsons, October 18, 1811, DPC.

28. *The Scourge* was published in Boston by M. Butler under the pseudonym of "Tim Touchstone, Esq." Only one volume was published. "Book of Chronicles" appeared in issues of November 5 and November 11, 1811.

29. C. W. Parsons *Memoir*, p. 5; F. L. Pleadwell, "Usher Parsons (1788–1868), Surgeon, United States Navy," *Naval Medical Bulletin*, 17:423–460, Sept., 1922. Capt. Pleadwell published several documents relating to Usher Parsons's early medical and naval career, including the full text of his certificate from the Massachusetts Medical Society. The original of all except the latter have been located.

30. Charlotte Parsons to Usher Parsons, December 2, 1811, DPC.

31. Richard Hazeltine to Usher Parsons, January 5, 6, and 13, and February 21, 1812, DPC.

32. Samuel Lord to Usher Parsons, February 29, 1812, DPC.

33. C. W. Parsons *Memoir*, pp. 5–6; Usher Parsons, "Diary Kept During the Expedition to Lake Erie Under Captain O. H. Perry, 1812–1814," RIHS. Extracted from Foreword to Diary.

34. Personal communication from Philip Cash, Professor of History at Emmanuel College, Boston, to the author. In his *Jack Tar and Commodores, The American Navy, 1783–1815* (Boston, Houghton Mifflin Co., 1984), William M. Fowler, Jr. noted that O. H. Perry arrived at Lake Erie on 27 March 1813 "with a large contingent of Rhode Islanders." Of some 36 officers and midshipmen in the Battle of Lake Erie, Usher Parsons identified 13 as New Englanders, of whom 9 were from Rhode Island ("Brief Sketches of the Officers Who Were in the Battle of Lake Erie," *New England Historical and Genealogical Register*, 17:17–29, 1863).

35. Pliny Hayes to Usher Parsons, April 10, 1812, DPC.

36. George W. May to Usher Parsons, April 17, 1812, DPC.

37. Isaac C. Day to Usher Parsons, May 23, 1812, DPC. Day was replying to a letter Usher had sent to him on May 20.

38. Charlotte Parsons to Usher Parsons, June 27, 1812, DPC.

39. The original order was signed by one F. S. Tibbets, Captain of New Hampshire Militia, dated Dover, June 11, 1812, DPC.

40. Usher Parsons to Josiah Bartlett, May 22, 1812, DPC.

41. Josiah Bartlett to Usher Parsons, May 30, 1812, DPC; Josiah Bartlett to Paul Hamilton, WRDNA. Bartlett's letter was accompanied by a certificate dated January 12, 1812 and signed by John Warren of Boston, attesting to three full years of study "under physicians of approved and established reputation," and further as to Parsons's diligent application, proficiency, and "immaculate" moral character.

42. Abiel Hall, Jr. to Usher Parsons, June 22, 1812, DPC.

43. Usher Parsons to George W. May, June 15, 1812, DPC.

44. This information comes from WRDNA.

45. George W. May to Usher Parsons, June 29, 1812, DPC.

46. C. W. Parsons *Memoir*, p. 6.

47. *Ibid.*

48. WRDNA; Paul Hamilton to Usher Parsons, July 10, 1812, DPC.

49. C. W. Parsons *Memoir*, p. 6.

50. Usher Parsons to Paul Hamilton, July 23, 1812, WRDNA; Ms. dated July 24, 1812, sworn before Moses L. Neal, Justice of the Peace, WRDNA.

51. George W. May to Usher Parsons, July 19, 1812, DPC.

52. Usher Parsons, "Diary Kept During the Expedition to Lake Erie," Foreword; Abiel Hall, Jr. to Usher Parsons, September 20, 1812, DPC.

CHAPTER TWO

Surgeon's Mate, U.S.N.

On Sunday morning, September 20, 1812 Commodore Isaac Chauncey came aboard the *John Adams*, and all hands were assembled. Chauncey, then forty years of age and a veteran of thirteen years in the navy, had recently been made commander of naval forces on Lakes Ontario and Erie. He had established his headquarters at Sacket's Harbor, New York, on Lake Ontario. Despite his well-deserved reputation as a skillful naval officer, earned during the successful attack on Tripoli in 1804, he was hardly a prepossessing figure. Having gone to flesh, he was pear-shaped, with a pear-shaped head, double chins, and sleepy eyes. Although a consummate organizer, he was to prove cautious to a fault.[1]

Wrote Usher, he "spoke to us of a secret expedition of two or three months and expressed a wish that the crew would volunteer to join him. Whereupon all hands stept forward & tendered their services. From this [day] till Thursday we were preparing to leave the ship and sailed on the Thursday following not knowing, most of us, what was our destination—though it was conjectured to be some part of the lakes."[2] On the day he departed, Usher began a diary. With keen and vivid powers of observation, he recorded the story of the expedition into the north country.[3]

On the 24th of September the bulk of the officers and crew of the *John Adams* were ordered to be in readiness to embark on a packet for a trip up the Hudson to Albany. Their ultimate destination was unknown to them or "to any except Commodore Chauncey," but it was "generally supposed to be Sackets Harbor." At three o'clock that afternoon all hands gave out with three lusty cheers, and they set sail. By nightfall, with the wind and tide turning against them, they anchored for the night. They had made some twenty miles.

19

Usher was impressed with the beauty of the scenery, particularly the rocky palisades on the New Jersey side, thrusting up perpendicularly for a hundred feet, laced by evergreen sprouting from the crevices.

At ten a.m. they got under way, passing Tarrytown, where Major John André, the British spy, had been captured on September 23, 1780, and Fort Stony Point, captured by General "mad" Anthony Wayne on July 6, 1779, as Usher noted in his diary.

At sunrise on the 26th they passed West Point, and then moved on to Putnam, where several of the men went ashore and "brought off great quantities of fruit." He was obviously impressed by the handsome country seats and the rich farms on the New York side of the Hudson, which to a farm boy from modest York County in Maine were "delightsome." On Sunday, the 27th, they reached Hudson, a town of "elegant appearance," and could hear the church bells ringing. At four o'clock, while "beating against the wind, the steamboat passed bearing our commander and other officers," certainly an early use of that newfangled craft for military transport. It may well have been Robert Fulton's *Clermont*, built in 1807 for Robert H. Livingston to ply the Hudson between New York and Albany.

They arrived at Albany at ten o'clock on the evening of the 28th. He noted that "the crew is very healthy," with only three names on the sick book, but "we discovered among the crew a female clad in sailor's apparel!"

He spent the next day exploring the town. The townspeople were mostly Dutch, and many of their homes were in the Dutch style. Despite the fact that the streets were lighted at night "as in Boston and New York," the "only elegant edifices are the statehouse and bank." "The people," he observed, "very well understand trading and speculating."

At eleven a.m. on the 30th, fifteen officers and 137 men with baggage wagons "were escorted from Albany with musick." They reached Schenectady that night after a very rough trip. "The purser's and hospital stores were very much injured," he wrote, in traveling only 14 miles. He slept on the floor of an open army barrack close by the Mohawk River. During the night several of the men swam the stream and "returned with an abundance of fruit, poultry, etc.," while others took from a neighbor's hog-pen "the larger hog undiscovered," while two of the party kept watch in an adjacent barn.

On October 2 they continued past Amsterdam and spent the night at Shepard's Inn on the banks of the Mohawk. "There are," he observed, "146 publick inns between Albany and Utica." The men took the opportunity to bathe in the cool waters of the river. He was not impressed with the local belles: "The females I have met since leaving Schenectady possess healthy countenances, robust persons, uncomely forms and airs, and are apparently destitute of every charm."

The party continued on for several days, drenched in rain, riding over hills, valleys, rivers, and broken bridges, and "twice across canals of the Mohawk near locks." There was, he wrote, "Great disorder and confusion among the officers, waggoners, and sailors; the keys of the medicine chest were lost; myself destitute of money; to compleat all, it was with difficulty that I avoided a challenge [to a duel] from one of the midshipmen . . . received without giving him occasion for offence." He, however, was able to find some comfort: "I purchased a drink for $1.00." The sailors, all the while, continued to plunder.

At Herkimer, 77 miles west of Albany on Sunday, October 4, a cold and rainy day, they took a left fork in the road leading to Buffalo on Lake Erie and away from Sackets Harbor. They turned in their uncovered wagons for covered ones and continued on their muddy way. At one point Usher was distressed by the breakdown of the medicine wagon, which had to be repaired before they could continue.

After a rest in Utica, they plodded on in the unrelenting rain. Usher was fascinated by an encampment of Oneida Indians 2,000 strong, who had volunteered their services to the United States in the war with Canada. He observed their dress and mode of living in considerable detail. "The conversation of the warriors," he wrote, "I could understand, but not that of the squaws," who, he observed, had less contact than their men with the white man.

They arrived at Lake Cayuga on the 10th, crossed the lake on scows, and then proceeded to Batavia, 161 miles from Utica. There on the 14th they were met by men bearing dispatches of the disastrous American defeat of the day before at Queenston Heights on the Canadian side of the Niagara River. Some 1,000 United States troops commanded by Colonel Stephen Van Rensselaer had attacked the heights across the river.[4] Usher noted laconically: "Killed 400. Surrendered for want of ammunition 400." The discredited Van

Rensselaer resigned his command, but the British general, Sir Isaac Brock, was killed in action.[5]

The roads continued to be bad beyond description. "We break about 2 waggons per day," noted Usher. On the 16th he walked a brutal 22 miles, arriving that afternoon at Black Rock, strategically located at the junction of Lake Erie and the Niagara River. There he could hear the sound of cannon in the distance, fired, it was reported, at the burial of General Brock.

Usher was assigned to the military post at Black Rock, which had been established as a staging area for the Great Lakes campaign, and would spend the next eight months there. Although he found leisure to visit Buffalo and explore the nearby woods, he was now in the combat zone and would be increasingly preoccupied with the care of patients and military matters.

The United States had declared war on Great Britain on June 18, 1812 in reprisal for the impressment of American seamen and enforcement of the hated Orders in Council, which forbade neutral trade *between* ports held by Napoleon. Furthermore, America was in a prolonged depression, which the Americans attributed to British actions. They were also spurred on by the expansionist War Hawks of the West. The highly provocative policy of the British, pursued in their desperate struggle with Napoleon, and the volatile political climate in the United States inspired James Madison to hurl the American armies at the Canadian border to chastise the British for their arrogance. Madison soon learned how ill-prepared his country was to fight a major war. As the United States undertook the conquest of Upper Canada, the long peninsula extending from Lake Ontario to the Detroit River, its initial strategy had been to split Canada in two by advancing up the Champlain-Richelieu corridor. With the miserable failure of this strategy, any hope of annexing Canada, an objective of many and especially of the War Hawks of Kentucky, was dissipated.

General William Hull commanded an army at Detroit and General Stephen Van Rensselaer another on the Niagara River. Hull was captured at Detroit and Van Rensselaer, as was noted, was defeated at Queenston Heights. The British now held possession of Lake Erie with five armed vessels and had captured the U.S.S. *Adams*, the only American armed vessel on the lake. The British vessels could at any time strike a serious blow with sailors and Indians on settlements on the southern side of the lake. The surrender of Hull at

Detroit exposed the territory at the head of the lake, and an attempt to counter the British there resulted in the ignominious capture of General James Winchester at Frenchtown, near Detroit.

The failed Champlain Valley campaign and the disastrous defeats at Detroit and Queenston Heights, and the ensuing one at Frenchtown on January 22, 1813 confronted the Americans with the necessity of reviewing their strategy of the first year of the war. They had learned a costly lesson, that whoever controlled the lakes controlled the war. On Lakes Erie and Ontario both sides were engaged in a frantic shipbuilding race. On Lake Ontario the British were building frigates at Kingston and York (now Toronto), while the Americans were rushing to complete a fleet at Sackets Harbor on the New York side. With no vessels at all on Lake Erie in 1812, time was of the essence, since whichever side won the shipbuilding contest would control the lakes. The Americans at breakneck speed were building an entire fleet at Black Rock, two miles north of Buffalo on the Niagara River in New York, and at Presque Isle at Erie, Pennsylvania. During the winter of 1812–13 the keels of five vessels were laid at Erie, and five merchant schooners, the only ones then plying the lake, were purchased and arrived with two or three guns each. The work was carried out by able ship's carpenters imported from the East Coast. Among the ships were two stalwart brigs, the *Lawrence* and the *Niagara*, each of twenty guns. The balance of power was so delicate that the side which managed to destroy a vessel or two of the enemy's might well achieve naval supremacy.[6] This was to be Usher Parsons's war.[7]

Usher reported that upon his arrival at Black Rock navy Lieutenant Jesse Elliott was in port after a daring escapade in which he and his men had seized the British ships *Caledonia* and *Adams* (formerly American) by boarding them at night. This was the only victory that they could celebrate among a dismal string of defeats. On October 17 "A flag of truce came over" from the British side with the "intelligence that any attempts to take guns from the *Adams*" would be treated by the British "as a violation of the armistice which now exists" along the Niagara River. "Notwithstanding," he noted, "2 guns were taken from her in the evening." The *Adams* had been burned, but the brig *Caledonia* was taken as a prize and became part of the American fleet on Lake Erie. There were about seven wounded in the expedition. He reported later that two more guns were seized from the *Adams*.

On October 22 he noted that "An eruption is complained of among the crew, and likewise a dysenteria." He found that "A solution of nitric acid cures the former and large doses of Calomel the latter." During this period he cared for several soldiers wounded at Queenston Heights in the absence of their surgeon. One died of "inflammation of the intestines."

Near Black Rock the men were engaged in erecting a fortification to be called Fort Adams. During the excavation several Indian skeletons were found, which Usher culled over with great interest. At the same site he discovered some real flint stones, and recalled that in his medical lectures in Boston Doctor John Gorham, professor of Chemistry at the Harvard Medical School, had "called himself the first discoverer of flint stone in the United States and that he [had] found it at Niagara Falls."[8]

The wounded and sick, who had been scattered around in various billets, were moved to the hospital at Black Rock. On the 27th he attended some 49 patients, including soldiers. Among them was Colonel John Fenwick,[9] who was wounded at Queenston and whose wounds, numbering no less than four, he had assisted in dressing. He was also very busy with an epidemic of dysentery, but found time to spend an occasional few hours "gunning" or "sporting." He performed a postmortem on the body of a soldier found on the lake shore who had died of a gunshot wound of the chest, "the lungs destroyed by suppuration."

The British ship *Queen Charlotte* on October 25 had entered Fort Erie, on the Canadian side of the Niagara River, an area included in the armistice then in effect. On the 28th she sailed into Lake Erie, and that evening three boats went in pursuit. The next morning Usher reported that "The crew engaged in last night's expedition returned this morning at 7 o'clock, having rowed 18 miles up the lake and found nothing." The crew, nevertheless, were "quite impatient to be engaged in hostile operations."

All of his casualties were not wounds and fevers. On November 5 he noted: "Ben Baily [a member of the crew], who has laboured under delirium for several days, was restored to perfect collectedness of mind by drinking his usual allowance of whiskey." Usher spent his evenings writing a paper on epilepsy.

On the 6th Usher visited Buffalo, where he made small payments on his debts: six dollars to G. W. May in Boston and ten dollars to Abiel Hall, Jr., in Alfred. Young Hall replied,[10] "I . . . have informed almost every person I saw that I had received a letter from you. The same evening I visited your father's family; your brother John was present and read to them the letter. What can be more pleasing than a letter bearing good news from a distant and beloved friend? from a dutiful and darling son? O Usher! your parents' countenances express more than words."

With the approaching winter, the weather began to thicken, and military action became sharper. On a visit to Buffalo on November 11, Usher saw posted a proclamation by General Alexander Smyth "calling on the men of New York to repair speedily to this place to assist in planting the American Standard on the Canadian shore," no doubt recalling the miserable performance of the New York militia at Queenston Heights. The weather remained extremely wet and "the roads are hardly passable for man or horse." A 32-pound cannon for the navy yard, nevertheless, had gotten through. News arrived on the 17th that Commodore Chauncey, cruising Lake Ontario with a brig and nine schooners, had cleared the lake, taken 2 brigs, and destroyed the *Royal George*. The armistice, still in effect, would expire on the evening of the 20th in accordance with a declaration by General Smyth. This was followed by an attempted crossing of the river by 120 sailors and 200 army regulars. As Usher reported: "Good order prevailed and they proceeded [only] a few yards, when they were counter-ordered to return." While the navy appeared to be doing well, failure dogged the land forces. Another attempted armed crossing on the 28th also ended in disaster, with many taken prisoner, although they succeeded in spiking all of the enemy cannon. The men made a considerable fuss about Smyth's poor leadership.

Usher reported the death from pleurisy of one of the naval officers, "which is the first case that has occurred." Physicians then believed that a daily issue of spirits was essential to the good health of the troops, in spite of which many died from measles, malaria, typhus, typhoid, influenza, and a variety of other diseases, which went, according to Berton, under the vague collective designation of "ague" or "lake fever." Usher listed the naval casualties from the recent engagements as seven dead (including two officers) and sixteen wounded, some seriously. One amputation was required because of a compound fracture of the leg. There were also several wounded soldiers.

Usher and a party of Americans under a flag of truce crossed the

river on December 2 to recover the body of a "Mr. Watts," killed
in the storming of the British batteries. They were met by two
companies of infantry. They had a "sociable" conversation with the
officers, but the request was curtly denied. After expressing great
resentment over the burning of their houses, they however permitted the Americans to take back in their boats the soldiers wounded
in the engagement.

Usher's concern about the growing sickness among his men is
reflected in his diary:

> Saturday 5th. High wind. The pleurisy prevails so as to be very
> alarming. In some patients typhoid symptoms attend it.
> Cullen's[11] description of it is very accurate. Moderate depletion
> is the usual, though unsuccessful, treatment.

On December 10 Usher wrote to Isaac Day[12] in Saco describing
his situation as generally advantageous. Although there were in-
conveniences, even privations, his "pecuniary prospects" were good
and his medical experience was valuable, particularly in surgery
with the continual, if sporadic, arrival of casualties.

Many wounded during the sharp action of November 27–28 remained under treatment for some time. Always preoccupied with
the weather, Usher noted with pleasure on December 30 that it was
an "Indian summer" day, while a few days later it snowed enough
to provide "good sleighing." "Having obtained a subject," he found
time in the evenings to do a little dissecting. On January 9, 1813
he noted: "The pneumonia, which a short time since subsided in a
small degree, now rages again among the sailors with redoubled
violence." On the 10th, Commodore Chauncey took leave of the
post. Shortly thereafter Usher recorded the deaths of two seamen,
probably victims of the pneumonia epidemic. By the 18th, the pleurisy had begun to abate. "Repeated bloodletting," he wrote, "is the
only remedy to be relied on."

Usher's first medical communication, his observations on epidemic pleuro-pneumonia, appeared in the *Buffalo Gazette* of January 19, 1813:[13]

> Dr. John Ross:—. . . I am led to disagree with you on the pro-
> priety of laying aside the blood letting. . . . You altogether mistook
> the seat of the disease in considering it to be in the right hypo-

chondrium [the region of the liver], when it is in the thorax, and is nothing more nor less than pneumonia or pleurisy.

In confirmation of this, I will venture to say a more accurate description of the disease now prevailing cannot be given than the one by Dr. Cullen in his treatise on pleurisy. Besides, of more than seventy cases that have fallen under my care, but little variation in the symptoms has been observable, except in violence and duration. And that the seat and nature of the disease might be thoroughly understood, the bodies of six patients, which were nearly all that died, . . . were carefully examined. The following were the appearances in the thorax: the lungs highly inflamed, adhered firmly to the pleura, in some places so sphacelated [gangrenous sloughing] that no vestige of organic structure remained.
. . .

In attempting the cure of the pleurisy, "the remedy chiefly to be relied upon is that of bleeding at the arm." With this I have commenced the treatment of every case that has come under my care, and have invariably found it relieves the most distressing complaints.

This interesting analysis of the cases is convincing in several respects. Usher's contention that the epidemic was one of pneumonia, rather than disease of the right hypochondrium (perhaps infectious hepatitis, also epidemic under military conditions), he confirmed by careful clinical studies and detailed postmortem examination in six cases. He found all of the abnormalities in the chest and none in the liver. His exceptionally low mortality in this severe epidemic, six of seventy cases, would be creditable even in a day of wonder drugs. He used niter and tartar emetic as adjuvants to "promote perspiration and expectoration." Usher's enthusiasm for the lancet was consistent with the practice of the time, while Doctor Ross, in his disdain for bloodletting, was more perceptive.[14]

Bleeding had originated as a means of letting out the demons causing disease, but later, as it was decided that weakness and fatigue were the cause rather than the result of the disease, patients were bled in order to get rid of the impurities which presumably resided in the blood.

Usher himself later changed his views regarding bleeding. We can assume that his careful, good general care, rather than the therapeutic shedding of blood, was the major factor in his success. In his later surgical experiences, both military and civilian, this was certainly true. In concluding his letter to Doctor Ross, he sought to soften somewhat the appearance of arrogance. One might even suspect a fear of malpractice suits, which, however, were not likely in those days:

> This mode of practice both theory and experience teach me to be the most rational and successful; and it has the sanction of perhaps every writer of medicine. You will not receive these remarks, Sir, as an attack on your professional character, nor as expressive of a wish to commence newspaper controversy. I am actuated principally by a desire to remove from the minds of my patients any undue prejudice against the use of the lancet, which the publication of your sentiments may occasion.

Usher sent copies of the newspaper to Abiel Hall, who replied:[15] "I perused . . . and was very much pleased with your remarks, which appear to me . . . to be correct, and I think you have the advantage of Doct. Ross. Though he may think you severe upon it."

Usher had not yet seen one of the wonders of America, only a day's ride away, but he now found time to view that spectacle:

> [Jan.] 24th. Took a view of the Falls of Niagara. Their perpendicular descent is 160 feet. The view of the rapids above the falls when standing near the pitch is more majestic, novel, and curious than that of the perpendicular descent of the water.

The severe weather and hard life on the rugged frontier created problems of morale and discipline. On January 29 Usher made the following notation in his diary: "News this day arrived . . . by a flag of truce from the other shore that Gen. Winchester with 600 regulars of the Kentucky militia were killed & taken." This was the first intimation of the third disastrous defeat of the year, that at Frenchtown in Michigan.

Usher wrote a surprisingly accurate account of the battle in a letter to his family in Alfred. The Americans under Major General William Henry Harrison were assembling troops to recapture Detroit, which had been surrendered to the British on August 15, 1812. Brigadier General James Winchester of Tennessee had sent 650 soldiers to occupy Frenchtown (now Monroe, Michigan) on the Raisin River below Detroit and himself led 300 more men to the settlement. On January 22, 1813 the Americans were attacked by a superior force of British led by General Henry A. Procter, together with their Indian allies. One wing of the American forces was routed. The remainder, including General Winchester, surrendered. A British promise of protection from the Indians was disregarded, and the Indians massacred the Americans. Known as the Raisin River Massacre, this event so stirred American public opinion that "Remember the Raisin River" became a rallying cry for the rest of the war. Winchester himself was imprisoned in Canada for over a year.

According to Usher, the intelligence "emerging along the line" indicated that 200 were killed and wounded in the "severe conflict," and some 400 surrendered and were taken prisoner. The enemy loss, however, was greater, and of seven surgeons only one survived. The prisoners were paroled and crossed the Niagara River not far from Black Rock. There was a report that "the conduct of the savages" was "barbarous beyond description." Later, however, the Kentucky volunteers passing through Black Rock on their way home spoke of the behavior of the Indians as not "so bad as was reported here."[16]

On February 11 Usher noted in his diary that he was "learning the vocal musick." He wrote to his family [17] that he was enjoying good health and his situation was favorable enough that he was unlikely to leave the service in the spring "unless some better establishment than Dover should offer itself." He hoped, however, to be ordered to the United States Naval Hospital at the Boston Navy Yard at Charlestown, Massachusetts, which being nearer home would suit him better than remaining "so far beyond the sunset."

Usher was reasonably affluent now. There were few expensive pastimes in this raw country, but he suffered occasional losses at cards. On February 15 he received from the purser the substantial payment of $150, half of which he sent on account to Doctor John Warren in Boston in payment for his preceptorship. Usher noted in his diary that he had given it to a Mr. Farewell "to pay him & take a receipt, the same to be endorsed on my note." He sent an additional $25 to his cousin, John U. Parsons, who had also loaned him money.

During February Usher visited neaby Buffalo several times and made a trip to Batavia, New York, some forty miles distant. Upon returning to the barracks, he had his first obstetrical experience at Black Rock, delivering one of the neighboring young matrons of a healthy baby daughter. He continued to do a little dissecting. His diary for the month ended with entries describing the strengthening

of the defenses at Black Rock and the arrival of news of a signal
naval victory, the destruction on December 29 of the British frigate
Java by the *Constitution* off the coast of Brazil. The men were
healthier than they had been for several months. There were some
25 on the sick list, but among them were no two patients "admitting of the same treatment."

During this period Usher had been boarding with a Mrs. Webb,
who was burdened with a bad case of dropsy. He was called upon
to minister to her professionally and performed "the operation of
paracentesis" (tapping her abdomen for fluid), relieving her of no
less than fourteen pints of water. This heroic procedure availed
little, as the poor woman expired eight days later. Usher attended
her funeral.

Usher was a guest at a ball in Buffalo for army and navy officers,
to which "13 citizen ladies" were invited as their escorts. On March
23 he recorded in his diary a significant event: "Capt. Perry, appointed to the command of Lake Erie, arrived today on his way for
Presque Isle." While the countryside took on a brighter aspect with
the coming of spring, illness lingered on and Usher himself was
confined to bed with a cold. The snows were melting away, and
tremendous rains broke up the ice on the river and lakes. The men
were now able to seine for fish and hunt for geese and ducks to
supplement their military rations.

Undeterred by the heavy responsibilities of his sick and wounded
and despite much military coming and going, Usher found time to
read, currently Milton and the romance of Abélard and Héloïse. He
even bought a share in the library at Buffalo and later attended
another ball there.

On May 10 Thomas Holdup, a young naval lieutenant, together
with a small detachment of men from Presque Isle came to Black
Rock to pick up a supply of ammunition. Holdup brought a letter
from Surgeon Joseph G. Roberts containing some timely advice for
Usher:[18]

> Since I arrived at this place, I have been constantly employed,
> the men being very sickly. . . . It gives me such pleasure to hear
> of your being left at Black Rock in charge of the sick (which are
> numerous) as it was your wish. You mentioned in your letter that
> it would be agreeable to you to be attached to this station, pro-
> vided you could obtain the appointment of acting Surgeon on

board one of the brigs. I think your best way would be, as soon as your sick are sufficiently recovered, to write to Capt. Perry informing him of it and of your being desireous to be attached to this station under his command. . . . I shall use every exertion in my power, in endeavouring to obtain for you the appointment you wish, and think the prospect flattering, as I am confident there is no one ordered as yet. . . .

Until now the military activities in this theater had been hardly more than skirmishes to secure tactical advantage. The overriding strategic objective was control of the Great Lakes frontier. Preliminary moves now in progress were drawing the line for a decisive battle.[19] Usher's own later account set the stage for the campaign.

As the war began, a squadron of seventeen gunboats was stationed at Newport, Rhode Island for the protection of Narragansett Bay, under the command of Oliver Hazard Perry, a native Rhode Islander, then 27 years of age. Since the area was essentially inactive, Perry volunteered for service on the lakes. He was ordered to take charge of the outfitting of the Lake Erie fleet. He brought with him many of the officers and seamen from Newport, arriving at Erie, Pennsylvania in March of 1813. This accounted for the large number of Rhode Islanders in the force.

Perry[20] was born in South Kingstown, Rhode Island of Quaker stock on August 23, 1785. Very delicate in health in his youth, he gave no promise of a vigorous manhood. He began his naval career as a midshipman aboard a ship commanded by his father, Captain Christopher R. Perry. He sailed with the American fleet in the war with the Barbary States and early showed signs of his bravery. He was promoted to lieutenant and was given command of the flotilla at Newport. He was a handsome figure of a man and was loved and respected by his men.

On May 24 Perry left Erie in a four-oared boat bound for Buffalo, where he and his crew arrived in twenty-four hours, a distance of 100 miles! He was on his way to assist Commodore Isaac Chauncey in the amphibious assault of May 27 on Fort George, on the Canadian side of the Niagara River near Lake Ontario. His heroic leadership as a junior officer assisted greatly in the successful but bloody assault on the fort. At a critical point in the battle Perry, standing upright in an open boat, tall and stern, in full uniform and oblivious of enemy rounds, directed fire from the schooners. The sound of cannonading from the attacking forces could be heard clearly at Black Rock. After the capture of Fort George, the British abandoned the Niagara frontier, including Fort Erie opposite Black Rock.

On May 28,[21] after the assault on Fort George, Usher and a party of twenty men crossed to the Canadian side and marched to Fort Erie unimpeded. They took a few prisoners on the shore, and on arriving at the fort met two more carrying a flag of truce, anxious to surrender! They then entered the fort, where they "were treated with great hospitality." They sent word back by boat to Colonel John Patton Preston of the Black Rock army garrison of the situation at Fort Erie. The Colonel and a regiment crossed over and took possession of the fort that evening. Usher "tarried all night" at the fort, with not a single "hostile person remaining near the fort." On many occasions in later years, Usher relished retelling the story of how he, as the ranking officer of the landing party, had received the surrender of Fort Erie. Among his papers was a handbill dated May 28, printed by the *Buffalo Gazette,* announcing the "capture of Fort George!" copies of which he sent home. He noted that, if Colonel Preston had crossed a few hours earlier, he might have recovered large amounts of provisions, clothing, furs, and ammunition, which had in the meantime been destroyed.

On returning to Black Rock he learned that the ship's carpenters, having completed work on the vessels at Erie, had passed through on their way to Sackets Harbor on Lake Ontario the previous evening.

While in Black Rock en route to the action at Fort George, Perry took measures to hasten the arming and outfitting of the five merchant schooners there, and on his return to Erie brought with him two companies of infantry from the army and a few sailors from Chauncey's fleet to man the vessels. He accomplished the Herculean feat of dragging the vessels by land past the Niagara rapids at Black Rock into the lake. This required nearly a week and the efforts of two hundred strong men, who laboriously warped the ships upstream by dragging them with ropes over their shoulders. They were all brought safely into the lake.

Early in June Usher "concluded to go to Presque Isle (Erie)." Whether he was ordered to proceed or requested transfer is not clear. He packed his gear and personal belongings and went into Buffalo to settle bills "and prepare for a departure from this place" after a "residence of 8 months." While in Buffalo he learned of another American disaster at Stoney Creek in Ontario.[22] Usher listed the commanders of the five vessels as Perry of the *Caledonia*, Almy of the *Somers*, Dobbins of the *Ohio*, Holdup of the *Tripp*, and Darling of the *Amelia*. After a false start on Sunday the 13th due to "want of wind," the squadron finally sailed into the sunset on the evening of June 14.

On the first day out of Buffalo, as they skirted the Ontario shore, Usher was called to see Perry, who had come down with a high fever. Worried about his captain and feeling that strong measures were necessary, Usher applied a "blister" to the back of his patient's neck. This remedy consisted of a plaster bandage on which was daubed an irritant blistering medication, usually cantharides or ground-up Spanish fly. This, it was thought, would draw away the inflammation from the lungs or other involved organs.[23]

Along with several other naval officers and years before the birth of Pasteur, Usher, surmising that the dysentery, and fever as well, prevailing among the men was caused by drinking of lake water, directed that all lake water used by the crews be boiled, an order that was generally followed.

On June 17, as they were approaching Presque Isle, two men rowed out from the shore bringing intelligence that the enemy had appeared there and were probably in pursuit of the squadron. Perry, although recently ill, took to the deck and ordered the other vessels to prepare for action and board the enemy craft should they appear. Fortunately, the Americans were not discovered, and the next evening safely piloted their little squadron over the bar and into the harbor at Erie. The bar at the harbor's mouth provided security from enemy ships. On arrival they learned that the British had recently launched the *Detroit* at Amherstburg. The largest ship ever to sail the lake, it was built in anticipation of the expected American effort to control the waters of Lake Erie.

Usher, extremely busy caring for the sick on board the several vessels, reported, "The men are very unhealthy." But he found time on occasion to dine on shore (once on turtle soup and later on wild turkey), and also to go "gunning" and "strawberrying." On June 23 he experienced for the first time the bane of sailors ("was seasick in the afternoon"). On the 25th, "The enemy made their appearance this morning at the mouth of the harbour, discharged one gun and sailed." A post hospital was opened on July 2 in the county courthouse.

Since the Fourth of July fell on a Sunday, the traditional celebration was held the next day. Usher took the occasion to write to his parents. On the fifth he and the officers attended a public dinner and in the evening a ball at a Colonel Forster's, to which some fifteen couples had been invited.

Usher was well informed about the progress of the conflict and kept a running account of it in his diary. The war was not going well on Lake Ontario. The enemy had shot up Sackets Harbor, Oswego, and other places on the New York shore. The enemy still had naval superiority on the lake. They had retaken and again fortified Queenston and Fort Erie on the Niagara River, which had been evacuated when Fort George fell to the Americans. Only Fort George was still in American hands. They boldly crossed the Niagara and raided Black Rock, burned the soldiers' and sailors' barracks, carried off provisions, killed and wounded some militia, and took prisoners.

Orders arrived from the Secretary of War dispatching most of the marines attached to the fleet at Erie to Fort George as reinforcements to strengthen that now isolated garrison. That left only a hundred seamen and a few marines to man the fleet of vessels, although more seamen were expected to arrive. One of two brigs had been completed and was ready for the sea, while the other brig and a pilot boat would be ready in ten days. The enemy troops at Malden on the Detroit River had been reinforced with regulars and Indians to exceed 6,000 men. "The prospect," Usher wrote, "of ever taking upper Canada is fainter now than ever." This strategic judgment, made by a junior medical officer, was extraordinarily perceptive.

He was, nevertheless, preoccupied with more mundane pursuits. He spent Friday, July 16 "reading Locke and practising the violin." On Sunday, the 18th of July, two "respectable missionaries," who were passing through Erie, were invited on board a ship by Captain Perry, where they addressed such officers and men as could be spared from duty. They offered fervent prayers for the success of the expedition, that they might gallantly subdue the hostile fleet, and "wrest from savage hands the tomahawk and scalping-knife. . . . so cruelly wielded against the defenseless settlers on the frontiers." They pleaded that in the event of victory "mercy and kindness . . . be shown to the vanquished."

The next few weeks passed rapidly as the men made final preparations to go to sea. Usher graphically described the laborious task of getting the brigs over the bar into the open waters:[24]

> The bar of Erie had thus far served as a fortification to prevent the enemy from entering the harbour where our fleet was preparing, but it now presented a serious obstacle to our egress. The two large brigs drew three feet of water more than there was on the bar. On Sunday, the 1st of August, the work began of clearing the *Lawrence* of cannon balls to lighten her; and immense scows called "camels" were placed under her sides, and being sunk to the water's edge, timbers were passed through from side to side of the ship, the ends of which were blocked up, resting on these floating foundations. Plugs were now put into the scows and the water bailed out, and as they rose they lifted the ship two feet, and this not being enough, the ballast and other heavy articles were taken out, till she was raised another foot, when she was able to pass over the bar. The *Niagara* was served in like manner, but the smaller vessels had previously passed over without the aid of camels. Before the large vessels were fairly over, the enemy hove in sight, and fired a few balls, which did not reach us. The Pennsylvania regiment paraded, and the small vessels that were out returned the enemy's fire. Had they come near enough to do execution while we were struggling over the bar, they might have destroyed our fleet with little difficulty.

On August 6 the fleet with barely half its complement of officers and men sailed across the lake, hoping to encounter the enemy before their large new brig *Detroit* had joined the fleet. The enemy, however, had sailed to Malden, and the Americans returned to Erie. There they were delighted to find Lieutenant Jesse Elliott, just arrived from Lake Ontario with one hundred officers and men. They again sailed up the lake in pursuit of the enemy, but found no trace. On the 17th they entered Sandusky Bay and fired cannon to signal the shore of their arrival.

Brigadier General Edmund P. Gaines came aboard that evening with a number of officers and Indians. Gaines reported that General Harrison with an army of 8,000 militia, regulars, and Indians was twenty-seven miles from Sandusky. General Harrison himself came aboard on the evening of the 19th, accompanied by his aides, Colonel Duncan McArthur (later governor of Ohio) and Colonel Lewis Cass (later United States senator from Michigan), together with many officers, two hundred soldiers, and fifty Indians, including the chiefs of several nations.[25] It must indeed have been a colorful sight! They remained on board for two days to settle plans for future operations.

The crews were so weakened by sickness that General Harrison sent some thirty or forty army volunteers to serve with the sailors. Commodore Perry and half of the officers were on the sick list with "lake fever." The two senior medical officers were confined to their berths. Usher, the junior medical officer, was so sick that he was unable to climb up the ships' sides when visiting the sick on the various vessels. He "was hoisted in and out like a barrel of flour or a cask of water."

Nevertheless, he felt somewhat better on the 20th and went ashore. He procured "some apples, pigs, &c.," and came upon the body of a man recently scalped, a remnant of some past Indian depredations. On the 21st the generals departed, "having stripped us of our provisions!"—no doubt including some apples and pigs.

Between August 23 and September 1 the squadron sailed back and forth between Put-in-Bay and Malden at the mouth of the Detroit River, reconnoitering enemy shipping, but not attempting to engage in combat. On the 26th Commodore Perry reported sick, and on the 29th one of the soldiers on board the *Trippe* died. Usher noted in his diary, "People becoming very sick," and on the following day, "Very sick myself." He had now been ill for some ten days.

On September 1 they sailed within a few miles of Malden, and could make out there "2 ships full rigged, 2 brigs, 1 schooner, & 1 sloop." "We now looked into the harbour of Malden," wrote Usher, "by way of returning the civilities the enemy had shown us at Erie. This kind of polite attention was repeated two or three times."

With Perry still laid low with fever on August 31, a welcome and unexpected reinforcement of one hundred Kentucky riflemen, clad in linsey-woolsey hunting shirts, arrived, dispatched by General Harrison. Avidly curious, most never having seen a ship before, they clambered over the decks, climbed the masts, and invaded the sick bay and officers' cabins. Perry gave them their freedom for a while, but eventually took them in tow and lectured them on ship's etiquette and discipline. Their mission, he explained, would be to act as marines and sharpshooters in the impending battle.[26]

On September 2, they sailed past Put-in-Bay to Sandusky, where they found the *Ohio* and Captain Dobbins recently arrived from Erie. Thirty-six men and four officers of the fleet were now unfit for duty, increasing to fifty-seven within the next two days. As for Usher himself, he reported that "I was never so much emaciated." However, he roused himself sufficiently to visit Sandusky Island with one of the officers and "found it to improve my health very much." He brought back to ship a considerable amount of fruit which he discovered on shore and later reported that he was also "well supplied with vegetables." This was important, as we shall see later, since he was convinced of the great value of fresh food in healing the sick and wounded.

Usher was obviously much concerned with the large number of sick officers and men on the various ships. On the 6th the squadron sailed from Sandusky to Put-in-Bay through the islands. Usher reported that "Dr. Dunham moved to the *Caledonia* being very sick." On the 7th he was called out of bed before daybreak to see one of the officers and late that evening to see Doctor Barton on the *Niagara*. He again visited Barton and others on the *Niagara* twice the next day. On the 9th eighty-seven persons in the squadron were sick, "all of whom I had sole charge of."

This, of course, was a serious matter, particularly with both senior fleet surgeons, Samuel Horseley and Robert R. Barton, down with fever. Despite his own indisposition Usher was burdened with this very large number of sick non-combat casualties. As he recorded these gloomy facts, he could not know that a decisive bloody battle was impending and that he alone would have thrust upon him the entire load of wounded.[27]

NOTES

1. Pierre Berton, *Flames Across the Border: The Canadian-American Tragedy, 1813–1814* (Boston, Atlantic-Little, Brown, 1982), pp. 71–72.
2. Usher Parsons, "Diary Kept During the Expedition to Lake Erie," Foreword.
3. Usher Parsons, "Diary Kept During the Expedition to Lake Erie," from which much of the narrative that follows is extracted.
4. The assault on Queenston Heights on the Canadian side of the Niagara River (October 13, 1812) was led by Major General Stephen Van Rensselaer of the New York militia. Brigadier General Alexander Smyth (1765–1830) in command of a brigade of regulars refused to take orders from or cooperate with Van Rensselaer. Believing that the assault should be made above the falls (Fort Erie) rather than below (Queenston), he held his troops at Buffalo. Van Rensselaer gained a foothold

on the Canadian shore, but, without support of Smyth's brigade, he was compelled to surrender with the loss of nearly 1,000 men. Van Rensselaer resigned his command and Smyth took over on October 24, 1812. Smyth's assaults on Fort Erie on November 28 and December 1 were no more successful due to lack of transport.

5. Sir Isaac Brock (1769–1812), British general in command of all military forces in Canada, was fatally wounded during his successful defense of Queenston.

6. Pierre Berton, *Flames Across the Border*, preface to the American edition, and pp. 21–31; Allan S. Everest, *The War of 1812 in the Champlain Valley* (Syracuse, Syracuse University Press, 1981), pp. 21–31.

7. Much of the following narrative is extracted from Parsons's "Diary Kept During the Expedition to Lake Erie."

8. John Gorham (1783–1829), A.B. 1801, M.B. 1804, and M.D. 1811 (all at Harvard University) was Erving Professor of Chemistry at Harvard from 1816 to 1827.

9. John R. Fenwick (1780–1842), Lieutenant Colonel of Light Artillery, Regular Army, was breveted a full Colonel for gallantry in the action of Oct. 13, 1812.

10. Abiel Hall, Jr. to Usher Parsons, December 7, 1812, DPC.

11. William Cullen, M.D. (1710–1790) was Professor of the Institutes of Medicine at Edinburgh Medical School and author of such standard works of medicine as *Synopsis Nosologiae Methodicae, Institutions of Medicine, Lectures on Materia Medica, First Lines of the Practice of Physic,* and *Clinical Lectures.*

12. Usher Parsons to Isaac Day, December 10, 1812. This letter is not known to exist, but it is mentioned in a letter from Isaac Day to Usher Parsons, January 21, 1813, DPC.

13. This was reprinted in C. W. Parsons *Memoir*, pp. 61–63. There is a manuscript copy of this letter in the Rhode Island Medical Society with the notation in Usher's hand: "this being my first attempt at medical writing."

14. Usher may have been influenced, as were many others of his day, by the writings of Doctor Benjamin Rush of Philadelphia, although it is generally agreed that New England doctors did not characteristically subscribe to Rush's doctrine. Rush, a persuasive exponent of bleeding, had studied medicine at Edinburgh under William Cullen and John Brown, who taught that fevers were due to debility, which increased irritability to a critical degree. Rush concluded that there was only one kind of fever, treated logically by reducing the "excitement" of the blood vessels. This he accomplished by a low diet, purging, and bleeding to the point of faintness and exhaustion—an excellent way, of course, of producing critical dehydration. The New Englanders maintained that bleeding produced its effects by relaxing excess tension in the blood vessels, nerves, and the body as a whole. Rush's enthusiastic bloodletting had no doubt contributed substantially to the demise of

George Washington. See Ralph H. Major, *A History of Medicine* (Springfield, Ill., Charles C. Thomas, 1954, 2 volumes), pp. 589–594, 724–730. See also W. F. Norwood's *Medical Education in the United States Before the Civil War,* pp. 69–75; *Medical America in the Nineteenth Century—Readings from the Literature,* edited by Gert H. Brieger (Baltimore, The Johns Hopkins Press), 1972, p. 95; and George W. Corner, *Two Centuries of Medicine: A History of the School of Medicine, University of Pennsylvania* (Philadelphia, J. B. Lippincott Co., 1965), pp. 39, 46, 67.

15. Abiel Hall, Jr. to Usher Parsons, March 10, 1813, DPC.

16. Following Gen. William Hull's disastrous surrender of Detroit to British Gen. Isaac Brock on Aug. 16, 1812, Maj. Gen. William Henry Harrison (1773–1841) was given command of all ground forces in this area, including a contingent of Kentucky militia recently raised by Brig. Gen. James Winchester (1752–1826) at Cincinnati. With Detroit as his objective, Harrison planned to move his army westward across Ohio in three sections and coordinate their crossing of the Maumee River. Winchester reached the river on Jan. 10, ahead of the main body and crossed into southeast Michigan unsupported. Surprised and overwhelmed by a superior force of 2,000 on the Raisin River south of Detroit on Jan. 22, 1813, Winchester's entire army was killed or captured, and Winchester himself was taken prisoner. Harrison thereupon went into winter quarters at Fort Meigs (near present-day Toledo) on the Maumee.

17. Usher Parsons to William and Abigail F. B. Parsons, February 11, 1813, DPC.

18. Joseph C. Roberts to Usher Parsons, May 3, 1813, DPC.

19. Usher Parsons, *Battle of Lake Erie. A Discourse Delivered Before the Rhode Island Historical Society, on the Evening of Monday, February 16, 1852* (2d ed., Providence, Bejamin T. Albro, printer, 1854) p. 3.

20. Alexander Slidell Mackenzie, *The Life of Commodore Oliver Hazard Perry* (New York, Harper & Brothers, 1840, 2 volumes), v. 1, pp. 21–69 *passim.*

21. The following text is extracted from Parsons's "Diary Kept During the Expedition to Lake Erie" and his Rhode Island Historical Society discourse *Battle of Lake Erie.*

22. The indecisive Battle of Stoney Creek (near Hamilton, Ontario) was yet another American attempt to invade upper Canada. Ineptly carried out, it was repulsed with considerable losses. Brig. Gen. William Henry Winder (1775–1851), lawyer and soldier and father of Brig. Gen. John Henry Winder, who was the hated commandant of the Confederate prison at Andersonville, and Brig. Gen. John Chandler, U.S.A. (1762–1841) were both captured.

23. Benjamin Rush taught that "Purges, vomits, blisters, sweats, and laudanum have all their precise days [and] hours" when they are effectual.

Whether because of or in spite of this drastic treatment, the Commodore appears to have recovered.

24. Usher Parsons, *Battle of Lake Erie, A Discourse . . .*, p. 6.

25. Edmund Pendleton Gaines (1777–1849) was later promoted to Major General. Colonel Duncan McArthur (1772–1839) was involved in the defense of Fort Meigs. Lewis Cass (1782–1866) was taken prisoner in Hull's capitulation at Detroit, but was released in Jan. 1813. Cass was Secretary of War under Andrew Jackson and Secretary of State under Buchanan. Fort Meigs, called the "Gibraltar of the West," was located on the Maumee River.

26. Pierre Berton, *Flames Across the Border*, p. 152.

27. Usher Parsons, "Surgical Account of the Naval Battle on Lake Erie, on the 10th of September," *New England Journal of Medicine and Surgery*, 7:316, 1818. The duties and responsibilities of a naval surgeon are well described in several publications of J. Worth Estes, M.D., notably, *Naval Medicine in the Early Nineteenth Century* (Boston, Education Department, USS Constitution Museum, 1981), and "Naval Medicine in the Age of Sail: The Voyage of the *New York*, 1802–1803," *Bulletin of the History of Medicine*, 56:238–253, 1982.

CHAPTER THREE

The Great Battle

Usher's own vivid story[1] of the strategic Battle of Lake Erie was written almost twenty-nine years after the event. Based as it was on his own diaries and his sharp memory of his personal experiences, it has stood the test of time for accuracy. Such standard contemporary accounts as those of historians George Bancroft,[2] Henry Barton Dawson,[3] Benson John Lossing,[4] and Alexander Slidell Mackenzie, Perry's biographer,[5] borrowed from it freely.[6] Usher, the sole medical officer available for duty during the battle, was stationed aboard the flagship *Lawrence*. This is his account of the battle:[7]

[On] the evening of the 9th of September [1813] . . . we anchored in Put-in-Bay. On the following morning at sunrise there was a cry from the masthead, "sail ho!" All hands sprang from their berths, and ere we could dress and reach the decks the cry was repeated again and again, until six sail were thus announced. Signal was made to the fleet, "Enemy in sight! Get under way!" and the hoarse voice and shrill pipe of the boatswain resounded through all the ships, "all hands up anchor."

The wind at this time was from the southwest, light and baffling, which prevented our weathering the island in our way, and it continued so until ten o'clock [a.m.], when it veered to the southeast, which enabled us to clear the island [South Bass Island, the site of Put-in-Bay], and stand out upon the lake. We now discovered the English squadron, five or six miles to the leeward, hove to in a line, and equidistant about a half cable's length. The vessels were freshly painted, and their red ensigns gently unfolding to the breeze, they made a very gallant appearance. [It was now a "clear pleasant day"].[8] Our squadron bore down to engage them, with the wind on our larboard quarter. . . .

41

The Commodore next produced the burgee, or fighting flag, hitherto concealed in the ship. It was inscribed with large white letters upon a blue ground, that could be read throughout the fleet, "DON'T GIVE UP THE SHIP"—the last words of the expiring Lawrence and now to be hoisted at the masthead of the flagship bearing his name.[9] A spirited appeal was made to the crew assembled upon the quarterdeck, who returned three cheers that were repeated along the whole line of our vessels, and up went the flag to the top of the fore-royal.

The Commodore brought me a package of papers, having a piece of lead attached to them, and gave orders in the event of his falling, to throw the papers overboard; they were instuctions from [the] Government, and letters from Mrs. Perry.

The grog ration being served out, drums and fifes struck up the thrilling air, "all hands, all hands, to quarters," calling all to their respective stations. The Commodore was on the quarter deck, with two young officers, Thomas Breese and his own brother, Alexander Perry, whose duty it was to run with his orders to every part of the ship: for in the din and uproar of battle no officers can be heard ten feet off. The hatches were now closed excepting a small aperture ten inches square, through which powder cartridges were to be passed up from the magazine by boys nimble of foot during the battle, and through which light was admitted into the surgeon's room, where the wounded were to be brought. The floor of this apartment was on a level with the surface of the water outside, and consequently the wounded were as much exposed to the enemy's cannon balls as if they were on deck. Six men were directed to bring the wounded below, and to assist the surgeon in moving them.

Every preparation being made, and every man at his post, a profound silence reigned for more than one hour—the most trying part of the whole scene. It was like the stillness of the atmosphere that precedes the hurricane. The fleet moved on steadily till a quarter before Meridian [11:45 a.m.], when the awful suspense was relieved by a cannon shot aimed at us from the flagship *Detroit*, one mile distant. It was like an electric shock, and was soon followed by another. . . .

The enemy fire was concentrated on the flagship *Lawrence*. In time it was completely crippled and dropped astern, "a perfect wreck." Abandoning the *Lawrence*, Perry took off in a boat for the *Niagara*, which then became his flag-ship; the *Lawrence* hauled down her flag and ceased firing. The battle, however, progressed to complete victory for the Americans, with the action terminating at about 4:00 p.m. Usher's viewpoint is from his own battle station below deck:[10]

The wounded began to come down before the *Lawrence* opened her battery, and for one I felt impatient at the delay. In proper time, however, as it proved, the dogs of war were let loose from their leash, and it seemed as though heaven and earth were at loggerheads. For more than two long hours little could be heard but the deafening thunders of our broadsides, the crash of balls dashing through our timbers, and the shrieks of the wounded. These were brought down faster than I could attend to them, farther than to stay the bleeding, or support the shattered limbs with splints, and pass them forward upon the berth deck. Two or three were killed near me, after being wounded. . . .

Among those early brought down was Lieutenant Brooks, son of the late Governor Brooks of Massachusetts, a most accomplished gentleman and officer; and renowned for his personal beauty. A cannon-ball had struck him in the hip, he knew his doom, and inquired how long he should live; I told him a few hours. He inquired two or three times how the day was going, and expressed a hope that the Commodore would be spared. But newcomers from deck brought more and more dismal reports, until finally it was announced that we had struck [our flag]. In the lamentations of despair among the wounded, I lost sight of poor Brooks for a few minutes, but when the electrifying cry was heard that the enemy's two ships had struck, I rushed on deck to see if it were true, and then to poor Brooks to cheer him, but he was no more—he was too much exhausted by his wounds to survive the confusion that preceded this happy transition.

When the battle had raged an hour and a half, I heard a call for me at the small sky-light, and stepping toward it I saw it was the Commodore, whose countenance was as calm and placid as if on ordinary duty. "Doctor," said he, "send me one of your men," meaning one of the six that were to assist me, which was done instantly. In five minutes the call was repeated and obeyed, and at the seventh call I told him he had them all. He asked if any could pull a rope, when two or three of the wounded crawled upon deck to lend a feeble hand in pulling the last guns. When the battle was raging most severely, Midshipman Lamb came down with his arm badly fractured; I applied a splint and requested him to go forward and lie down; as he was leaving me, and while my hand was on him, a cannon-ball struck him in the side, and dashed him against the other side of the room, which instantly terminated his sufferings. Charles Pohig, a Narragansett Indian, who was badly wounded, suffered in like manner.

The destruction and carnage aboard the *Lawrence* were appalling. In his report[10] to the Secretary of the Navy, Perry stated: "Every brace and bow line being soon shot away she became unmanageable, notwithstanding the great exertions of her sailing-master. In this situation she sustained the action upwards of two hours within canister distance, until every gun was rendered useless, and the greater part of her crew either killed or wounded." Guns were dismounted; the killed and wounded were strewn about. But amidst these terrifying scenes the irrepressible Yanks saw things to smile about and ways to relieve the tension:[11]

> There were other incidents that were less painful to witness. The Commodore's dog had secreted himself in the bottom of the closet containing all our crockery. A cannon-ball passed through the closet, and smashed crockery and door, covering the floor with fragments. The dog set up a barking protest against the right of such an invasion of his chosen retirement.
>
> Lieut. Yarnall had his scalp badly torn, and came below with blood streaming over his face; some lint was hastily applied and confined with a large bandanna, with directions to report himself for better dressing after the battle, and he insisted on returning to deck. The cannon-balls had knocked to pieces the hammocks stowed away on deck, and let loose their contents, which were reed or flag-tops, that floated in the air like feathers and gave the appearance of a snow-storm. These lighted upon Yarnall's head covered with blood, and on coming below with another injury, his bloody face covered with the cat tails made his head resemble that of a huge owl. Some of the wounded roared with laughter that the devil had come for us.

Concerning his management of the casualties Usher wrote:[12]

> [The ward-room] being only nine or ten feet square, this floor was soon covered, which made it necessary to pass the wounded out into another apartment, as fast as the bleeding could be stanched either by ligatures or tourniquet. Indeed this was all that was attempted for their benefit during the engagement, except that in some instances division was made of small portions of flesh, by which a dangling limb, that annoyed the patient, was hanging to the body. . . . of about one hundred men reported fit

for duty in the morning, twenty-one were found dead, and sixty-three wounded. The wounded arteries occupied my first attention, all which, except where amputation was required, were secure before dark. Having no assistant . . . I deemed it safer to deter amputation till morning, and in the meantime suffered the tourniquets to remain on the limbs. Nothing more was done through the night than to administer opiates and preserve shattered limbs in a uniform position.

Usher's diary contained a description of the action and this entry:

. . . Slept but little, & dressed about one third, & secured with tourniquets such as bled copiously. During the action I cut off 6 legs in the cock-pit, which were very nearly divided by cannon-balls. Most of these numbered among the dead.

His formal account continues:[13]

The hard fighting terminated about three o'clock. As the smoke cleared away the two fleets were found completely mingled, the small vessels having come up to the others. The shattered *Lawrence* lying to the windward was once more able to hoist her flag, which was cheered by a few feeble voices on board, making a melancholy sound compared with the boisterous cheers that preceded the battle.

About four o'clock a boat was discovered approaching the *Lawrence*. Soon the Commodore was recognized in her . . . returning to resume command of his tattered ship, determined that the remnant of her crew should have the satisfaction of witnessing the formal surrender of the British officers. It was a time of conflicting emotions when he stepped upon the deck; the battle was won and he was safe, but the deck was slippery with blood, and strewn with the bodies of twenty officers and men, some of whom had sat at table with us at our last meal, and the ship resounded everywhere with the groans of the wounded. Those of us who were spared and able to walk, met him at the gangway to welcome him on board, but the salutation was a silent one on both sides; not a word could find utterance.

And now the British officers arrived, one from each vessel to tender their submission, and with it their swords. When they had approached, picking their way among the wreck and carnage of the deck, they held their swords with the hilts toward Perry, and tendered them to his acceptance. With a dignified and solemn air, the most remote possible from any betrayal of exultation, and in a low tone of voice, he requested them to retain their side-arms,

inquired with deep concern for Commodore Barclay and the
wounded officers, tendering to them every comfort his ship afforded, and expressing his regret that he had not a spare medical
officer to send them, adding that he had only one on duty for the
fleet, [and he] had his hands full. . . .

Those who were killed in the battle were committed to the
deep at night-fall, the Episcopal service being read over them. . . .

Immediately following the cessation of hostilities Perry sent forward these historic communications famed for their terseness and
dignity; the first to General Harrison, and the second to the Secretary of the Navy:[14]

Dear General,—
We have met the enemy, and they are ours. Two ships, two
brigs, one schooner, and one sloop.
Yours, with great respect and esteem,

O. H. Perry.
P.S. Send us some soldiers to take care of the prisoners who are
more numerous than ourselves.

*　　*　　*

U.S. brig *Niagara*, off the westernmost Sister head of Lake Erie,
Sept. 10, 1813, 4 p.m.
Sir,
It has pleased the Almighty to give to the arms of the United
States a signal victory over their enemies on this lake. The British
squadron, consisting of two ships, two brigs, one schooner, and
one sloop, have this moment surrendered to the force under my
command, after a sharp conflict.
I have the honour to be, Sir, your obedient servant,

O. H. Perry

In his later report to the Secretary of the Navy, Perry noted:[15]
"The *Lawrence* has been so entirely cut up, it is absolutely neces-
sary she should go into a safe harbor; I have therefore directed Lieut.
Yarnall to proceed to Erie in her, with the wounded of the fleet and
dismantle and get her over the bar as soon as possible."
Usher's diary resumes on the day following the battle:

Saturday, September 11th. Very early I commenced operating.
Found that four of those whose legs I amputated yesterday and
laid on the berth deck were either afterwards killed in action or

had died of their wounds. Before breakfast, had dressed one amputated leg, James Tompson of New York.

After breakfast I amputated the leg of George Varnum of Wiscasset [Maine]. In both these cases I deceived myself in applying the tourniquette [sic] not sufficiently taut and was compelled to turn it after having made the incisions. At ten o'clock I amputated the arm of James Moses of Falmouth [Maine]. This case was a compound fracture of the humerus within 2 inches of the head. . . . Was unable to apply the tourniquette [because of the high level of the injury] and used compression on the first rib [to compress the subclavian artery]. After dividing the bone, found the artery had retracted so much that it was 15 minutes before I could arrive at it and then only by dissection. Secured it and made a tolerable covering.

By seven o'clock he had completed all of the amputations. "The impatience of this class of the wounded," he wrote, "rendered it necessary to take them in the same succession in which they fell." He next attended to the compound and simple fractures, luxations, lacerations, and contusions in that order, "all which occupied my time till twelve o'clock at night." His account continues:[16]

The day following [September 12] I visited the wounded of the *Niagara*, who had lain till that time, with their wounds undressed. I found the surgeon sick in bed, with hands too feeble to execute the dictates of a feeling heart. Twenty-one wounded were mustered, most of whom were taken on board the *Lawrence* and dressed, and afterwards such as were lying in like manner on board the small vessels. In the course of the evening the sick were prescribed for, which was the first attention I had been able to render them since the action.

In his entry for the day in his diary, he added:

. . . Trepanned[17] John Newen, Quarter Master, [and] removed several pieces of bone from the cerebrum, and a piece of leather hat. Found him sinking during the operation and dressed him immediately. A violent gale this day carried away all the masts of the *Detroit*, and the forward mizzen of the *Charlotte*. Funeral of the officers.

That evening, he later recalled,[18] "the officers of the small vessels came on board the *Lawrence* . . . and all of them, without exception, expressed but one opinion on the conduct of Elliott [Captain of the

Niagara] in keeping out of the battle, that he held back more than two hours from engaging his antagonist the *Queen,* that when the *Lawrence* was much crippled and began to drop astern, the *Niagara* then came up abreast of her and the enemy, but far away outside, much farther from the *Lawrence* than the *Lawrence* was from the enemy." Elliott's tactics resulted later in a serious controversy between himself and Perry.

Usher described the officers' funeral in his history of the battle:[19]

> On the following morning [after the battle] the two fleets sailed into Put-in-Bay where the slain officers were buried on the shore. The scene was a solemn one. Equal respect was paid to the slain of the two fleets. Minute guns were fired from the fleet, a martial band preceded performing a funeral dirge, and the corpses were ranged in alternate order of American and British, and the procession followed in like order to the graves, where the funeral service was read.

Again from the diary:

> Monday 13th. Called the British surgeons in consultation today, viz. Dr. Young & Kennedy. Much pleased with them. Amputated limbs doing well. I am unable to attend the sick [presumably because of his own indisposition].
> Tuesday, Sept. 14. Wounded [i.e. the remainder] removed from the *Niagara* to the *Lawrence.* Officers from Gen. Harrison's army arrived on board. Dr. Crow was sent to assist me with the wounded from Harrison's army. Thursday 16th. Had not time before today to make out an official report of wounded. . . .
> Friday 17th. John Newen [his trephine case] died this morning & am unwell myself. We are just able to dispense with the wounded from morning 'til night. Amputated limbs doing extremely well. Saturday. Sept. 18th. Troops are coming in to Put-in-Bay from Sandusky, &c. Am very low spirited. Writing up the sick book. Sunday 19th. Unwell. Hardly able to attend duty. Monday 20. All impatient to sail. Market boat came along with fresh provisions from Cleveland & Sandusky. I bought for the wounded a barrel of pumpion [*sic*] pies.
> Tuesday, September 21st. Gen. Harrison on board. Dr. Martin, Surgeon General, consulted with me on all the desperate cases. We got under way for Erie and proceeded six miles. Wednesday 22. . . . [Two men] died with fever. Pleasant. Got under way at daylight, going 31 knots.

On the same day he wrote his first letter to his parents since the great battle. It contained the earliest reference in Usher's own hand to Elliott's ambiguous conduct, which generated Elliott's later bitter conflict with Perry:[20]

> Before the arrival of this, an account of our victorious engagement with the British Squadron on this Lake will reach you. I can only add a few particulars . . . .

After briefly describing the action, he continued:

> It may seem mysterious to one how some of the other vessels could see us slaughtered in such a manner [and remain out of the action], but it is equally so to us. Nor can the commanders of some of them offer satisfactory reasons for remaining behind [i.e. Elliott and the *Niagara*]. Unfortunately for the wounded, the two Surgeons had been confined for some days with fever and could render them but little assistance. It however has operated in my favour, as I have had all the amputating to perform and it affords me the greatest pleasure to reflect that in no case have I failed of the best success. This has impressed the Commodore with so favourable opinion toward me that I have not the least doubt of his rendering me assistance to a better situation. He is the first warm friend I have met in the service capable of assisting me. I am now on my way in the *Lawrence* for Erie, having all the sick and wounded on board, and shall continue with them in the hospital 'til the most of them recover, and then intend to shape my course for Cape Home. Gen. Harrison was on board the *Lawrence* this morning,[21] and his army was on an island within half a mile of the vessel consisting of about 7,000. Since the loss of the British fleet the Indians have deserted Detroit after burning the place and (as is reported) massacring the inhabitants. I had some narrow escapes for my life during the action. Five cannon balls passed through the room in which I was attending to the wounded. Two that I had dressed and laid aside were afterwards killed during the action. The enemy's squadron mounted more guns than ours and carried at least one fourth more men. In the course of a year I hope to obtain a little prize money. I have enjoyed very bad health during the cruise and am reduced to a skeleton, and will never cross this or any other lake again.

Samuel, Usher's elder brother, was also in service on the Lakes, but was not mentioned in the diary. Usher, however, informed his family that "Samuel's steady and well." At high noon on the 23rd the *Lawrence* arrived at Erie and was greeted by a seventeen gun salute. The wounded were brought ashore and removed to the courthouse hospital. Usher was now extremely busy caring for the casualties, but there was inevitable sadness. On the 28th Usher wrote in his diary: "Mr. Claxton very low." Thomas Claxton,[22] a midshipman whom Usher considered one of the most promising young officers, had received a mortal shoulder wound in the battle. His father, Doorkeeper of the United States House of Representatives, was unaware of the tragic event and had written from Washington relating news of the family and expressing pleasure at hearing that "you were well." Usher had the painful duty of informing Claxton's father of the untimely death. Young Claxton died on October 8. He appears again in this story, but briefly, many years later.

On the 24th of September Usher learned from G. W. May[23] that the remittance of seventy-five dollars forwarded to Doctor Warren by "Mr. Farewell" in February in partial payment for his preceptorship had never arrived. May chided Usher for not sending the money by mail; or, if he had obtained the fellow's Christian name and address, he might be found and the money recovered. "Write to Dr. Warren," he advised, "and give him all the particulars." Usher complied.

Usher found time for relaxation, tarried ashore with his new acquaintances, including a "Miss H," and visited the various ships for both professional and social reasons. On October 22 Commodore Perry and the defeated Commodore Robert Barclay arrived at Erie and were welcomed with a gun salute. That evening the houses and streets were illuminated, and a street procession was accompanied by the sound of cannon, "musick &c., &c."

Usher's finances were considerably bolstered by an "acceptance" from the Navy of $442 and later an additional unexpected $100. On the 13th he "took thorough rounds at the hospital" and later "operated on [one] George Platt for stricture," a hazard of the sailors' dalliances.

The 21st dawned a rare pleasant day, inspiring Usher to go sightseeing at Waterford, fifteen miles away on the French River, which sported "4 publick inns, very reputable," where he "passed the evening merrily." The 25th, he recalled, was "Thanksgiving in Massachusetts," his second away from home. He played cards often, sometimes winning and sometimes losing. As winter deepened, he indulged in "good sleighing." Midshipman Senat and Sailing Master

Birthplace of Usher Parsons in Alfred, Maine. Built by his father, William Parsons, about 1781, and called by him "The Mansion," it is located on Kennebunk Road, just outside the village proper. Photograph (1984) by the author.

Left: John Warren (1753–1815), preceptor of Usher Parsons and first professor of anatomy and surgery at Harvard. From a painting by Rembrandt Peale, lithographed by John Pendleton. Countway Library, Harvard Medical School.

Right: Massachusetts Medical College, the medical department of Harvard University. Located on Mason Street, Boston, not far from the Boston Common, between 1816 and 1846. From an engraving by Ammin R. Smith, 1820. Countway Library, Harvard Medical School.

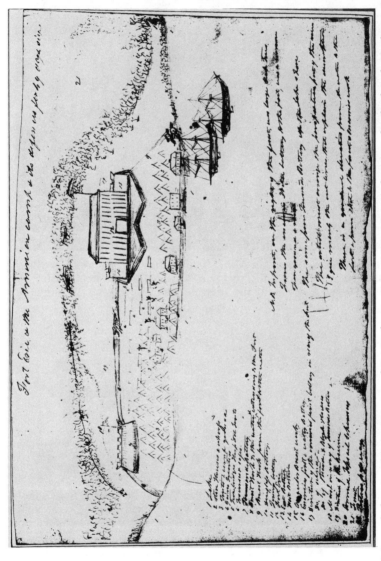

"Fort Erie and the American Camp and its Defenses." From an unsigned pen and ink sketch made in 1860 by Usher Parsons and sent to W. W. Dobbins of Erie, son of Captain Daniel Dobbins. The original is in the Buffalo Historical Society. From a photostat in the Rhode Island Historical Society Manuscript Collection.

View of Put-in-Bay Harbor and Put-in-Bay Island. The smoke on the horizon to the left indicates the location of the Battle of Lake Erie. Wood engraving from a drawing "made on the spot in 1859 by Captain Van Cleve," a veteran steamboat commander on the lakes. This, and the other illustrations on this plate, are from *The Pictorial Field-Book of the War of 1812*, by Benson J. Lossing (1869).

Left: Captain Daniel Dobbins (1776–1856), a sailing master during the War of 1812. Woodcut from a painting by Moses Billings of Erie, Pennsylvania, c. 1851.

Right: Commodore Stephen Champlin (1789–1870). He was one of a number of Rhode Islanders whom Oliver Hazard Perry brought to the Lakes to help him man his squadron during the conflict. Woodcut copied after an unidentified source.

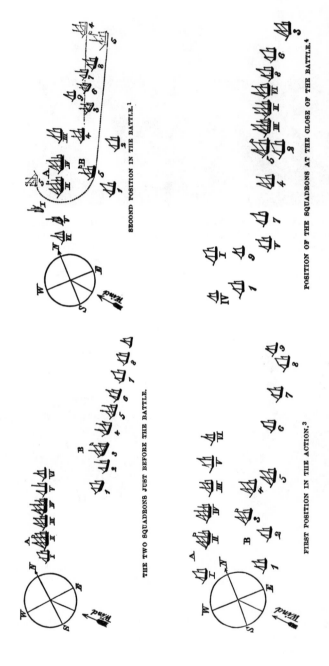

Diagrams showing the positions of the two squadrons during various stages of the Battle of Lake Erie. The British vessels (A) are designated by Roman numerals and the Americans (B) by Arabic. The British ships were I. *Chippewa*, II. *Detroit*, III. *Hunter*, IV. *Queen Charlotte*, V. *Lady Prevost*, and VI. *Little Belt*. The American ships were 1. *Scorpion*, 2. *Ariel*, 3. *Lawrence*, 4. *Caledonia*, 5. *Niagara*, 6. *Somers*, 7. *Porcupine*, 8. *Tigress*, and 9. *Trippe*. The diagrams were furnished to Lossing by Stephen Champlin.

The Battle of Lake Erie, September 10, 1813. Engraving in *The Life of Oliver Hazard Perry* by John M. Niles. Published separately by William S. March, Hartford, 1820. Rhode Island Historical Society.

"Perry's Victory on Lake Erie." Chromolithograph by Kurz and Allison, Chicago, 1880 period. Shows Perry transferring his command from the disabled brig *Lawrence* to the unblemished brig *Niagara*. Rhode Island Historical Society.

Left: Usher Parsons at about the time he joined the Navy as a surgeon's mate in 1812. From a miniature by an unknown artist in the Dwight-Parsons Collection, Brown University Archives.

Right: Commodore Oliver Hazard Perry (1785–1819). Painting by John Wesley Jarvis. Courtesy of the U. S. Naval Academy Museum. From a photograph in the Rhode Island Historical Society.

Unidentified American frigate, early nineteenth century. Copy of an engraving by Baugean from "Récueil de Marines," titled "Frigate of the United States of America, preparing to anchor and taking in topsails." Probably the *Macedonian*, but also possibly the *Guerrière* or *Java*, all of the same class. U. S. Naval Historical Center.

McDonald fought their first of several duels, somehow related to the Perry-Elliott controversy. No one was hurt, but a year later McDonald ultimately succeeded in killing Senat.

Usher made daily hospital rounds and looked in at sessions in the courthouse. He attended an amputation in a neighboring hospital and observed the first dressing of the stump. As his patients convalesced, they were returned to duty on the ships or in the field, and he certified pensions for the wounded of the *Lawrence*. With the luxury of more leisure, he resumed his medical reading, concentrating on chemistry, and worked at cleaning his pet skeleton. The hospital was now functioning well, and he was at last in "high spirits."[24]

Usher made his final entry for the year 1814 on December 11 and soon thereafter went on detached duty. It is fitting here to review his own account of his surgical experience and results:[25]

> In the battle of Lake Erie, on the 10th of September, 1813, nearly a hundred were wounded—sixty-one of them on board the *Lawrence*, twenty-three on board the *Niagara*, and about a dozen in the smaller vessels. There were eleven cases of compound fractures, besides simple fractures, many gun-shot wounds and extensive lacerations; among them all several amputations were required. Those wounded on board the *Lawrence* were ranged on the upper deck in the spaces occupied by the cannon and gun carriages, which were removed from both sides of the deck to afford room for mattresses. . . .
>
> To the wounded of the *Lawrence* were added, after two days, those of the *Niagara* and of the small vessels. The whole number of patients requiring a recumbent posture on the deck was about fifty. They remained in the ship fourteen days after the action, and were then landed at Erie and lodged in a large unfinished courthouse, and remained there until cured. Of the ninety-six wounded only three died, and these were cases of so severe a nature that a surgical operation was not deemed justifiable, and they were left to linger out a few days of misery.

Usher attributed[26] his success to a number of factors (not discounting, of course, "a generous supply of wine and cordials," or the "barrel of pumpion pies"):

> The recovery of so great a proportion of the wounded may in a great measure be attributed to the following causes: *First* to the purity of the air. The patients were ranged along on the upper

deck, with no other shelter from the weather than a high awning
to shade them. They continued in this situation for a fortnight,
and when taken on shore, were placed in very spacious apartments, well ventilated. *Secondly*, to the supply of food best
adapted to their cases, as fowls, fresh meat, milk, eggs, and vegetables in abundance. The second day after the action, the farmers
on the Ohio shore brought alongside every article of the above
description that could be desired. *Thirdly*, to the happy state of
mind which victory occasioned. The observations, which I have
been able to make on the wounded of three engagements, have
convinced me that this state of mind has greater effect than has
generally been supposed; and that the surgeon on the conquering
side will, *caeteris paribus*, always be more successful than the
one who has charge of the vanquished crew [the effect of morale
on recovery is not far-fetched, and has often been noted in civilian
practice]. *Lastly*, to the assistance rendered me by Commodore
Perry and Mr. Davidson. The latter gentleman was a volunteer
soldier among the Kentucky troops, and engaged to serve on board
the fleet during the action. After the action he rendered the
wounded every aid in his power, continuing with them three
months. And the Commodore seemed quite as solicitous for their
welfare as he could possibly have felt for the success of the battle.

Since Usher was the only surgeon on duty during the battle, the
pressure of work was so great that he was obliged to confine his
efforts to lifesaving measures. He administered generous amounts
of cordials and anodynes as sedatives and allowed his wounded
charges to rest through the night. The cordials were aromatized
alcoholic liqueurs, while the anodynes contained mostly opiates.
The delay yielded an unexpected dividend; he explained it thus:[27]
"Now as all but the hopeless cases recovered, it was proved satisfactorily that the delay of amputations and other severe operations
for one and even two days had no unfavorable effect upon the
chances of recovery. Probably some lives were saved by it which
would have been lost had the operation taken place on the day of
injury."

Many years later he wrote:[28] "[A] cause of success worthy of
special notice was the *delay of severe surgical operations until the
system was entirely recovered from the shock of the injury.*" This
astute evaluation of his experience in 1813 was written just before
the outbreak of the Civil War; its significance would not be fully
realized until the classical studies on traumatic shock of World War

I. Another incredible success was his case mortality of little more than three per cent. During the Korean War, the mortality among treated casualties was estimated to be about 2½ per cent, the lowest in history up to that time. Yet this impressive feat had been matched by a twenty-five year old, inexperienced, and partially trained physician more than a hundred years earlier. In attending to ground casualties later on he did not fare as well. In a report to the Secretary of the Navy written in January 1814, Perry stated:[29]

> Of Dr. Usher Parsons, surgeon's mate, I cannot say too much. In consequence of the disability of both the other surgeons, Drs. Horsely and Barton, the whole duty of operating, dressing, and attending nearly a hundred wounded, and as many sick, devolved entirely on him; and it must be pleasing to you, sir, to reflect that, of the whole number wounded, only three have died. I can only say that, in the event of my having another command, I should consider myself particularly fortunate in having him with me as a surgeon.

NOTES

1. Usher Parsons, *Battle of Lake Erie, A Discourse . . .*

2. George Bancroft, *Oliver Hazard Perry and the Battle of Lake Erie. Together with the Addresses of Dr. Usher Parsons, Fleet Surgeon Under Commodore Perry, and of Governor William Sprague of Rhode Island, Delivered in Cleveland, Sept. 10, 1860, and Other Papers of Interest* (Newport, R.I., Mercury Publishing Co., 1912).

3. Henry Barton Dawson, *Battles of the United States, By Sea and Land; Embracing Those of the Revolutionary and Indian Wars, the War of 1812, and the Mexican War; with Important Official Documents* (New York, Johnson Fry, and Co., 1858, 2 volumes), v. 2, pp. 274–287.

4. Benson John Lossing, *The Pictorial Field-Book of the War of 1812, of the History, Biography, Scenery, Relics, and Traditions of the Last War for American Independence* (New York, Harper & Brothers, 1869, 3 volumes), pp. 1242–1243.

5. Alexander Slidell Mackenzie, *The Life of Commodore Oliver Hazard Perry*, v. 1, pp. 222–269.

6. It was also the basic source for the recent excellent narrative of the battle by Pierre Berton, *Flames Across the Border.*

7. Usher Parsons, *Battle of Lake Erie, A Discourse . . .*, p. 8, *et seq.*

8. Usher Parsons, "Surgical Account of the Battle on Lake Erie."

9. The ill-fated American naval hero, James Lawrence, was mortally

wounded when the U.S.S. *Constitution* was captured by the British outside Boston harbor on June 1, 1813.

10. Usher Parsons, *Battle of Lake Erie, A Discourse* . . . , Appendix, p. 35.

11. Usher Parsons, *Battle of Lake Erie, A Discourse* . . . , p. 8, *et seq.*

12. Usher Parsons, "Surgical Account of the Battle on Lake Erie."

13. Usher Parsons, *Battle of Lake Erie, A Discourse* . . . , p. 8, *et seq.*

14. Alexander Slidell Mackenzie, *The Life of Commodore Oliver Hazard Perry*, v. 1, p. 261.

15. Oliver Hazard Perry to Navy Secretary William Jones, September 13, 1813 (second letter of that date), printed in Charles Oscar Paullin, *The Battle of Lake Erie: A Collection of Documents Chiefly by Commodore Perry* . . . (Cleveland, The Rowfant Club, 1918), p. 97. See also J. Russell, Jr., *The History of the War Between the United States and Great Britain, Which Commenced in June, 1812, and Closed in February, 1815 . . . Compiled Chiefly from Public Documents* (2d ed., Hartford, B. & J. Russell, 1815), pp. 219–221.

16. Usher Parsons, "Surgical Account of the Battle on Lake Erie."

17. A trepan is a crown saw for removing a button of skull for decompression or exploration. The modern term is trephine.

18. Usher Parsons, *Battle of Lake Erie, A Discourse* . . . , p. 16.

19. *Ibid.*, p. 15.

20. Usher Parsons to William and Abigail F. B. Parsons, September 22, 1813, RIHS.

21. Harrison took Detroit on Sept. 15, 1813 and on Oct. 5 defeated Procter in the Battle of the Thames, in which Tecumseh was killed.

22. Usher Parsons, *Brief Sketches of the Officers Who Were in the Battle of Lake Erie* (Albany, N.Y., J. Munsell, 1862), p. 7. This was preprinted from the *New England Historical and Genealogical Register*, 17:17–20, 1863.

23. G. W. May to Usher Parsons, September 12, 1813, DPC.

24. Usher Parsons, "Diary Kept During the Expedition to Lake Erie."

25. Usher Parsons, "Letter on Some Points of Military Surgery, Addressed to Professor Frank H. Hamilton of Brooklyn, New York," *Communications of the Rhode Island Medical Society*, 1:97–99, 1861.

26. Usher Parsons, *Battle of Lake Erie, A Discourse* . . . , p. 6.

27. Usher Parsons, "Letter on Some Points of Military Surgery."

28. *Ibid.* The issue of prompt versus delayed amputation was being argued at the time. Whether or not Parsons would have preferred to amputate earlier is not relevant, since delay was forced upon him by the extreme pressure of work. In retrospect he felt that it had been beneficial. Larrey, Napoleon's surgeon, maintained that amputation should be performed early, certainly within twenty-four hours. Although his first monograph *Dissertations sur les Amputations des Membres à la Suite des Coups de Feu* appeared in 1803, the first English translation of his

memoirs did not appear in America until 1814, after the Erie battle. See his *Memoirs of Military Surgery and Campaigns of the French Armies, Translated by Richard Wilmot Hall* (2 v., first American from the second Paris edition, Baltimore, Joseph Cushing, 1814), v. 1, p. 333 and v. 2, p. 350. Larrey performed 200 amputations at the Battle of Borodino alone. The British naval surgeon, James Yonge (1647–1721), had written on amputation as early as 1679.

29. C. W. Parsons *Memoir*, p. 10.

CHAPTER FOUR

Great Lakes Cruise

After Perry's great naval victory, Erie became an American lake. Since he could now cruise its waters at will, the British would have considerable difficulty holding the territory captured in 1812. While they took up defensive positions along the Thames River Valley in Upper Canada, the United States reverted to its original strategy of cutting the lifeline between the two Canadas.[1] American armies at Fort George and Sackets Harbor would comprise the main attack force, while a third at Plattsburgh on Lake Champlain would either support a massive assault down the St. Lawrence or create a diversion.[2]

Shortly after the Erie battle, the British retreated from Detroit and Malden, enthusiastically pursued by William Henry Harrison, the hero of Tippecanoe, with a force larger than William Hull had had in the previous action in that area. In the ensuing Battle of the Thames River,[3] fought near Chatham, Ontario on October 5, 1813, the great Shawnee chief Tecumseh, swarthy hazel-eyed nemesis of Harrison, was slain, and the British command was put to flight.[4] The American invasion did not proceed much farther, but at war's end the Indians had been completely humbled and the northwestern border was in American hands.[5] Other combat on the Canadian frontier had produced nothing more startling than the burning by the Americans of the parliament buildings at York (Toronto),[6] while the British would take Fort Niagara[7] on the American side.

Efforts by the British during 1814 to invade the United States were inconclusive. In the Niagara area, where most of the fighting took place, the Americans on July 25 fought a stubborn engagement at Lundy's Lane,[8] west of Niagara Falls. The American forces under the command of the vain, but able General Winfield Scott and led in the field by the fine-looking but stubborn General Jacob J. Brown, pushed into Canada, encountering British troops posted along Lundy's Lane. After a night-long engagement with heavy casualties on both sides, the Americans withdrew to Fort Erie on news that the British had received significant reinforcements.

The Lake Champlain invasion route was rendered useless to the British when a small flotilla of American ships under the command of the able Captain Thomas Macdonough defeated a British squadron off Plattsburgh Bay,[9] while the big-chested blue-eyed General Alexander Macomb defeated a superior force of British under the ill-fated Sir George Prevost. While the Americans could no longer hope to gain control of the Canadian land mass, the northern frontier of the United States now appeared to be reasonably secure from invasion.

Usher made no entries in his diary during the period December 12 through January 21, but upon resuming his daily log inserted a resumé of military actions that had taken place in the interim. In October and November the despised General James Wilkinson had failed in a full-scale attempt to take Montreal. General George McClure, inept commander of a New York militia force, on December 10 had without orders burned Newark and then evacuated Fort George on the Canadian side of the Niagara, while on December 18 the British had destroyed Fort Niagara on the American side, burned the village, and took copious supplies of arms.

On December 29 the British crossed the upper Niagara and burned Black Rock and Buffalo.[10] When this intelligence reached the village of Erie, it was thrown into understandable confusion. Responding to an urgent appeal for help, General David Mead, commander of the Pennsylvania militia stationed at nearby Meadville, sent 200 men to aid in the defense of Erie and the fleet. Further, construction of a blockhouse and hospital on the peninsula at Presque Isle was started, and all British prisoners in the hospital at Erie were transferred to Pittsburgh.[11]

On New Year's Day of 1814 Usher was ordered by General David Mead to temporary duty as surgeon of the 17th Regiment, Pennsylvania Militia now stationed at Erie, probably in addition to his naval duties.

He wrote on the 10th to his friend Surgeon McReynolds at Sackets Harbor, complaining of the threatening military situation in the area. McReynolds replied:[12] "Your defenseless position (for such I may call it when militia are your only aids) is truly alarming. When will things be better conducted? I fear not until a change takes place elsewhere." While Usher was thus occupied, romance first appeared in his eventful life. McReynolds reacted skeptically: "Your talk of *love*. My God! Is it possible that you have seen any jade worthy of your attention in the woods of Erie? I am disposed to believe it not *honorable* love you talk of. Be it as it may, [I] have only to wish you success."

In the meantime, Usher had at last been promoted to the well-deserved rank of Surgeon and was ordered to duty on board the *Lawrence,* now completely repaired and returned to the fleet. Usher vacated his quarters on shore on January 19 and resumed his old billet aboard ship.

Usher continued to mix professional duties with lighter diversions. Late in January "women visited the fleet," and he "saw them on shore with Mr. Turner." The next day he made another overnight trip to Waterford with Turner and others, and on returning attended an evening party to which he "carried Miss C.F." The young lady, it seems, was the daughter of his friend Colonel Foster (more properly Forster), a resident of Erie with whom he boarded when on shore. Whether this lass was the principal object of his attentions is left to conjecture. On February 2, after attending the funeral of young Midshipman James Bliss, who had died of fever, he "commenced a journal of practice." He alone was "attending all the sick, which numbered about 50."

The journal of his medical experience in the Navy, titled *Day Book of Practice,* and his naval diaries have been in the custody of the Rhode Island Historical Society for more than a century. He kept the Day Book faithfully until the termination of his later cruises in European waters. On February 3 he wrote: "My month as Militia Surgeon expired. Dismissing the militia." He was paid through the 5th.

During February and well into March, Usher was occupied with daily routine aboard ship and on shore. He made many friends in the civilian community, where he visited frequently, and found female companionship among its eligible daughters. He often attended Sunday church service ("meeting"), usually that of the Reverend Robert Reid (whom he variously referred to as Reed and Read). Usher became closely attached to Reid, who, in the absence of a chaplain, also conducted burial services. On one Sabbath, after writing letters home and to his friends, he concluded the day "reading bible."

One of Usher's chores as a medical officer was the putting up and marking of medicines, in which connection he reviewed his books on materia medica. He brushed up on anatomy, having "had bones brought from the hospital," kept his journal of surgical cases up to date, and saw patients on the ships as well as on shore. Once, upon returning to the fleet, he noted laconically, "Found no one dead as I had expected." Seeking greater mobility, on February 14 he "bought 1/2 a horse & gave watch" in payment. The next day he "bought the other half for $35.00" However, after a week and without explanation, he sold the nag to one of the sailors, Ben Baily, for an unnamed price.

On the 17th he "went on shore with Mr. Turner" and "conducted with great impropriety in the evening!" It is not surprising that the next day he was "attacked with faintness." Later, he attended a ball with other officers. For change of pace he read *Democracy Unveiled*,[13] an attack on Thomas Jefferson and the Democrats by Thomas Green Fessenden, and "had some verbosity with Lieut. Webster." While in later years he was known for his abstemious habits, these were not evident at this stage of his life ("Drank apple toddy in the evening" and later, "Gentlemen drank with me A.M."). He also drank tea, as he reported on several occasions. At least twice he fell through thin ice attempting to board ship during a thaw. He enjoyed listening in at the county court, which was then in session. "I intend," he wrote rather cryptically on March 10, "to go to New Orleans in April." This plan never materialized.

On March 12, Usher confided in a letter to McReynolds that he was thinking of marrying. His mature and experienced confidant gave him fatherly advice:[14] "You mention that you think of taking [a] wife. The ladies of Erie must be very interesting. I expect to learn next that you are spliced." He then addressed Usher in the third person: "If matters are not too far advanced, I should be induced to tell him what he no doubt knows, that he is young, has many days before him, that before he reaches the meridian of life, his wife will be an old slouch with 1/2 dozen brats about." He allowed that such advice is "seldomly attended to, much less from one who acts on the other extreme." We do not know which of the several "ladies" mentioned by Usher was the apple of his eye, nor do we know the fate of this romance.

The officers greatly treasured the Reverend Reid's unwavering warmth and sympathy and appreciated his kindness in conducting services for their deceased comrades. On Monday, March 14 Usher recorded in his diary, "Presented Rev. Mr. Reed a black cloak in behalf of Navy officers." The gift was accompanied by a graceful little note drafted by Usher.[15] Reverend Reid acknowledged[16] with gratitude the thoughtful gift and expressed his appreciation for the opportunity of participating in their "devotional exercises."

From time to time Usher administered to the medical needs of his civilian friends. On one special occasion he "attended" a "parturition at Johnston." For some weeks he had been looking after "Eliza S's eye," presumably the daughter of Thomas H. Sill, a local citizen. Usher was considerably worried about her trouble and made several visits "to see Eliza's eye." On March 15, he made special notations in his diary, titled "Diseases of the Eye." His interest was obviously stimulated by his concern for Eliza. The notes, based on text-book reading, comprised mainly definitions of medical terms related to the eye, such as hypopyon, chemosis, leucoma, and albugo (respectively pus in the anterior chamber of the eyeball; swelling of the membrane covering the eyeball; milky-white opacity of the transparent corneal membrane; and also a white corneal opacity), and remarks on their Greek derivation. Happily, matters soon took a turn for the better, for on March 17 he observed, "On shore in the morning; found Miss S's eye better than I had expected."

After an interlude of two or three warm spring-like days, foul weather again set in. Yet the coming of the vernal equinox brought news of quickening military activity:

> Monday 21st. Overcast. Stormy. News arrived that the British are building a naval force on Lake Huron.

On the twenty-second he "rec'd cash of Dr. Wallace,—94 dollars for services as Surg-n of militia." This amount (actually $92.63 1/3) represented back pay for service with the Pennsylvania militia, of which Doctor Wallace was the medical officer.[17] The generous payment enabled him to settle some debts and make a loan besides. The nature of his debts is not mentioned, but there was much borrowing back and forth among the men:

Wednesday, 23 March. At Dr. Wallace's vesp. [in the evening] playing cards. Lost [$]30. Sent letter to Dr. Warren of Boston enclosing $50[18] Paid Mr. Seth Reed $31.50 in full,—also lent him $23.00. Paid Baily $8.82, Knox $1.00.

Usher received another payment of $200 from the navy on April 16. It came none too soon, as a few days before he had had another disastrous evening at cards ("lost 25"). Yet he promptly loaned or otherwise disposed of the whole amount to Ben Baily ("Hired Baily $200") to whom he had just paid $8.82. The nature of this transaction with Baily, not related to the horse episode, is unexplained.

This is the same Ben Baily who once aroused from a delirium to "perfect collectedness of mind" by drinking his "usual allowance of whiskey," and who on another occasion was wounded in the chest during the attack on the Canadian shore opposite Black Rock. Parsons described[19] Baily as a "robust seaman, aged about thirty seven." In the Black Rock affair he "was wounded by a canister shot which entered the chest about one inch from the sternum, passed through the right lung, and out between the fifth and sixth ribs, both of which it fractured." He convalesced "so rapidly, that in a fortnight he was able to do partial duty," and four weeks later "was perfectly sound and as active as any sailor in the battle of Lake Erie."

Usher was always keenly aware of world events and of their impact on the local situation. On April 14 he took note of a political act of great importance in the war ("The Embargo & Non-Intercourse are removed"). He added: "Reading newspapers." On the 28th, "News arrived of the defeat of the allies under Blucher." Cultural needs were not neglected, as he was also "reading a bk. re Philosophy."

Since Usher's relations with Captain Elliott were still outwardly cordial, it was not surprising that on April 23 Elliott invited him on board to dine. Usher, however, later strenuously opposed him in the controversy with Perry. Two days later Usher noted a "fray with Mr. Hyde & Mr. McDonald," probably over the Elliott-Perry affair. On the same day news arrived that Elliott would be replaced, and he finally left the station on May 4.

Another long-awaited dispatch arrived on April 25—announcement that the prize money, awarded for the capture of enemy ves-

sels during the battle of September 10, would amount to the handsome sum of $255,000. There was considerable delay before the
actual distribution, however, and then, because of the large number
of persons involved, individual awards were small.

The advent of spring and assurance of good weather brought
increasing activity at the base. A general muster was held on board
the *Niagara* on May 1 for the issuance of newly arrived orders and
resolutions. Usher was busily engaged in putting up medicines and
taking inventory. During the first ten days in May, the ships were
eased over the bar of Erie harbor into open water. On May 5 Usher
recorded with satisfaction: "I received my commission as Surgeon
of the Navy. Dated April 15th."[20]

Finally on May 12 Usher received a letter from Doctor John
Warren of Boston regarding the payment for his preceptorship and
the Ben Farewell business, which confirmed his worst fears:[21] "I
have never, either from Mr. Farewell [*sic*] or any other person, received any other money on account of your note. Should it come
to hand I will immediately apprize you thereof." In his diary that
day, Usher noted, "Wrote . . . to a lawyer near Merrimack [N.H.]
requesting him to get my money of Ben Farewell." Usher himself
had written to Farewell on November 7, but received no answer.
His recourse to legal help also proved to be unavailing.

In mid May a gossipy letter arrived from friend Pliny Hayes[22] in
Boston, a student at the Harvard Medical School, disclosing plans
for the new Harvard Medical School building in Boston and the
eventual establishment of the Massachusetts General Hospital:

> Some changes in the medical line have taken place or rather
> are about to take place in Boston since you went away. The
> legislature have made a grant of the Province House (Marlborough
> St.) and a committee have been appointed . . . to establish a
> general hospital, provided they procure by subscription the sum
> of $100,000. . . . and this confidently expected. . . . The medical
> department will be under the direction of the Professors. As soon
> as the subscription is filled, the Province House will be made use
> of until a new building is erected. They will give up the Alms
> house [then the only clinical facility available] next month. A
> grant has also been made to Harvard University of $50,000—
> 20,000 of which goes to the medical department, and will be
> appropriated to the erection of a medical college in Boston. The

building will be large and complete. The site is not yet fixed upon [ultimately Mason Street].

This information, of great interest to Usher, proved to be quite accurate. Hayes also reported: "The medical journal [predecessor of the venerable *New England Journal of Medicine*] goes on well. . . . Dr. Warren, jun. performed the operation of lithotomy last winter—the boy is nearly well."

During this time preparations were in progress for a raid on Long Point, Ontario, directly across the lake from Erie.[23] Four hundred regulars and 500 militia were loaded onto several vessels, ostensibly in accordance with official orders, to destroy "publick property." The ships moved out on the 14th, carried out their raid on the 16th, and straggled back during the next couple of days. Usher recorded that "Reports are current that many depredations were committed on private property." Depredations indeed were committed. Every house, barn, and private building for a distance of ten miles from Port Dover to Turkey Point was burned to the ground. This unauthorized exploit was carried out with gusto as revenge for the burning of Buffalo and other malicious deeds perpetrated by the enemy.

On the 19th Usher amputated the arm of one Scrowder, seemingly a casualty of the recent foray. Such amputations were usually the consequence of compound fracture or gangrene from a gunshot wound. There were at this time sixteen men on the sick list. Ten days later he dressed Scrowder's arm and loaned him three dollars! He learned at this time that Purser Humphrey Magrath[24] was dismissed from the service. Thus abruptly, for reasons unstated, ended the naval career of a brave sailor, who, in the absence of senior officers, had commanded the *Calendonia* during the Battle of Lake Erie. Magrath did not long survive his dismissal, for "In 1814 he blew his brains out in a fit of insanity."

As the season progressed, the apple trees lost their blossoms and the weather turned warm and summery. The arrival of the first rations of rum signaled the quickening of naval activity. New replacements arrived in the persons of a sailing master, several midshipmen, and a covey of sailors. Usher moved his personal belongings to the *Lawrence* and, with the help of Surgeon Barton, transferred the hospital stores to the *Detroit*. He then attended to labeling his medicines.

On the 29th Usher complained impatiently that "I am very desirous to get ordered from this Lake." His wish was soon fulfilled, for on the very next day he was invited by navy Lieutenant August H. M. Conklin to apply for orders to join the squadron for a mission to Mackinac, where Lake Huron meets Lake Michigan. Conklin, who had commanded the *Tigress* during the Erie battle and whom Usher later described as "an elegant officer in appearance, but too convivial even for the navy,"[25] undoubtedly received an enthusiastic response.

Strategic Fort Mackinac on Mackinac Island (pronounced both Mackinac and Mackinaw and variously spelled in the diary) was taken by the British early in the war. The *Lawrence* was later ordered to the northern lakes to participate in the campaign to retake it. The *Caledonia* and the *Ohio* sailed for Mackinac on June 3 with Conklin aboard the former. For the present Usher remained at Erie with the *Lawrence.*

About this time Usher received a letter from Abiel Hall, Jr., dated May 16:[26] "Your letter of the 21st [April] is received in which you state that you are under no engagements to the fair sex of the western quarter. But, sir, since your letter, a report is in circulation that you are married. To whom? I know not, perhaps some squaw. This news came in a letter from Mr. McIntire to Mr. Holmes." While this was an obvious exaggeration, it is clear that Usher's occasional dalliance had not gone unreported in his home town.

During the next few days Usher attended to getting provisions on board, including a barrel of wine, and procured medicines for his dispensary. While all hands were preparing for departure, Usher learned of a momentous event, the capture and the abdication of Napoleon on April 12, which in the long run would have a considerable bearing on the war in America. He was busy looking after his patients, and reported that he had extracted a tooth, a necessary chore for surgeons in those days. At a time when the first dental school in America was still a quarter of a century in the future, every surgical kit contained a dental extractor.

On June 10 and 11 all of the sick were removed from the *Lawrence* and the *Niagara* in preparation for the impending move. Usher settled his debts and borrowed some maps and books which would be useful on the trip. On the 18th he turned over the sick list, took leave of Erie, and went aboard in a rainstorm. The next afternoon the *Lawrence* got under way, doubled the peninsula off Erie at 4 o'clock, "and sailed for Mackinac with a full breeze." At the time Usher had five men on the sick list. He whiled away his time pleasantly reading Charlevoix's travels (*Histoire de la Nouvelle France*) and Bonaparte's tracts.[27]

Twenty-four hours out of Erie they passed Sandusky Island, close by the site of the Great Battle. At 6 a.m. on the 21st they came in sight of the Detroit River and at 10 o'clock reached Malden, "where the destruction of the public buildings was clearly evident." They later sighted Windsor, Ontario, a "handsome settlement exhibiting marks of antiquity." On the opposite side of the river was Detroit; Usher recalled Hull's ignominious defeat and later court-martial. That evening he went ashore on the Canadian side and visited "a dozen houses to find sallad, &c." He found only one person who could speak English and from him "obtained the article I was in pursuit of" (presumably "sallad, &c."). Usher offered him half a dollar and received in return a quarter dollar in "cuts." The practice there, he explained, was to cut pieces from large coins to pass for small change. "The dialect of the French," he observed, "is very different from that used by modern Frenchmen of Paris." At that time Canada was already two hundred years old.

During the next several days they were tied up off Sandwich, which he visited several times. There were many fine orchards visible on both sides of the river. The buildings in Sandwich, now a part of Windsor, were very fine, including the Catholic church and an academy, converted during the war into barracks and barricaded. The church was attractive, but ancient in appearance. On Sunday the 26th he attended mass there. The congregation numbered some 400. "The furniture was handsome," the "musick bad," and the "ceremonies not very solemn," he reported. An Indian officiated in breaking the bread, while another carried around the box. There were only three communicants. The "drawings were bad," probably primitive. The priest, who preached in French, "appeared respectable." A young lady carried around the contribution box. "The ladies have elegant persons," he noted, "but many have bad complexions," and he added, "Several Indians attended, dress'd elegantly, tho' in Indian fashion." On the 29th he rode three miles down river to Spring Wells, where he examined some Indian bones, a fascination and preoccupation of his throughout his life.

During this period the *Scorpion* had returned from Lake Huron with intelligence that the enemy were preparing to meet the Americans on the lake with a large force. A boat was hurriedly dispatched to recall the *Ohio* and the *Calendonia*, which had just set out for Erie. The Americans had a force at Sandwich numbering about 400 men. A couple of them were found scalped on the shore. Several rangers were sent out forthwith to search for the perpetrators, and they soon returned with three prisoners.

While the fleet was awaiting a fair wind to sail north, Usher was preoccupied with trivia. He bought a pair of moccasins ashore for $1.50. On board he witnessed a flogging, a cruel punishment, against which he would agitate for many years until it was ultimately outlawed. Medical practice was light, as there were only four men on sick call.

Usher received a welcome letter from McReynolds,[28] congratulating him on his recent promotion to surgeon. While McReynolds himself had had almost enough of naval service, he nevertheless advised Usher to be patient:

> I take the liberty of advising you to hold out longer. You are much younger than myself. Your situation, being now respectable in point of rank, will extend your acquaintance & celebrity. Though should you in the pursuit of your duty at any place find a woman that was worthy of you (mind that she has money), in a place where your practice will be at first as good as your pay, & every prospect of it improving, then and in that case you may do as you please.

On July 2 the wind changed to the southwest, favorable for sailing. Troop reinforcements arrived from Sandusky, and at 9 p.m. on Sunday the 3rd they sailed from Detroit for Mackinac. The 240 soldiers on board were attached to Colonel George Croghan's expedition, which was assigned to recapture and destroy any shipping encountered on the upper lakes. The next morning they passed through Lake St. Clair and approached the mouth of the St. Clair River. Ahead lay the bar of the St. Clair River, a hazard to the heavy brigs *Lawrence* and *Niagara*. Both, in fact, went aground in shallow water. The soldiers were sent ahead on foot to lighten ship, and ballast was removed. By the 6th all ships, with considerable difficulty, were over the bar and again took on their ballast. During the next few days they slowly worked their way up the St. Clair River.

The men were now beginning to be sick, and on that day four patients were added to the sick list. Usher whiled away the long hours reading Samuel Butler's *Hudibras*[29] and fishing. William Eustis, a member of the crew, died on the evening of the 9th and was buried the next day five miles from where they were anchored, as there was no nearer site suitable for burial. At the grave he "examined the body . . . and found the aorta had been worn through by its constant attrition on a calculus as large as a robin's egg. The rupture of the aorta was very small & within the pericardium. The chest contain'd at least 4 lbs. of blood. He was sick 26 hours." The al fresco postmortem examination yielded interesting results. This was doubtless a ruptured calcified aortic aneurysm.

On Sunday, July 10 at two p.m. they reached the point up-river where the previously disembarked troops were encamped. The men were again taken aboard, and the *Lawrence* continued up the meandering river. "Mosquitoes," Usher noted, were "very troublesome." The troops again debarked as the ships negotiated the rapids of the St. Clair and marched to Fort Gratiot at the head of the river. The fleet arrived at Lake Huron on the evening of the 13th. Early the next morning all of the troops were taken on board, including a regiment of Ohio militia stationed at Gratiot, the whole now numbering about 750 rank and file. More than 300 of them were aboard the *Lawrence*. During the next day and night they made about 100 miles in a brisk wind, which, according to Usher, was halfway to their first destination and mission of attacking Matchedash Bay, the southeastern arm of Georgian Bay, on which a new British base was located.[30]

The attempt to take Matchedash Bay turned out to be a fiasco. No one, it transpired, knew how to get there or had thought to bring along a pilot who could guide the squadron through the maze of fog-shrouded islands, shoals, and sunken rocks, behind which the bay was concealed. They never did, in fact, find the bay and frittered away a week in the vain attempt. Frustrated in the venture, Croghan was anxious to get on to Mackinac without delay. The fleet commander, Captain Arthur Sinclair, however, in an ill-advised command decision arrogantly ordered the out-ranked Lieutenant Colonel Croghan to attack and burn the deserted British fort on St. Joseph's Island, forty miles to the north of Mackinac, before proceeding to their primary objective.[31]

During the next several days they sailed first in a northerly direction and then to the northwest, keeping an eye out for the enemy. On one occasion a sail was discovered and the fleet gave chase, but lost their quarry. The weather was clear and pleasant, and the health of the men improved, although Usher himself suffered somewhat from seasickness.

"At about noon" on Tuesday, July 19, Usher reported, they "made sight of land on our starboard quarter and ahead, represented to be the mainland on the starboard side of the River St. Joseph" (i.e. St. Joseph Channel). In the afternoon they entered the channel and in every direction saw fires, the smoke of which, Usher surmised, was intended as a telegraphed warning to the enemy on Mackinac. Fort Joseph was sighted a few miles ahead, commanding the strait. Near the fort were a dozen houses, while three or four miles up the strait stood the village. That evening the ships anchored in sight of the fort and sent in a flag of truce demanding surrender, but not a soul was to be seen. The buildings, however, were in good condition and gave evidence of recent occupancy, possibly within twenty-four hours. Although some spies were sent ashore to pick up a straggler or two in the hope of gaining intelligence about Mackinac, not a person could be found.

The next morning a landing party of some two hundred men went ashore and thoroughly pillaged and burned the fort and all public buildings. The men were able to bring aboard a wild variety of loot (Usher called it "plunder"), including old furniture, a trunk of officers' clothing ("of inferior quality"), forty barrels of resin, nails, coffee, a fire engine, old muskets, several birch-bark canoes, and valued livestock in the way of three beeves and six sheep.

Early the next morning a strange sail was sighted at the mouth of the strait. The whole squadron, except the *Lawrence,* immediately gave chase. When the enemy ship discovered the pursuers as she entered the strait, she attempted to escape, but, realizing that to be hopeless, turned about, approached the fleet, and surrendered. She proved to be the British schooner *Mink,* laden with 230 barrels of flour bound for St. Mary's. Soon thereafter another strange sail was discovered coming about the point. The *Scorpion,* together with two launches carrying sailors and soldiers, set out in pursuit, but failed to catch up to it. "It," in fact, later proved to be two Indian canoes with sail, which were abandoned as the Indians fled.

On the 22nd two launches carrying sailors and soldiers were dispatched to Fort St. Mary's at Sault Ste. Marie. Under the command of navy Lieutenant Daniel Turner and army Major Andrew Holmes, they were directed to seize any furs deposited there. Usher reported that a number of men were "very sick," two or three of whom were dangerously ill with pleurisy. As if there were not enough trouble, an infantry captain and a navy lieutenant fought a duel, the latter being wounded in the chest. Later that day a signal was raised to prepare for departure, but a change in the wind delayed the sailing. Usher grasped the opportunity to explore ashore and recorded his observations on the native flora ("juniper trees, birch, fir in quantity, beech . . . [and] flowers of the species of daisy of light blue color").[32]

On July 24 the squadron, except for the *Scorpion*, finally got under way, the latter having been left behind to pick up Lieutenant Turner and the crews of the two launches. After sailing south and then to the northwest, the squadron sighted Mackinac ten or fifteen miles ahead at sunset and were within six or seven miles of the island by nightfall. Usher was feeling ill and, despite doses of an emetic and a cathartic, was unable to attend to duty. The next morning, as the fleet approached within two or three miles of the island, Indians could be seen ashore on nearby Buttonwood Island. Still not well on the 26th, Usher had himself bled by a fellow surgeon, which, miraculously, "immediately removed my complaint."

As the squadron maneuvered off Mackinac Island, there was an exchange of shots between the *Niagara* and the blockhouse of the fort and other random firing as well. A boat dispatched from the *Lawrence* to pick up provisions from the *Niagara* drew fire. Although the army aboard the *Lawrence* was almost out of rations, the boat failed to return. The crew and soldiers were, in fact, on three-quarter and half rations respectively. Two men set a trout net in an attempt to supplement the scant supplies.

On the 30th the *Scorpion* finally rejoined the squadron after an absence of several days, longer than had been expected. She had sent boats up St. Mary's River to within fifteen miles of Lake Superior. There they found a small vessel containing 2,000 pounds of sugar, 50 kegs of liquor, 40 skins, and some bales of clothing. The houses of the Northwest Fur Company were burned, along with all of the spoils which they were unable to carry with them. As the prize vessel was being eased over the rapids, several holes were punched in her hull, rendering her useless, so that she was abandoned and burned. The launches, together with several boats seized in the raid, made their way back to the *Scorpion*, anchored off the village of St. Joseph near the mouth of St. Mary's River.

Amid the excitement Usher found time to iron his clothes, a fastidious note, all things considered.

On the 31st Colonel Croghan and other officers came aboard the *Lawrence* to report on a raid on nearby Point St. Ignace, the northern promontory of the Straits of Mackinac. From the French inhabitants there it was learned that there were about 300 regulars, 100 militia, and 400 Indians on Mackinac Island. Colonel Croghan returned to the fleet determined to fight. Sailing Master Stephen Champlin, who had participated in the raid on St. Ignace, returned with some fishnets and also some fish, which was a welcome addition to the short rations.

On August 1 Usher had the crew and Champlin sign power of attorney papers, a traditional custom in the military before combat. Champlin reported sick the next day, but appears to have rallied after a dose of castor oil ("oleum ricini" in Usher's diary). The next couple of days were occupied with seemingly aimless jockeying about, while the *Mink*, which carried the all-important artillery, was lost in the fog, her plight compounded by a faulty compass. A landing party in the meantime went ashore, but returned immediately when it was fired upon by the Indians. A sailor and three soldiers were wounded in the action.

Finally, on August 4, with everything seemingly in order, the attack on Mackinac finally got under way. Usher recorded the battle graphically in his diary:

> August 4th. Off Mackinac. Pleasant. At about 9 o'clock signal was made for armed vessels to get under way. At about half past 11 came to anchor in line of battle abreast the N.W. side of Mackinac Island, where there is a spot partly cleared on which the British landed when they took the fort from us [July 27, 1812]. The land is low. At one [p.m.] the troops began to disembark. At two a firing commenced from the vessels which cleared the shore. At three o'clock the troops were formed at a short distance from the shore and at quarter past three firing commenced with field pieces, and shortly after musketry.

During the ensuing two-and-a-half hours the fluctuating fortunes of the invaders were indicated by the rise and fall of the sounds of battle. Usher's account continues:

At half after five, however, the direction of the firing indicated
that our army was on the retreat. At 5 o'clock firing ceased, and
most of the troops were on the shore from which they had
marched. Boats were on shore ready to receive them. Maj. Holmes
was killed early in the action,[33] and Capt. Desha wounded. Capt.
Vanhorn was mortally wounded and [also] Lieut. Jackson. The
report of killed & wounded of the regulars stands thus: [12 killed,
40 wounded, 3 missing]. . . .

Lieut. Jackson was wounded through the bowels a little below
& to the left of the navel; the ball passed out a little above the
[os] innominatum [part of the pelvic bone] on the left of the spine;
a small portion of omentum passed through the front [abdominal]
wound. Capt. Vanhorn was also wounded in the same manner. A
sergeant was wounded through the stomach and died in the night.
A private [wounded] through the left lung bids fair to recover.
The other wounds were slight, that occurred to the men on board
the *Lawrence*. Weighed anchor & stood off about one mile. The
retreat was well conducted.

In later years Usher wrote a terse summary of the ill-fated Mackinac campaign: "Our squadron carried the army of Col. Croghan,
for the purpose of recapturing the fort which was lost early in the
war. After failing in this enterprise, the squadron returned to Erie
for winter quarters." The response to treatment of the casualties
was more discouraging than he would have expected from his earlier
experience:[34] "In an attack on Mackinac . . . the number of wounded
was less than half that [in the Battle of Lake Erie]. Our vessels were
crowded with troops and afforded no suitable lodging for patients.
The air became foul. Diet mostly salt meat with no fresh vegetables,
and added to this was defeat in the enterprise, for we were repulsed.
Consequently the wounds acted unkindly, and some died that under
more favorable circumstances might have recovered." It is more
likely that the greater degree of wound contamination under infantry combat conditions as compared to naval, when added to the
inevitable delay in evacuation of the wounded, contributed importantly to the disheartening results.

Lieutenant Jackson and Captain Vanhorn died the next day. A
flag of truce was sent to the fort with a request for the body of
Major Holmes. The party was received politely, and the request was
granted. The British commander, Colonel McDowell, offered the
squadron provisions and fruit, which were gratefully accepted. That

evening the body of Major Holmes was found unmolested, since fortuitously it had not been discovered by the Indians. When brought on board, examination revealed that two balls had entered his chest. The other bodies had been scalped and buried.

Later that day they were joined by a new vessel, arriving after a seventeen-day passage from Detroit. She brought news that "General Brown had gained a signal victory over the enemy at Queenston." This cheering report buoyed up the flagging spirits of the men, but despite its tonic effect was really only partially accurate. While Jacob Jennings Brown, a handsome figure and one of the better American generals, had in this third and last invasion of the Niagara frontier won a bloody victory at Chippawa, permitting him to occupy Queenston Heights, and also prevailed in a later engagement, he nevertheless was unable to follow up his victory, and, as so often happened in this dreary war, the campaign ended indecisively.[35]

On August 6 the squadron weighed anchor and skirted adjacent Bois Blanc Island. The British sent off a flag of truce demanding that the Americans pay 888 dollars for the cattle killed at St. Joseph. The bill was paid, but Usher wondered whether an I.O.U. to the British commander might not have been wiser in view of the scarcity of specie. The following day they sailed north in a fog for St. Joseph. That evening Usher watched a "flogging mast" for the crew, a strange sequel to a disastrous battle, and further reinforcement for his advocacy of the abolition of this primitive and cruel punishment. On August 8, a warm and pleasant day, the fleet departed from Fort St. Joseph, cleared the mouth of the channel, and sailed southward to return forthwith to its base at Erie.[36]

The next evening they anchored overnight off Middle Island, near Thunder Bay on the Michigan coast. The men were allowed to go ashore for a welcome bath. On the 18th, Usher's birthday, he reported that there were twenty-two sick aboard. The squadron arrived at Detroit on the 20th. Some of the troops and the bodies of the dead were unloaded. The *Niagara*, which had captured the British brig *Nancy* at Matchedash Bay, had lost all of her boats in a gale and had sprung her mainmast. She was to be refitted at Detroit.[37]

The *Lawrence* in the meantime sailed from Detroit on the 22nd and by the 25th had made Put-in-Bay, where she was forced to lay over because of head winds. Usher took the opportunity to do a little sightseeing in the environs. A favorable wind the next morning permitted them to proceed, and they reached the Cleveland area two days later, where they landed more of the men.[38]

On Sunday the 28th the *Niagara*, with Commodore Sinclair on board, overtook the *Lawrence*. Sinclair reproached the *Lawrence* for not having made more headway which, Usher thought, was very "ungenerous." "Commodore Sinclair," Usher complained, "has no regard for the feelings of his officers," which he observed "is universally admitted." The next day with a very brisk tail wind, they out-sailed the *Niagara*, but the race for Erie remained nip and tuck. Usher, despite twenty-two sick men aboard, found time as they scudded along to read about the French Revolution.[39]

On the following day the *Niagara* again outsailed the *Lawrence*. When she arrived off Erie at eight a.m. on August 31, the *Niagara* was already in port. The Commodore ordered the *Lawrence* forthwith to make the rest of the way to Buffalo, which was in serious danger of being attacked, according to a ship recently arrived from there. They set out immediately, arriving off Buffalo the next afternoon. Usher visited his old haunts at Black Rock, which, during his long absence, had been burned to the ground by the British. "The situation," he wrote, "excited melancholly sensations." Sporadic skirmishing and cannonading prevailed about Fort Erie in Canada, now held by the Americans, but under British siege. Aboard Usher's ship everyone felt tension and "alarm lest we should be attack'd." Usher observed great numbers of militia crossing in the direction of the fort. From the East came reports that both Washington and Baltimore had fallen (actually Baltimore held out) and that Spain had declared war on the United States. Amid the commotion Usher found time to read geography and naval history and to catch up on back issues of newspapers. After two weeks in the area, the *Lawrence* was ordered to sail to the west. She got under way on September 16, soon encountering very heavy weather which delayed her passage:

> Wednesday 21st. The wind favoured us yesterday and this morning we made sight of Erie. Came to anchor about 11 o'clock. . . . Reported that [Gen.] Brown had sallied out at Fort Erie and taken 700 prisoners. Since have learned that he took 400. It was on Sunday.[40]

Commodore Perry had turned the Erie squadron over to Jesse Elliott on October 25, 1813 and made a triumphal journey to his home town, Newport, Rhode Island. He was happy to be spared a winter of discontent, having been frustrated in his effort to obtain an independent command on the lake, and was no longer under the thumb of Isaac Chauncey, who had so stubbornly begrudged him an adequate complement of seamen. In July of 1814 Perry was ordered to Baltimore to take command of the new frigate *Java*. Captain Arthur Sinclair, who had replaced Elliott, ran a much tauter ship than Perry and accordingly was a good deal less popular:

> Thursday, Sept. 22nd. Erie. Commodore Sinclair arrived in the *Niagara* and hoisted flag prohibiting communication with the shore. This deservedly produced much dissatisfaction.

Usher nevertheless went ashore to procure supplies for his patients and to take care of personal matters among familiar surroundings. The next evening in moderating weather the *Niagara,* the *Lawrence,* and the *Lady Prevost* sailed once again for Malden to pick up more troops. Delayed by unfavorable winds at the Put-in-Bay group of islands, the *Lawrence* arrived at Malden on the twenty-seventh:

> Wednesday 28th. [Malden]. Went on shore and dined with the army officers. Got beastly drunk with the others. Fine pleasant day.
> Thursday 29th. Malden. Sick in consequence of yesterday. Walked on the island [probably Grosse Isle]. . . . It is more dangerous for the inhabitants residing in the neighborhood of Detroit [and] Malden than it ever has been. People residing in the suburbs have moved into the villages. Two men were lately scalped in sight of the fort at Detroit. A lieutenant at Fort Gratiot was scalped with some of his men, being in a garden after apples. Communication between Fort Gratiot & Detroit [is] cut off.

After a delay due to confusing commands, sailing orders were finally issued. The three ships, carrying over 700 troops, arrived at Buffalo in the remarkably short time of four days. Favored by strong winds astern, they made an impressive run of 160 miles in twenty-four hours. With the weather turning cool, Usher "commenced living in the cabin." Taking advantage of the opportunity, he began "writing on pleurisy." This appears to have been the essay on pneumonia which he later presented as his M.D. thesis at Harvard. Early on October 6 the squadron anchored off Buffalo and promptly discharged the troops. Usher hurried ashore to learn the latest news about the war. In his diary he recorded some good tidings: "Preparing in the forenoon to get to Boston on furlough. In the afternoon heard the very pleasant intelligence that I am to be ordered to join the *Java* in Baltimore." That evening they sailed for Erie.[41] The U.S. frigate *Java* had been under construction at Baltimore. Perry, as its future commander, had been granted the privilege of naming his own officers and had selected Parsons, whom he held in great respect and affection, as his surgeon.[42]

The following evening the *Lawrence* arrived at Erie. On Saturday, the 8th, a "very fine day," Usher "pass'd the greater part . . . on shore with the ladies." At Erie orders were issued to cruise to the Portage River, west of Sandusky and south of Put-in-Bay, to pick up prisoners for transport to Long Point, Ontario, where they would be exchanged for Americans. They set sail late Saturday afternoon in company with the *Lady Prevost* and the *Porcupine*. The weather was pleasant, and Usher worked on his paper on pleurisy. The ships passed Cleveland Monday morning and anchored off Sandusky early that afternoon. Later, in attempting to find the mouth of the Portage River, they went aground on a reef, which held them until the following morning. During the next several days they made repeated but vain attempts to locate either the Portage River or the prisoners.[43]

On Wednesday they entered a small river and ascended through a marsh for four or five miles, making way with great difficulty on account of the "weeds and mire." "Ducks and geese," reported Usher, "were in great plenty in the marsh." After withdrawing, they sailed westward toward the Maumee River, but found nothing except a pleasant shore, on which they discovered the body of a sailor killed in an earlier action, "nearly consumed by turkey buzzards."[44]

They were informed by persons on shore that the prisoners had been sent to Sandusky. Returning there on Thursday evening, they were again eluded, the prisoners having been sent farther east to Cleveland. They weighed anchor for Cleveland on Saturday and, sailing through a heavy gale and high seas, arrived there on Sunday:

Sunday, Oct. 16. The wind abated early and we put in to Cleveland. Anchored within 2 miles of the shore. . . . I went on shore. Cleveland is a small village called a city, has about 12 dwelling houses. The land is very new. Almost every house is a tavern. Inhabitants are immigrants from Connecticut [this, of course had been the Western Reserve of Connecticut]. Found the prisoners [at last!]. There [were], among 700 U.S. troops & prisoners, 200 cases of fever, & ague [possibly malaria; several of the prisoners died].

They got under way on the 22nd and arrived at Erie with the prisoners on Sunday, the 23rd.

After the prisoners had been landed, Usher resumed his routine activities. He hoped to be sent to Pittsburgh for medicines, but orders for this trip did not arrive. On October 30 he left power of attorney with Thomas H. Sill, as did several of the other officers and men, designating him as agent to collect their prize money.

During the next few days Usher devoted as much time as possible to medical reading, particularly Cullen, having begun to study his *Synopsis.* He also read William Saunders'[45] work on the liver and found time to catch up on his newspapers. Champlin, who had been taken prisoner, turned up after his release, now partially recovered from his wound. Usher visited him and engaged a room for him on shore at Colonel Forster's. He secured a signed requisition for medicines, and then (in a curious transaction) "began to collect the men's grog to exchange for Hospital stores." As the week closed he recorded the outcome of a court-martial he had attended a week earlier:

> Friday 11th. Warm, clear morning. Commenced raining at 11 o'clock. Execution of prisoners. . . . James Bird, Corporal [of] Marines, was sentenced to be shot for deserting his post on sentry and James Rankin for deserting with him. Henry Davidson was sentenced to be hung for the same crime, it being the 5th time for him. All the crews were collected. The Marines were shot & [the] sailor hung at the same moment. Prayer was made by the Rev'd Mr. Reed.

The execution gave rise to a popular ballad of the day, the "Ballad of James Bird."[46] For the next twenty years, it is said, there was never a corn-husking, log-rolling, or quilting bee which did not end with the singing of this pathetic song. According to the story then current, James Bird had enlisted in Perry's fleet, but before it sailed from Erie he was given furlough. He stayed too long with a woman he was going to marry. By the time he returned to Erie, his ship, the *Niagara*, had sailed, but he managed to get aboard the *Lawrence* in the nick of time. He was wounded during the great battle, but fought on. Later he was tried for desertion, found guilty, and ordered executed. On the day of execution he was made to kneel on his coffin and was shot by a squad of sailors. Perry, who knew nothing of the court-marital, eventually sent a reprieve, but it arrived too late. Whatever the true facts, this romantic version was believed implicitly by the thousands who sang the sad ditty.

Anxious about his new assignment, Usher wrote to Purser Hambleton, now in Washington, "to ascertain when I will be ordered to the *Java.*" He finished Cullen's *Practice of Physick* and read from the works of James M. Meikle (1730–1799), a Scottish naval surgeon in the Royal Navy, whose writings were more religious than medical, and also from the medical writings of Robert Thomas.[47] He did some further shopping in preparation for his departure, buying material for more pantaloons and a vest. Operations were undertaken for getting the *Lawrence* back over the bar at Erie on November 21. On the same day Usher was shown a letter from Hambleton "mentioning the squadron of Baltimore Flyers." The "Flying Squadrons," as they were called, were organized to harass British shipping. Perry, doubtful that he could ever get the *Java* out of blockaded Chesapeake Bay, had volunteered to take a Flying Squadron to the Mediterranean.

The *Lawrence* was finally eased on to the bar on the 26th, but then some spars gave way and had to be replaced. On the 27th Usher recorded in his diary that he had "Dress'd Mr. Champlin's leg"; also, "The *Lawrence* rigged new spars yesterday, and got over the bar about 4 o'clock this morning. Came aboard at noon." The wound Usher mentioned bothered Sailing Master Champlin all his life. In 1816 "his wound breaking out afresh, he had to submit to a very severe operation." More than 45 years later, Usher wrote:[48] "He continues to be a great sufferer from his wound which he received in 1814, but is otherwise hale and hearty." With the *Lawrence* safely moored in winter quarters, her great days were over. Usher's travel orders were not long delayed. Issued in Washington on November 19, they were, in fact, already on their way.[49]

In his entry for the 28th Usher recorded two recipes for "purifying foul air in ships," a chronic need in the small, close-quartered, and bilgy wooden craft. This involved the generation of nitric or muriatic acid "vapours" through the action of sulphuric acid on niter or common salt, and by increasing the volume of vapors if the "virulence of the contagion" were high, or "if the air is foul and peculiarly offensive."

For the third time since leaving home, Usher noted on Thursday, December 1: "Thanksgiving Day in Massachusetts & Rhode Island. Pass'd the evening [on shore]." This was the first time that Usher identified himself, however tentatively, with the hearty Rhode Islanders with whom he served and whose native state he was destined to make his home.

> Friday, 2nd. . . . Orders arrived for Messrs. Holdup, Breese, and myself to repair to Baltimore and report ourselves to the Commander, Capt. O. H. Perry on board the *Java*. High Glee! . . . Sunday 4th. . . . Bought horse 100 dollars.

During the next few days Usher "carried things ashore" and was busily engaged in "settling bills, &c." and "packing up to be off." He also "returned the horse," and then borrowed $300 from Champlin to bolster his finances for the long trip to Baltimore. He was entertained ashore at a whitefish supper (a traditional Great Lakes delicacy) and was presented with gifts of a pair of moccasins and $20. Then, as he put it, he "settled with everybody," collected $620.21 from the purser, took leave of his shipmates, and bade farewell to all "my friends with painful feelings."

He set out for the East, and it appears that, after all, he had acquired a horse for the journey:

> Traveled 10 miles to Morehead's tavern. . . . The settlements are numerous on the road. Saturday, Dec. 10th, 1814. Rode 10 miles before breakfast to Harrison's. Cool, cloudy. Pass'd an elegant farm. . . . Made 28 miles and put up at dark.

Thus abruptly ends the diary of Usher's war on Lake Erie.

NOTES

1. Pierre Berton, *Flames Across the Border*, p. 175.
2. *Ibid.*, p. 209.
3. *Ibid.*, p. 189–204.
4. *Ibid.*, pp. 110–111, and 203–206.
5. *Ibid.*, p. 208.
6. Allan S. Everest, *The War of Eighteen Twelve in the Champlain Valley* (Syracuse, N.Y., Syracuse University Press, 1981), p. 103.

7. Pierre Berton, *Flames Across the Border,* pp. 257–262.

8. *Ibid.,* pp. 333–342.

9. Allan S. Everest, *The War of Eighteen Twelve in the Champlain Valley,* pp. 179–187.

10. Pierre Berton, *Flames Across the Border,* pp. 262–268.

11. Usher Parsons, "Diary Kept During the Expedition to Lake Erie."

12. J. D. McReynolds to Usher Parsons, January 28, 1814, DPC.

13. [Thomas Green Fessenden], *Democracy Unveiled; or Tyranny Stripped of the Garb of Patriotism* (Boston, Printed by David Carlyle, for the Author, 1805). This was published under the pseudonym "Christopher Caustic." Fessenden was a journalist and satirical poet. This poem was a celebrated virulent, coarse, and libelous attack on Thomas Jefferson and other Democratic leaders.

14. J. D. McReynolds to Usher Parsons, April 15, 1814, DPC.

15. Usher Parsons to Robert Reid, March 14, 1814, DPC. Usher's letter, written aboard the U.S. brig *Lawrence,* reads:
    Reverend Sir: The Navy officers on this station offer you their warmest thanks for your friendly attendance and devotional services at the funeral of their deceas'd brother officers, and as a token of their high esteem beg you will accept this cloak. With a sincere [hope] for a more intimate acquaintance, they are Your assured friends. [signed] Usher Parsons, pr. request of the N[avy] officers.

16. Robert Reid to Usher Parsons, March 14, 1814, DPC.

17. Receipt from Dr. Wallace for $92.63/3 for service from Jan. 1 to Feb. 5, 1814, DPC.

18. This represented another substantial payment on his debt. In this letter he inquired whether Dr. Warren had ever received the previous payment of $75 entrusted to Ben Farewell for delivery. Usher Parsons to John Warren, March 23, 1814. The original letter has not been located, but in his diary Usher recorded that he had written to Doctor Warren on that date. See note 21 for Warren's reply.

19. Usher Parsons, "Cases of Gunshot Wounds through the Thorax, with Remarks," *New England Journal of Medicine and Surgery,* 7:209, July, 1818.

20. Usher Parsons, "Diary Kept During the Expedition to Lake Erie." His commission is also recorded in his service record, WRDNA.

21. John Warren to Usher Parsons, April 24, 1814, DPC.

22. Pliny Hayes to Usher Parsons, May 12, 1814, DPC. Pliny Hayes received his M.D. degree from the Harvard Medical School in 1815. He practiced in Cambridge until his untimely death in 1831.

23. Pierre Berton, *Flames Across the Border,* p. 292.

24. Usher Parsons, *Brief Sketches of the Officers Who Were in the Battle of Lake Erie,* p. 10.

25. *Ibid.,* p. 11.

26. Abiel Hall, Jr. to Usher Parsons, May 16, 1814, DPC.

27. *Histoire de la Nouvelle France,* by Pierre François Xavier de Charlevoix (1682–1761). Published initially in 1744, it contained in an appendix a detailed journal of the author's trip through the interior of America and a full description of the area. Usher may have read an English translation entitled *Journal of a Voyage to North-America,* published at London in 2 volumes in 1761. "Bonaparte's Tracts" refers possibly to the *Collection Générale et Complète de Lettres, Proclamations, Messages, &c. &c. de Napoléon le Grand . . . Accompagnée de Notes Historiques, Pub. par. Chr. Aug. Fischer,* which was issued at Leipzig by H. Gräff in 2 volumes between 1808 and 1813. However, since Usher, by his own account, did not commence the study of the French language until his first European cruise a year or so later, he more likely could have read the edition of the *Military Journal of General Buonaparte; Being a Concise Narrative of His Expedition from Egypt into Syria* that was issued by Warner and Hannah at Baltimore in 1799. No other editions of Napoleon's writings appear to have been published in America before the War of 1812, and very few came into print in England in translation until after that time.

28. J. D. McReynold to Usher Parsons, June 28, 1814, DPC.

29. *Hudibras,* a mock romance by the English poet and satirist, Samuel Butler (1612–1680).

30. Usher was fascinated by the coldness and clarity of the Huron waters. "The water is colder than any I ever saw," he recorded in his diary, perhaps ten degrees colder than that of Lake Erie and colder than any spring water he had ever encountered. In fact, owing to its extreme coldness, "it cannot be held in the mouth, nor used to clean the teeth, 'til warmed." Bubbles were seen distinctly ten feet below the surface, and an object as small as an egg, he guessed, could be recognized sixty feet under water. They could make out fish, which they took to be salmon trout, perfectly plainly some thirty yards away and fifteen feet below the surface. The water, he added, was "as clear & transparent as the atmosphere."

31. Pierre Berton, *Flames Across the Border,* p. 308; also, B. J. Lossing's *The Pictorial Field-Book of the War of 1812,* p. 850.

32. Usher Parsons, "Diary Kept During the Expedition to Lake Erie."

33. Usher Parsons, *Brief Sketches of the Officers Who Were in the Battle of Lake Erie,* p. 6. A small cemetery on Mackinac Island contains the remains of the Americans killed in this ill-fated battle. The grave of the heroic Maj. Holmes is marked.

34. Usher Parsons, "Letter on Some Points of Military Surgery."

35. Usher Parsons, "Diary Kept During the Expedition to Lake Erie;" Pierre Berton, *Flames Across the Border,* pp. 307–314.

36. Usher Parsons, "Diary Kept During the Expedition to Lake Erie."

37. *Ibid.*

38. *Ibid.*
39. *Ibid.*
40. Gen. Jacob Jennings Brown (1775–1828), who led the troops in the field at Lundy's Lane, was based at Fort Erie. The sortie Usher reported in his diary took place on September 18 and actually netted 385 prisoners.
41. Usher Parsons, "Diary Kept During the Expedition to Lake Erie."
42. *Ibid.*
43. *Ibid.*
44. *Ibid.*
45. Reference is to *A Treatise on the Structure, Economy and Diseases of the Liver,* by William Saunders (1743–1817). This was first published at London in 1793. Usher was probably using a copy of one of the two American editions, published at Boston in 1797 and at Brattleboro, Vermont in 1810.
46. Charles J. Dutton, *Oliver Hazard Perry* (New York, Longman, Greene and Co., 1935), pp. 289–292.
47. Reference is to *The Modern Practice of Physic, Exhibiting the Characters, Causes, Symptoms, Morbid Appearances and Improved Method of Treating the Diseases of All Climates,* by Robert Thomas (1753–1835). This was initially published at London, with three American editions appearing between 1811 and 1815.
48. Usher Parsons, *Brief Sketches of the Officers Who Were in the Battle of Lake Erie,* p. 11.
49. Usher Parsons service record, WRDNA.

CHAPTER FIVE

Cruise of the Java *and Stateside Interlude*

Two weeks after Usher departed from the Lakes the war officially ended. The Treaty of Ghent was signed on December 24, 1814, and ratified by the United States Senate on February 17. In the interim, unaware of the treaty, Andrew Jackson had fought the Battle of New Orleans, virtually a postscript to the war. The Treaty ended British aspirations for control of the Great Lakes, but left unsettled the question of impressment of seamen and the rights of neutrals in time of war, two major causes of the conflict.

During the previous summer and fall Perry had busily studied plans for the 44-gun frigate, the *Java*, to be constructed at Baltimore; it promised to be a first-class ship. He had been appointed her commander and in recognition of his brilliant victory at Lake Erie was awarded the privilege of selecting his own officers. This could have been an empty honor. A month before, the British had landed in force in Maryland and Virginia. Baltimore was under siege, and the shores of the Chesapeake were threatened. The British were anxious to capture the *Java*, but fortunately Baltimore held out and she remained in American hands.[1]

With the war over and Flying Squadrons forgotten, Perry's interest in the *Java* was renewed. She was virtually completed before he was able to give his full attention to her structural qualities. Government supervisors, who had assumed this role in the interim, proved to be slipshod and irresponsible. Though impressed by the *Java*'s handsome lines, Perry, who was an astute and experienced sailor, worried about inferior workmanship, poor materials, faulty rigging, and more particularly the safety of the masts. To satisfy his doubts, he had requested a survey of the ship, which confirmed his own findings of defective rigging and numerous other faults. Secretary of the Navy William Jones ordered the *Java* to New York for refitting, but unwisely rejected the request for new masts. Perry's judgment was later justified with a vengeance.

The *Java* did not actually leave Baltimore for New York until August 1815. During this period, and after an absence of over two years, Usher visited his home town and family. From Alfred he traveled to Boston, then sailed to Newport to meet his friend and shipmate Thomas Breese.[2] They journeyed to Providence by stagecoach to meet the Commodore. On this, his first visit to Providence, Usher lodged at the Manufacturers Hotel, a venerable and historic edifice located on Market Square opposite the old Market House.[3]

Usher reported to the *Java* at Baltimore during the early weeks of 1815. On May 5 he prepared a list of medical and hospital stores, and on July 1 entered into his "Day Book of Practice"[4] his first sick list for the *Java*. The roster for the day showed a wide assortment of disorders: pleurisy, lues venerea, contusions, gonorrhea, fever, sarcocele [testicular swelling, probably gonorrhea], dysenteria, and fractured foot. Visits to the sick bay numbered as many as thirty daily. Usher was acquiring a substantial and varied clinical experience.

The medical complement of the ship consisted of Usher as Surgeon, Thomas V. Wiesenthal as Surgeon's Mate, and Doctor Richard Stevens, a volunteer. On August 1 Usher received a letter from Doctor Thomas Whittington of Baltimore concerning the health of his Surgeon's Mate.[5] Whittington related that his friend Wiesenthal, a young gentleman of many talents and a member of one of the first families of Maryland, had recently been under his care, suffering from an affliction of the mind. Wiesenthal, he informed Parsons, was sailing against his advice. An entry in Usher's "Day Book of Practice" identified the illness as epilepsy. Later, in August a Doctor C. G. Stevenson of Baltimore wrote further to Usher concerning Wiesenthal.[6] He reported that he had consented but reluctantly to Wiesenthal's return to the ship, and had in fact advised him to apply for a furlough. Disregarding this advice, Wiesenthal was aboard six months later when the ship sailed. He completed the cruise without incident.[7]

On August 5 the *Java* moved down the bay to Annapolis to take aboard additional supplies.[8] Perry and his officers were invited to a public dinner by the social leaders of that wealthy and elegant town, but Perry, impatient to move on, declined. On leaving port, the *Java* paid her respects by firing a salute.

After picking up a supply of extra spars at Hampton Roads, she remained in the lower Chesapeake until early in September. During this time officers and men, including Usher to be sure, frequented Norfolk, always a good navy town. The perils of shore leave were reflected in Usher's sick list for August 26, which contained no less than twelve cases of "lues venerea," from which neither officers nor midshipmen were immune.

An anecdote about Perry written by Usher bears on the conduct of officers on leave. Usher related[9] that Perry

> had a fine sense of honor in regard to female character. He frowned indignantly on any who trifled with the affections of a lady—and his whole deportment towards the fair sex was most courteous, circumspect, delicate & graceful. He was never licentious, like many navy officers. In examining, when on board the *Java*, a swelling of his knee joint, I observed that such swellings were sometimes caused by mercury. He assured me he had never gone through a course of mercurial treatment, nor contracted any disease that required it.

In those days mercury was given for both gonorrhea and syphilis, which had not been clearly differentiated. Joint swelling as described by Usher was more likely attributable to a gonorrheal arthritis than to the mercury treatment. Perry's disavowal accords with his unblemished character.

After being detained in port for more than a week by a succession of heavy gales, which dismasted several vessels and drove aground others at anchor, the *Java* finally put out to sea on September 6. As she sailed from the harbor on this maiden cruise, she was pronounced the most beautiful frigate at sea, and Perry most certainly agreed. Yet he was haunted by those rugged looking but treacherous masts. She arrived off Sandy Hook on September 9, but was unable to get into New York harbor for another two days. Eventually she tied up at the Navy Yard in the East River, where a complete new set of standing rigging was installed. The main gun carriages and miscellaneous ship's gear were also replaced. Many other defects came to light later.

Perry was visited by Commodore David Porter, who was interested in promoting a voyage to the northwest coast, Japan, China, and the South Sea Islands for discovery and the protection of commerce. He invited Perry to join his squadron with the *Java,* but Perry, always reluctant to accept a subordinate command, declined.

The *Java* remained in the New York area until early in the New Year, her destination and time of departure still in doubt. A cruise to the Mediterranean was under serious consideration because of renewed trouble with the Dey of Algiers. Years ago the Dey had exacted tribute from the United States government, but the practice had been terminated by treaty in 1805. During the War of 1812 and the Napoleonic Wars, Algerine cruisers resumed preying upon American commerce. Congress was determined to deal with the problem effectively. A squadron under Commodore Stephen Decatur, consisting of the famed frigates *Constitution, Guerrière,* and *Macedonia,* and several smaller vessels, in June of 1815 had compelled the Dey to restore all captured American property, to release prisoners, and to relinquish forever any claims to yearly tribute.[10]

The depredations of the Barbary pirates nevertheless continued, and reinforcements were ordered to the Mediterranean. On December 16, 1815 Perry was advised to ready the *Java* for Mediterranean duty and to pick up additional crew at Newport. While riding out a modest gale in the East River, the *Java* sprang a beam and was detained while repairs were made. Before she could clear New York, the private contractor insisted on immediate payment. Washington ignored requisitions for cash, and the government's credit was so poor that money could not even be borrowed. The ship was released when Perry agreed reluctantly to leave his purser behind as collateral.

On New Year's day of 1816 Usher began his diary[11] of the cruise of the *Java,* prefacing it with quotations from Doctor Johnson and the French philosopher, Condillac, whose maxims might be a suitable guide for his own conduct.[12] For the next few days the *Java* lay at anchor off Sandy Hook, awaiting favorable winds and tide to cross the bar into open water. Finally, on the morning of January 6, she sailed for Newport, making the run in the excellent time of sixteen hours. Whatever failings she might have, the *Java* was a smart sailer.

Perry, a native of South Kingstown, Rhode Island, lived in Newport with his wife and two young sons. On several occasions the handsome Commodore and his lovely wife entertained the officers.

A dramatic incident involving Perry occurred on the morning of January 9. A Providence newspaper reported:[13]

On Tuesday morning last about 6 o'clock, the schooner *Eliza*, Captain C. Gordon, of this port [Newport], from Havana, with a cargo of molasses, (in consequence of there being no light in Beaver-tail Light House) went on Brenton's Reef, near the entrance of the harbour, and in a few minutes went to pieces. The quarterdeck separated from the wreck, on which with great difficulty, Captain Gordon, his passengers and crew, 11 in number secured themselves. Soon after daylight they were seen floating out to sea on the quarterdeck, when by the spirited exertions of several of our citizens, a boat was obtained, which towed them to the shore of Brenton's Neck, where they were all landed. The severity of the weather was such, that had they not been thus relieved, they must have perished in a short time. Several of the crew are much frozen. No part of the cargo was saved.

Not mentioned in the report was the fact that Commodore Perry was the hero of the story. While at breakfast with his wife, he was informed of the impending tragedy. Without hesitation he set out in his own rugged barge, which fortunately was at the wharf with its crew of twenty seamen. Despite almost capsizing several times, he succeeded, at a distance of five miles from shore, in carrying out the exciting rescue and returned with all hands safe.[14]

Despite an outbreak of "cynanche tonsillaris" [quinsy sore throat, or more likely acute tonsilitis] which kept Usher busy, he still found time to make several visits ashore, including calls at the Perry home and Fort Adams.

The *Java*'s purser rejoined the ship when the president of the Exchange Bank of New York patriotically accepted responsibility for payment of the repair bills. He came aboard on January 21, along with Lieutenant Dulany Forest, carrying the ratified treaty of peace with Algiers, dispatches for William Shaler, consul to the Barbary States, and orders for the *Java* to proceed to its destination.

Buffeted by high winds and stormy seas, the *Java* raced across the Atlantic at a record-setting pace, while the crew was beset by both sickness and lack of sleep. The stormy seas deluged the ship, and Parsons's stateroom was usually covered with several inches of water. On February 6 Usher noted: "This dampness has occasioned much sickness, such as dyspepsia, slight fever, &c. But of 30 men now on the [sick] list probably twenty are disabled by contusions, sprains, lacerations, &c., principally occasioned by falls, slips &c. from the pitching of the vessel."

One hundred miles east of Cape St. Vincent, Portugal, as the storm mounted in fury, tragedy struck. Perry's misgivings regarding the masts were indeed vindicated:

> Wednesday 7th. At about 10 o'clock this morning while the ship was making a heavy roll, the main topmast broke off, which tore the mizzen spars and main top gallant mast & spars from their situations. One man, Johnson, was lost overboard, two, viz. Caleb Lippencutt and Robert Court, were killed. . . . Thomas Dunn & Wm. Falkhouse [were] mortally wounded. The ship was laid to during the day. The roll and swell were very heavy. Rain and sunshine alternately.

After a run of unsurpassed speed, it became necessary because of the driving wind to take in sail. Ten men had been sent aloft to furl the main topgallant sail when the catastrophe occurred. They were standing on the yard when the wind suddenly freshened, parting the main topmast, carrying the main topsail yard with it. One man, thrown against the muzzle of a maindeck gun, fell overboard and immediately sank. Another struck the keel of a boat turned bottom up and split his skull. Three others lost their lives, and several were mutilated. Five or six men clung to the topgallant yard, the topmast, crosstrees, and other rigging. Some were crushed in the wreckage on the decks. There were shrieks and groans from the wounded and dying and cries for help from those aloft.

The ship, in peril of foundering, soon righted herself and steadied. While helping to move the wounded, Usher was thrown between decks and sustained a fractured patella (kneecap), for which years later he received a pension. He was soon absorbed in dressing the wounded and carrying out emergency surgery. The harrowing scenes made a deep impression on a wide-eyed thirteen-year-old midshipman, Alexander Slidell Mackenzie, who had joined the crew at Newport. Young Mackenzie, who would one day be Perry's biographer, years later described the disaster:[15]

> The after part of the main-deck on the starboard side became a temporary cockpit, and Doctor Parsons . . . had for some hours occupation for all his skill. Almost every operation in use in

surgery was required to alleviate sufferings of the wounded. The man who had fallen on the boat was quickly trepaned [trephined], though scarcely any hope existed of his recovery, and he soon died. Ere long four of the killed were decently laid out, dressed in white frocks and blue trousers, and placed side by side on gratings standing upon shot boxes, and on the following morning, they were sewed in their hammocks, and committed together to the deep. From the gloom occasioned by this dreadful casualty, the ship was long in recovering, and the impression can never be effaced from any one who witnessed it!

Later investigation revealed that the mast was completely honey-combed with dry-rot and previously had been exposed for almost two years to the sun and weather. Other spars found to be in the same shameful condition were replaced as soon as possible with those which, with foresight, Perry had procured at Hampton Roads.

The remaining voyage to Gibraltar, where they arrived on March 13, was much more pleasant and largely uneventful. After Perry delivered two Newport youths to their uncle, a Gibraltar merchant, the *Java* made sail for Malaga. En route Usher noted that "ophthalmia is becoming very prevalent," which he attributed to long hours on watch and the attendant "fatiguing of the eyes." The men besides had nothing like sunglasses to protect their eyes from the brilliant Mediterranean sunlight. On the whole, however, he found the climate "delightful" and was pleased that the crew were becoming healthier "from the pleasantness of the weather."

On Saturday, March 2, Usher noted in his diary: "Entered Port Mahon [Minorca] about 12 o'clock. . . . Met with old acquaintances." The "old acquaintances" were aboard other American warships already in the harbor. Early in November Commodore John Shaw[16] had brought his squadron there for winter quarters. Most likely the *Java* made rendezvous according to plan. The squadron consisted of Shaw's flagship the frigate *United States*, the frigate *Constellation*, the sloop *Erie*, and the sloop *Ontario*.[17] This small force, joined by the frigate *John Adams*, later undertook the mission to Algiers for which the *Java* had been dispatched to the Mediterranean.

On Sunday, March 3 Usher contentedly observed: "Ship throng'd with officers. The weather is clear, but rather chilly. The crew is becoming very healthy. The ship is surrounded by boats containing oranges, almonds, hazelnuts, cauliflowers, radishes, lettuce, beets, &c. I commenced the study of French."

The following day he

> Visited the American hospital in charge of Dr. McReynolds [his old friend], and took thither two men. It is situated on an island at the lower lazerette [i.e. lazerette or lazaret—a quarantine station]. The buildings on this island are intended for those who are quarantined in the river. They are surrounded with stone walls of 20 or 25 feet height, and 3 or 4 feet thick. In the centre is a garden owned by the Governor of Minorca. In this I observed fig trees, also the lemon, orange, &c., with all kinds of salad & flowers.

Usher visited the naval hospital several times to bring in patients and to see McReynolds. While all hands were busily engaged in refitting the ship, the officers entertained on board the governor of the island and his family. Hearing that an American ship, the *Alert*, was about to leave for the United States, Usher wrote several letters home. On the 12th he noted: "On Sunday last three cases of pleurisy occurred. This is an epidemic peculiar to this island at this season, & it is to be feared it will take off a great many of our sailors. Cleghorn's[18] practice, when here [as a British Army Surgeon 1736–1749], was to bleed to a great extent in the first two days, 'til the pain subdued."

Early on the morning of March 14, a party consisting of Commodores Shaw and Perry, Consul William Shaler, several officers, Usher, and a guide took an overnight sightseeing tour of the island on horseback. Usher was fascinated by the narrow roads hemmed in by stone walls seven feet high. En route they visited a limestone cave, where he took note of the stalactites and columns of "petrified stone." "The cave had nothing in it unusually met with in such caves," he observed, comparing it in his mind's eye, no doubt, with those at Put-in-Bay.

After an overnight rest at the village of Ferrerias, they set out early the next morning, first visiting the village church, where the paintings were "indifferent and the images poorly sculptured." Before noon they had climbed nearby Mount Toro, 1400 feet high, topped on its very summit by a convent of friars, whose life, he thought, was "very uninteresting and uncongenial . . . while in a state of celibacy." After dining in the village on roasted & boiled fowls, veal, sausages, and eggs cooked all ways, fruit, &c. ("I have not [previously] met with such an entertainment in Spain"), they returned to Mahon over roads strikingly covered with purple stones of porphyry. "In this excursion," he noted with a touch of envy, "those who rode jackasses were less fatigued."

On March 16, H.M.S. *Boyne*, a British 110-gun sloop, together with several 74-gun ships and frigates, arrived at Mahon on a secret expedition. It was reported that they in cooperation with a large Spanish fleet in the area planned an operation against Algiers and other Barbary powers. The admiral of the British squadron, Edward Pellew, Lord Exmouth, and several of the British officers visited aboard the *Java*. The British sailed from Port Mahon on the 23rd followed shortly by the *Java*. The cruise to Algiers was uneventful:

> Monday, April 1. In the afternoon we arrived off Algiers. Found the British fleet here which sailed from Mahon. Stood off in consequence of heavy wind. . . . Sick list 21, 11 fevers.
> Wednesday 3d. Wind died away and weather became calm. Anchored off Algiers. A salute was fired of 21 guns, which the *United States* returned with 18. Capts. Perry and Gordon endeavoured to avoid all communication with the shore in order to avert the quarantine of 30 to 40 days when we arrive in a Christian port. In this, however, they did not succeed.[19]

The weather was pleasant, and Usher and the other officers went ashore at every opportunity. While in port he wrote a long intricate sketch of the geography and bloody history of Algiers, much of it obviously taken from the texts in Perry's library. He also recorded observations of the contemporary scene.[20]

The ensuing events are best understood in the light of the diplomatic posture of the United States at that time. The Moslem Algerians were restive under the treaty of 1815 and resented humiliation at the hands of Christians. At the earliest opportunity after the withdrawal of the United States forces, the Dey informed Consul Shaler that he had denounced the treaty. The British squadron under Lord Exmouth, which had left Mahon ahead of the Americans, was in the harbor at Algiers when the Americans arrived. Exmouth was anxious to win terms as favorable as those granted to the Americans by agreeing to pay a heavy ransom for twelve hundred Neapolitans and Sicilians.

When Commodore Shaw and Shaler presented the ratified treaty brought over on the *Java*, the Dey declared it null and void on the ground that its terms had not been complied with. Usher noted in his diary:

> Monday 8th. Late last evening it was made known that the Dey of Algiers had refused to accept . . . the treaty in its present terms. The bone of contention appears to be this. Decatur and Shaler [had agreed verbally, but] not in the treaty, . . . to return the ship [a frigate] and brig captured [by the Americans] as a present. The ship did return, but the brig was brought back by the Spaniards. They therefore say they are indebted to that Govt. and not to the United States for said brig; that the United States must now give a new sloop of war before the treaty will be ratified.

Actually the United States had been unable to fulfill its commitment, since the brig had been seized by the Spaniards and could not be recovered. Usher went on:

> A war is expected to be declared today and an expedition is now preparing to burn the enemy's shipping laying within the mole. Volunteered my services to go in Capt. Perry's boat, and prepared both for fighting or doctoring. Late in the evening a letter came off stating from the consul that the negotiation was still going on tho with no favourable prospects.

As the Dey stubbornly refused to concede, Shaler hauled down his flag and retired to the flagship in the harbor. Plans were then made for a night assault landing by twelve hundred men:

> Tuesday 9th. Today signal was made [for] all Capts. [to] repair on board the flagship, where the consul [evidently the Swedish consul] & Mr. Shaler reported that the Dey had finally rejected the treaty. This is equivalent, it is said, to an open declaration of war. Prepared the ship for immediate action. The consul came on board for a permanent residency.

The elaborate preparations for the attack, intended to be secret, were discovered by a recently arrived French frigate. The French, unfriendly toward the United States at the time, promptly reported these activities to the Dey. Although deprived of the element of surprise, the bellicose tactics nonetheless impressed the Dey. Perry and the Swedish Consul Noderling went ashore under a flag of truce to sound out the Dey. "He express'd surprise at the flag," wrote Usher, and "said he did not dream of war, and finally assured . . . that hostilities would not be commenced by him under three months, allowing that time . . . for a vessel to go to the United States & return." He was, he said, in favor of preserving peace. The Dey declared that the treaty must nevertheless be considered void, but Perry was thus allowed time to communicate with Washington for instructions, while Consul Shaler was invited to remain. Perry agreed, and Shaler returned to the consulate. Encouraged by the jealous consuls of Britain, France, and Spain to be recalcitrant, the Dey proposed to the President of the United States renewal of the unfavorable treaty of 1795, which required payment of tribute.

The Dey then sent out word that all officers were welcome to visit the shore. Usher noted in his diary:

> Saturday 13th. The post Captains visited the Dey, and were politely treated. . . . The *Washington*, 74 [guns], is hourly expected from the United States . . . . The Turks are fitting out their publick vessels. It is pretty well ascertained that had the expedition been attempted on the 8th [as planned] we might have succeeded in cutting out or burning the Algerine vessels. But on the 9th, the Dey became alarmed and had the batteries well supplied, and on the 10th slept at the batteries, himself and guard.

The *John Adams* was ordered to America with the Dey's letter to the President and other dispatches. The *Java* and other American ships were ordered to visit Tripoli and Tunis in the meantime to assure that everything was quiet there. The final denouement of the story occurred some months later.

On April 16 the American squadron, including the *Java*, sailed from Algiers and headed for Tripoli. En route they anchored in Tunis Bay for a few days, allowing Usher and a dozen other officers to visit the ruins of Carthage, where Usher "collected more antiques." While at Tunis, Usher related, "The squadron obtained several rare animals, [such] as hares, opossums, antelopes, guinea pigs, pigeons of various kinds, chameleons, &c."

On Sunday, April 28, the squadron anchored off Tripoli. Usher continues the story in his diary:

A boat returned with the consul. No news. The British fleet, which we have followed, we find here. The admiral has treated favourably with them. Several officers went on shore.

Monday 29th. The remainder of the officers on shore. Tripoli appears in a declining state, houses going to decay, people very indigent. They have very little commerce compared with Tunis, and the number of inhabitants does not exceed say 10, or 15,000. Our officers met with a Turk on shore of the name of Wilson, who is a native of Salem, Massachusetts. He turned Mohometan after being prisoner, in order to remove him[self] from slavery and ameliorate his condition. He sustains the office of Painter General, and receives handsome pay. His character is infamous, worse than that of a Turk, using oppression and violence against the defenceless Jew, and particularly the females, which a Turk would abhor. The Jews are in an abject condition throughout Barbary, neither their property or persons being secure from violence. They nevertheless are the most monied class of people, and . . . mercantile business is mostly conducted [by them].

Usher learned that Christians were tolerated, but were obliged to purchase the privilege of worshiping at a high price. There were two Christian churches in the area, one in Tunis and one in Tripoli. The Mussulmen, despite their supposed devout faith, imbibed liquor freely when unobserved; furthermore, the Turks eat pork, "which Mahomet forbids, when they can do it with impunity." He also discussed sexual and other customs of the region:

The abominable crime mentioned in the 27th verse of the first chapter of Romans ["men with men"] is often committed with impunity, and sodomy is often practiced. Polygamy is allowed and every rich man is entitled to four wives and any number of concubines. The Bey of Tunis has 4. He is particularly attached to one who has borne him two sons. He locks her in a closet and carries the key with him. All husbands keep their wives under lock. It is very seldom that a Turkish woman is seen in the streets.

They bury their dead in Christian form. There are no doctors among them except three or four from Europe. The consul of Tunis rates its number of inhabitants at 100,000. . . . Provisions in Tripoli are cheap. Eggs sell for 10 cents the hundred . . . [and] oranges 75 the hundred, of a very large size. A very few European goods are sold here. There is no tavern. Money is scarce, and the credit of the United States bad. Our consul gives 4 per cent per month, or 48 per cent per annum. At Tunis it could be obtained for 12 per cent.

Regarding relations with the United States, Usher observed that

Our treaties with Tunis and Tripoli are highly disgraceful to us and more favourable . . . than they are able to obtain from any other nation. We pay a tribute of 4,000 dollars on the arrival of a new consul, are not saluted unless we give a barrel of powder for each gun. Our merchant vessels can be impressed in their service, whenever they choose to demand their use. We, however, make no annual presents as some nations do. The Bashaw, or Bey, alone administers justice. The Alcoran [Koran] is the only code of laws.

The *Java* sailed for Syracuse on the island of Sicily on the evening of Monday, April 29, skirted the island of Malta, and sighted the coast of Italy and historic Mount Etna on May Day, 1816. The *Constellation* and *Erie* arrived shortly after the *Java*, the *Ontario* from Marseille a little later. Meeting unexpected difficulty in obtaining pratique (lifting of quarantine), they were ordered to proceed to Messina, where "prattic [as Usher termed it] could be obtained sooner." Usher regretted that he would not have an opportunity to visit this ancient city. The *Java* cleared Syracuse for Messina on the 11th.

After lying at anchor off Messina for several days, Usher was granted shore leave for an "excursion to Mount Etna." At 5 a.m. on May 18 he set out with Doctor Hoffmann of the Navy, a civilian friend, and a servant for the trip to Etna. He was impressed by the many hill towns which they passed en route and explained that "The villages on the summits of the mountains are rendered inaccessible [to the ravages which the barbarians were in the habit of committing] by the lofty and perpendicular acclivities." He was fascinated by the Greek and Roman antiquities of Taormina, "the site of a respectable ancient Roman city," and considered its famed amphitheater "well worth the traveler's inspection." In his diary he described the ruins in considerable detail.

On the 19th he and a small party climbed Mount Etna, ascending to the cone on mules and the last three-quarters of a mile on foot. At the base of the cone the snow was six feet deep while below it was already late spring. Ascending the cone was "most fatiguing," the difficulty due to the steepness and lightness of the ground. "The feet in advancing 1/2 a yard recede half of it." He brought along a thermometer and was impressed that the air temperature at the summit was 30° Fahrenheit, while at the base it was 70–80°. He found the temperature of the volcanic matter at the margin of the crater to be 140°. After inspecting the crater, the party returned to the mules and made a rapid descent to Messina on the same day.

The next three weeks were uneventful. "I have not been able," he wrote, "to visit the shore of Calabria opposite this. All that country is in a state of quarantine, so that a person landing there is prohibited from returning 'til he has rode quarantine 30 days." The *Constellation* withdrew from the squadron and proceeded to Malta. About the 8th of June the *Java* sailed from Messina past the Lipari Islands and arrived off Palermo on the 9th.

Certain American merchants in Sicily urgently requested help from the United States government because of fear of renewed seizure of American ships by Tunis. This nervousness was understandable in view of intelligence which soon reached the *Java*. The squadron was ordered to return to the Barbary coast. The diary continues:

> Thursday, June 13th, 1816. Sailed from Palermo. In the afternoon fell in with *Constellation* [just in] from Malta. We learned from her that the Turkish soldiers at Tunis had manned and slip'd off with six vessels belonging to the Dey . . . , are now cruising in the Levant, and have captured several merchantmen. [They reported] that a difference had arisen between Lord Exmouth and the Dey of Algiers respecting the terms of the treaty with England, which occasioned some threats from the Lord toward the Dey's city. . . . the Dey dispatched a courier to Bono . . . with orders to the Turkish soldiers to capture all the Englishmen to be found there. . . . On the following day, he sent countermanding orders which arrived too late, the execution of the order having already been attempted, but fortunately without success. The Christians [had] armed and defended themselves, and repulsed the Turks.

> Thursday, June 20th. Arrived off Tunis. Here we learned that, since the disturbance in which several vessels were lost, everything remained quiet. The consul did not land, and we sailed for Algiers.

> June 28th. Arrived off Algiers. The *Constellation* and *Erie* proceed to Gibraltar, pursuant to orders left here with the consul about four weeks since by Commodore Shaw. Capt. Perry received

Mr. Shaler on board, which has again placed us in quarantine.
Salutes were exchanged between the ship & Algiers. Saturday,
June 29th. Capt. Perry on shore.

On Sunday, June 30, as Usher reported in his diary, he went on
shore at sunrise to procure some fresh provisions for the sick. A
gentleman residing with the consul conducted him to the Turkish
baths, which he described in detail:

These are steam. I was conducted into a small dressing apartment
where I exchanged all my clothes for a robe. I was then led into
a dark room filled with steam of a moderate temperature, say
100°, through this room into another of a higher temperature, and
then to a third. My robe being remov'd, two or three servants
commenced rubbing and pressing my flesh with the hand. I was
then spread out on a marble slab and 3 flesh brushes with hot
water were exercised over my body for at least half an hour. The
rolls of scarf skin which these instruments removed were the size
of a small quill, and the number of them [was] astonishing. I was
finally washed down with soapsuds, and wiped, and then enclosed
in several sheets, and conducted back to the dressing room. A
slight degree of debility had pervaded my system, but, with a
little repose on a bed and a cup of coffee, I soon recovered vigor.

Running low on provisions, the *Java* was ordered to Gibraltar,
where she arrived about July 8, 1816. There the officers and crew
were delighted to find the U.S.S. *Washington*, just arrived from the
States. On board was the American diplomat, William Pinkney,[21]
on a special mission to Naples.

The *Java* was directed to carry recent dispatches from the United
States to Algiers, while other units of the fleet proceeded straight-
way to Naples. She sailed on Thursday, the 10th of July, calling
briefly at Algiers over the weekend. Becalmed off Sardinia for two
days, she made sight of the Italian coast on the twentieth. Usher
noted:

Sunday July 21. At 11 A.M. made the city of Naples as we
pass'd the Island of Capri. From this [point] it is about 15 miles
to the bottom of the harbour where we discover the *Washington*
at anchor. We anchored in the afternoon. In the evening there
was a grand display of fireworks making a part of some church
ceremony. Here we are quarantined with the *Washington*. . . .

The *Erie* arrived on the following day, completing the squadron. The *Java*, now in good order, attracted attention in the harbor as a most beautiful ship. Pinkney was landed under a salute of guns. Although Usher's diary of the cruise ended abruptly with the entry of the 22nd, the *Java* remained in Naples for a month and in the Mediterranean for another half year.

Late in August the squadron, commanded by Commodore Chauncey, sailed for Messina. It called later at Tripoli and Tunis, making Algiers early in October. During the absence of the Americans, the combined British and Dutch fleets under Exmouth had subjected Algiers to an unmerciful bombardment, destroying the Algerine navy and severely damaging the fortifications. Consul Shaler had been an eyewitness to the shelling; his house, in fact, was heavily damaged.

The appearance of the American squadron caused the Algerians to fear a further attack, but Shaler gave assurance that the visit had only peaceful intentions. He then sailed with the fleet to Gibraltar to await the President's instructions. These arrived aboard the brig *Spark* with orders appointing Shaler and Chauncey commissioners to treat for peace with the Dey. The *Washington* and the *Spark* carrying Chauncey and Shaler returned to Algeria, where on December 9 the Dey was handed an ultimatum. Agreements satisfactory to the United States were concluded on December 23. A year later the unhappy Dey was assassinated.

The *Java* was not present during the negotiations, as it was already in winter quarters at Mahon. When Chauncey returned to that port in January, the *Java* and the *Ontario* were dispatched to the United States with separate copies of the treaty.

The younger officers and midshipmen were loath to leave the seductive pleasures of the balmy Mediterranean. Serving with the cultured and enlightened Perry had been, after a fashion, like going to school. At every port he granted leaves and urged the men to visit art galleries, museums, and famous buildings. The midshipmen went ashore with other officers as guides and were encouraged to use the commander's large library, which contained historical and geographical works dealing with the countries visited. Two teachers were engaged to give lessons in French and Spanish, and classes were held on board every morning. The young officers were taught swordsmanship and were required to take dancing lessons.

"An officer in the Navy," Perry asserted, "should be a gentleman, accustomed to the social graces."

The *Java* had probably the finest band of any ship in the navy; music was a passion with Perry, who himself played the violin after a fashion. The band played several times during the day, since Perry believed that music was effective in maintaining the morale and spirits of his men. Striving to discover any talents or accomplishments, he encouraged the men to participate in special bi-weekly concerts. These activities were doubtless effective in furthering Usher's education, assurance, and polish.[22]

The *Java* sailed from Port Mahon on the morning of January 14, 1817, stopping at Malaga the next day to take on stores from the U.S. storeship *Alert*. She arrived off Gibraltar on the 26th. She lay at anchor only a few hours, received additional supplies for her long voyage home, and on the same evening stood out to sea before a brisk easterly wind. For several hours that night she made a lively twelve knots running with the prevailing trade winds. The weather was delightful during the initial stages of the voyage, no one suspecting that disaster lay ahead.[23]

Before leaving the Mediterranean, Parsons summed up his medical experience: "The average of sick per day for the last year . . . is 22 . . . [the] total reported being 8,142. There have been no deaths, and the only death on board the ship within that time from sickness is that of a Mr. Baldwin, who left the United States in an advanced stage of consumption with the hope of deriving benefit from the Mediterranean climate, but he died shortly after his arrival in this sea off Algiers, March 12, 1816."[24]

Smallpox was widespread in the Mediterranean during the *Java*'s visit. Fortunately, with characteristic foresight and with Usher's emphatic approval, Perry had ordered his men vaccinated before leaving the United States. It was not common practice at the time, nor had it been done on any of the other vessels of the fleet.[25] Just before departure from Mahon some forty seamen, medical casualties from the fleet and others whose terms of service had expired, were taken aboard. An equal number of the *Java*'s men were left behind as replacements. Smallpox promptly broke out among the new men. Perry reported on the harrowing experience to Navy Secretary Benjamin W. Crowninshield immediately upon arriving at Newport on March 3, 1817. He enclosed a report drawn up by Usher:[26]

... The day following our departure from Gibraltar, and eleven days after our separation from the squadron at Mahon, a seaman was attacked with this disease in its most malignant form. This man was among those whose term of service had expired and who were transferred to this ship to be discharged on their arrival in the United States. On mustering the others, eighteen reported themselves to have never had either the small or kine pox. By your order they were immediately vaccinated, but with matter that I had brought from the United States a year previous, and its age had rendered it inert. As soon as it was ascertained that the vaccination would fail, I inoculated them and by the use of medicine with strict attention to diet and regimen, they all underwent the small pox in its most benign form, none of them being confined more than two or three days.

Unfortunately for others, who failed to report themselves for inoculation, eighteen men were attacked with the disease the natural way. Four of them died, and the recovery of many of the others was long despaired of. I am, however, happy to inform you, that only six now remain on the list, all of whom are convalescing. You have prevented its spreading among our own crew by ordering their vaccination before we left the United States. By a similar precaution on board the other ships in the Mediterranean, the serious calamity we have witnessed might have been prevented.

Usher's report concluded:

Besides those who died on our passage with the small pox, we have lost three with pulmonary consumption, making in all seven deaths; an unusual loss to be sure for one ship, but considering, Sir, that in addition to your own sick, we had to take home all the incurable patients of the squadron and hospital to the number of forty or fifty, and with a long winter passage, the number of deaths will seem as moderate as could have been expected.

For days the ship had been a virtual pesthouse, but Perry did what he could to make the men comfortable, visiting them daily in both hold and cabins. He was warned of the risk, but disclaimed any concern since he himself had been vaccinated. Followed by the steward, he distributed extra rations of food and wine, some from his own stores. Despite his sympathetic ministrations and Usher's care, he had the unhappy task of reading the burial service seven times on the voyage home.

As if this were not trouble enough, the *Java* encountered a boisterous and terrifying gale as she neared the coast of the United States. She leaked badly, and the pumps were manned without let-up. Perry encountered several ships that had been severely battered by the storms, one of which had been fifty-nine days out of Bristol, England. To those in obvious distress, he brought men and supplies to relieve the exhausted and hungry crews, and Doctor Parsons's skills were much needed.[27]

When the *Java*, with flag at half mast, arrived off Newport just thirty-six days out of Gibraltar, she immediately went into quarantine. Of the total of eighteen new cases of smallpox, all but six had either died or convalesced sufficiently to be discharged. The town authorities granted permission to "land a number of persons from on board the said ship with the small pox at Coasters' Harbor Island," the marine quarantine facility at Newport. On the following day five cases were brought ashore, officially ending Usher's first Mediterranean cruise.[28]

The treaty was immediately dispatched to Washington, together with a copy of a circular letter sent by Commodore Chauncey to all consuls in the Mediterranean area.[29] The good news was announced at an Inauguration Day celebration (for President James Monroe) in Providence on March 4 amid much jubilation.[30]

Immediately upon arrival in the United States, Usher wrote to his parents. He received a prompt and salty reply from his father:[31]

> Yesterday we had the pleasure of receiving yours of 3d instant and can bid you a hearty welcome to the United States and hope to see you at Alfred. We have received a letter from your brother Thomas.[32] He is settled in New Spain and has a family. He is married, doing well, settled on the banks of the river about 50 leagues from Buenos Aires. Keeps a hatter's shop.
>
> If you are not like to come home soon, send us a letter, but do not send the smallpox in it. . . .

While at Newport Usher found time to appear before the Censors of the Rhode Island Medical Society in Providence, hedging his bets in case he eventually decided to settle there. On March 25, 1817, "he was duly examined" and was granted a license "to practice Physic & Surgery." As in Massachusetts, this was[33] a certificate of competence rather than a legal license to practice.

The *Java* was ordered from Newport to Boston, arriving on April 4, 1817. Perry, relieved of command, was transferred back to the

Newport station as its commandant. The ship was eventually dismantled. The officers sent Perry a moving letter of appreciation, which Usher was unable to sign since he was absent from Boston when Perry departed. To express his sincere personal gratitude and friendship, he wrote to Perry:[34]

> Understanding you have relinquished the command of the *Java*, in which I have had the honor of serving you for more than two years, permit me, on our separation, to tender you my grateful acknowledgments for the friendly and generous solicitude with which you have at all times regarded my best interests and happiness. It is but just to say, that the mere performance of my duty has ever given me a certain passport to your friendship and favour, and I shall ever regard it as the happiest incident of my life that I was fortunate in being placed under a commander who has ever been exceedingly active in advancing the improvement and welfare of his officers.
>
> Permit me also to express the feelings with which I shall ever bear in mind your treatment to sick and wounded seamen. In you they have ever found a kind, attentive commander and sympathizing friend. Your prompt attention at all times to whatever I could suggest for the preservation of health, or the benefit of the sick, your diligent inquiries into all their wants, and frequent appropriation of all your private stores for their comfort, are among the numerous acts of beneficence which can never be forgotten by them or me. In short, to your humane exertions is attributable any extraordinary success that has ever attended my practice during the four years I have been under your command.

Usher could write with grace and dignity when circumstances demanded and when he took the time. Giving serious thought to the desirability of furthering his medical education while in Boston, he sent the following to the Navy Department:[35]

> If consistent with the good of the service, I would ask for orders to remain attached to the *Java*, or if this indulgence cannot be granted, I would like to be continued on this station in some other situation. My object in this is to avail myself of the advantages which the town of Boston affords for professional improvement.

Eventually he was able to accomplish this.

Usher was very concerned with finding a suitable location for practice. With this in mind, he made extended visits to Portsmouth,

New Hampshire and to Providence. Charles O. Handy, a *Java* shipmate, wrote to him from Newport:[36]

> I think it would be well for you to cast your eye to Providence.
> I am told there never has been a better opening for a physician—
> two vacancies. I only state this generally as I am not qualified to
> go into particulars.
> . . . The Commodore is well & very happily situated. His home
> is to be abandoned to the President for his accomodation while
> in Newport[37] . . . . The ladies are as fascinating as ever—I have
> repromised them the pleasure of your company shortly. You must
> not disappoint them.

Usher investigated Portsmouth first during several weeks in the
early summer.[38] Discouraged with the prospects there, he set out
for Providence late in July, fortified with letters from Perry and
other navy associates.[39] For some four months he boarded with
Revolutionary War pensioner Major Samuel McClellan, whose
house at 75 Benefit Street was frequented by prominent lawyers,
judges, and politicians.[40] McClellan exposed Usher to much stimulating and entertaining conversation. While in Providence, Usher
corresponded actively with his friends. Doctor Hoffman, now in
New York, had advised him to send specimens to Doctor S. L.
Mitchill,[41] director of the new Lyceum of Natural History there,
thinking this might aid him professionally. In his reply,[42] Usher
indicated that he would follow through on Hoffman's advice,
mainly to achieve "a niche in that gentleman's acquaintance."
Charles Handy, writing to Usher from Newport,[43] expressed chagrin
that the "faculty" at Providence (i.e. the medical profession) had
not shown greater friendship to a young man of Usher's character
and qualifications. He affirmed his belief that Usher would eventually triumph, despite the "gloomy selfishness" pervading the
medical community of Providence. He offered a few useful suggestions and enclosed a letter of introduction to Senator James Burrill
couched in the handsomest terms.

In his assault on Providence and the Medical School at Brown
University, Usher sought help wherever he had friends. He received
an informative letter from Thomas Chichester, a friend of his preceptor days in Boston in reply to an inquiry (August 26):[44]

> On reading [yours of the 24th] . . . I went immediately over to
> Dr. Inglese [English] to execute your request. . . . and on arriving

in his house, delivered to him your letter. He read it with interest and pleasure, and said that he should the next day lay it before Dr. Baldwin, who had more influence over the Providence institution than he had.

He acknowledged that in consideration of your opportunities and character he had suggested the thing to you and that he was happy to find that you had considered his suggestion. . . . That he should use all the influence he had (which he signified he feared was not great at the Providence institution) in your favour. He stated moreover some difficulties that he thought . . . you would have to contend with in carrying on dissections, resulting from an unfortunate affair that occurred in Providence last winter respecting a female subject that was taken up there, and a severe law[45] that had been passed by the legislature of R.I. in consequence of this affair, the prejudice of the people of the place, &c. But notwithstanding all these, if you could get the approbation of the President of the college and would conduct your dissections with proper caution, he had no doubt but you would succeed.

He seemed, however, to think that in order to obtain the approbation of the President of the college, it would be best for you to propose to give your demonstration course to the class in College. . . .

This revealing letter gave the first intimation of Usher's desire to settle in Providence and to participate in its academic life.

Usher had on deposit with one Charles Lawton, an Erie veteran now in business in New York, the considerable sum of $737.09, with further interest due, for all of which he could take a note or cash.[46] His fortunes had improved since the impoverished days of his youth. Taking stock of his financial assets, Usher inquired of Thomas H. Sill at Erie about his share of the prize money from the victory on Lake Erie. Sill's tart reply was disastrous. Considering that Congress had appropriated a handsome $255,000 for this purpose, Usher's share, amounting, according to Sill, to a mere $15.73,[47] was laughable. On this melancholy note the saga of the prize money came to an end.

Usher returned to Boston in November to attend lectures at the Harvard Medical School, called the Massachusetts Medical College at that time. The edifice, completed in December 1816 and located on Mason Street near the Boston Common, is no longer in existence.

It was here that Usher at long last studied medicine under formal auspices. The Medical Faculty had been increased in April 1815 by the addition of two lectureships, one in Materia Medica and Botany and another in Midwifery. Each lecturer received as compensation only the fees collected from their students, "which fee[s] shall be charged agreeable to regulations determined by the [Harvard] Corporation." Jacob Bigelow was elected to the lectureship in Materia Medica and Botany, and Walter Channing to that in Midwifery. The eminent John Warren, who had recently died, was succeeded by his son John Collins Warren as Professor of Anatomy and Surgery. The lectures in chemistry were given by Doctor John Gorham, and those in Theory and Practice of Physic by Doctor James Jackson.[48]

On the whole this was an able and distinguished faculty. Bigelow, who had earned his M.D. degree at the University of Pennsylvania, was a participant in the first United States Pharmacopoeial Convention and wrote a perceptive introduction to the first compendium. He was an ardent collector of botanical specimens and attained an international reputation in his field. Channing was an amusing and interesting lecturer. He attended Harvard College, but his undergraduate degree was withheld because he had been involved in the notorious student Rebellion of 1807. He had M.D. degrees from both Harvard and the University of Pennsylvania. John Collins Warren (the first), the son of John Warren, was the second generation of a long line of Warrens at Harvard Medical School extending to the present era. A graduate of Harvard College, he studied with his father and extensively in Europe. While not as facile a lecturer as his father, he prepared his talks with exquisite care and was an enthusiastic dissector. His specimens later formed the basis for the Warren Anatomical Museum at Harvard Medical School. A very busy surgeon, he conducted a clinic at the Almshouse, which was a valuable teaching aid in surgery. Some thirty years later he became famous for performing the first operation under ether anesthesia at the Massachusetts General Hospital.

Gorham was a popular and very successful teacher. A graduate of Harvard College with an M.A. degree, he studied with his future father-in-law, John Warren, and received his medical degree at Harvard Medical School. He gave courses both at the College in Cambridge and at the Medical School and was the author of two of the basic books on chemistry of that era. Jackson, a very good teacher, was friendly and sympathetic with both students and patients. A graduate of Harvard Medical School, he spent two years studying in Europe and was a founder of the Massachusetts General Hospital. It was an interesting and stimulating time for Usher, studying under a group of young men, all of whom would later attain both national and international stature.[49]

There were some fifty-odd students in the School at that time, the majority of whom would not receive a degree. In fact, Usher was one of only twelve who received degrees in 1818. Of his class, nine were from Massachusetts and three from Maine, which at that time was still a part of Massachusetts. Eight settled in Massachusetts, and one each in Rhode Island, New York City, and New Orleans. While ten ultimately practiced medicine, one became a wholesale chemist and the other a dentist. Several became prominent in their chosen communities.[50]

The course of lectures began on the third Wednesday in November and lasted three months. The fees were $20 for Anatomy and Surgery, $15 each for Theory and Practice and for Chemistry, and $10 each for Materia Medica and for Midwifery. The catalogue for 1818 stated, "During their residence in Boston the students have opportunities of seeing actual practice, either by entering their names with some physician in the town or by attending the Almshouse which is usually accessible for a small fee. The Physician of the Marine Hospital (Dr. Townsend) has liberally invited them to attend." This feature, of course, was less vital to Usher, who already had had considerable clinical experience. The Almshouse, like its counterpart in most of the principal towns of New England, was primarily an asylum for the poverty-stricken, the care of the sick being an inevitable, but of necessity a secondary consideration. In a symbolic gesture, the Boston Almshouse set aside but eight beds for the sick and insane of the entire town. The Marine Hospital provided shelter and medical care for the sick and fevered seamen who regularly arrived in this seaport town from all over the world. Doctor Solomon David Townsend, its physician, then a young man of twenty-five, would later become a prominent Boston clinician and one of that small but distinguished group who watched the first induction of ether anesthesia at the Massachusetts General Hospital in 1846.

Usher's military status during this period caused concern in Washington. To set matters straight he wrote to Secretary of the Navy Crowninshield:[51]

Having understood that it has been represented to the department that I have entered upon the practice of physick in Rhode Island with the intention of leaving the Navy, I beg leave to state that I have ever held myself in readiness to obey orders from the Department or from the Commander of the *Java*, and have not been absent from this town a single day for nearly three months.

Having been at considerable expense in purchasing tickets for the medical lectures in Boston, I shall consider it a favour to be continued in my present situation till those lectures close in March, and as much longer as is perfectly consistent with the good of the service.

Presumably the request was granted, since he completed the lectures and entered the examinations.

Each candidate for a degree was examined privately for eight minutes on each subject, or "in doubtful cases" as long as the examiner "judges necessary." Directly following the examination a vote was taken on each candidate, and a majority determined the candidate's success or failure. Candidates such as Usher, who were not college graduates, were also examined in Latin and Natural Philosophy. At the public examination which followed, ten minutes was allowed each candidate for the reading of his dissertation. A graduation fee of $20 was charged for those students who had not taken a bachelor's degree, but only $15 for those who had.[52] Usher's doctoral dissertation was based on "the epidemic pneumonia of 1812–13, as it appeared about Lake Erie." The text of the thesis has not been found. Usher passed the examinations satisfactorily and was awarded the degree of Doctor of Medicine by Harvard University in March 1818.[53]

During this period Usher sent to *The New England Journal of Medicine and Surgery* two clinical papers based on his military experience. The first, titled "Cases of Gunshot Wounds Through the Thorax, with Remarks," appeared in the July 1818 issue and included an account of the injury of his old comrade Benjamin Baily. The second, a "Surgical Account of the Naval Battle on Lake Erie, on the 10th of September, 1813," appeared in October.

While awaiting orders, Usher corresponded with the Navy Department concerning back pay held up by red tape.[54] He eventually received a satisfactory reply,[55] and was also advised that Captain Thomas Macdonough had requested his assignment to the U.S. frigate *Guerrière* (not to be confused with the British frigate of the same name destroyed by the *Constitution* in 1812). Macdonough, as described earlier, was the hero of Lake Champlain, which victory equaled in strategic importance that of Lake Erie. The letter concluded, "I think it confers great honour on you that you should be selected by so excellent a man." On May 12 he was ordered[56] "to report to Com. Bainbridge for duty on board the *Guerrière,*" which was in Boston preparing for a Mediterranean cruise. Captain William Bainbridge, a respected officer, had commanded the *Constitution* from September 1812 to July 1813.

Late in May Usher's father wrote that Mrs. Parsons was seriously ill with dropsy.[57] By early June he had some intimation of the itinerary of the forthcoming cruise, for a letter from Doctor George W. May, his friend of student days in Boston, noted, "I was glad to hear that you were going to Russia. . . ."[58] With his departure for Europe imminent, Usher was granted leave to visit his family. He reached Alfred on June 12 and spent the next couple of weeks there.[59]

On the 28th he returned to Boston, stopping with relatives in nearby New Castle, New Hampshire[60] to bring them news of his mother's illness. Although Mrs. Parsons rallied a little from time to time, she was failing rapidly. Usher soon received somber news from his father:[61]

[Wed., July 1] Your dear Mother is almost gone. She may continue two or three days, but we look every hour that she will leave us. . . . She was taken with puking which left her in a short time, but she grows weaker fast. Our hearts are ready to burst. . . . Pray for our help; we do not forget you.

Thurs. 2nd. She seems to be more comfortable this morning. . . . She was wandering in her mind, but seems now composed a little. . . . She requests me to write you that her water continues to run more than heretofore. Her thighs are very much swollen. . . . I am press'd down and know not what or how to write. If you are going, I wish to hear when you expect to sail.

Mrs. Parsons died on Saturday, July 4, and was buried on Sunday.[62] The Reverend Nathan Douglas, who officiated at the burial, wrote promptly to Usher to inform him of the sad event.[63] Usher's brother-in-law, General Leighton, attended the funeral, which he described in a melancholy letter to Usher.[64]

In the meantime, Usher had learned[65] from Erie comrade Dan

Turner in Newport that Captain Elliott was making "a stir about the Lake Erie business," a renewal of the controversy over his conduct in the battle. Elliott had challenged Perry to a duel; Perry had preferred charges against Elliott and requested that he be court-martialed. At Perry's request, Usher traveled to Newport, where he swore out an affidavit strongly supporting the commodore. This deposition and those of other officers who had rallied to Perry's aid were forwarded to Washington on August 10 with the formal charges.[66]

The charges were never pressed and were eventually pigeonholed by President Monroe. They did not come to light again until 1840, when Perry's biographer, Alexander Slidell Mackenzie, disclosed the whole correspondence. Perry in 1819 at the age of thirty-four had succumbed tragically to yellow fever contracted on a naval mission to Venezuela. He was buried in Trinidad.[67]

NOTES

1. These events are discussed in detail in Charles J. Dutton's *Oliver Hazard Perry*, p. 232 *et seq.*, and in Alexander Slidell Mackenzie's *Life of Commodore Oliver Hazard Perry*, v. 2, p. 86 *et seq.*

2. Thomas Breese to Usher Parsons, December 10, 1814, DPC.

3. C. W. Parsons *Memoir*, p. 5.

4. Usher Parsons, "Day Book of Practice," RIHS. This was kept during the cruises of both the *Java* and *Guerrière*. A separate manuscript of Usher's in DPC records the list of medicines and hospital stores which were turned over to him at this time.

5. Thomas Whittington to Usher Parsons, August 1, 1815, DPC.

6. C. G. Stevenson to Usher Parsons, undated (but September, 1815), DPC.

7. Thomas Van Dyke Wiesenthal, the son of Dr. Andrew Wiesenthal, was born at Chesterton, Maryland in 1790. After attending medical lectures at the University of Pennsylvania in 1811, he was appointed Surgeon-Major of the Sixth Infantry in July, 1813 and subsequently was commissioned a Surgeon's Mate in the navy. Between 1814 and 1819 he saw sea duty on the U.S.S. *Ontario, Java* and *Independence*, with later shore and sea duty following. He was separated from the service on April 7, 1829, and he died at Portsmouth, Virginia in 1833. In addition to a medical career, he was a composer and song writer of more than local fame. A list of his musical compositions before 1826 covers nearly four pages in Richard J. Wolfe's *Secular Music in America, 1801–1825, A Bibliography* (New York, New York Public Library, 1964), v. 3, pp. 963–967.

8. Alexander Slidell Mackenzie, *Life of Commodore Oliver Hazard Perry,* v. 2, p. 99 *et seq.*

9. Usher Parsons, Manuscript fragment, undated, apparently notes for a biography of Oliver Hazard Perry, RIHS.

10. Gardner W. Allen, *Our Navy and the Barbary Corsairs* (Boston, Houghton, Mifflin and Co., 1905), p. 294 *et seq.*; Ray W. Irwin, *The Diplomatic Relations of the United States with the Barbary Powers, 1776–1816* (Chapel Hill, University of North Carolina Press, 1931), p. 182 *et seq.*; Glenn Tucker, *Dawn Like Thunder; the Barbary Wars and the Birth of the U.S. Navy* (Indianapolis, Bobbs-Merrill Co., 1963), pp. 447–465.

11. Usher Parsons, "Diary Kept During the Cruise of the U.S. Frigate *Java,* 1816–1817, and During the Cruise of the U.S. Frigate Guerrière, 1818–19," RIHS. The two manuscripts are bound together.

12. From Johnson: "A man of letters requires a publick library and periodical publications . . . , new acquaintances to converse with, professional associates to whom he can communicate his various discoveries. [He] spends in . . . study that season of life in which the manners are . . . softened . . . , and polished into elegance; and when he has gained knowledge enough to be respected, has neglected the minuter acts by which he might have pleased." From Condillac: "In composing a work we should avoid long periods, because they fatigue the mind . . . , digressions . . . , and repetitions, because they tire the reader. A thing once said in its proper place is [sufficient]."

13. *Rhode Island American & General Advertiser* (Providence, R.I.), January 16, 1816.

14. Alexander Slidell Mackenzie, *Life of Commodore Oliver Hazard Perry,* v. 2, p. 99, *et seq.*

15. *Ibid.,* p. 105 *et seq.*

16. John Shaw, U.S.N., 1773–1823.

17. U.S. frigate *Constellation,* Captain Charles Gordon; U.S. sloop *Erie,* Commander William Crane; U.S. sloop *Ontario,* Commander John Downes.

18. George Cleghorn, M.D. (1716–1789), a Scottish physician stationed on Minorca 1736–1749 as army surgeon. He was author of *Observations on the Epidemical Diseases in Minorca from the Year 1744–1749.*

19. The incubation period of smallpox is under twenty-one days, and that of the plague much shorter; yet ships carry rats, and rats carry plague, perhaps justifying that length of quarantine. The first quarantine, for 30 days, was instituted in Ragusa, Dalmatia, in 1377 for all persons coming from a plague-infected area. Since this period was insufficient, it was increased to 40 days, *quaranti giorni,* and was called *quarantena,* hence the English word "quarantine."

20. Usher Parsons, "Diary Kept During the Cruise of the U.S. Frigate *Java,*

1816–1817, and During the Cruise of the U.S. frigate *Guerrière*, 1818–1819." Usher's account reads:

The expulsion of the Turkish Bashaw in 1710, and the union of his office with that of the Dey, introduced the present form of government in Algiers. It is a pure military aristocracy at the head of which is the Dey. The Dey is always chosen out of the army, to every order of which that dignity is open. His authority is as absolute as that of any monarch in the world. He is chosen by the military, and every soldier votes. A dowan, or council, consisting of 30 yiah bashaws [or colonels], is a sort of cabinet, but generally coincides with the wishes of the Dey. . . .

Military strength 20,000; 6 or 7,000 of whom are Turks, and the rest Colouglis or Moors. . . . The commerce is trifling. Exports are grain, ostrich feathers, copper, rugs, silk, ashes, embroidered handkerchiefs, dates, and Christian slaves. . . . In religion the Algerines agree with the Turks. They hold to the Koran. . . . All affairs of moment . . . are submitted to the Dey himself. Some of the punishments are exceedingly cruel. A Jew or Christian guilty of any capital crime is carried without the gates and burnt alive. A Moor or Arab is hung by the neck over the battlements or thrown down upon hooks, fixed in the wall below, where they sometimes hang in exquisite torment for 30 or 40 hours. The Turks are punished in private. They are either bastinaded [beaten on the sole with a stick] or strangled. Females, if guilty of Criminal Conversation with a Christian, are tied up in a sack and thrown into the sea alive.

Population: Turks rank as first. They are proud, indolent, voluptuous, jealous, revengeful, and avaricious, at the same time sincere, faithful and courageous. . . . Next in dignity . . . are Colouglis, who are the children of Turks by female Moors. . . . They are more active than the Turks, but more depraved, false, revengeful, cowardly, fanatical, and avaricious. The Arabs . . . inhabit the mountains. The number of Jews is not considerable and their condition is deplorable. The Christians are transient residents. Renegadoes of either Jews or Christians, i.e. those who renounce their own religion for that [of] the country, if possessed of talents, acquire office and a high standing.

21. William Pinkney (1764–1822), lawyer, statesman, and diplomat, was en route to St. Petersburg to assume his duties as Minister to Russia. His objective in the Naples mission was to obtain compensation from the present government of Naples for shipping seized under the régime of Joachim Murat, late King of Naples. The mission was unsuccessful.

22. Alexander Slidell Mackenzie, *Life of Commodore Oliver Hazard Perry*, v. 2, p. 140; Charles J. Dutton, *Oliver Hazard Perry*, p. 255 *et seq.*

23. Alexander Slidell Mackenzie, *Life of Commodore Oliver Hazard Perry*, v. 2, p. 142; Usher Parsons, "Day Book of Practice."

24. *Ibid.*

25. *Ibid.* Dutton stated (p. 256): "Before sailing, Perry ordered all his seamen vaccinated. It was not the usual practice of the time, nor done on other vessels of the fleet; but he talked the matter over with Doctor Parsons, and thought it worth a trial." Alexander Slidell MacKenzie in his *Life of Commodore Oliver Hazard Perry* uses similar language. It appears that the idea originated with Perry himself. According to Robert J. T. Joy (personal communication), "That Perry *ordered* vaccination is *most* interesting. The Royal Navy still did it voluntarily. Except for Washington at Valley Forge in 1777, acting on advice from Shippen and Morgan, *no* commander had *ordered* immunization. This is an important piece of public health history." Dr. Joy is Professor of Medical History at the Uniformed Services University of the Health Sciences.

26. Usher Parsons to Oliver Hazard Perry, March 3, 1817, manuscript file copy, WRDNA.

27. Charles J. Dutton, *Oliver Hazard Perry*, p. 255 *et seq.*

28. C. W. Parsons *Memoir*, p. 15. Also Usher Parsons to Oliver Hazard Perry, March 3, 1817, WRDNA.

29. *Rhode Island American and General Advertiser* (Providence), March 21, 1817.

30. *Providence Patriot and Columbian Phenix*, March 8, 1817.

31. William Parsons to Usher Parsons, March 10, 1817, DPC.

32. Thomas Parsons to "Dear Brother" and parents, July 10, 1815, DPC. Only a typed copy appears to have survived.

33. The charter of the Society provided that it "shall have full power and authority to examine all candidates for the practice of physic and surgery," and, if found skilled and fitted, "they shall receive the approbation of the said society." This was weaker than it may have appeared, as it did not prevent unqualified and "irregular" practitioners and quacks from hanging out a shingle. That reform was not accomplished until state licensure was enacted with some opposition in 1895. As one of the older members of the Society had put it: "It was the inalienable right of the people to be humbugged if they should so choose." See *The History of the Rhode Island Medical Society and Its Component Societies, 1812–1962*, by various authors (Providence, the Society, 1966), pp. 3–5 and 51–54.

34. Alexander Slidell Mackenzie, *Life of Commodore Oliver Hazard Perry*, v. 2, p. 149.

35. Usher Parsons to Benjamin Crowninshield (Secretary of the Navy), May 13, 1817, WRDNA.

36. Charles O. Handy to Usher Parsons, June 14, 1817, DPC.

37. President Eisenhower during his summer visits to Newport occupied the commandant's house at Fort Adams. The building is now known as Eisenhower House.

38. Jeremiah Goodwin to Usher Parsons, July 24, 1817, DPC. John Holmes

to Benjamin Penhallow and John Holmes to Clement Stoner, July 22, 1817, DPC.

39. C. W. Parsons *Memoir*, p. 15.

40. *Ibid.*

41. Samuel Latham Mitchill, M.D. (1764–1831), physician and eminent chemist, was currently professor of natural history at the College of Physicians and Surgeons in New York City and was a founder and the editor of the *Medical Repository*. Usher met him later on a medical pilgrimage to New York.

42. Usher Parsons to R. R. Hoffman, August 1, 1817, DPC.

43. Charles O. Handy to Usher Parsons, August 6, 1817, DPC.

44. Thomas Chichester to Usher Parsons, August 26, 1817, DPC.

45. "An Act to prevent the violation of the sanctuary of the dead." *Acts and Resolves*, Rhode Island General Assembly, session of Feb. 1817. It provided a mandatory fine of one to five thousand dollars *and* imprisonment of one to six years for body snatching.

46. Charles Lawton to Usher Parsons, September 2, 1817, DPC.

47. Thomas H. Sill to Usher Parsons, September 28, 1817, DPC. This is highly ironical, since Elliott, despite his ambiguous and controversial conduct during the battle, and Perry each was awarded $7,140. Furthermore, Chauncey, who had never sailed Lake Erie during this critical period (so far as the record shows) and who had sorely tried Perry's patience by begrudging him an adequate supply of seamen, received an incredible $12,750. Congress made up for this inequity, however, by voting Perry another $5,000. Cf. John K. Mahon, *The War of 1812* (Gainesville, University of Florida Press, 1972), p. 176; Charles J. Dutton, *Oliver Hazard Perry*, p. 209; and Pierre Berton, *Flames Across the Border*, p. 173.

48. Thomas Francis Harrington, *The Harvard Medical School*, pp. 405–406.

49. William Frederick Norwood, *Medical Education in the United States Before the Civil War*, pp. 176–182; Henry K. Beecher and Mark D. Altschule, *Medicine at Harvard, the First 300 Years* (Hanover, N.H., University Press of New England, 1977), pp. 29–49 *passim*.

50. Thomas Francis Harrington, *The Harvard Medical School*, pp. 1454–1455.

51. Usher Parsons to Benjamin Crowninshield (Secretary of the Navy), January 30, 1818, WRDNA.

52. Thomas Francis Harrington, *The Harvard Medical School*, pp. 412–415.

53. C. W. Parsons *Memoir*, p. 15.

54. Usher Parsons to Benjamin Homans, May 8, 1818, WRDNA; Usher Parsons, Service Record, WRDNA.

55. Edward Fitzgerald to Usher Parsons, May 30, 1818, DPC.

56. Usher Parsons, Service Record, WRDNA.

57. William Parsons to Usher Parsons, May 20, 1818, DPC.

58. George W. May to Usher Parsons, June 16, 1818, DPC.

59. "Diary of Gen. Samuel Leighton, 1818–1848," Maine Historical Society, Portland. Mimeographed copy in Parsons Library, Alfred, Maine. Gen. Leighton kept this diary without missing a single day for thirty years. See entries for June 12–28, 1818.

60. James Alfred Spalding, *Dr. Lyman Spalding, The Originator of the United States Pharmacopoeia* (Boston, W. M. Leonard, 1916), p. 306 *et seq*. Dr. Spalding reported that "Dr. Parsons at this time had been at Alfred on leave and had visited Portsmouth to see relatives in New Castle, his Mother having been Miss Abigail Frost Blunt of that village."

61. William Parsons to Usher Parsons, July 1, 1818, DPC.

62. "Diary of Gen. Samuel Leighton, 1818–1848," entries of July 4–5, 1818.

63. Nathan Douglas to Usher Parsons, July 1, 1818, DPC.

64. Samuel Leighton to Usher Parsons, July 7, 1818, DPC.

65. Dan Turner to Usher Parsons, June 8, 1818, DPC.

66. Alexander Slidell Mackenzie, *Life of Commodore Oliver Hazard Perry*, v. 2, p. 245. Perry preferred charges on August 8, 1818 and forwarded the documents on August 10. Usher Parsons's affidavit, undated, was sworn out before Justice of the Peace Holmes Weaver of Newport. See also *Documents in Relation to the Differences Which Subsisted Between the Late Commodore O. H. Perry and Captain J. D. Elliott* (Washington, 1821; reprinted at Boston, 1834). Captain Elliott was to be brought up before a Court-Martial which would examine his conduct at the Battle of Lake Erie, and Perry had transmitted documents to the Navy Department to support his charge. However, because many of the witnesses were on the Mediterranean Station, a Court-Martial was never convened, for Perry died in the interim. When Perry was about to sail on the cruise which terminated his life, he requested Commodore Decatur to take charge of copies of those documents in order to keep Elliott in check during his absence; and, should any accident befall him while on the cruise, he requested that they be published as the most effective means of guarding his character against Elliott's false claims. These were published by his family and friends in the above collection two years after his death.

67. Alexander Slidell Mackenzie, *Life of Commodore Oliver Hazard Perry*, v. 2, pp. 218–226.

CHAPTER SIX

Disciple Abroad

The *Guerrière*, commanded by Captain Thomas Macdonough, sailed from Boston on July 26, 1818.[1] Usher left home burdened with grief over his mother's death and fearing that, faced with a cruise of possibly two years, he might never again see his aged father. The trip across the Atlantic was uneventful. Cowes on the Isle of Wight was the first port of call. From there the ship proceeded to Elsinore in Denmark, whence Usher wrote a sprightly account to his friend, John Holmes, now in the United States Congress. Congressman Holmes thought enough of this letter and subsequent letters to send them to the *Eastern Argus*, a Portland newspaper, for publication.[2]

From Elsinore the *Guerrière* entered the Gulf of Finland, making calls at Port Baltic in Estonia on September 13 and at Kronstadt off St. Petersburg on the 19th. On board, for passage to the Russian capital, was George W. Campbell, newly appointed minister to Russia.[3] Usher carried a letter of introduction from Copenhagen to one Jacob Kruhse, a court physician. They spent about ten days in the Russian capital, during which Usher went sightseeing. His son Charles recalled his "very full accounts of remarkable objects in that city, and of peculiar customs." After leaving St. Petersburg, the *Guerrière* recrossed the Gulf of Finland and returned to Copenhagen.[4]

During a layover there Usher wrote to Campbell about a rumored vacancy in the diplomatic service. Usher asked the Minister if he might serve him in the position that Charles Pinkney, Chargé d'Affaires, had vacated. He admitted that he was ignorant of court etiquette and the duties of such an office, but pressed his

120

proposal nonetheless.[5] Then he told Campbell about his alternative plans:

> The plan I have determined to prosecute is this—on entering the Mediterranean to try for the hospital surgeoncy, which however I have no reason to expect will be vacated. Failing in this, I shall next enquire into the state of the Barbary Consulates though with very little expectation of meeting with encouragement to apply for one of them. In the meantime I shall apply for a furlough, which will probably reach me in March [correct], and if nothing has then occurred to invite my stay in the Mediterranean, I shall set off for Paris and London, and embark from the latter for the United States in May with the intention of settling in private practice at the South or Westward. Now, sir, it would comport with my inclination to go from London to Petersburg, and return to the United States with you; and a certain prospect of obtaining Mr. Pinkney's situation might induce me even to relinquish the other objects of pursuit which I have mentioned. . . . I shall not make known to the commodore any part of my plans till my furlough has arrived, as it would be in his power to thwart me in them. . . .

Although nothing came of his inquiry concerning the ministerial post, it is obvious that Usher was an opportunist. It is not clear whether he was then afflicted with a "liver complaint" which he later mentioned in his request for leave. The fact is that his future activities were predicted quite accurately in this plan.

Usher recorded his observations of St. Petersburg in a letter to his scholarly friend, John Pickering of Salem, Massachusetts, written from Copenhagen. He was struck by the contrast between the dazzling and opulent treasures of the Hermitage and the profound and depressing illiteracy of the masses:[6]

> I have been highly gratified with my visits in Petersburg, and regret that it was of only ten days' duration. The appearance of the city is magnificent beyond anything of the kind I ever expect to see again. . . . no house is erected till the plan of it is submitted to the examination of the Emperor's council, who have power to make any alterations in the position and style that are calculated to render it an ornament to the city. So that . . . you are here presented with the symmetry and uniform majesty of style arising from the judicious taste of a single individual, who possesses the

means and inclination to make it the rival city of the world. Unfortunately I arrived too late to see the Emperor [Alexander I].

... The Russians, however, still wear a more savage aspect than I expected, and seem entirely destitute of integrity and magnanimity. I apply this to about nine tenths of the population. . . .[7]

From Copenhagen the *Guerrière* sailed the Kattegat and the Skagerrak into the North Sea, thence south to the Mediterranean. Usher's sporadic diary of the cruise opens with this entry:

November 12th, 1818. Arrived at Gibraltar from Russia &c. Being in ill health I have applied for permission to ask the Secretary of the Navy for a relief. In Gibraltar I met with some old acquaintances of 1816 and found the place had very little altered.

On information that the squadron was at Syracuse, the *Guerrière* sailed for that port late in November, making rendezvous on December 12. Usher found no "perceptible alteration" in the town since his previous visit. They proceeded to Messina, where on December 22 they "moored ship" and went into winter quarters.

On January 16, 1819 Usher's brother-in-law, General Leighton, wrote[8] that on a recent visit to Alfred he had "found your Father much more comfortable as to his health than I had expected to find him." Father Parsons, he reported, "hoped you would get clear of the ship in the spring . . . , but he was afraid . . . we should hear that you did not expect to be home under a year or two."

A month later Usher wrote to Captain Perry:[9] "I am affected with a chronic disease of the liver which renders one unfit for duty while at sea and, if I continue in my situation a few months longer, will probably be incurable. . . . I am now certain that nothing will effect a complete cure, but long continued exercise in traveling, and for this purpose wish for permission to return to the United States through France."

Although supposedly ill and in need of a leave, Usher saw a fine opportunity to further his medical education and broaden his horizons at navy expense. Knowing that departure was imminent, he requested permission of Captain Macdonough[10] on April 1 to transfer six "incurable" cases from the *Guerrière* to a "hospital where some of them may recover and all of them be more comfortably situated." Macdonough's endorsement read, "This report was handed to Commodore Stewart and he returned for answer that the hospital at Pisa would be established somewhere else in the course of a month and that the sick must remain as they are until that is done."

The extended visit at Messina seems to have been uneventful. The log of the *Guerrière*[11] notes that on April 15 she "stood to the northward" through the straits of Messina, and "stood in" to Palermo on the 17th, a distance of 120 miles. They remained there until May 10. Usher made effective use of the time, conscientiously visiting hospitals, museums, and universities. He described these experiences at length:[12]

> Palermo (Sicily), May 1819. Dr. Weber, to whom I gave a letter [of introduction], made many appointments to meet me and assist me to a sight of the hospitals, &c. in the city. . . . I called this day at the Venereal Hospital to see the Surgeon of it and to make my respects to him. The first surgeon was absent, but the second accompanied me through the wards in which there were about 100 patients of both sexes. The house is about 150 feet square with a large court in the centre & a fountain. The ward makes a circuit on the first chamber floor through the building and the only separation between the sick is that between the sexes, and this is separated to the height of about 15 feet which is about half the height of the story or room. . . . The beds are about 8 feet apart ranged along each side of the room with the head to the wall. . . . The bedsteads are made of iron . . . on which are laid painted boards. . . . On these are laid mattresses of hair, then of wool, brown linen sheets are used. . . . At the side of each bed is a little closet, large enough for the table furniture of each patient.

He discussed in detail the excellent provisions for ventilation. A preoccupation with this problem was characteristic of the pre-Pasteur era, as it was thought to have much bearing on the transmission of disease. The head physician was currently Professor of Anatomy at the University of Palermo. Usher then visited the Military Hospital, which impressed him greatly:

> The Military Hospital I found much better. There was a large court in the centre as in the other with a fountain. . . . A sentinel was placed at the door . . . , who prevented every person from entering but such as the superintendant or doctor permitted. The wards were not so large as in the other, but the beds were ranged in the same manner. The linen looked much cleaner & floor & walls as white as snow.
> There was one room—for such as had got wounded in unnec-

essary quarrels, which had an iron door, and a sentry was kept to it. Another room was appropriated to the blind, and this could be darkened at pleasure. [There was also] a surgery with a table in it and good light, four very neat rooms for officers, and two for the doctor of the day. There were two head physicians, one head surgeon, & 6 under doctors, who kept day's duty in turn. One room was appropriated to venereal patients, one to convalescents, and to very sick men, &c. . . .

[There was] a walk for convalescents aloft on the house. At the head of each bed the place of birth of each patient, the age, company, battalion, &c. was attached to a board, & also the time of entry & disease. A piazza, or walk encircles the inner side of the building around the court on the same floor . . . , and this may be closed up or opened at pleasure. This walk is like that around the court in the Exchange at Boston.

This elaborate and well-run institution was impressive to a country boy from America, where established hospitals were still a rarity. He also visited the "hospital for paupers of the town:"

Here I met a sentry and was pass'd by the superintendant. The sick were on the second story [in] a ward extending like those in the Venereal Hospital, from one end of the building to the other. . . . The side of the walls are whitewashed and a grape vine runs the whole length, top and bottom of the room, which looks very well. Contains about 70 patients and might accommodate 300. One room is appropriated to men with fevers, another to convalescents, & another to surgical cases. It has a surgery or operating room for men, another for women, and a small room with the likeness of Aesculapeus in which consultations are held. The sick women sleep on a floor over the men. A room far apart from all others is appropriated to lying-in women.

A tour of the Medical School followed:

This building I visited with the Professor of Anatomy. It embraces a school for Anatomy, Surgery, Theory & Practice of Physic, [and] Chemistry. The laboratory is hardly yet commenced. There is besides a room for the different branches of fine arts & other sciences, and one for a small collection in natural history. Subjects are dissected.

There is a handsome collection of wax representations of dissections. [These include] a figure to exhibit the veins & blood vessels, very large; two or three for the muscles; one for the bones and ligaments, and one for the viscera like that of Dr. Warren's in Boston, which very much resembles it in every respect, except that it is not half so nice. They are all injured more or less. In cases there are representations of parts only of the body. . . .

Among these he enumerated the brain, sectioned in about twenty pieces, skin showing the papillae of the thumb and fingers, nerves, muscles, and bone. He concluded: "Degrees are not conferred here as in Catania. A knowledge of the dead languages is not required at all." He was much impressed by an "Astronomical apparatus," Piazzi's telescope.[13]

On May 4 he wrote to John Holmes from Palermo:[14]

We are commencing a summer's cruise to Naples, Leghorn, [and] Marseilles, from which the squadron will proceed up the Adriatic and thence along the coast of Barbary. Having myself obtained permission from the Secy. of the Navy to return home, and desirous of returning through France, I shall probably leave the squadron in Marseilles. . . .

He then reported that they were expecting the arrival of Commodore Bainbridge in the *Java* to succeed Commodore Stewart in the *Franklin*, and that Bainbridge would probably take the squadron to Constantinople. Should this happen, it was hoped that none of the American officers there

would follow the example of one of our Marine officers here by assuming the turban of Mahomet and entering the Turkish ranks as a Mussulman. This gentleman you may perhaps have heard of. His name is English of Boston, graduated at Harvard, turned Methodist preacher, then wrote a Deitistical work of some celebrity, afterwards entered the Marine Corps, and arrived here about two years since. He left this [place] on leave of absence for Tunis to exhibit to the Bey a new weapon of warfare of his own invention. From thence he went to Constantinople and turned Turk!! . . .

On May 8 Usher wrote[15] to Jacob Bigelow, Professor of Materia Medica at the Harvard Medical School, describing the Royal Botanical Garden of Palermo and a tour of it, personally conducted by its Director. The college edifice was "superb," and the college was "furnished with books, prints, herbariums, &c. &c. in abundance," bearing, in short, "the impress of royal munificence." On entering the library, the Director handed Usher a book and asked him if he knew its author. Usher continued, "he was much gratified with my reply, as well as with one of your papers . . . which I had taken care to have in my pocket."

Usher's Navy Department file[16] indicates that permission "to return to the U.S." had been granted on January 30. He remained another ten weeks with the *Guerrière*, which cleared Palermo on May 10 and entered the Bay of Naples with the sloop *Erie* on the 13th. Usher resumed his sightseeing with enthusiasm seemingly not handicapped by his ailing liver. Several entries at Naples are undated. In one such, he described a visit to the Grand City Hospital for Incurables:[17]

> On inquiring for the head surgeon and expressing a wish to obtain his permission to visit the wards of the hospital, I was told he was out, and a priest offered to conduct me around.
>
> The hospital is 3 stories high and contains about 980 patients, all chronic cases & venereals. Of the latter there were about 60 of each sex, . . . the men in the lower story and the women in the upper. This particular separation of them was to render it more safe and convenient to use mercury without its interfering with other diseases.
>
> Ulcers on various parts of the body and a sad want of noses [a stigma of lues] were the most observable taint. There was one large ward of about 30 men with phthisis pulmonalis [tuberculosis] and as many women. . . . [One] room [was set aside] for those in a moribund state, containing about a dozen. [There were] two ranges of rooms on each side of a long entry for lying-in women. In one of these rooms I was shown a drawing of a female near the time of parturition . . . with a distorted or malformed pelvis occasioned by rickets. In consequence of this the Caesarean operation was performed with success to the child, but the mother died on the 7th day after the operation of peritonitis. The child was healthy & beautiful, about 2 months old [and] of full size. The mother's height was about 3 feet 4 inches, the abdomen below the knees. The surgeon, who I found in this room, informed me the incision in the mother was made along the linea alba from the navel to the pubis.

The wards were much like those in the other hospitals, except that some of the tile floors were covered with sawdust. In this well-equipped institution, Usher found an operating room where the cutting for bladder stone was a frequent occurrence, an operating room for diseases of the eye, a darkened room for operated eye cases, a dispensary, a chapel, and other facilities.

Usher was impressed by the quality of the care at the Hospital for Diseases of the Eye, which contained about 150 patients, more than half of whom were blind. Cavaliere Paolo Assilini,[18] to whom he had been introduced by letter, invited him to attend an operation there. Professor Quadri[19] conducted them into an apartment where about 150 men and boys were at dinner. He showed Usher three or four patients who had been operated on to create an artificial pupil for albugo of the cornea. Usher described the operative procedure:

His plan of operating is to make an incision on the edge of the cornea with the cornea knife about one third of the circuit of the eye in the manner that is done for extracting the cataract. This is made in that edge of the cornea where the albugo is least apparent. With a pair of fine finger forceps, a little curved, he takes hold of the iris in a very easy & apparently careless manner, draws it out through the incision, and with a pair of curved scissors cuts out a large patch without any regard to form or size, then lets the iris return, closes the lid, & confines it with a piece of court plaster & ribband.

There was, of course, no anesthesia, either local or general, and surgery of this delicacy is remarkable under the circumstances. He continued:

I saw several patients with a spot in the centre of the cornea much larger than the old pupil and as white and impervious to the light as ivory, but by loosing a large portion of the iris under a sound part of the cornea could now see perfectly well. He operated on one patient in the above manner in my presence.

He afterwards took us into another apartment where blind men were at work polishing furniture. [Others were] learning musick, . . . weaving, webbing, . . . making trigonometrical figures, composing musick notes, cyphering, making flowers, &c.

Usher did not miss the rich cultural opportunities of worldly Napoli, visiting museums and galleries during his stay. He learned that the city harbored twenty archbishops and one hundred and seven bishops. The Kingdom of Naples supported an incredible 600,000 ecclesiastics and, Usher added irrelevantly, 300,000 lawyers. In 1783 the government had dissolved 466 convents. Naples was impressive in other ways:

A well clad stranger no sooner lands than he is surrounded by panders in female employ, whose importunity to follow them he is able to quell only with blows. I have myself been surrounded by no less than twelve of these despicable characters at a time. And in further proof of the depravity of the female sex, a large foundling hospital maintained by donations is crammed with the fruits of their lasciviousness.

While in Naples he visited Pompeii, as he had during the *Java* cruise, and found that in the interim there had been further progress in the excavations.

Medical duties were not neglected, and regular entries appear in Usher's "Day Book of Practice." He was responsible for the proper nourishment of his patients, as evidenced by an order for olive oil, Indian meal, sago, arrow root, eggs, and fowl, as well as ten pounds of rags (perhaps for bandages).[20]

In a long letter to Doctor Lyman Spalding written from Naples on May 30,[21] Usher reported that he had been "favoured with an introduction to some of the leading members of the medical faculty." Assilini, he reminded Spalding, had written on the plague and extensively on the eye. He had not only devised instruments for making an artificial pupil, but had applied his genius to improving nearly all surgical instruments. Usher characteristically had shown Assilini a circular of the projected pharmacopoeia (which would be compiled mainly by Spalding and Jacob Bigelow), and, of course, his host "desired to possess [a copy] as soon as it was published." Usher mentioned that the Chevalier had been an intimate companion of Larrey, Napoleon's Surgeon-in-Chief, and had received the same honorary titles from the Emperor. He reported that he had learned of a recent Caesarean operation on a mother greatly deformed with rickets. "The operation," he noted, "is a rare one and seldom more successful," despite the loss of the mother, although it had been performed in France within the year with complete success for both mother and child.

On June 1, 1819 the *Guerrière*, in company with the U.S. ships *Franklin* and *Erie* and the brig *Spark*, stood out under full sail from the majestic Bay of Naples, heading for Algiers. She entered Algiers harbor on the 11th for a brief stay.[22] While at sea, Usher wrote to John Pickering[23] of Salem, for whom he had purchased books in Naples: "We are now running down the Barbary coast to the Rock. On arriving there I shall commence a tour of Leghorn, Florence (Rome perhaps), thence to Marseilles, Paris, London & Boston."

On June 16 the *Guerrière* anchored overnight in Malaga Bay, and on the 17th went on to Gibraltar, arriving there the same day. Usher promptly applied[24] to Commodore Charles Stewart, Commandant of the United States Mediterranean Squadron, for leave: "I am too unwell to wait on you in person . . . my disease, a liver complaint, has returned within the last 20 days and is daily increasing. I am of no further service, and believing a change of climate necessary to my recovery."

While at Gibraltar he wrote to his friend Richard Hazeltine,[25] describing his recent visit to Pompeii (his fourth) and further progress in the continuing excavations. He was particularly fascinated by the surgical instruments found at the site and could recognize probes, finger forceps, and spatulas. "These instruments," however, he noted, "prove . . . that surgery has undergone great changes since the days of Galen."

His "liver complaint," very probably infectious hepatitis, has an unpleasant propensity to relapse under stress, but no currently recognized relationship to climate. Failing to receive a satisfactory response to his application for leave, he repeated his plea to Commodore Stewart on July 14.[26] In the meantime Captain Mcdonough had been relieved of command and was preparing to depart. The officers sent him a gracious note of appreciation, penned by Usher:[27]

> It is with the deepest regret that the ward room officers of this ship see themselves deprived of a commander to whose character they have been accustomed to look as a worthy pattern for their imitation, whose mild and equitable discipline has filled them with admiration, and whose personal kindnesses demands their warmest acknowledgements.

On July 17 Usher prepared a complete inventory of medicines and hospital stores for transfer to his replacement[28] and made his last entry in the *Day Book of Practice*. Both he and Macdonough remained on board as passengers when the *Guerrière* sailed from Gibraltar on July 20, 1819.[29] They arrived off Leghorn about August 4. From there Usher wrote:[30]

> . . . My reasons for leaving the squadron are that the Mediterranean climate disagrees with my health on account of the heat and confined air of a berth deck, and secondly because I am desirous of making the tour of Europe for the purposes of professional improvement, and do not expect to meet with another opportunity so favorable as the present. Lastly, I am so exceed-

ingly tired with the monotonous scenery of a man o'war, of the
perpetual jarrings that occur, and of the restrictions that are im-
posed on officers, that a change seemed desirable for the health
of the mind as well as body.

I leave this tomorrow for Pisa, Lucca, Pistoia, and Florence,
where I shall remain for some days to examine the anatomical
representations in wax, the gallery, academy, &c., and thence
proceed to Rome by water as the passage is short.

On the following day Usher started his grand tour.[31] Commodore
Macdonough "favored me with his company" as far as Pisa, where
they parted. Usher was fascinated by Pisa's perennial tourist mag-
net: "The most curious monument of architecture here is the Leaning Tower, which seems to be always ready for falling, but still
stands." "The city," he noted, "wears a dismal aspect from the
scarcity of inhabitants, which, he explained, had been drawn away
by the rapid growth of neighboring Leghorn. Continuing his travels
by various conveyances, he journeyed from Pisa, through Lucca and
Prato, and on to Florence on August 18. There he was overjoyed to
discover that the consul, a Mr. Tudor of Boston, was an old acquaintance from the U.S.S. *Franklin*. Tudor, to whom Usher handed
letters of introduction, had been in the city for some time and "was
able as well as willing to aid me in seeing all the curiosities."[32]

Usher visited the hospital in Florence and also the Medical
School, where he found the wax preparations at the anatomical
museum of great merit:

> The wax museum, [which] I mentioned first deservedly, is of
> itself worth a tour from the United States to inspect. I, however,
> cannot say that it contains a single figure superior in beauty, if
> equal to, the one owned by Doctor Warren. But the various organs
> and portions of the human body separated, the beautiful repre-
> sentations of the lymphatic system, and the gravid uterus in its
> various stages of gestation render the collection highly valuable
> and interesting. Sixteen apartments are filled without having a
> duplicate of any one piece. I observe this sort of work is very
> common in every part of Italy. . . .[33]

From Florence Usher proceeded by carriage to Rome, arriving
about August 30.[34] He spent a feverish week traveling on foot and
by carriage through that vast storehouse of antiquities, viewing the
Forum, St. Peter's, the Pantheon, and the Coliseum. Tremendously
impressed by the riches and the "vast number of objects," he used

such terms as elegant, colossal, immense, grand, exquisite work-manship, very fine, well-preserved, and exquisite beauty. Archeo-logical excavations were everywhere in progress. He was fascinated by a curious activity in the Tiber River: "We went to see the boat, or machine, employed by some English and others to dig into the bed of the Tiber. They are now at work, but do not disclose their discoveries." Elsewhere he described it as "a steam boat with ap-propriate machinery" for "ploughing up" the river bed.[35]

On Friday, September 3 he viewed the Pope "who always appears out at 5 o'clock"; and "thence to the Pope's Garden where an organ goes by water & two trumpets blown by angels and various other works of curiosity" could be seen. He was charmed by "the Pope's coffee house which is a delightful summer house."[36]

On Saturday he made the rounds of several hospitals, including the facilities for incurables, venereal patients, the insane, and fi-nally, near St. Peter's the San Spirito on the banks of the Tiber, which sheltered six hundred patients. He also visited the "Trinity of the Pilgrims, where [wayfarers] lodge three days free, and where the poor of the hospitals are received 3 days, when discharged cured from their hospital, to confirm their strength." Later he viewed the Ripa Granda, "where the vessels lay, to get a passage to Leghorn," and "thence home." On Sunday, he visited the Vatican museum.[37]

His notes carry on the narrative. On September 6, knowing he must soon leave Rome, perhaps forever, he could not refrain from taking a last look at the Pantheon, Coliseum, and Roman Forum, all of which he had already visited.[38]

At 3 p.m. on the 6th, Usher left the city for Ripa Granda, where he embarked on a small schooner for Leghorn. She drifted down the Tiber River, passing in sight of Ostia, to Fumicino, 21 miles from Rome. His "accommodation for sleeping was the hard deck for a feather bed and without any covering." A covering would not really have mattered much "on account of the millions of fleas on the vessel"—"my eyes were closed for probably half an hour that night." The river near Fumicino, where they lay over for a few days, was cut through marshland "so very unhealthy that every habita-tion was deserted," due, no doubt, to malaria. The rain was inces-sant, and he spent "another wretched night." He dallied on shore, where he was "called to see an aged female afflicted with partial blindness and another with fever." His ministrations, if any, were not mentioned. The former lived in a large house and offered to board Usher while he was ashore, which he accepted with alacrity. During this interlude he came to know the village doctor: "A jolly old bacchanalian is physician to about 20 soldiers who are stationed here and to the few inhabitants. He professed great veneration for the Brunonian system of medicine, and his bloated face indicated the sincerity of his faith, tho' his apparel gave him the appearance of a Shakespeare's apothecary."[39]

Usher was reluctant to leave "the comfortable habitat of my hostess for another visit of the fleas." The captain, procrastinating because of capricious winds, finally took his boat out at 4 p.m. on the 9th, but did not arrive at Leghorn, a distance of only 20 miles, until the evening of the 10th, "a day and a night ever riveted in my recollection," wrote Usher. En route they passed "within a few rods of Elba," a "rough and barren" island, not long ago the abode of Napoleon in his brief first exile. During part of the frustrating and wretched journey Usher had the companionship of a Roman officer traveling to England, who "spoke good English and was good company for me."

From Leghorn Usher traveled to Genoa, Switzerland, and Nice, reaching Marseille by sea on September 19. From Marseille he proceeded overland up the Rhone Valley through Aix, Avignon, and Lyon, arriving in Paris on September 29.[40] At Marseille he wrote to his brother William:[41] "If robbers spare me on the road from Marseilles to Paris, you will probably hear from me there or from London." Spared, he reported from Paris to Professor John Gorham of Harvard:[42] "There is very little in the south of Europe to interest a chemist; and excepting the anatomical museum of wax in Florence, a few botanical gardens, and hospitals, a medical gentleman finds nothing worthy of his notice in any branch of his profession south of Paris." He continued:

> The hospitals in Rome, Florence, Genoa & Lyons are I think in as good, if not better, condition than those in Paris. They are, however, not so large as the Hôtel Dieu or St. Louis, nor headed by such able men; for, with the exception of Scarpa, I cannot learn of a single Italian surgeon or physician of great eminence.
>
> But if this southern tour has been unprofitable in a professional point of view, it has not been so in other respects. The splendid monuments of antiquity in Rome, its museums of statuary, and academies of fine arts, as well as those of Florence, the magnificent cathedrals, and the colossal building of St. Peter's make up

for every disappointment [in] medical advantage. To give . . . even a catalogue of all the remains of temples, theatres, obelisks, triumphal arches, &c. would require a large shelf of books. . . .

Early in the nineteenth century, the leadership of medical thought was shifting from Edinburgh to Paris,[43] where a number of able physicians were discarding the theoretical "systems" of the 18th century in favor of the study of disease processes by careful observation of clinical signs and symptoms, which were then meticulously correlated with the postmortem findings. Soon to join this distinguished coterie was Pierre C. A. Louis,[44] then a young man of 31 and still studying in Russia, who would combine the clinical-pathological correlation with a "numerical method" of careful collection and analysis of facts, followed by logical classification, in modern parlance a statistical analysis. Utilizing data in this way greatly advanced the recognition of specific diseases, previously lumped together under such general terms as recurrent, malignant, or putrid fevers.[45]

As Usher set out for Paris in the fall of 1818, he was virtually in the vanguard of a significant movement in American medicine.[46] He carried letters of introduction,[47] but, as it turned out, managed quite well without them while in Paris. His notes and letters unfold an exciting panorama of the brilliant French School of medicine at the height of its vigor. He describes the teeming activities in considerable detail:[48]

La Charité (Paris: October 13). Went through the wards with [Alexis] Boyer,[49] his son-in-law [Philibert Joseph] Roux,[50] and about thirty students. Saw nothing but bad ulcers and those badly managed. The French surgeons are neither neat, scientific, nor successful in their treatment of ulcers, wounds, &c. They rarely attempt to heal by the first intention; even in amputations below the knee, the first surgeons are in the habit of stuffing the stump with lint to prevent its closing by the approximation of the skin of the opposite sides. This practice is condemned in England, and must ere long be in France. . . .

While some French surgeons showed great gentleness and care, others displayed a gross inhumanity and disregard for life:

[Dominique Jean] Larrey's [51] manner of operating is pleasing. He uses the knife adroitly and gracefully, and is neat in his dressings. He is humane and solacing in his behavior to the patients, differing in this respect very much from [Guillaume] Dupuytren,[52] whose behavior to them is savage. This is the more remarkable when it is considered that D. has always been in civil life, while L. has always been in military practice, where sympathy and fine sensibilities are less known [he had formerly been surgeon-in-chief of Napoleon's Grande Armée]. Their stature is much alike, both being very stout and very stately in their appearance. Larrey is very ready and pertinent in his remarks.

November 11. Went early to the hospital Salpétrière [a psychiatric hospital] to attend the physician in his rounds. Enquired for M. [Philippe] Pinel,[53] who is physician-in-chief and at the head of the institution, and sent in to him my address, with a request that I might accompany him through the hospital. He invited me into his study, and after some enquiries about American hospitals, &c., we made a tour first through three large wards full of women past sixty years of age, and who were ill. After prescribing for these, we visited the lunatic apartments in which are women in every state of mental disorder, from slight melancholy to furious mania. Those of the latter description were many of them chained, and others shut up in prisons. . . . I found in this instance, that introducing myself to the professor had as good if not better effect than a letter would have had.

On November 15 Usher received a written invitation to visit the hospital of Baron [Nicolas-René Dufriche] Desgenettes [the Val-de-Grâce military hospital].[54] Sensible of the honor, he sent a formal reply, written with exceptional care (November 16),[55] in which he explained that he had to decline this offer because of prior commitments.

Usher remained in Paris for another two weeks. Shortly before his departure, he again wrote to Doctor Lyman Spalding. A New Hampshire boy and Harvard Medical School graduate, Spalding was then living in New York City, and was involved in preparing the first United States Pharmacopoeia:[56]

Having been . . . engaged for two or three months in attending hospitals and medical schools, I have thought . . . you might feel some curiosity to know how I have found them. These establishments are so numerous and employ so many lecturers and professors that a stranger . . . would believe the attention of the whole city is directed toward them. I have collected the names of rising sixty professors and lecturers in medicine and its collateral branches and am everyday hearing of others. I have attended the lectures of some whose names are familiar to you, particularly [Paul] Dubois', Boyer's, Dupuytren's, [Anthelme Balthaser] Richerand's, [Jean Louis] Alibert's & Larrey's on surgery; and [Louis Nicolas] Vauquelin, [Jean Antoine] Chaptal, [Jean Louis] Gay-Lussac, [Louis Jacques] Thénard, and [René Just] Abbé Haüy on Chemistry.[57] It is difficult to determine which surgeon to rank first—Dubois, Boyer, or Dupuytren. They are each at the head of a hospital and continually engaged. The two first are older and consequently more experienced, but Dupuytren has been at the head of the Hôtel Dieu for several years and . . . has performed more operations than all the other surgeons in Paris. I . . . acknowledge him the best operator I have yet seen. . . . Boyer is more known abroad than the others, by his system of anatomy and surgery. The latter will . . . consist of 8 volumes.

Richerand is still a young man, say 35 or 40, and has written several works equal to his physiology, but he is a miserable lecturer. His subject is *médicine opératoire* (or surgical diseases). [Charles Michel] Billard,[58] a young anatomist, and [Louis Jacques] Thénard, the chemist, are the most popular lecturers, and not more than three fourths of those who go to hear Thénard can gain admittance.

I have not learned that any popular work has appeared on medicine of late, excepting an elementary work on Phlegmasia by a [François Joseph Victor] Broussais, [François] Magendie's Physiology, [Jons Jacob Count] Berzelius' work on Mineralogy, and some few pamphlets.[59] Abbé Haüy is promising something on chemistry. Larrey is surgeon of the hospital of the King's guards, which is but a small establishment. An opinion prejudicial to him prevails that he is too fond of cutting; and that he frequently amputated when it was not necessary; and scandal says he has emasculated half of the King's guard.

In reply to this canard, Usher wrote that he "performs . . . surgical operations in a very elegant style" and added, "You however see much more of this man in his writings." He then told Doctor Spalding that

Medical gentlemen are permitted to see his patients every Thursday, when he gives a particular history of every case and performs some operations. The last time I was there I took the liberty of introducing myself to him, which he gave me no reason to regret doing. He enquired about the hospitals in the United States and asked if I was acquainted with you & when I saw you last.

I have found the people here very ignorant of the state of medical science with us and yet very desirous to be better informed. This circumstance has induced me to supply one of the journals with a short description of our contemplated dispensatory, a translation of which is subjoined. I have had the honor of becoming acquainted with Drs. [François Xavier] Swediaur, Pinel, & Cuvier [Georges Léopold Chrétien Frédéric Dagobert, Baron de la Cuvier], each of whom have contributed their part to medical science. . . .[60]

I proceed from this to London in about two days and, after a month pass'd in that city, shall return to the United States. Dr. Packwood, a young gentleman from New York, accompanies me.[61]

Usher had several other interesting experiences in Paris.[62] As luck would have it, Sir Humphrey Davy, the famed English physicist and chemist, was passing through Paris on his way to Naples to undertake a delicate and arduous task, the unrolling of the Herculaneum manuscript scrolls. While there, Davy was elected to the Institut de France as a foreign member. Usher, with his uncanny knack of being at the center of action, was present at the election. While in Paris, Usher formed an acquaintance with William Clift, "a genial and accomplished Englishman." Clift, a pupil of the great British surgeon John Hunter, was Conservator of the Royal College of Surgeons. "This acquaintance, renewed in London," wrote Charles Parsons in his *Memoir* of his father, "ripened into a lifelong friendship with Mr. Clift and his son-in-law, Professor Richard Owen, the eminent comparative anatomist," who was then but a boy of fifteen years.[63]

Before leaving Paris Usher bought medical books and instruments, including Laënnec's classical treatise on auscultation and a stethoscope of the master's own design, certified to have been "examined and used by Laënnec."[64]

Although Paris had replaced London as the favored European center of study for young American physicians, many were attracted as well to the vital and varied medical world of the British capital, where the English language gave them the comfortable feeling of being home. Usher eagerly joined their number and unabashedly rubbed shoulders there with the medical élite. Using notes which have not survived, his son Charles described Usher's profitable and eventful stay there:[65]

He went from Paris to London, arriving there December 4, and remaining till Christmas. In those three weeks he became acquainted with many of the most eminent surgeons and savants of London, Sir Astley Cooper,[66] [John] Abernethy,[67] and others. He attended the levee of Sir Joseph Banks.[68] He breakfasted with Sir Astley Cooper, but found him pressed with business. He gave considerable attention to the Hunterian Museum at the College of Surgeons, and contemplated the formation of a museum of anatomy founded on a principle suggested to him, viz: that of bringing together specimens of corresponding organs and sets of organs from as many as possible of the different classes and orders of the animal kingdom [in other words, a museum of comparative anatomy]. He attended two meetings of the Royal Society. Beside the usual sightseeing, he saw Kean play Hamlet at Drury Lane, and heard a debate in the House of Lords by Russell, Castlereagh, and others on the subject of the "rotten boroughs," and the expediency of admitting representation from the large manufacturing towns in the House of Commons.

The following entries in Usher's original diary have also been preserved only in his son's *Memoir*:[69]

December 9. Examined the Museum of the College of Surgeons. This collection is calculated for physiological purposes alone. Every organ of the animal machine is exhibited in as great a variety of animals as they have hitherto been able to collect. The separate organs are preserved in spirit, and are arranged from those of the most simple to those of the most complex structure. The museum begins with a simple muscular fibre, [i.e.] rectilinear; then follow single and double penniform muscles, sphincters, &c. Then the organs of digestion and assimilation beginning with the stomachs of all sorts of animals; then the various organs of mastication, &c., &c.
[December] 20. Went to St. Bartholomew's and heard Mr. Abernethy lecture on organic diseases of the heart to about three hundred pupils, the most interesting lecture I almost ever heard. His manner is peculiar, and the most engaging and amusing as well as impressive I ever heard. Dr. Mason of New York makes somewhat such a figure in the pulpit as Mr. Abernethy does here.[70] He is full of illustrative anecdotes which he tells with

such a quaintness as to make one laugh. He is about fifty years old, of middle stature, head powdered, dressed in black.

Usher had been commissioned to deliver to William Thomas Brande, Professor of Chemistry at the Royal Institution, a chest of American minerals, a gift from Professor John Gorham of the Harvard Medical School. As the *Guerrière* had failed to stop in England, Usher shipped the specimens from the continent. Usher wrote Gorham from London:[71]

> I arrived here about a fortnight since. The first Thursday evening after my arrival I met with Mr. Brande at the Royal Society and being introduced to him, I took the occasion to speak about the minerals you sent him by me. He informed me they were received early last spring. . . . He appeared gratified with the notice you had thus taken of him . . . and invited me to see the Institution. I am sorry the box did not reach him sooner, but no exertion was wanting on my part. . . .
>
> I can give you nothing new respecting the medical schools or hospitals in London or the physicians & surgeons, who are at the head of them. . . .
>
> The hospitals here differ from those in Paris . . . in the apparent respectability of the students. Every medical student I have seen in London will pass anywhere for an accomplished gentleman, while in Paris about half I saw in the hospitals were very little short of accomplished blackguards.

Usher sailed from Liverpool on December 28 aboard the merchant vessel *Harmony*. While at sea he wrote a final letter to Doctor Spalding recounting some highlights of his memorable stay in London:[72]

> I called at the book store in St. Paul's Church Yard as you desired, and inquired for [William Fordyce] Mavor's Travels, but found the old bookseller you mentioned had discontinued business, and that the book store had not a single volume . . . of that work.[73] . . . I have passed a month in the medical schools and hospitals of London much to my satisfaction and, I hope, improvement. Although I think better of the Paris schools for Anatomy and Surgery, yet the other branches, particularly Pathology and Therapeutics, are better understood and taught by the London professors. . . . Were I to be asked which surgeon of London enjoys the highest reputation, it would puzzle me to answer. Mr. Abernethy is undoubtedly the most engaging and valuable lecturer.

Mr. A. Cooper has the most practice. Charles Bell[74] has contributed most for the Press. Yet Sir Everard Home,[75] Sir William Blizzard [*i.e.* Blizard],[76] and Mr. [Henry] Cline, Senr.[77] are considered by the profession as equal if not superior to either of the above ... their writings are ... superior.... There are [also] a host of young surgeons striving for eminence, as Lawrence[78] [and] young Cline.[79]

Usher then mentioned a subject which must have been of great interest to his New York compatriot:

Among the American books on medicine and its collateral branches ..., no one has been so well received as [Parker] Cleaveland's[80] "Mineralogy," and Gorham's "Chemistry." ... Mr. Brande told me that he considered Gorham's "Chemistry" a most excellent and complete digest of everything at present known on that science.[81] Rush "On the Yellow Fever" and "On the Mind" are, however, from their greater age in more circulation. I have met with the latter in the medical libraries of Russia, Denmark, Tuscany, Rome, Naples, France, and England.[82]

... I shall probably pass through N.Y. in the course of a month or two. ...

NOTES

1. C. W. Parsons *Memoir*, p. 16.
2. Usher Parsons to John Holmes, August 31, 1818, transcript, unsigned, Published in the *Eastern Argus*, Portland, Maine, on December 22, 1818. Usher described mainly the Isle of Wight, at which the *Guerrière* arrived after a thirty-five day passage from Boston, and the visitors who were attracted to come on board and see an American man of war. He concluded with a few remarks about Elsinore.
3. George Washington Campbell (1769–1848), U.S. Congressman, Secretary of the Treasury, and U.S. Senator, served as Minister to Russia for two years. He resigned when two of his children died of typhus within a single week.
4. C. W. Parsons *Memoir*, p. 16; Usher Parsons, "Day Book of Practice Kept During the Cruise of the U.S. Frigates *Java* and *Guerrière*," RIHS.
5. Usher Parsons to George Washington Campbell, October 8, 1818, G. W. Campbell Papers, Library of Congress.
6. Usher Parsons to John Pickering, October 14, 1818, DPC. John Pickering (1777–1846), was a legal authority who also acquired fame in linguistics and philosophy.
7. While at sea Usher also wrote long, detailed letters to Professor John

Gorham of the Harvard Medical School faculty describing the wonders of St. Petersburg and the peculiarities of the Russian people. Usher Parsons to John Gorham, November 4 and November 11, 1818, draft copies, DPC.

8. Samuel Leighton to Usher Parsons, January 16, 1819, DPC.

9. Usher Parsons to Oliver Hazard Perry, February 18, 1819, DPC.

10. Usher Parsons to Thomas Macdonough, April 1, 1819, DPC.

11. "Log of the U.S. Frigate *Guerrière*," entries for January 1, 1819 to July 20, 1819, WRDNA.

12. Usher Parsons, "Diary Kept During the Cruise of the U.S. Frigate *Guerrière*," RIHS.

13. Invented by Giuseppe Piazzi (1746–1826), the Italian astronomer.

14. Usher Parsons to John Holmes, May 4, 1819, DPC.

15. Usher Parsons to Jacob Bigelow, May 18, 1819, DPC.

16. Usher Parsons, Service Record, WRDNA.

17. Usher Parsons, "Diary Kept During the Cruise of the U.S. Frigate *Guerrière*."

18. Assilini (1780–1851) had been a Napoleonic army surgeon and first court surgeon under Napoleon.

19. Gian Battista Quadri (1780–1851), famed oculist and director of the Clinica Oculista at Naples. Jacques Daviel (1696–1762), French surgeon and oculist, had invented the operation of cataract extraction a half century before these events. See his monograph *Lettres sur les Avantages de l'Opération de la Cataracte par Extraction* (Paris, 1756).

20. Usher Parsons, Requisition to Thomas Macdonough, May 23, 1819, DPC.

21. Usher Parsons to Lyman Spalding, May 30, 1819, transcribed and published in James Alfred Spalding's *Dr. Lyman Spalding*, p. 307.

22. "Log of the U.S. Frigate *Guerrière*," January 1, 1819 to July 20, 1819.

23. Usher Parsons to John Pickering, June 10, 1819, draft, DPC. See also C. W. Parsons *Memoir*, p. 17.

24. Usher Parsons to Commander Charles Stewart, draft copy, undated, DPC.

25. Usher Parsons to Richard Hazeltine, June 22, 1819, DPC.

26. Usher Parsons to Commander Charles Stewart, June 14, 1819, draft copy, DPC.

27. Probably a draft copy, in Usher's hand, of a communication of the Ward Room Officers to Thomas Macdonough, July 11, 1819, DPC.

28. Usher Parsons, "Inventory of Medicines and Hospital Stores," July 17, 1819, DPC.

29. C. W. Parsons *Memoir*, p. 18.

30. Usher Parsons to an unknown correspondent, August 14, 1819, draft copy, DPC.

31. Usher Parsons, three pages of manuscript notes, August 17 and 18, 1819, possibly a draft copy for the letter of the following note, DPC.

32. Usher Parsons to an unidentified correspondent, headed "Mon Caro Amico" [*sic*], August 18, 1819, DPC.

33. *Ibid.*

34. Usher Parsons, fragments of a diary, August 30 (probably August 31) to September 11, 1819, DPC.

35. *Ibid.* Also Usher Parsons to William Parsons (his brother), September 19, 1819, DPC.

36. *Ibid.*

37. *Ibid.*

38. *Ibid.*

39. Brunonianism was a controversial system of medicine according to which all diseases arise either from a deficiency or an excess of excitement and must be treated with stimulants or sedatives. It was named after its founder, John Brown, M.D. (1735–1788) of Edinburgh, whose favorite remedies were whiskey and laudanum, of which he himself partook freely. "Shakespeare's apothecary" probably refers to the apothecary in *Romeo and Juliet*, who sold the fateful poison to Romeo (Act V, Scene 1): "In tatter'd weeds, with overwhelming brows, culling of simples; meagre were his looks, sharp misery had worn him to the bones." See also note 40.

40. C. W. Parsons *Memoir*, p. 19.

41. Usher Parsons to William Parsons (his brother), September 19, 1819, DPC.

42. Usher Parsons to an unknown correspondent (but probably John Gorham), November 1819 (no further date), DPC.

43. Henry K. Beecher and Mark D. Altschule, *Medicine at Harvard*, pp. 16–18.

44. Ralph A. Major, *A History of Medicine*, pp. 671–673.

45. Lester S. King, *The Medical World of the Eighteenth Century* (Chicago, University of Chicago Press, 1958), pp. 123–154 *passim.*

46. During this period of about half a century Paris became the educational and scientific center of western medicine, attracting between 1820 and 1861 nearly 700 ambitious young American physicians who went there to observe and study. Many of them, such as Elisha Bartlett, John Collins Warren, Oliver Wendell Holmes, Henry Ingersoll Bowditch, George Cheyne Shattuck, Jr., John B. S. Jackson, and William Wood, became the leaders of American medicine. See Henry K. Beecher and Mark D. Altschule's *Medicine at Harvard* and Russell K. Jones, "American Doctors in Paris, 1820–1861: A Statistical Profile," *Journal of the History of Medicine and Allied Sciences*, 25:143–157, 1970, as well as that same author's "American Doctors and the Parisian Mediworld, 1830–1840," *Bulletin of the History of Medicine*, 47:40–65, 1973.

47. For example, Usher had such a letter of introduction written by James Ombrosi to John Rathbone, August 24, 1819, now in DPC.

48. C. W. Parsons *Memoir*, pp. 20–22. According to Usher's son, these are extracts from a notebook kept by his father titled, "Surgical notes and observations made in different cities in Europe, particularly in Paris and London." The original manuscript has not been located.

49. Alexis Boyer (1757–1833) was appointed to the Charité in 1787, having previously (1781) gained the gold medal at the college of surgery. He was a brilliant operator and a productive writer.

50. Philibert Joseph Roux (1780–1854) was, among the French surgeons of the nineteenth century, second in importance only to Dupuytren. He performed staphylorrhaphy (the plastic operation of uniting a cleft palate) as early as 1819 and sutured the ruptured female perineum (perineorrhaphy) in 1832. He is also remembered for a method of resection of joints.

51. Dominique Jean Larrey (1766–1842) was formerly Surgeon-in-Chief of Napoleon's Grande Armée.

52. Guillaume Dupuytren (1777–1835) was Surgeon-in-Chief of the Hôtel Dieu. He was one of the premier surgeons of the nineteenth century. He had a large private practice and was surgeon to Louis XVIII, who created him a baron, and Charles X.

53. Philippe Pinel (1745–1826) was Physician-in-Chief at the Salpétrière, famed hospital for nervous and mental diseases. He is particularly remembered for abolishing restraint of the mentally ill and as a pioneer in humane treatment. It is of interest that almost two decades after the publication of Pinel's celebrated monograph *Traité Médico-Philosophique sur l'Aliénation Mental ou la Manie* (Paris, 1801), in which he proposed his concepts of the compassionate treatment of the insane, Usher found some of the more violently psychotic patients still in chains.

54. Baron Nicolas-René Dufriche Desgenettes (1762–1837) was professor on the faculty of medicine at Val-de-Grâce military hospital.

55. Usher Parsons to Baron Desgenettes, November 16, 1819, draft copy, DPC.

56. Usher Parsons to Lyman Spalding, November 29, 1819, DPC. The pharmacopoeia was published in 1820.

57. Paul Dubois (1795–1871) was an obstetrician; Anthelme Balthasar Richerand (1779–1840) was professor of surgical pathology at the Faculty of Medicine of Paris; Jean Louis Alibert (1766–1837) was a physician who made several classical contributions to dermatology; Louis Nicolas Vauquelin (1763–1829), a chemist, was professor of chemistry at the Faculty of Medicine and chemist to the Jardin des Plantes; Jean Antoine Chaptal (1756–1832) was also a chemist; Jean Louis Gay-Lussac (1778–1850) was professor of physics at the Faculty of Sciences and professor of chemistry at l'École Polytechnique; Louis Jacques Thénard, a chemist, was professor at the Collège de France and later

dean of the Faculty of Sciences; René Just, the Abbé Haüy (1743–1822), a mineralogist, was professor at the Museum of Natural History of Paris.

58. Charles Michel Billard (1800–1832) was a physician and anatomist.

59. François Joseph Victor Broussais (1778–1832) was a celebrated physician whose advocacy of bleeding, leech treatments, and fasting dominated Parisian medical practice early in the nineteenth century. His work on inflammation of the veins (phlegmasia) was written in 1808; François Magendie (1783–1855) was an experimental physiologist who did pioneer studies on the nerves and on the effects of drugs on various parts of the body; Jons Jacob Count Berzelius (1779–1848), Swedish chemist, developed the table of atomic weights.

60. François Xavier Swediaur (1748–1824) was an Austrian physician; George Léopold Chrétien Frédéric Dagobert, Baron de la Cuvier (1769–1832), a famed naturalist, was professor at the Collège de France.

61. Samuel W. Packwood was a recent graduate of the College of Physicians and Surgeons of New York (later Columbia University), class of 1819, and one day would be president of the New York State Medical Society.

62. In a letter written earlier to Professor Gorham of the Harvard Medical School in November (see footnote 42), Usher mentioned other medical and scientific stars of the French galaxy whom he had seen in action: Jean Nicolas Corvisart, physician of La Charité; François Chaussier, anatomist; Jean Baptist Jacques Thillaye, surgeon; Jacques Louis Moreau de la Garthe, medical historian; Claude François Lallemand, physician; and Georges Balthasar Sage, chemist and mineralogist, now an old man, whom Gorham had known when he himself had been a student in Paris.

63. C. W. Parsons *Memoir*, p. 22. Sir William Clift (1775–1849), an apprentice and protégé of the great anatomist and surgeon, John Hunter (1728–1793), took charge of Hunter's famed anatomical collection upon Hunter's death. When that collection went to the Royal College of Surgeons in 1800, Clift was appointed Conservator. Richard Owen, M.D. (Edinburgh) (1804–1892), joined Clift at the Hunterian Museum in 1827. In 1835 he married Clift's daughter, Caroline Amelia. He became Hunterian Professor of Comparative Anatomy at the College in 1836, Joint Conservator with Clift in 1842, and his successor in 1849. In 1856 Owen became director of the Natural History branch of the British Museum.

64. René Théóphile Hyacinthe Laënnec (1781–1826) invented the stethoscope in 1816 and published his classic treatise on diseases of the chest and physical diagnosis, *De l'Auscultation Médiate*, in 1819. Usher's copy of this classic of cardiology is now, along with many others of his books, in the historical collection of the Rhode Island Medical Society.

65. C. W. Parsons *Memoir*, p. 22.

66. Sir Astley Paston Cooper (1768–1841), anatomist and surgeon at Guy's Hospital, was one of the premier English surgeons of the nineteenth

century. He was attached to St. Thomas's Hospital as well, and he made many classic contributions to his specialty.

67. John Abernethy (1764–1831) was surgeon at St. Bartholomew's Hospital.

68. Sir Joseph Banks (1743–1820), naturalist, wealthy patron of science, collector of books and specimens, is known mainly for his patronage and promotion of science rather than for his own original researches.

69. C. W. Parsons *Memoir*, p. 23. The original manuscript appears not to be extant.

70. The reference is to John Mitchell Mason (1793–1827), a distinguished New York educator and clergyman, who was noted for his commanding and magnetic presence on the pulpit.

71. Usher Parsons to an unknown correspondent (but probably John Gorham), November 1819 (no further date), DPC.

72. Usher Parsons to Lyman Spalding, transcribed and published in James Alfred Spalding's *Dr. Lyman Spalding*, p. 311.

73. *The Voyages, Travels and British Tourist*, by William Fordyce Mavor 1758–1837), consisted of no less than 30 volumes!

74. Sir Charles Bell (1774–1842), anatomist, was then surgeon to the Middlesex Hospital. He was later professor at Edinburgh.

75. Sir Everard Home (1756–1832), pupil and brother-in-law of John Hunter. He was surgeon to the King and professor at the Royal College of Surgeons.

76. Sir William Blizard (1743–1835) was surgeon at St. Bartholomew's Hospital and founder of the London Hospital Medical School.

77. Henry Cline, Sr. (1750–1827) was surgeon at St. Thomas's Hospital. His son, Henry Cline, Jr. who succeeded him in 1811, died of tuberculosis in 1820 shortly after Usher's letter was written.

78. Sir William Lawrence (1783–1867), surgeon at St. Bartholomew's Hospital and lecturer at London Hospital Medical School, wrote a classic treatise on the surgery of the eye and one of the earliest works on anthropology.

79. See note 77.

80. Parker Cleaveland (1780–1858), Harvard College 1795, was professor of mathematics and natural philosophy at Bowdoin College. When its medical school began operations in 1820, he taught materia medica.

81. Doctor John Gorham, Erving Professor of Chemistry and Mineralogy at both Harvard College and the Harvard Medical School, had just published his two-volume *Elements of Chemical Science*, the first systematic textbook on chemistry written by an American and published in America. It had found its way to England in short order.

82. Benjamin Rush was well known in his day for his treatment of yellow fever, which called for copious bloodletting. His early treatise on the

subject, *An Enquiry into the Origin of the Late Epidemic Fever in Philadelphia*, first published in 1793, was reprinted in the early nineteenth century in several editions of his *Medical Inquiries and Observations*. His *Medical Inquiries and Observations Upon the Diseases of the Mind*, published initially in 1812 and again in 1818, was the first American treatise on psychiatry.

CHAPTER SEVEN

Charting a Course

The *Harmony* arrived in Portsmouth, New Hampshire on the last day of January, 1820. Usher spent the night in Eliot, across the Piscataqua River, with his sister and brother-in-law, the Leightons. On the afternoon of February 2, amidst a drifting snowstorm and the coldest weather of the season, Usher and his sister, Mrs. Leighton, set out by sleigh for Alfred twenty-five miles away, where for the first time in nineteen months Usher was able to visit with his ailing father.[1]

On February 8, in fine clear weather, Usher departed for Boston. Immediately upon arriving there, he set about mending fences. He dispatched the following to Navy Secretary Smith Thompson:[2]

I hereby report my return from the Mediterranean, which I left on account of ill health, by the authority of the enclosed letters. . . . The failure of Doctor Sproston to relieve me and my consequent prolonged detention on board the *Guerrière* increased my disease to such a degree, that it was considered unsafe for me to attempt a passage across the Atlantic . . . , and I was advised to try the climate of the north of Europe, which the commodore permitted. The expenses . . . incurred in traveling, for medical advice, & passage across the Atlantic have been very considerable; to defray a part of which I ask . . . your approval of the enclosed account. . . .

My health is now so far restored as to permit my doing duty on shore, and would be perfectly reestablished if I could pass the summer in a northern climate. Captain Hull has . . . advised me to ask for the surgeoncy of the Marine Barracks in Charlestown [Massachusetts], the duties of which I am now able to perform.

146

Usher, characteristically, attempted to extract every advantage
from his situation—shore duty near his beloved Boston and allow-
ances for personal expenses while on leave. He had been ill, he was
now a veteran of some years, and his combat and sea duty had been
extensive, at times arduous. This he carefully detailed in a long and
plaintive letter to Representative John Holmes. While awaiting a
reply, he was notified by the Secretary of the Navy that he and
eight other officers of the Erie campaign had received a citation.[3]
When neither orders nor his silver medal arrived, Usher turned to
Holmes:[4] "I will thank you to take charge of the medal and bring
it in such a manner that it may not be defaced."

In a letter to Holmes a few days earlier Usher had sought his
help:

> I reported my return here to the Secretary by letter and re-
> quested orders for duty at the Marine Barracks in Charlestown,[5]
> but have received no answer, and have lately learned that the
> Secretary is invariably silent to all such applications unless they
> are forwarded by the commander of the station. Captains Hull &
> Shaw, the commanders here, refused to consider me under their
> command and advised me to address the Secretary myself; so that
> between their refusal to forward my letters and the Secretary's
> peculiar manner of doing business, I am left in ignorance of my
> destiny and of the source whence I am to receive pay.
>
> The Secretary is unacquainted with my services and probably
> thinks me as undeserving of favor or notice as some of the sur-
> geons are, who have managed to keep on shore station without
> ever going to sea at all [the eternal lament about stateside offi-
> cers]. Therefore, should it be convenient . . . to correct any wrong
> impression . . . by a word respecting my services, I will thank
> you to say it.

Holmes replied:[6] "The silver medals have not arrived for the Erie
victory, but will before the end of the session. As soon as the Secy.
shall return I shall receive an answer to your enquiry as to pay &
station, & will immediately transmit." Usher pursued the matter
with Isaac Hull,[7] but still received no reply, the frustrating weeks
stretching into months.

He had, however, hit the mark. A later communication to Hull
is filed in Navy archives in Washington, evidence that it had indeed
been forwarded: an order of May 8[8] directed Usher to "Report to

Capt. Hull for duty at Marine Guard." Appended was a notation (underlined in the original): *"No extra pay allowed."* He had won half his cake. Captain Hull ordered him to report on May 19.[9]

"While holding this appointment," writes son Charles,[10] "he resided much of the time at Cambridge, enjoying opportunities of study, and mingling in the learned society of that place." His "mingling" surely included visits to the gracious "gambrel-roofed house," which was the home of the Reverend Abiel Holmes and his family. The scholarly parson, whose forthcoming comprehensive history, *Annals of America*,[11] would contain complimentary references to Usher's Lake Erie exploits, was not, we can be sure, the principal attraction. Holmes's charming, vivacious, and cultured daughters, Ann and Mary, were a powerful allurement. That summer at Commencement time Usher received an honorary A.B. degree at neighboring Harvard, a distinction which certainly did not go unnoticed in the Holmes ménage, especially by the reverend's astute elder daughter Mary.

Soon thereafter, "through the influence of acquaintances gained in Cambridge," according to Charles,[12] Usher at last "realized his youthful dream" of becoming a teacher of anatomy. He was appointed Professor of Anatomy and Surgery in the Medical Department of Dartmouth College. Established in 1797 by Nathan Smith, the school appeared to have a bright future despite its remote location. Smith, a native of Rehoboth, Massachusetts, had studied with John Warren and received an M.B. degree from Harvard in 1790. He continued his education at Glasgow, Edinburgh, and London before undertaking his project at Dartmouth. For the first ten years he gave almost all of the lectures, held all of the examinations, and made all of the recommendations for graduation.[13] Oliver Wendell Holmes later described him as filling "a settee of professorships."[14] He was assisted briefly by Lyman Spalding, and later by Alexander Ramsay in anatomy. In 1820 the faculty consisted of Reuben Mussey, a graduate of the medical school, who was Professor of Surgery, Obstetrics, and Medical Jurisprudence; James F. Dana, Harvard educated, Professor of Chemistry; and Daniel Oliver, Harvard College graduate with an M.D. from the University of Pennsylvania, Professor of the Theory of Physic, Materia Medica, and Botany. To be eligible to take the examination in medicine, a candidate must have apprenticed in medicine for three years and completed two courses of lectures of twelve weeks each. There was no infirmary or clinic available to the students. Of perhaps a half a hundred students in the school at any one time, the number of graduates per year prior to 1824 ranged from eight to eighteen. Among the more eminent graduates of the early years were Mussey, George C. Shattuck of Boston, and Henry Bond of Philadelphia.[15]

At the annual meeting of the Trustees of Dartmouth, "holden at said College on Tuesday, the 22nd day of August, A.D. 1820," the following action was taken:[16]

> Voted & chose unanimously Usher Parsons, M.D., Professor of Anatomy & Physiology on the conditions agreed to by him (viz.):
> That Dr. Parsons advance one thousand dollars for commencing a museum in human & comparative anatomy,—that he engage for one season only & that, if his mode of instruction be satisfactory, he continue the connection as long as it shall be considered mutually advantageous,—that in the event of separation, he will leave the anatomical preparations for the benefit of the School, if the College wish it, at such price as disinterested persons shall establish,—and that the residence of Dr. Parsons at all times, except during the lectures be at Boston.

While it is curious that Usher should have been expected to finance the museum, his willingness to do so accorded with his aspirations. Since a medical professor's income depended on lecture fees paid by the students, it was to his advantage to make the course as attractive as possible. Usher wrote pretentiously that his "motive for engaging in the business of lecturing was a desire to establish a museum of anatomy, human and comparative, on the plan of the late John Hunter's." As the main feature of the collection, he hoped to import preparations from Florence like those he had seen there. The transaction, however, was not completed during his tenure. Usher spent most of the year close to Boston, but visited Hanover in September to acquaint himself with the college. He called on Doctor Daniel Oliver of the faculty, who drove him about the countryside to acquaint him with the environs.[17]

On returning to Boston, Usher wrote to his niece Frances Leighton, daughter of the General:[18] "You have probably heard of my appointment at Hanover. I have not yet accepted, and shall not go there, provided I do accept, till a year from this." He approved of the General's plan to sell his unprofitable farm in Eliot and move to Alfred, and he sent money for school books to nephew Usher Parsons Leighton.

The Navy became understandably nervous about the Hanover business and inquired whether it was compatible with Usher's duties at Charlestown. He sent the following explanation to the Secretary of the Navy, dated Ocober 9 at the Marine Barracks:[19]

> In reply to the enquiry whether it be my determination to resign my commission as Surgeon in the Navy, in consequence of having received an appointment of professor in Dartmouth College, I have to observe that said appointment has not yet been accepted, and that it is my purpose (the department being willing) to continue on duty in my present situation another year, or till one attempt more shall have been made in Congress to improve the condition of Navy surgeons.

Somewhat later he received from Thomas Appleton, his agent at Leghorn, Italy, information regarding the wax models, which proved to be a particularly troublesome business:[20]

> I received a few days ago your favor of 10 Aug. inclosing an order . . . for one hundred dollars & which I now return inclos'd. I wrote immediately to Mr. Ombrosi [of Florence] on the subject of the wax preparations, to which he replied he had long since written you . . . that they could not be procur'd for the prices you limited & that he waited your further instructions. You will observe you have omitted to indorse the order to me, as it is in your name.

In the latter part of 1820 Usher published in Cambridge a small volume which attracted favorable notice throughout his life. A medical guide for use at sea, it had this comprehensive and incredibly prolix title,[21] *The Sailor's Physician, exhibiting the symptoms, causes and treatment of Diseases, incident to seamen and passengers in merchant vessels; with directions for preserving their health in sickly climates; intended to afford medical advice to such persons while at sea, where a Physician cannot be consulted.* The author identified himself as a "Fellow of the Massachusetts Medical Society and Surgeon in the United States Navy." The book was announced in *The New England Journal of Medicine and Surgery* of January 1821 and was reviewed at length in the April issue.

Usher was convinced that it was necessary to "supply the forlorn sailor with some directions for relieving his pains and preserving his health, when tossing upon the dreary ocean, where no physician can be consulted," to allay "human suffering . . . without any interference with the dignity or interest of the profession. . . . The book being intended exclusively for seafaring people, nautical diseases only are included." For want of a few simple directions, he wrote, "sailors are often crippled for life . . . there is scarce a marine hospital in the country that does not exhibit noseless faces [syphilis] and mutilated bodies, the sad vestiges of a long protracted disease which, with suitable instruction, the patient himself might have [relieved]."

Though written almost seventy years after the classic treatise[22] on scurvy by the British naval surgeon James Lind, Usher's comments on that disease were still pertinent:

> Among the most celebrated and infallible remedies [for scurvy] are succulent fruits, of which oranges, lemons, limes, and apples are the best. Unfortunately, however, these articles are with difficulty preserved on long voyages, and consequently least likely to be found when most wanted. Perhaps, then, no article after these is so valuable in long voyages, both for its efficacy and imperishable quality, as potatoes, which have moreover the advantage of being cheap and easily supplied in almost every port.[23]

He described the antiscorbutic properties of "the concrete salt of lemon," a dried concentrate of lemon juice, and a sort of primitive vitamin C preparation. This, he said, "should be introduced into every medicine chest in large quantities, since it is imperishable by long keeping, and may therefore be carried to sea for years, and serve as a last resort when every other acid and anti-scorbutic in the ship is exhausted." He emphasized his point with an anecdote:

> It is remarkable that this disease should at the present day be suffered to prevail in merchant ships, often to the destruction of half their crews, when preventatives are so well known and so easily supplied. In crossing the Atlantic in a frigate in 1818, we fell in with a French ship bound from South America to Havre, where this disease had prevailed to such a degree, that one third of her crew were dead, another third at the point of death, and the other survivors more or less diseased; all which calamity might have been prevented by a supply of potatoes and lemon juice of the value of five dollars, . . . or the concrete salt of lemon.

The *New England Journal* review of the book, generally favorable, concluded:

Dr. Parons has, we think, performed a valuable service to the public in this work. It does credit to his good sense, his practical skill and judgment, and the industry with which he has devoted himself to its completion. His official situation in the service has given him an ample field for experience and observation, and this he has improved with great assiduity and intelligence. . . . We have no hesitation in recommending it to the attention of the public.[24]

A second edition of two thousand copies appeared in 1824, and others in 1842, and 1851. He made additions, revisions, and improvements in the various editions and changed the title in 1842 to the more familiar (and perhaps more accurate) *Physician for Ships.*[25]

Usher had long contemplated a trip to New York, Philadelphia, and Baltimore to visit their medical schools, and shortly after Christmas of 1820 found an opportunity to do so. He kept a diary of the journey which provides a lively picture of contemporary medical teaching and vivid sketches of some of the great figures of American medicine.[26]

Usher departed from Boston by stagecoach at one p.m. on December 27 and arrived in New York at 7 a.m. on the 29th. He found himself in a medical environment which was well established, sophisticated, and urban, contrasted with the isolated and undermanned school at Dartmouth. The medical school at Columbia University (formerly King's College) had been initiated in 1767 with a faculty of six able teachers, all of whom had received some or all of their education in Europe (Trinity College in Dublin, London, Paris, Edinburgh, and Leyden). The sole surviving member of the original faculty (teaching theory and practice) was Samuel Bard, now president of the College of Physicians and Surgeons at Columbia, successor to the original school. Also founder of New York Hospital, Bard was now in the final year of his flourishing administration.

In 1820 the regents declared the school, with an attendance of some two hundred students, to be "in a state of rapid improvement." In 1819 the school had graduated seventy-seven physicians, the number having risen rapidly from a mere eleven in 1815. The faculty at the time of Usher's visit contained, in addition to Doctor Bard, the eminent but turbulent David Hosack, Wright Post, Valentine Mott, John Wakefield Francis, William James Macneven,

Samuel Latham Mitchill, William Hamersley, and John Kearney Rodgers.[27]

Despite the long and exhausting journey from Boston, Usher immediately set about making contacts, attending clinics and lectures, and immersing himself in this teeming medical environment. After calling on his old friend Doctor Hoffman, he went to hear Valentine Mott lecture on tumors and the extirpation of cancerous breasts. "The doctor lectures without any notes in an easy and profitable manner," Usher recorded, adding, "The only thing against elegance is a too frequent repetition of the same idea." He next heard Doctor Wright Post, whose manner of lecturing he described as remarkable for ease of precision: "His voice is feeble but very agreeable." John Wakefield Francis lectured at 4 p.m. Usher thought him wholly prepared, though wandering in his subject, flying from one thing to another and offering nothing new to the class.

On Saturday, December 30th, he attended David Hosack's lecture on Theory and Practice in plague and yellow fever. Usher recorded the following impressions of Hosack in his diary:

> He is exceedingly animating and imposing in his manner, very positive, and not a little vain, for a great share of his lectures was taken up in sounding his own fame and detracting from others, using harsh and reproachable language against many respectable practitioners, impeaching even the honesty & veracity of such of them as differed in opinion with him on contagion. Spoke of the translations of Desgenette's & Assilini's works as base misrepresentations of those gentlemen's opinions. Alluded also to a mutilation of a paper which the editors of the *Repository* had made on the subject of the yellow fever at Havana, saying that he had detected it and published the same, having been able to do so by comparing it with a duplicate of the same paper rec'd from the same source himself.

Usher also attended lectures by Doctors Mott and Post and visited the anatomical museum, which he found small and uninteresting: "There were several arterial preparations in rather a bad state of preservation and some wet preparations. None of wax, of fine injection, or corroded; none of quicksilver except some of a turtle & rabbit. The collection is not worth half so much as Warren's." On the other hand, Usher found the collection of minerals very good, and the chemical apparatus appeared nearly perfect. He examined a private collection of anatomical preparations at Mott's, and he noted that of the dry ones "some of them are very handsome, but the number is very small."

On Sunday, December 31 he breakfasted with Doctor Hosack, examined his anatomical museum, and again found little of interest. His diary records additional impressions of this visit:

> His study is an octagon with a dome of light and is filled with a choice and very large collection of books. He has a very small private study for the common reception of persons [i.e. patients]. In this he has a small library. On one of the shelves is an elegant volume of Thomas' *Practice*, dedicated to Hosack, which I had heard he always took pleasure in showing; and to gratify his humor I anticipated his putting it into my hands by taking it down and asking what work it was. I at once saw what I had often heard, that he took a heartfelt satisfaction in perching upon this book to crow.
>
> It is required in the medical school of New York that each candidate for a degree shall have attended only one course of lectures of each of the professors, but they must be two seasons in doing it. . . . Number of students is about 120.

Usher left New York on New Year's day of 1821, crossed the Hudson River by steamboat, traveled by stage to Trenton, where he stopped overnight, and arrived at Philadelphia on the morning of the 2nd. This was the cradle of academic medicine in America. Pennsylvania Hospital, sponsored by Benjamin Franklin and the first and only permanent general hospital in the colonies, opened in 1752. The City Almshouse, the infirmary of which later became the Philadelphia General Hospital, had already been in existence since 1732. The medical school was established in 1765 by Doctor John Morgan, an Edinburgh medical graduate, who had also studied in London under the Hunter brothers and Cullen. He was joined in the project by William Shippen, also educated at Edinburgh. Now passed from the scene were Benjamin Rush and Caspar Wistar, the latter as professor both of chemistry and physics, and anatomy and midwifery. They also had studied in Europe.

Now the leading medical institution in America, it required degree candidates to have completed two years of preceptorship (three years for local residents), attendance at lectures for two years, attendance on the wards of Pennsylvania Hospital, and presentation of a thesis. There were well over three hundred matriculants at the time, a third of whom would be awarded degrees. The faculty was strong. The professorship of the theory and practice of medicine and the institutes (physiology) was held by Nathaniel Chapman (1780–1837), a pupil of Rush's who had studied in London and Edinburgh. (Like Rush, Cullen, and John Brown, he carried purging and bleeding to great extremes.) Chapman was a fair lecturer, but his speech was marred by a defect of the palate. He was to become the first president of the American Medical Association in 1847.

Philip Syng Physick (1768–1837), a graduate of the University of Pennsylvania, a house surgeon under John Hunter at St. George's Hospital in London, and recipient of an M.D. degree from Edinburgh, was professor of anatomy at the medical school as well as surgeon at the Pennsylvania Hospital. William Edmonds Horner (1793–1853), a graduate of the University of Pennsylvania medical school, who had trained in anatomy under Wistar, was adjunct professor of anatomy and assisted Physick by skillfully conducting dissections in the amphitheater.[28] Professor of materia medica was John Redman Coxe (1773–1863), an apprentice of Rush's. Doctor Coxe had studied abroad and was the first physician in Philadelphia to adopt vaccination for smallpox. He was a poor lecturer, whose discourses were considered by the students to be irrelevant and antiquated. William Gibson (1788–1868) had but recently, at the age of thirty-three, been appointed professor of surgery. A graduate of Edinburgh and a pupil of two great British surgeons, John Bell of Edinburgh and Charles Bell of London, he was a skilled operator and a fine teacher, who lectured effortlessly and extemporaneously. (He was unpopular with his colleagues, however, because of a volatile temper and a sharp tongue.) Robert Hare, Jr., not a physician, was professor of chemistry. Inventor of the oxy-hydrogen blowtorch, he was an outstanding chemist. Thomas Chalkley James, a medical graduate of the University of Pennsylvania, who had trained in London and Edinburgh, was professor of obstetrics. Finally, professor of botany in the college, but denied a chair in the medical school, was William P. C. Barton, a nephew of the late eminent professor of botany, Benjamin Smith Barton, and himself an excellent medical botanist.[29] Like Usher, Barton had been a naval surgeon during the War of 1812.

Usher set out promptly to sample this varied menu and succeeded in meeting all of the faculty except Barton, who was burying a child at the time of Usher's visit. Usher committed many of the exciting details to his diary:

> Wednesday 3rd. At 10 o'clock met Dr. [Nathaniel] Chapman at the door of the college. . . . Asked permission to attend his lectures, introduced myself as surgeon of the Navy. The janitor was ordered to let me pass to all the lectures. The doctor's lecture was on Dyspepsia, delivered to about 350 students. His voice is bad in consequence of having lost the palate of his mouth, and he speaks like one having a bad harelip. He is, however, very animated and gives great satisfaction. He, however, deals too much in superlatives and, if I am not mistaken, occasionally exaggerates.

After the lecture Chapman introduced Usher to Doctors Physick and Horner. To the former he gave a letter of introduction from Lyman Spalding, which resulted in a "very pretty reception." He then took a seat in the amphitheater where nearly four hundred students were assembled. The lecture by Doctor Horner was on the basis of the brain [the basis cerebri]. An actual brain was dissected, and there was also a model for comparison purposes which was magnified about ten times that of the actual organ. Usher found Horner's lecture very interesting and his manner pleasing and instructive. Regarding Doctor Horner's lecturing, Usher recorded that

> He has not the ease and entire readiness of Dr. Post. Yet he takes more pains to make everything thoroughly understood. Every object that was pointed out was repeated from three to five or six times to the different sections of the class, holding the object up to view . . . to each [of them respectively]. I never saw half so intelligible a demonstration of this before intricate part of anatomy. On my return home I went over every part in my own mind with perfect perception of every part. The Dr., however, occasionally hesitates, but this is in such a manner that it rather benefits than counfounds the hearer since it rather serves to keep alive the attention in a more eminent degree.

After the lecture Usher inspected the anatomical museum, which he found more elegant for its size than any in the world. He was particularly pleased with the corroded preparations and the wet minute injections, which he felt were unsurpassed. On the following day he attended Doctor Coxe's lectures, which were on anthelmintics (remedies for intestinal worms). During his lecture Coxe spoke frequently of Jacob Bigelow's *American Medical Botany*, but never once mentioned William P. C. Barton's rival publication, his *Vegetable Materia Medica*.[30] He quoted many passages from the Bigelow work. Usher found Doctor Coxe a better lecturer than he had expected.

Afterwards he went into Doctor Horner's room and was introduced to Doctor Gibson, whom he had previously met. After attending Gibson's lecture on the diseases of the eye, Usher recorded in his diary that he was "slow, very correct & precise, but rather monotonous and fixed in his posture." While Gibson lectured without notes, Usher concluded that his presentation had previously been written and committed to memory.

Usher then heard Robert Hare deliver a lecture on the chemistry of chlorine, and Physick on the spinal marrow and the integuments of the eye. In the afternoon he attended a lecture by Doctor James on obstetrics and finally, in the evening, observed experiments on the air pump at the museum.

Usher left Philadelphia by stage at 7 a.m. on the 5th of January, crossed the frozen Susquehanna River at 8 o'clock that evening, and arrived in Baltimore the next morning at 5 a.m. As usual, he wasted no time in looking about.

The College of Medicine of Maryland, later the University of Maryland College of Medicine, much younger than those of New York and Philadelphia, was founded in 1807 by an able triumvirate consisting of John Beale Davidge (1768–1829), a Glasgow graduate, professor of anatomy, surgery, and midwifery; John Shaw, who had studied at both the University of Pennsylvania and Edinburgh, professor of chemistry; and John Cocke, a pupil of Sir Astley Cooper at Guy's Hospital in London, professor of physiology. Other members of the early faculty were Thomas E. Bond in materia medica, George Brown in practice and theory of medicine, and William Donaldson, institutes of medicine (physiology and pathology).

The medical school in 1822 had about three hundred matriculants, only a fraction of whom would receive degrees. (Usher gives a smaller number.) A degree candidate must have had two years of apprenticeship (increased to three years in 1824), and attendance at two yearly courses of lectures. He was also required to read and study a specified list of books and to write, publish, and defend a thesis in Latin or English. Baltimore at the time had several medical facilities—the infirmary and the teeming Almshouse, which harbored some five hundred city and county paupers, the Marine Hospital, and the Baltimore (later Maryland) Hospital, which had recently received a gift of life-size anatomical models costing $20,800. The Baltimore General Dispensary treated four thousand patients a year, while the Baltimore Infirmary (later University Hospital) was to be completed in 1823.

In 1822 two members of the original faculty, Davidge and Nathaniel Potter (1770–1843), the latter having succeeded George Brown after a few months, were still teaching. Davidge was professor of surgery, while Potter, a medical graduate of the University of Pennsylvania and a pupil of Rush's, was professor of the principles and practice of medicine. Maxwell McDowell (1771–1847), college graduate trained as a physician by apprenticeship, taught the institutes of medicine (physiology and pathology). The most learned member of the faculty was Granville Sharp Pattison, formerly professor of anatomy, physiology, and surgery at the Andersonian Institution in Glasgow. A controversial figure, having emigrated to the United States because of domestic difficulties, he nevertheless, as professor of surgery, imbued the school with his energy and dynamic personality. Richard Wilmot Hall, a medical graduate of the University of Pennsylvania and professor of obstetrics, had translated from the French Jean Larrey's works and published them in 1814 as the two-volume *Memoirs of Military Surgery*. The chairs of materia medica and chemistry were held respectively by Samuel Baker (1785–1835) and Elisha DeButts (1773–1831). Baker and DeButts, a native of Ireland, had both received M.D. degrees from the University of Pennsylvania.[31]

Usher's notes on his Baltimore experience were brief, but he touched all the bases:

> Went to the Medical College at 12, introduced myself to Dr. [Nathaniel] Potter, prof. of Theory & Practice of Physic, was politely welcomed to his lectures, which today was on asthma. He said emetics were of no service, that flannel next to the skin was good, [also] a sea voyage, blood letting, drastic purgatives, &c. At 1 [p.m.] attended Dr. [John Beale] Davidge's lecture on the anatomy of the liver, stomach, and pancreas. He is free from embarrassment, is rather slow, is very clear in demonstration, is fond of traducing others, particularly Rush. No. of students about 130.

After recording the weekly schedule of lectures in his diary, Usher wrote:

> A student for a degree must attend only one course of each, but must do this in two seasons. By attending one course, however, at any other college on any of the above branches, he need only attend the others here. Each professor has 20 dollars. 7 professors at $20—$140.00. Board $4.00. Fee to dissecting room $10.00. Subjects $4.00 each. Dissecting room badly managed. No Museum.

Usher thus concluded the diary of his medical pilgrimage. Before heading north he had some business at the Navy Department in Washington. He was back in Boston by the middle of January. On March 4 he wrote to Chief Clerk Benjamin Homans of the Navy Department:[32]

> Perhaps I am giving myself unnecessary concern. . . . You recollect my bringing you a letter from Dr. Marshall and my asking of you . . . to stand between me and the surgeoncy of the *Constitution*. Since I saw you, my liver complaint has returned and threatens to entirely disqualify me for duty; and as it commenced in the Mediterranean I fear a voyage there in the *Constitution* would very soon prove fatal. I will thank you therefore to bear this in mind and prevent the issue of orders . . . to me for any sea duty for the present.

Usher's "liver complaint" was evidently convenient as well as troublesome. The Department did not, in fact, order him to sea duty at that time, and he remained attached to the Marine Barracks.

While at Charlestown Usher corresponded[33] with his friends at Dartmouth and learned a few weeks later that he would at last fulfill his ambition to give a course of lectures at Hanover. His abilities and contributions to the college were recognized by honorary degrees awarded at the Dartmouth commencement that summer. The Trustees' Records for August 1821 state: "That the degree of Master of Arts and Doctor of Medicine be conferred on Usher Parsons, who has been admitted to the degree of Bachelor of Arts in Harvard University."[34]

The Records of the Faculty of Medicine of Dartmouth for September 20, 1821 contain the following entry: "The Medical Lectures commenced this day. At a meeting of the Faculty of Medicine,— Present: R. D. Mussey, U. Parsons, J. F. Dana, Professors." It further noted that "the Introductory Lecture on Anatomy was delivered at 3 P.M. by Prof. Parsons." Usher attended only one other meeting of the Medical Faculty, that of December 19.[35] Upon completion of this one course, he returned to Boston and did not again lecture at Hanover. While Dartmouth was essentially a country school which touted "its pleasant location and freedom from temptations and demoralizing influences of the city,"[36] the remoteness of Hanover from the seductive pleasures of the east coast very likely discouraged Usher from settling there, as it also did many other potential leaders in medicine. In March of 1822 he submitted his resignation, ostensibly because he found it difficult to serve two masters at so great a distance. His letter arrived too late for action by the Trustees at that time.[37] He then set about laying the groundwork for a teaching career in Providence, requesting an extended leave from the Navy:[38]

My duties at the Marine Barracks being small, and the expense of living on this station greater than my pay, I beg permission to ask for leave of absence for one year, that I may reside in a less expensive situation, and have time to attend some private concerns of importance, which my constant employment in publick service for ten years has compelled me to neglect. I should like to continue attached to the Marine Barracks during said time, the duties of which can be performed by the surgeon & mate of the yard.

He was granted leave by Captain Hull effective April 13, 1822.[39]

Usher had written earlier to Daniel Oliver at Dartmouth asking him to forward to Boston the wax anatomical preparations, some of which had now arrived from Florence, so that he could take them to Providence. After some delay Oliver replied[40] that he was not able to get the models because they were then entirely at the disposal of Doctor Mussey. Mussey questioned the propriety of sending them to Boston, as he thought it imprudent to deprive the Hanover museum of them, especially since he wanted them to be used by his students in the coming summer months. As a final excuse for not sending them, Oliver related that he hesitated to take the responsibility of packing these frail items and trusting them to the conveyance of a public stage.

Usher later decided that he did not need his anatomical preparations after all and presented them to the medical school at Dartmouth.[41] The remainder of the wax models never arrived from Florence, and Usher was "in great want of the money paid for them more than two years since." There is no evidence that he ever received it. He decided to short-cut his letter of resignation previously forwarded to Dartmouth (but arriving too late for a meeting of the trustees) by returning the original appointment letter with notes on the back of it, including a statement that he could not "perform the duties of his station at Hanover and in the Navy at the same time." This seems hardly ingenuous, since in the meantime he had already moved to Providence. He apparently kept his Navy commission as a sheet to windward in the event that his new endeavors did not work out advantageously. He posted the above communications to Hanover from Boston while on his way to Alfred, the first of many summer visits to Maine.

Some time after April 13, Usher had made his fateful move to Providence, where he immediately joined in partnership with Doctor Levi Wheaton, a prominent practitioner of the town and Professor of the Theory and Practice of Physic in the Medical School at Brown University. Their partnership survived for several years and provided Usher with the opportunity of establishing himself in the community both professionally and socially.

On September 5, 1822, at the annual meeting of the Corporation of Brown University, Usher was appointed "adjunct Professor of Anatomy and Surgery in this Institution."[42] On the 23rd, in a quiet wedding, he married Mary Jackson Holmes of Cambridge, daughter of the Reverend and Mrs. Abiel Holmes and older sister of Oliver Wendell Holmes, who was then thirteen years old.

The first tentative budding of their romance is hidden by a veil of youthful modesty and reticence, but by the late summer of 1821 their affection had blossomed into something more than casual. Some seventy-five letters to or from Mary Holmes for the years 1818–1821 are extant.[43] It is significant that, in a close and confidential correspondence between Mary and several of her intimate girl friends, there is no reference to Usher before the late summer of 1821. The first suggestion of romance appears in a letter which Mary wrote on Harvard Commencement Day, Wednesday, August 29, 1821 to Ariana Smith of Exeter, New Hampshire.[44] She told of a beau waiting for her, and in later letters mentioned parties, one of them on Fresh Pond. Of this she wrote: "Never did I go to such another! Just in the midst of a sail, it began to rain most violently—

we had three beaux to nine ladies." Her letter also mentioned an illness she had endured during the summer.

A few weeks later Mary received a significant letter from Hanover, which goes far in explaining the exciting events that had taken place in her life.[45] Although only a week had elapsed since their parting, Usher told Mary how exceedingly impatient he was to exercise the privilege she kindly allowed him of writing to her. In an eventful interview with the Reverend Holmes, it would appear, Usher had asked his consent for his daughter's hand in marriage. Because of the resulting turmoil in his mind, Usher had neglected to take leave of Mary: "My mind was too much distracted by the encouragement and discouragement that alternately succeeded each other during the interview, to make it desirable to see any one that evening, or I should have seen you once more."

"Pray how did I acquit myself on the momentous occasion?" he asked. "You can no doubt inform me." Indecision on the Reverend's part was apparent, he went on, "and a qualification given to every expression of consent, which makes the probable result somewhat doubtful." Usher went on:

> The great objection to me seemed to rest on the ground of my having been in the Navy. That there is, Mary, much to condemn in the habits and character of Navy officers I admit, and have never concealed from you, and that a man-o'-war is destructive to virtuous habits and impressions no one can deny—but I cannot conceive that the character of an individual should be undervalued who resides in such exposed situations without yielding to the force of their influence; indeed I have had the vanity to arrogate some little credit to myself for having preserved integrity of character amidst the allurements that have surrounded me, and am more indebted to this circumstance than to any other for the situation I hold in this institution.

Usher expressed his appreciation for the many kindnesses extended by Mary's parents and pressed on to plead his case:

> Your father's enquiries and objections were, however, made with such delicacy and apparently good feeling, that whether ultimately successful in obtaining his consent or not, I shall always think of the interview with satisfaction and hold him in higher esteem than ever, and shall cherish hopes that his unfavourable impressions will be effaced by time and further acquaintance. To your mother I am unable to express half the gratitude

I feel for the polite attention and numerous civilities conferred on me while a sojourner in Cambridge, and more particularly for the favourable view she has been pleased to take of the subject that so deeply concerns us. Should the few clouds that gathered over my prospects during the interview with your father be dispersed, and my wishes crowned with success, I shall ever take great satisfaction and delight in showing myself worthy in some degree of the good opinion and confidence with which she has been pleased to honor me, by my attention to whatever will promote your happiness. But what, my dear Mary, shall I say to you, and what return make for consenting to confide all your prospects of earthly happiness to my influence, and condescending to embark on the ocean of life with so unworthy a pilot. . . . I am confident your generous heart and tenderness of feeling will prompt you to do it.

He again expressed his impatience for a letter from her that might brighten his hopes of a favorable outcome to his plea. He also mentioned the lively picture her father had drawn of their characters, situations, and circumstances in life and the vivid colors with which he drew a contrasting picture incompatible with a harmonious union. Usher then begged Mary to take care of her health, and reported on his new teaching career. "I am well pleased with my new avocation," he continued, "preaching as I call it. . . . Considering the novelty of the business, the magnitude of my audience, which is greater than before [I came], and the natural diffidence in speaking which I have to contend with, I have no reason to complain. . . ." He concluded the long letter, "Affectionately yours U.... ...."

Mary's letters to her friends provide glimpses of some of the events that followed. On New Year's night (January 1, 1822) Mary and her younger sister had entertained thirty of the neighborhood children at a party and cotillion. "Dr. Parsons," she wrote to Ariana Smith,[46] "arrived the night before from Hanover, so he was admitted to see the beautiful little creatures." She spoke of a ball that took place on the following evening, which Usher attended in her party. It was most fortunate, she wrote to Ariana, that Mr. J. D. Gourdin handed her into her carriage, "for the whispers on every side which awaited Dr. P. would have been quite sufficient to have crimsoned my cheek for a fortnight." She recounted the byplay of this intriguing evening:

Mrs. Fay (entre nous) was really mischievous. She rose and
came to me bringing Dr. Parsons. 'Shall I introduce you to Miss
Holmes', she said to him, and insisted on his dancing with me.
It [had been] agreed that we would not, as every eye . . . was bent
upon us. But the lady was irresistible, and many were the roguish
smiles and glances cast upon us. We had a most pleasant dance.
Next morning we had calls, of course. The ball was discussed,
the dresses, &c. In the evening Dr. P. & myself went to Mrs.
Hedge's where the previous evening's exertions tended to make
us more brilliant than ever.[47]

In mid-February Mary, and perhaps the Reverend Holmes as well,
at long last capitulated to Usher's persuasion. Mary later wrote to
her friend Amelia Leavitt:[48] "I have just written a letter to the
doctor, whom I suppose you know is my prince—Dr. Parsons."

In July, after spending a few days in Boston and Cambridge, Usher
visited Alfred, and on the journey he escorted Mary's sister Ann to
Exeter, where she planned to stay several weeks with Ariana Smith.
They left after the July 4th festivities, as Mary explained in a letter
to Ariana on the 5th:[49]

Rain . . . detained Ann who was intent on going. But the Doctor
was anxious to join the procession on the Fourth & to attend the
Mayor's levee in the evening—beside its being generally disagree-
able to be on a journey when so much firing is going on. . . .
Yesterday . . . in the evening the Doctor & I rode in to the Mayor's
party. The house was devoted to company; a band of music
[played]—a perfect rout à la mode de Washington. But I must say
my adieu for they are going. . . . Receive my Ann from my hand,
or rather from the hand of my Doctor.

Usher arrived at Alfred on July 6, as General Leighton recorded in
his diary.[50] The next day Leighton called on him, after attending
Sunday meeting. On the 9th Usher took his father for a ride to the
General's house where "We hoed the corn by the road above the
house & some potatoes. . . ."

Usher returned to Providence via Boston on July 10, apparently
after discussing wedding plans with Mary and her family. On July
19, in a letter to Amelia Leavitt, Mary reported that the Doctor
planned to spend several weeks in Providence before making another visit to Cambridge.[51] "I think it is very probable," she added,
"that I may [not] be . . . Mary *J. H.* . . . [after] this autumn."

In August Usher was summoned to testify at the court-martial of his commanding officer, Captain Isaac Hull, commandant at Charlestown. Although Hull was highly respected, a morose young subordinate named Joel Abbot had charged him with defrauding the Navy and with oppressive treatment of his men. One Benjamin H. Fosdick, a clerk, had embezzled a considerable sum of money by manipulating the payroll; Hull was allegedly implicated. In due course Lieutenant Abbot himself was tried and found guilty of unjustly and scandalously defaming a superior officer. Despite the implied vindication, Hull requested an investigation, and a court of inquiry was convened on August 12.[52]

Usher was but one of many witnesses who had served in various capacities during Hull's command. He did not reach the stand until August 26. Court records noted that Parsons "resides at Providence, where he has three patients dangerously sick, to whom his personal attendance is of importance at this time." Since he knew "but little on the subject of the present enquiry," he asked "to be examined now, in order that he may return immediately to Providence." After completing his testimony, Usher was excused and hastened back to Providence to care for his sick patients and to await impatiently a very eventful day in his life. Hull, of course, was exonerated.[53]

In September Mary discussed her plans in a letter to Amelia Leavitt:[54]

> You may know already that I expect to live in Providence, & you will please to direct letters to the care of Dr. Usher Parsons, Providence, Rhode Island. Whenever I shall be there, you must continue writing. . . . I shall not go to housekeeping for a year or two, I think, as I expect to board with the physician & his wife with whom Dr. Parsons practices in partnership. And although I have the most encouraging accounts of Dr. P's success in business, we think it best for him to be well established there first. I like the idea extremely, as I shall be free from care for some time. A friend of Ann's, Louisa Gindrat, a very amiable young lady of independent fortune, considerable accomplishments, & pleasant connections, expects in the spring to marry one of the first merchants in Providence, Mr. Richard Arnold, a fine young man [Class of 1814 at Brown University], who has traveled a great deal, is genteel, handsome, accomplished, & highly respectable, beside having a large fortune. They will probably live in a handsome style. . . . I think it very probable this letter is the last you will receive from me with my present name.

Amelia wrote to Mary on the 24th of September, addressing her letter to "Miss Mary Holmes" at Cambridge, unaware that the wedding had already taken place. Delivered by cousin Stiles Gannet to Cambridge, it was redirected to "Mrs. Mary Parsons" in Providence and sent by the same "Baggage Waggon" that brought Mary's things to Providence.[55]

The *Manufacturers and Farmers Journal* of Providence for Monday, September 30, 1822 carried an announcement of the wedding: "In Cambridge, Mass. on Monday evening last, by the Rev. Dr. Holmes, Usher Parsons, M.D. of this town, to Miss Mary Holmes, daughter of the Rev. Dr. Holmes." Mary was in her twenty-first year, and Usher in his thirty-fourth.

NOTES

1. "Diary of Gen. Samuel Leighton, 1818–1848."
2. Usher Parsons to Smith Thompson, February 12, 1820, WRDNA.
3. Ms. file copy of Order dated February 10, 1820, WRDNA. The communication to Usher read: "In compliance with, &c. &c., the President directs me to present you a silver medal in testimony of the high sense, &c., of your good [this reads 'galant' in the case of the line officers, and certainly should have applied to Usher who had earned and deserved equal recognition] conduct of service in the decisive & glorious victory gained on Lake Erie on the 1st of September ([sic] *was 10th of September*) in the year 1813 over a British Squadron of superior force. . . ."
4. Usher Parsons to John Holmes, March 9, 1820, Maine Historical Society.
5. Usher Parsons to John Holmes, March 7, 1820, WRDNA. Holmes, it appears, forwarded Usher's letter to the naval authorities.
6. John Holmes to Usher Parsons, March 21, 1820, DPC.
7. Usher Parsons to Isaac Hull, April 5, 1820, DPC. Usher Parsons to Isaac Hull, May 2, 1820, WRDNA.
8. Usher Parsons service record, WRDNA.
9. Isaac Hull to Usher Parsons, May 19, 1820, DPC.
10. C. W. Parsons *Memoir*, p. 24.
11. Abiel Holmes, *American Annals; or A Chronological History of America From Its Discovery in MCCCCXCII to MDCCCVI* (2 v., Cambridge, H. Hilliard, 1805). A second edition was issued by the firm of Hilliard and Brown at Cambridge in 1829.
12. C. W. Parsons *Memoir*, p. 24.
13. Ralph A. Major, *A History of Medicine*, pp. 765–767.
14. Holmes's remark is quoted in Emily A. Smith's *The Life and Letters*

of Nathan Smith, M.B., M.D. (New Haven, Yale University Press, 1914), p. 97. Dartmouth was apparently thought to be a good place for an aspiring teacher of anatomy to get his feet wet. Oliver Wendell Holmes started his academic career there in 1838, teaching anatomy in Hanover until he was appointed Parkman Professor of Anatomy and Physiology at Harvard in 1847.

15. The largest and most complete history of the Dartmouth Medical School is Carleton B. Chapman's *Dartmouth Medical School, the First 175 Years* (Hanover, N.H., The University Press of New England, 1973). The early history of the school is reviewed on pp. 7–27. An earlier account of the first years of the school is provided in Phileas S. Conner's *Dartmouth Medical College: Centennial Exercises. Historical Address* (Hanover, Dartmouth Medical College, 1897), pp. 3–17 *passim.*

16. Dartmouth College Archives, Baker Library, Hanover, N.H.

17. Daniel Oliver to Mrs. William D. Peck, September 23, 1820, Dartmouth College Archives. Doctor Oliver was Professor of the Theory and Practice of Medicine, and Materia Medica at Dartmouth. Mrs. Peck was the wife of William Dandridge Peck, Massachusetts Professor of Natural History at Harvard (1805–1822). Usher's visit to Hanover is described in this letter.

18. Usher Parsons to Frances Leighton, September 27, 1820, Parsons Memorial Library, Alfred, Me.

19. Usher Parsons to the Secretary of the Navy, October 9, 1820, WRDNA.

20. Thomas Appleton to Usher Parsons, October 30, 1820, Houghton Library, Harvard University.

21. This was published at Cambridge by Hilliard & Metcalf, who did the printing for Harvard University. It was reprinted under the title *Physician for Ships* through five editions and proved to be particularly reliable and widely used. It is significant that the United States Public Health Service still provides a similar manual, *The Ship's Medicine Chest and Medical Aid at Sea* (1984), which superseded PHS Misc. Pub. # 9 of the same title, reprinted in 1955 and 1978 (Sa Docs HE 20.8: M46-SN 917-010-00000-5).

22. James Lind's *Treatise of the Scurvy* was published at Edinburgh in 1753. Lind, a surgeon in the Royal Navy, proposed practical means of providing antiscorbutic items in the daily ration during long sea voyages.

23. Potatoes are a good source of iron and vitamins, especially vitamin C.

24. Unsigned review, *The New England Journal of Medicine and Surgery,* X (n.s. V), 166–173, April, 1821.

25. The second edition of Parsons's *Sailor's Physician* was printed at Providence by Barnum Field & Co. in 1824. On its title-page Usher described himself as "Formerly Surgeon of the U.S. Navy." The third edition, which, as was noted, appeared under the title *Physician for Ships,* came out in 1842 under the Boston imprint of Charles C. Little and James

Brown. A fourth edition, published in Boston by Damrell & Moore in 1851, also bore this title. In order to capitalize on the California gold rush, Usher concluded its title by stating that it contained advice for preserving health in sickly climates, "and also in California." In his *Memoir* of his father, Charles W. Parsons mentions a fifth edition, published in 1867, a year before Usher's death. However, such an edition does not seem to exist, for no copy can be located in Providence and no such edition appears in any library catalogue, including the *National Union Catalog of Pre-1956 Imprints.* On the other hand, a copy of a sixth edition, issued in New Bedford by Edwin Denz in 1877, has been located in the Rhode Island Medical Society library, and this contains in its preface a statement referring to it as the fifth edition. What appears to have occurred is this. Usher was undoubtedly preparing a fifth edition before his death, which must have intervened and canceled its actual publication. When writing the *Memoir,* Charles came across a reference to it (or the manuscript perhaps) and listed it as published. Years later, for some reason or other, but during Charles's lifetime, the sixth edition appeared, with reference to a fifth edition, which was actually a literary "ghost."

26. Usher Parsons, "Manuscript, comprising a diary of a trip to New York, Philadelphia and Baltimore, December 27, 1820 to January 5, 1821," DPC.

27. Information on the College of Physicians and Surgeons at Columbia derives from W. F. Norwood's *Medical Education in the United States Before the Civil War;* Ralph A. Major's *History of Medicine;* an oration by Thomas W. Blatchford titled *Our Alma Mater Fifty Years Ago,* delivered before the Alumni Association of the College of Physicians and Surgeons, Medical Department of Columbia College, at the Spring Commencement, March 14, 1861 (Troy, N.Y., 1861, pp. 5–38 *passim*); and Byron Stookey's *History of Colonial Education in the Province of New York, With Its Subsequent Development (1767–1830),* issued by Thomas at Springfield, Ill., in 1962.

28. Horner was a good teacher and a competent surgeon, and he had assembled a notable collection of specimens. He later became dean of the medical school.

29. The major source on the medical department of the University of Pennsylvania is George W. Corner's *Two Centuries of Medicine: A History of the School of Medicine, University of Pennsylvania* (Philadelphia, J. B. Lippincott Co., 1965); other information comes from W. F. Norwood's *Medical Education in the United States before the Civil War* and R. A. Major's *History of Medicine.*

30. In the 1817–1821 period both Jacob Bigelow of Boston and William P. C. Barton of Philadelphia issued medical botanies which were copiously illustrated with colored pictures of plants, the Bigelow work through color printing and the Barton work through hand-colored plates. See Chapter VII of Richard J. Wolfe's *Jacob Bigelow's American*

Medical Botany, 1817–1821 (Boston, Boston Medical Library, 1979), for details.

31. Eugene F. Cordell, *The Medical Annals of Maryland, 1799–1899* (Baltimore, The Medical and Chirurgical Faculty of the State of Maryland, 1903), pp. 58–83, 297–637, 675–688 *passim.* This was prepared for the Faculty's centennial. Additional information comes from R. A. Major's *History of Medicine* and W. F. Norwood's *Medical Education in the United States before the Civil War.*

32. Usher Parsons to Benjamin Homans, March 4, 1821, WRDNA.

33. Reuben D. Mussey to Usher Parsons, May 3, 1821, RIHS.

34. Material related to Usher Parsons's activities at Dartmouth College is preserved in the Dartmouth College Archives in the Baker Library at Hanover.

35. *Ibid.*

36. W. F. Norwood, *Medical Education in the United States before the Civil War,* p. 190.

37. Dartmouth College Archives, Baker Library, Hanover, N.H.

38. Usher Parsons to Smith Thompson, WRDNA.

39. Entry in Usher Parsons's service record, WRDNA.

40. Daniel Oliver to Usher Parsons, March 10, 1822, DPC.

41. Usher Parsons to Reuben D. Mussey, July 7, 1822, Dartmouth College Archives, Baker Library, Hanover, N.H.

42. Minutes of the Corporation of Brown University, v. 2, Brown University Archives.

43. These are a portion of the extensive private collection of family papers of Hugh Upham Clark of Arlington, Virginia, a direct descendant of Ann Holmes Upham, Mary's younger sister. The complete Clark collection is preserved on microfilm and in Xerox copies at the Countway Library of the Harvard Medical School. Most are available in Xerox copies at the Rhode Island Historical Society. The Hugh Upham Clark Collection is cited hereafter as HUCC.

44. Mary Holmes to Ariana Smith, August 29, 1821, HUCC. Among Mary's most intimate girl friends were Ariana Smith of Exeter, New Hampshire, the daughter of Judge Jeremiah Smith of that town, and Amelia Leavitt of Greenfield, Massachusetts. Amelia, whom Mary called "cousin," was actually not related, but was the niece of Maria Stiles Holmes, first wife of the Reverend Holmes and the sister of the distinguished Reverend Ezra Stiles, later president of Yale University.

45. Usher Parsons to Mary Holmes, September 22, 1821, HUCC.

46. Mary Holmes to Ariana Smith, January 28, 1821, HUCC.

47. Harriet Howard Fay, the charming and vivacious wife of Judge Samuel Prescott Phillips Fay of Cambridge, was later mistress of the lovely homestead which became the Fay House of Radcliffe College in 1885.

Her gracious entertaining was legendary. Mrs. Hedge was the wife of Levi Hedge, Professor of Philosophy at Harvard.

48. Mary Holmes to Amelia Leavitt, May 7, 1822, HUCC.

49. Mary Holmes to Ariana Smith, July 5, 1822, HUCC.

50. "Diary of Gen. Samuel Leighton, 1818–1848," entries of July 6 and 7, 1822. Leighton had by now moved to Alfred.

51. Mary Holmes to Amelia Leavitt, July 10, 1822, HUCC.

52. *Minutes of Proceedings of the Court of Enquiry into the Official Conduct of Capt. Isaac Hull, as Commandant of the United States Navy-Yard, at Charlestown in the State of Massachusetts, Convened at the Navy-Yard in Said Charlestown, on the 12th Day of August, 1822.* (Washington, Davis and Force, 1822). This was printed by order of the Navy Department, from the official record.

53. *Ibid.*

54. Mary Holmes to Amelia Leavitt, September 15, 1822, HUCC.

55. Amelia Leavitt to Mary Holmes, September 24, 1822, HUCC.

CHAPTER EIGHT

Young Professor

Usher took his bride to their new home in Providence. During the early months of their marriage they boarded at the residence of Doctor Levi Wheaton on Thomas Street, opposite the Baptist church and in the very center of this lively town. Mary carried on a running correspondence with her parents, her sister Ann, and her friends. Much of our knowledge of this period in Usher's life comes from her letters. Though often in a saccharine style typical of the times, the extravagant expressions of devotion were genuine and sincere. Mary was not lonely, thanks to Usher's many professional and academic acquaintances and her preoccupation with a voluminous correspondence. As time went on there was much visiting back and forth between Cambridge and Providence. Mary wrote to Ann on September 27, 1822:[1]

> . . . I am pleasantly situated here—a house which suits my ideas of ease, convenience, & a certain comfortable snugness, more than anything else—just such a house as I *should* like to board in. Dr. Wheaton—one of the pleasantest old gentlemen, & Mrs. W.—very much the sort of woman I expected to find—very kind, easy, good-natured, plain sense, character. Mrs. & Mr. H. Wheaton of New York I find very intelligent, agreeable people.[2] The rooms we occupy I find just what I should wish. Several ladies have called to see me, & we expect tomorrow evening to see several more. The doctor manages the business to admiration, & I let him do as he chooses. . . . Mr. W. is a lawyer of much respectability & high standing in N.Y. . . . Mrs. W. is weak having been very sick. My doctor had the pleasure & pain of bleeding her.

171

Mary had taken one walk since moving to Providence and found the town to be a beautiful place. She referred to the many Quakers living there:

> The next house contains a family of rich quakers [*sic*]—Brown is the name.[3] There is a quaker meeting here very frequently—a church appropriated to them. I intend going there—some of the fair ladies preach soon. There is a quaker college situated very prettily on a hill near here, which I shall go to see one of these days. . . .[4] There is a Universalist church [now] building here, which is to be in the style of . . . a theatre. I shall go to that too. . . . Miss Eliza Wheaton, a niece of Dr. Wheaton's . . . has been to see me, & says she will call & walk with me any time. . . . I shall find it pleasant, I think, as the doctor is continually engaged with one patient or another. He performed yesterday a surgical operation on Mrs. [Zachariah] Allen, Mr. Arnold's twin-sister, where Louisa is to stay when she comes here.[5] He took out a large piece from one of her arms.

Finally, she asked her mother to send on her bureau and a few books of hers as well. And she admonished Ann to make the girls write to her, and Wendell and John, too.

The boys did their best to oblige. John, age eleven, wrote that "Since you have gone we have all been very sober," with even Ariana, the family cat, "going into a melancholy." "You must make allowance for this letter," he begged, "as it is the first I ever wrote." Wendell, a big boy of thirteen, also tried his hand:[6]

> My dear Mary, our family is now made smaller by your absence, and Cambridge is deprived of one whom it will be long before she can forget. We still keep a communication which lights up the gloom we feel, and is the means of driving away a large part of our sadness. But still we cannot help feeling the absence of her who was the life of all our enjoyments. I am sitting now in the little parlour—on one side of me (in the back parlour) Miss Holmes [Ann] and Mr. Furness[7] enjoying a fine tête à tête, on the other Father and Mother, but a few moments ago sighing and groaning, now forming plans with all the brightness imaginable for an expedition to Providence. Before I end my sermon I must give you a compliment from one of your old admirers . . .—I carried some of Mrs. Parsons' wedding cake to him . . . he told me that he should remember Mrs. Parsons long after he had forgotten the cake. Our love to yourself, your dear husband and

our dear Brother. And now my dear Mary I must bid you good-bye—and beg you not to be too critical, remembering that it comes . . . From your loving Brother . . . O. W. H.

In these brief lines Usher's young brother-in-law Oliver Wendell Holmes early on revealed an aptitude for writing with style and charm.

Usher was attracting important patients. Mary, in a letter to her mother, wrote:[8] "The Doctor has been called to the rich Mrs. Brown's—all the old physicians are done with.[9] Mrs. B. has delayed her voyage to Europe for a month to see what Dr. can do with her. . . . The Doctor gives her letters, if she goes abroad, to his Sicilian & perhaps some other European friends. He has just been called to a new patient who is in great distress." She commented concerning their wedding, at which the Reverend Holmes had officiated: "Tell Father the doctor & I have determined that nobody could have performed the ceremony so admirably and well as he did, & that we love him more than it is . . . possible to tell."

That fall Usher and his bride had a visitor from Alfred. Usher's nephew, William Lewis (the son of Colonel Daniel Lewis and Usher's sister Abigail), was twenty-four years of age and the first of several nephews to study medicine in Providence under the stimulus of Uncle Usher. Although he attended lectures for two years, William did not obtain a degree from Brown University.

A letter from Mrs. Holmes to Mary, dated Tuesday, October 1, reflects a mother-daughter relationship poignant for any age.[10] She wrote that she was dispatching by baggage wagon a number of household effects and urged Mary to write frequently with "lines thick and close . . . no corner blank . . . two or three days' journals . . . nicely compacted" in each letter, and begged her to "be careful of your health and strength."

In obedience to maternal instructions, Mary's letters home were incredibly detailed and "compacted," and never was a corner left blank. Such was her letter of October 3 to her mother,[11] in which she described the topography of Providence and of her immediate neighborhood, gave further details about her accommodations, and reported some recent events:

Our house, as I already call it, faces south—two rooms about the size of our little parlour—one on the right hand as we enter, I receive company in & the other we dine & sup in. Directly back of the right-hand parlour is a little cunning room (in which I am writing) with two windows—one north, the other east—the north one looking out on the back yard where are the offices with little pavement walks through it, & quite surrounded by houses & outhouses. The east windows I keep always shut as Mr. Brown's, the quaker's house, overlooks.[12] We have a *comfortable* looking carpet, a *comfortable* sort of looking glass, & comfortable bed & bed curtains—not close bed-curtains . . . you know my aversion to close air. There are two good closets . . . , a mantlepiece, a card-rack, which is filling fast indeed. . . .

The Doctor has continual calls—& has had 4 students since he came home. He was sent for while we were at Judge Lyman's[13] to go to Oxford, of father's memory, 30 miles from here, but by some bad management of the trouble, lost the case.

Writing to Ann, Mary reported:[14] "Sunday morning . . . I went to the Episcopal church. . . . The church was filled with very respectable & many fashionable people. . . . I was much pleased . . . & think . . . I shall attend . . . regularly. In the afternoon I attended Mr. Edes' [First Baptist Meeting House] . . . he seems so much impressed himself with the solemnity of his subject.[15] . . . He is besides the most charming little man in the world in private. Mr. E's church is the most beautiful I was ever in—the outside is beautiful. . . . I know you will like Providence." Mary, daughter of a Cambridge Puritan parson, and Usher, a farm-boy from Maine, were much impressed by the opulence of plutocratic Providence, then enjoying the abundant fruits of a burgeoning industry and the China trade.

Mary and Usher were entertained that fall by some of the first families of Providence. On October 7 they attended an especially glittering affair at the home of the Zachariah Allens, Mrs. Allen apparently having recovered from her arm operation recently performed by Usher. Eliza Allen's parties, wrote Mary, were "among the very largest & most elegant given in Providence." Mary described the affair to her sister Ann[16] in superlative terms—the elegant and opulent home, the handsome and tasteful furnishings, and Eliza Allen's beautiful black dress. After a cordial reception, Mary and Usher danced to piano music played by a young lady, and Mary then danced with Eliza's brother, Richard Arnold. After cordials and lemonade, the gentlemen escorted the ladies to the dining room, where the table was set with an elaborate and exquisite table service of crystal and silver, and a delectable repast. After the meal, the ladies returned to the drawing room, leaving the table, as was the custom, to the gentlemen, who, no doubt, savored their cigars and brandy unencumbered by female chatter.

Later in the month[17] they attended another party at the elegant home of Miss Candace Allen, Zachariah's maiden sister, whom Mary described as "a very handsome lady of about 30 or 35" with "a large fortune" of her own and a "splendid establishment"—a large brick house in the federal style, set off by shrubbery, and "surrounded by a handsome iron fence." Mary again danced "a cotillion" and "had a gay time, I assure you." "Providence," Mary reassured Ann, "is sufficiently gay, but not dissipated."[18]

Mary wrote often of the cordial manner in which she was received by Providence's fashionable ladies and gentlemen. Usher's professional affiliations certainly helped to inspire the warm reception; but Mary, in her unselfconscious modesty, seemed unaware that her position as the daughter of one of Cambridge's best families and her own glowing personality were doubtless equally fascinating to the local society matrons.

Usher at about this time attended a very interesting medical case, doubtless known to Mary, as he often discussed with her his special problems. Doctor Artemas Johnson of Pawtucket had been called to Smithfield, Rhode Island, to visit a very sick elderly gentleman "of the denomination of Friends," suffering from both jaundice and intestinal obstruction. Because of the grave nature of the illness and the confusing symptoms, Johnson had called Doctor Wheaton in consultation. Wheaton saw the patient on October 23, but on the 24th, "Dr. W. being out of health, sent his partner in business Dr. Parsons." Usher made the long trip to Smithfield the same day and again on the 25th.

Johnson and Usher together, with considerable astuteness, arrived at the correct diagnosis. Although stomach obstruction from cancer was considered, they concluded that the symptoms were caused by "bilious concretions" which had passed into the bowel, causing bowel obstruction (known now to doctors as gallstone ileus). Usher never saw the patient again, but the diagnosis was later established when, on the day before Christmas, the patient passed a large gallstone. Although greatly relieved, he soon began to fail, went into decline, and died two months later. "Feeling much interest in the case," wrote Johnson, "and extremely anxious for a full demonstration . . . , I prevailed on the family for permission to examine the parts post mortem." On February 26 Usher performed an excellent and careful autopsy, which he described in full in the published report of the case. The clinical diagnosis, one often missed even in this age of scientific gadgets, was confirmed.[19]

In a letter to her mother, Mary gave an account of Usher's more routine professional life:[20]

> You would be surprised to find how well the Dr. gets along here. He gives a lecture every day at 12 o'clock of about an hour's length. He has eleven private students, together with Dr. Wheaton. He permits all these to attend the lectures at 10 dollars a ticket, the others, students of other physicians & from out of town, at 12 dollars. He has many patients; he has performed a surgical operation worth 15 dollars this week, & the visits & office come to much more. Dr. W is all goodness & kind feeling— & is so pleased with the engagement of the Dr. to be in partnership with him that he wishes . . . it to be five years—to which my Doctor has consented. This is very agreeable—I think it most probable, as my Doctor is so essential to Dr. W-n (& Dr. W. is no less to him in introducing him to families) that Mrs. W. would be willing to have him here a year, before we go to housekeeping— which I think would suit us. We cannot judge, to be sure, how we may feel next spring. . . . We are as well accommodated as we could expect to be anywhere. Mrs. W. keeps a fire upstairs, so that we have this little sitting-room quite to ourselves, except at meal-times.

Mary, in an enormous twelve-page letter to Ann,[21] again assured her family that Usher was "coming on finely," both with private students and practice. She apologized for his not having written to the Reverend Holmes, as he had been troubled with an infected mosquito bite of his hand, "which he had been obliged to poultice." Mary reported that she was taking long walks, which Usher felt were benefiting her health. One of her favorite jaunts was to Pawtucket, a distance of three or four miles. Pawtucket, she explained, was just north of the city, while Pawtuxet, to which she had also recently taken a long walk, was a village to the south.

"Cousin" Amelia Leavitt, who had not written to Mary since her belated note at the time of Mary's marriage, finally wrote on November 6 to correct this deficiency.[22] In her reply,[23] Mary told Amelia that she had received more than eighty visits from ladies since arriving in Providence and from many gentlemen as well. "I find very pleasant society here. I have been to nine or ten parties. . . . The walks around Providence are beautiful." Then, changing the subject, she added:

> My husband is chosen professor of surgery & anatomy in the College here—is lecturing to a class of 23 medical students—has nine young men, who are studying medicine with him. He has a good deal of practice & his time is fully employed. He desires his love to you.

Mary's letters continued to recount her social life and were full of news of parties. In a letter to her mother[24] she related that she had been to two parties since she last wrote—"at Mrs. Crocker's, a small one, & at Mrs. [Sullivan] Dorr's. . . . Mrs. Dorr's was quite an elegant party." She was very impressed with the Dorr establishment, in which, she related, "the walls of the drawing room, & of the entry are painted by an Italian, with views of the Bay of Naples & Vesuvius. . . . The Doctor says they give one the best idea of that beautiful spot & the neighboring mountain of any pictures he ever saw."[25]

Mary was again invited to the Dorr Mansion, this time to meet some distinguished guests. Among them were the eminent orator Daniel Webster and Mrs. Webster, and Judge Joseph Story of Massachusetts, Associate Justice of the United States Supreme Court. They were all in Providence in connection with a celebrated trial. Conscious of the occasion, Mary donned her very best gown and wore a crimson bow and chrysanthemums in her hair. Although in describing the event she does not mention Usher, it is likely that he escorted her that evening.[26]

Usher and Mary were beginning to find life in another's household more restrictive than they had at first surmised. Toward the end of the year Mary's correspondence with her family mentions hunting for a suitable place to set up housekeeping. Finally, arrangements were made for shipping from Cambridge more of her belongings to furnish the new home, especially her cherished piano.[27]

As Usher became better established in Providence, the Medical

School at Brown University, where he chose to build his career, became increasingly important to him. Although there had been a nucleus of well-educated physicians in Rhode Island throughout its early years, several with M.D. degrees from European universities, it was more usual for a physician to enter the profession through a preceptorship of three to four years with a prominent practitioner, as Usher himself had done. The apprentices helped in the preparation of medicines, participated in the care of the sick, and assisted at minor operations in return for instruction in the medical arts. Upon leaving, the pupil was given a letter of recommendation, his only credential.

During the second decade of the 19th century, the more advanced concept that medicine should be treated as a science rather than as an outgrowth of intuition gained increasing acceptance and was a significant factor in the establishment of the medical school at Brown during 1810 and 1811. The University's charter authorized it to "admit to and confer any and all the learned degrees which can or ought to be given and conferred in any of the colleges or universities in America," and several times under this authority the M.D. degree had been granted to already prominent physicians. Solomon Drowne, Pardon Bowen, and Usher's partner, Levi Wheaton, had received such degrees from Brown.

The medical school was formally established in 1811, the third oldest in New England following Harvard (1782) and Dartmouth (1798). Only four other schools existed in America at that time. Solomon Drowne[28] was professor of Materia Medica and Botany, William Ingalls[29] of Anatomy and Surgery, and William Corlis Bowen[30] of Chemistry. Later, Doctor Levi Wheaton[31] was appointed professor of the Theory and Practice of Physic, while Doctor John M. Eddy served a brief tenure as adjunct professor of Anatomy and Surgery when Ingalls resigned due to inadequate compensation. Eddy died prematurely two years later, and Usher Parsons eventually filled that vacancy. Finally, Doctor John DeWolf, Jr. in time replaced Doctor Bowen as professor of chemistry.[32] The school awarded its first M.D. degrees in 1814, two in number, increasing to a high of thirteen in 1825, and several of its graduates were later to achieve prominence.[33]

This was the medical school of which Usher was now an integral part. Initially, Usher met resistance from President Asa Messer in seeking a room of his own. He appealed to Nicholas Brown, a member of the Corporation, over the head of Messer. The Corporation, consisting of Brown, Judge Samuel Eddy, Stephen Hopkins Smith, and the Reverend Henry Edes, directed Messer to approve the request.[34]

After Eddy's death in 1817, the fortunes of the medical school reached a low ebb. With Usher's appointment in 1822 the school was "reorganized." Charles Parsons wrote: "The opening of courses by Doctor Parsons gave new life to the institution. He made arrangements through channels over which a veil of secrecy had to be thrown, for a supply of anatomical material. He was the owner of valuable and novel representations of human structure in wax models made in Italy. He had learned from Doctor Ramsay the methods of displaying and preserving the perishable organs."[35]

The college and its surroundings then had a rural aspect. When the medical school was opened, the only buildings on the campus were University Hall and President Messer's barn. Hope College was the only structure added during the life of the school. "No other street but Angell," wrote a contemporary,[36] "then led directly to the river. What is now Waterman Street was chiefly a pasture for horses." The area between Thayer Street and the Seekonk River "consisted of unoccupied meadows and pastures." There was only a scattering of houses in the environs of the college. At the head of College Hill, on the site of the present Rockefeller Library, the university in 1810 built (at a cost of $1,452) a brick building to house the grammar school which it had sponsored for many years. It was appropriated as an anatomical building when the medical school opened. Charles described it as follows:

> Its upper story was used for dissection, and the preparation of specimens for the lectures, and an opening or trapdoor allowed them to be lowered into the lecture-room beneath. The courses on anatomy appear to have been sometimes given—probably at an earlier period—in the upper rooms of Dr. Bowen's building at the corner of South Main and Leonard Streets. A certain anatomical tradition and aroma lingered round both these classic precincts. I think that most, if not all, the courses in other departments were delivered in University Hall. The audience frequently contained practicing physicians as well as pupils.

The organization of the school is described in a circular issued about 1823, now in the Brown archives:

Medical Lectures in Brown University

The Medical Lectures in Brown University will commence in the Anatomical Building, in Providence, on the first Thursday in February and be continued daily for nearly three months.

Theory and Practice of Physic and Obstetrics,
  by Dr. Wheaton. $10.00
Chemistry and Pharmacy,
  by Professor D'Wolf. 10.00
Anatomy, Physiology and Surgery,
  by Dr. Parsons. 15.00
                                                                                   $35.00

The public are informed that no pains have been spared to render the institution worthy of patronage. The Professor of Chemistry has, within the last year, made extensive additions to his apparatus, which render it very complete. A cabinet of minerals has been formed, and collections of specimens are making for teaching the other branches of natural history.

The Anatomical Museum has recently received very important additions from various parts of Europe, and now contains every preparation, plate and instrument necessary to a teacher of anatomy. Students will be accommodated with separate sets of bones, and allowed ample opportunities in Practical Anatomy.

A Medical Library is attached to the school, to which the students will be allowed full access.

The lectures on Surgery will comprise about one fourth part of the course, and nearly every instrument now in use will be exhibited and described. When practicable, students will be allowed to attend surgical operations, and cases of sickness.

Arrangements are made with the Steward of the College for boarding in the commons at $1.25 per week. Lodging rooms may be hired in the vicinity of the College at a moderate rent, which will make the price of board lower than at almost any Medical School in New England.

The conditions on which Medical Degrees are conferred are the following:

1st That the candidate sustain a good moral character.
2   That he furnish the Professors with satisfactory evidence of his possessing a competent knowledge of the Latin language and Natural Philosophy.
3   That he shall have attended two full courses of lectures on

Anatomy and Surgery, Chemistry and the Theory and Practice of Physic.

4   That he shall have studied three years (including the time of lectures) with physicians of approved reputation.

5   That he shall have submitted to a private examination held by the Professors during the last week of the lectures, or on the Monday and Tuesday preceding Commencement . . . and received their recommendation.

6   That he shall have written a dissertation on some medical subject and read and defended it in the College Chapel before the President, or such college officer as he may appoint, and the Medical Professors and such other professional or literary gentlemen as choose to attend. Where, however, the candidate can offer a satisfactory excuse for being absent at commencement, and has complied with all the other conditions, he will be allowed to send his dissertation, to be read publicly by some other person, all dissertations to be transmitted to one of the Professors at Providence at least four weeks before Commencement, and read on the Monday and Tuesday preceding that day.

Gentlemen wishing to become private pupils with Drs. Wheaton and Parsons are informed that they can be accommodated for one, two or three years; that Lectures will be given twice or thrice per week during the year, and that the use of a valuable Library will be allowed, with an extensive collection of Anatomical Preparations; . . . making the advantages for the elementary part of their education equal to those of any private establishment in the country. They have moreover made arrangements with the Professor of Natural Philosophy and the Professor of Botany, by which Medical Students will be allowed to attend their Lectures at the College.

A Brown University Medical Association,[37] established for the benefit of professors, students, and interested physicians, existed during most of the life of the medical school. Its first meeting was held on November 9, 1811, and subsequent meetings were held irregularly during the academic year. The association aspired to assemble a library and authorized the purchase of books. Discussions were in the form of debates, a typical proposition being, "Whether any diseases were produced by absorption." On September 4, 1816, the association adjourned *sine die*, and did not meet again for seven years—roughly the "disorganized" period between the death of John Mathewson Eddy and the accession of Usher Parsons. Zachariah Allen, Jr., during his brief interlude as a medical student, was a member of the Association in 1813.[38]

Procuring specimens for anatomical study was a continuing problem. Charles Parsons wrote:[39] "A full account of it would include tales of nocturnal adventure, the evasion or befooling of night watchmen, and a mysterious traffic." A notorious episode concerning this traffic has appeared in several versions. According to Charles,[40]

> A story is told of a certain skeleton in the course of preparation, which was left in a barrel in front of the 'anatomical building', and hence involved Professors Wheaton and Parsons in trouble. By some forgetfulness, it was allowed to remain out-of-doors till college students began to roll and kick it down the steep of College Street, and at the level of Benefit Street it ran against some obstacle, I think the steps of the old town house. Out came the head of the barrel, followed by another head, and great was the consternation and excitement. A startled crowd gathered around the spot; stories were soon astir of desecrated graves; search was even made in one place of recent burial, which was found not to have been disturbed. A medical student, who was supposed to be implicated, found it convenient to visit his uncle's house in the country, and remained there till the affair had blown over. Dr. Parsons . . . claimed the bones as his own property, but public opinion demanded a prompt and decent burial.
>
> The notoriety produced by this splattering of "armless trunks and trunkless head" attracted public attention to the rumored lack of discipline of the students, and according to tradition led eventually to the demise of the school.

These were satisfying years for Usher. He enjoyed a growing practice, fulfillment of his academic aspirations, and the contentment of a happy marriage. Mary now had a home of her own and the pleasure of frequent visits with her closely-knit family. As the year 1823 began, Usher and Mary were settled in their new home at 69 Cheapside, now North Main Street.

On New Year's Day of 1823, Usher wrote to his father-in-law:[41]

> After wishing you all a Happy New Year, we announce with much pleasure our commencement of housekeeping. We breakfasted at our house this morning for the first time, and during the forenoon our friends called in spite of the snow storm to tender their

anniversary felicitations. Our house is very comfortable and con-
venient and pleases us exceedingly. In short, we are delighted
with our new establishment and the novel cares that attend it.
The furniture . . . from Cambridge arrived safe and in good time.
. . . Should the weather be favorable & sleighing good next week,
I shall probably pass a day in Boston and a night in Cambridge.
Mary prefers remaining here. . . .

Mary added her own lines: "Do make my dear Mother happy by
telling her that I never was happier." She concluded: "Yesterday we
began housekeeping. I was determined to exert myself as much as
possible to date the commencement of my housekeeping from the
beginning of the year." She looked forward with pleasure to having
a home of her own.

Although Mary was envious of the gay goings-on in Cambridge,
life in Providence was most certainly not dull. Yet she was given
to spells of depression when separation from her family, the cares
of a new home, and possibly her delicate health seemed to over-
whelm her. Now, because of Usher's impending absence on a visit
to Boston and Cambridge, her loneliness was more poignant than
usual. Mary attended parties almost weekly, however, and by January had received since coming to Providence some twenty-eight
callers—and "many more on the Dr.'s account solely." The doctor,
she added, had a good practice and was never so happy "having a
home of his own."[42] She sought some solace during his absence by
attending a Quaker meeting, but sitting for an hour without a word
being spoken "has a singular effect."[43]

Early in February Mary visited Cambridge, and later Ann returned
the visit. During Ann's stay in Providence Mary wrote to her
mother[44] about an adventure in the culinary arts—a roast of veni-
son, which Usher judged to be "most excellent." His tastes on the
whole, however, were simple, a typical meal consisting of boiled
ham, topped off by a gin punch.[45] His habits were notably temperate,
"excepting that his professional visits [at times] lead him to take a
little more spirit." Usher was currently deeply immersed in William
Paley's *Natural Theology*,[46] reading it "night and day—at all seasons
and hours!" Mary and Ann visited about a good deal, but Mary was
most flattered ("the greatest compliment of all") by an invitation
to Ann to meet Mrs. Sullivan Dorr and by her gracious hospitality
as well.[47]

Early in April Usher received a long letter from his father-in-law gently chiding him for not writing:[48] "As you and your wife are one in *law*, I shall consider you *legally* holden, by the letters we wrote to her to write to us occasionally [about] . . . your health, progress, and prospects." The family regularly received accounts of the Wheaton connection ("I hope, as agreeable and advantageous as it promised"), and of Usher's lectures, practice, and surgical operations ("occasionally profitable"), but "I hope, you [yourself] will still be able to confirm [all this]." The Reverend emphasized his and Mrs. Holmes's desire to be informed about Usher's professional success and the Parsons's domestic happiness. Ann, he noted, was highly pleased with Providence and what she saw "of your happy settlement at a home of your own." "Your care of Mary's health," he concluded, ". . . we highly commend."

At a meeting of the Censors of the Northern District of the Rhode Island Medical Society on March 12, 1823, Usher Parsons, having passed "the necessary qualifications," was recommended for fellowship in the Society and was elected to membership at the annual meeting in Newport on June 25.[49]

On April 10, 1823 new orders were issued to Usher by the Navy Department:[50] "Proceed to Norfolk and report yourself to Captain Arthur Sinclair as Surgeon on board the U.S. Ship *John Adams*." Since this annoying and inconvenient order followed by exactly one year Usher's request for a year's leave, there is no question about its logic and fairness. Yet in his present favorable circumstances Usher could conceive of nothing more alarming or repugnant than to be uprooted and sent to sea. Consequently, he promptly resigned from the service. With acceptance of his resignation on April 23, an eventful period in his life came to an end.

A further inducement undoubtedly prompted Usher's resignation. A letter from Mary to her mother[51] refers to this in suitably delicate terms. Amid chit-chat about household minutiae, Mary, with characteristic Victorian circumlocution, reported that, while never in better health, she wanted to do "what I can now, that in the summer time I may be able to do another . . . kind of work—do you comprehend?" In a word, Mary was pregnant.

Mary's letters in the succeeding months are full of local interest and family news. In a letter to her mother in early May[52] she reported her less than enthusiastic reaction to the performance of James William Wallack, the great English actor, who was then visiting Providence for a week that spring and played Hamlet and

Shylock as well as Rolla in the play *Pizarro*. Mary had read in the Providence paper[53] of a rebellion at Harvard and begged for news of the incident.[54] Mary's friend Amelia Leavitt had indicated a possible visit to Providence,[55] to which Mary responded enthusiastically.[56] She informed Amelia that her mother had just spent a few days with her, which made her very happy, and then discussed her reaction to some of the religious controversies that were then raging:

> To avoid attending a Unitarian church, I attend the Episcopal, as the form of that church is almost the only difference between it & Father's church. The principles I hear preached are those I believe in—Orthodox as they are called—in distinction from liberal.

Mary's comments on orthodoxy reflect her father's unwavering convictions in religious matters. The split within the Congregationalist Church between the Orthodox Calvinists and the newfangled liberal Unitarians deeply affected the Reverend Abiel Holmes's own flock. At a later time he and a covey of his embattled brethren actually walked out of the First Parish in Cambridge and set up a separate congregation. Usher, who had been raised as a Congregationalist, had not been burdened before marriage with doctrinaire concerns. Marriage to the daughter of a minister, however, made a difference. Charles wrote:[57] "Soon after his marriage, he was admitted to the Episcopal communion at St. John's Church."

While Mary was busy writing letters, Usher's office was the scene on May 16 of a meeting of the rejuvenated Brown University Medical Association.[58] At its first meeting in seven years, held the week before, the constitution and bylaws had been read. The treasury contained $11.09, the last disbursement (for books) having been made nine years before. Doctors Barrows, Arnold, and Parsons were delegated "to revise the constitution & propose any alteration or amendment they may think proper & report at the next meeting." Their report was approved, and at a subsequent meeting, also in Usher's house, the committee was requested to alter "the form & diction of the Diploma" (i.e. the certificate of membership) as they might think desirable.

Amid these events Usher ventured into new surgical realms. Wrote Charles:[59] "He used to point out the house in Smithfield [Rhode Island] where he first operated for strangulated hernia in 1823. Being little acquainted with the operation, he studied it up, perhaps in Scarpa's treatise which he had bought in Paris, while the messenger was conveying him to the house." Elsewhere[60] Usher identified the patient as one Elisha Olney, aged 64. He reported: "Scrotal hernia of right side, intestine and omentum down, pain not severe, some nausea, hernia of many years' standing." He noted that the strangulation had existed forty-eight hours and listed the patient as "cured." Operation for hernia at that time was directed exclusively at relieving the fatal strangulation, attempts at definitive repair having to await the later development of adequate anesthesia and surgical asepsis. In the same year Usher performed his first "extirpation" of the breast for cancer on a "Mrs. Arnold, age 46." In this case, "the disease re-appeared in less than one year in the cicatrix, and soon involved the lung; she died within eighteen months." He was later to have some cures of this disease.

Usher was never reticent about his exploits as a military surgeon. On numerous occasions during his long residence in Providence, sometimes to the annoyance of his medical colleagues, he found opportunities to keep alive the story of his naval experiences. It is not clear why the editor of the *Rhode Island American and General Advertiser* (of Providence) took notice of Usher's essay on military surgery, published five years before. At any rate this is what the *American* of June 13, 1823 had to say:

> In the *New-England Journal of Medicine and Surgery* for October, 1818, we find an interesting surgical account of the celebrated naval battle of Lake Erie, by Usher Parsons, M.D., now of this town, but at that eventful period a Surgeon in the naval service of the United States. . . . the official reports of military commanders convey no adequate conceptions of the horrors of the battle scene. The [present] account, . . . is, however, of a different character—describing . . . with professional accuracy the dreadful consequences of even victorious strife. Everything connected with the fame of the gallant Perry awakens interest, and Dr. P.'s narrative illustrates both his humanity and his valor.

Early in the summer, Usher's old friend and anatomy teacher, Alexander Ramsay, arising like a shade from the past, sent a pathetic letter to "The Managers of the College in Rhode Island."[61]

> Being an utter stranger to you, and unacquainted with your Institution or its regulations, I must beg leave to refer you to my former pupil, Dr. Parsons, who presents this.

When, twenty years back, I was called by your colleges of New York, Dartmouth, &c., to introduce the youth to the manner and Doctrines of Anatomy, Physiology, Medicine and Surgery I had practiced and published in Europe, Professors were then fully aware of the necessity of Improvements. These are amply diffused by the numerous scholars I have had the honor of receiving on this continent. The expense and labour, however, of reducing the plan in shape of a Museum is the lot of very few. This has in some measure been effected in six years, by my pupils. I must esteem myself fortunate, were this institution rendered permanently useful under a pupil. My entire apparatus of Books, Drawings, Preparations, &c., estimate of $10,000. The preparations about $4,000, detached from the rest. I would willingly set the plan in motion on reasonable terms, and have the whole on equally easy purchase, provided, that the Institution was forever to be appropriated to the improvement of the Youth, which would not fail to commence a new era in Medical improvement. I beg leave, gentlemen, to assure of the high consideration of your obedient servant.

Under this same date he wrote a covering letter to Usher.[62] "During my Northern Tour, I had the pleasure of polite observations delivered by you, where I was concerned, from gentlemen who had attended your discourses." Son Charles writes that Ramsay "then gives directions for the preparation of a material which was to be thrown into the blood vessels, to render them distinct, and preserve them in a form for subsequent study. It is essentially the same material which I remember my father using many years later." Ramsay's letter to Usher continues:

By the Concord *Patriot* and Portland *Statesman* you notice that having collected a Museum, on the Plan so universally approved in Europe and America, as the medium of an arranged school, this is offered for sale, as a rudiment of National Improvement. The best proof of the efficiency of the Institution is that the entire mass is the produce of American labor under my direction, and that wherever my pupils settle, publick confidence is experienced by them. I could wish you came here, that we might converse on the subject, as this method cannot fail to raise any college which completely adopts it. I have addressed a card to your Managers of the College that you may not appear in the character of officious.

If indeed this request ever came before the Corporation, no action was taken. Unhappily Ramsay failed in his goal of preserving for posterity the fruits of his life-long labors. He died the following year.

Charles Upham, Ann's fiancé, visited Providence for a speaking engagement during the latter part of May. Mary had invited him to the Parsons home, signing her letter,[63] significantly, "Your affectionate sister." Mary was feeling poorly when Charles arrived, but roused herself with effort to make his stay a "tolerably happy" one.[64] Mary was also looking forward to having Amelia Leavitt as a house guest and hoped that Ann might join them. With Amelia as a companion for Mary, Usher was able to travel to Boston and Cambridge, assured that Mary would not be alone. Upon his return to Providence, he brought a letter from Mary's parents and also news that Ann would soon follow.

Mary, although big with child, was sitting for her portrait by Francis Alexander. The Reverend Holmes wrote to Mary that he was awaiting Usher, who was still in Cambridge, to join them for dinner. Mrs. Holmes added: "It delights me that you had your picture taken ... I long to see it in one of Daggett's handsome frames."[65]

Mary was a pretty girl, and the portrait conveys a sense of her charm and refinement. A contemporary portrait of Usher, executed by the same artist but unsigned, shows him to be a handsome, apple-cheeked young man with brown hair and eyes. They were indeed an attractive couple.[66] Delighted with her portrait, which all approved of and acknowledged to be a striking likeness, Mary later arranged for a sitting for Ann—"$15 for the smallest size & 20 for the next."[67]

Ann traveled to Providence by stage on July 9, Mary's friends Amelia Leavitt and Catherine Haven having already arrived. In the next few days the girls enjoyed a steamboat excursion down Narragansett Bay and attended a "super-abundance" of parties. Ann was her usual sparkling self. Upon Usher's return, he and Mary drove into the country, "a charming ride" of six miles, to attend a fashionable Quaker wedding in Cranston[68] of Anne Almy, daughter of William Almy, a business associate of Moses Brown in the firm of Almy, Brown, and Slater, which established the first cotton textile mill in America, the famed Slater Mill of Pawtucket, Rhode Island.[69]

Usher had been caring for the son of Judge Daniel Lyman, now quite recovered, when the judge's chaise arrived to fetch him to see his sister, who in turn had become ill. Lyman was Chief Justice of the Rhode Island State Supreme Court. In appreciation of Usher's attentive care, the judge gave him a three-volume set of Erasmus Darwin's *Zoonomia* (which anticipated his grandson's theory of evolution), inscribing it "Your affectionate friend."[70] About this time Mary reported on Usher's obstetrical practice: "Dr. is but 6 miles from here at Capt. Kelly's, whose wife wished him as an accoucheur, & ... [he] has been gone now eight hours!"[71] Also: "Mrs. Russell and all his patients are doing well [several related Russells were very wealthy merchants]."[72]

As her pregnancy progressed, Mary alternately felt quite well or poorly, especially as she suffered from the hot humid summer of Providence.[73] On August 31 Anna Bell Leighton, Usher's nine-year-old niece, arrived for a visit and proved quite a help as she "runs up and down for me."[74] Ann came from Cambridge by stage on September 1 after a dusty suffocating ride.[75] She brought with her, to share in the Brown Commencement gaiety, Ann Hulburt, another of the Cambridge girls. With her sister and little niece on hand, Mary was preparing for the eventful day, sewing her maternity wardrobe ("we made my last loose gown yesterday")[76] and interviewing her nurse-to-be ("active & apparently good-natured & motherly").[77] Mary was feeling content now: "I read & talk with my kind & gentle husband & upon the whole never enjoyed myself more than [now] in my retirement." [78] Surrounded by young females of various ages and size, Usher accepted his lot with monumental equanimity.

On the Sunday before Harvard Commencement Mary sent a note to Amelia[79] by Samuel Starkweather, on his way to Cambridge to attend the festivities. Young Starkweather, a graduate of Brown in the class of '22 and now a tutor at the college, had cast an admiring eye on Amelia. Despite his fondness for her, Amelia was reluctant to encourage his attentions while still undecided about certain others of her beaux, and Mary counseled her on her dilemma.[80] It appears that Samuel failed in his quest, since some time later he confided to Usher that he had sent a farewell letter to Amelia.[81] Amelia could have done worse, since Samuel Starkweather, a Pawtucket boy, was admitted to the bar, moved to Cleveland, became Mayor of the city, and later a judge.[82]

The Brown Commencement was held according to custom on the morning of Wednesday, September 3. Although Mary remained in semi-seclusion, she most certainly did not miss the commencement procession, her first in Providence. From her own front windows she had a fine view of the slowly moving column in full academic regalia, as it wended its way down College Hill and into the First Baptist Meeting House directly across the street from her front door. Marching with the faculty was young Professor Parsons. The girls, we can be sure, watched the proceedings from a better vantage point. Although a little cold for the season, the day was fine and clear. The ceremonies attracted an assemblage of citizens described as the largest in many a year. Visitors expressed great satisfaction with the general excellence of the program and the gaiety of the occasion.[83]

At a meeting of the Corporation of Brown University held the day after Commencement, Usher was "appointed Professor of Anatomy and Surgery in this Institution," thus attaining the rank of full professor.[84]

NOTES

1. Mary H. Parsons to Ann Holmes, September 27, 1822, HUCC.
2. Henry Wheaton (1785–1848) was a prominent American jurist and diplomat. He married his cousin, Catherine Wheaton, daughter of Dr. Levi Wheaton. Some of Mary's Providence acquaintances cannot now be positively identified.
3. Mary was referring to Obadiah Moses Brown, son of Quaker Moses Brown, one of the five famed Brown brothers of Providence—James, John, Joseph, Nicholas, and Moses. All except Moses were Baptists.
4. This is now the Moses Brown School.
5. Eliza Harriet Arnold and Richard J. Arnold were children of Welcome Arnold, Providence merchant. Zachariah Allen (1795–1882), husband of Eliza Harriet, was a leading Rhode Island industrialist. Richard J. Arnold was affianced to Louisa Gindrat of Bryan County, Georgia. Now engaged in the China trade, he removed to Georgia after his marriage to become proprietor of his wife's family plantation. He returned to Providence at the outbreak of the Civil War. See also Note 16.
6. Oliver Wendell Holmes to Mary H. Parsons, September 29, 1822, Houghton Library, Harvard University.
7. Horace Howard Furness, a graduate of Harvard College, class of 1820, was later a Unitarian minister. Furness, a friend of Ralph Waldo Emerson, was not as feared by the Holmes family a rival suitor for Ann's affections. At that very moment, in fact, he was telling her of his secret engagement to a Salem girl, while Ann's own favorite, Charles Wentworth Upham of Salem, remained unchallenged in her affections. See

E. M. Tilton's *Amiable Autocrat: A Biography of Dr. Oliver Wendell Holmes* (New York, Henry Schuman, 1947), p. 24.

8. Mary H. Parsons to Mrs. Abiel Holmes, September 29, 1822, HUCC.

9. Which of the several rich Mesdames Brown she does not say.

10. Mrs. Abiel Holmes to Mary H. Parsons, October 1, 1822, HUCC.

11. Mary H. Parsons to Mrs. Abiel Holmes, October 3, 1822, HUCC.

12. Dr. Levi Wheaton lived at 10 Thomas St. and Obadiah M. Brown next door at No. 11. In these houses, built by clock maker Seril Dodge, the Providence Art Club is now located. Obadiah M. Brown died on October 15, 1822 at age 52 only twelve days after this letter was written. Mary did not see fit to mention this in her letters. Obadiah was the only child of Moses Brown, who is mentioned in footnote 3. Moses established the Slater Mill in Pawtucket, Rhode Island, where the Industrial Revolution in America began with the manufacture of textiles using water power in the process.

13. Reference is to Daniel Lyman (1756–1830), Revolutionary War officer and Chief Justice of the Supreme Court of Rhode Island, 1802–1816.

14. Mary H. Parsons to Ann Holmes, October 7–8, 1822, HUC.

15. Nathan Bourne Crocker (1781–1865) was rector of St. Johns's, the Episcopal church. Henry Edes (1780?–1851) was pastor of the First Church, which was Baptist.

16. Mary H. Parsons to Ann Holmes, October 7 and 8, 1822, HUCC. Zachariah Allen, Jr., then only twenty-seven years of age and already showing promise of his future potent status in the business world of Rhode Island, was the son of a very wealthy mill owner. A graduate of Brown University, he attended medical lectures at Brown and studied law, but ultimately devoted his life to business, becoming a figure of great stature in Rhode Island involved in a multitude of enterprises. He was a founder of the Providence Institution for Savings (now the "Old Stone Bank") and originated the nationally important Factory Mutual Insurance group, now bearing the family-related name of Allendale Insurance. Eliza Harriet (Arnold) Allen was herself the daughter of a very wealthy Providence merchant, Welcome Arnold. The Zachariah Allens lived in the "Russell House" at 118 North Main St. Eventually elevated to install shops below it, it is still in existence, although much of the fine inside finish was removed to the Brooklyn Museum.

17. This is described in a letter from Mary H. Parsons to Ann Holmes of October 18, 1822, HUCC.

18. Candace Allen's magnificent house at 12 Benevolent St. is still standing and still gracious. Designed by the architect John Holden Greene, it had just been completed that year. For details see William McKenzie Woodward, *Providence 1984 Festival of Historic Houses* (Providence, Providence Preservation Society, 1984), p. 12. Candace Allen was the sister of Zachariah Allen (1795–1882) and daughter of the wealthy

Zachariah Allen, Sr., who introduced calico printing into New England. Candace remained a spinster all her life, her fiancé having been killed in the War of 1812.

19. "Johnson, Artemas: Case of Jaundice, Bilious Concretions, and the Passage of a Large Stone. Appearance on Dissection with Remarks, by Dr. Parsons," *New England Journal of Medicine and Surgery*, 14:165–169, 1825.

20. Mary H. Parsons to Mrs. Abiel Holmes, October 26, 1822, HUCC.

21. Mary H. Parsons to Ann Holmes, October 30, 1822, HUCC.

22. Amelia Leavitt to Mary H. Parsons, November 6, 1822, HUCC.

23. Mary H. Parsons to Amelia Leavitt, November 10, 1822, HUCC.

24. Mary H. Parsons to Mrs. Abiel Holmes, November 10, 1822, HUCC.

25. Sullivan Dorr (1778–1858), later president of the Providence Washington Insurance Co., was a native of Boston and son of the Ebenezer Dorr who participated with Paul Revere in the famous events of April 18, 1775.

    The Dorr mansion, one of the most elegant of the Federal period houses in Rhode Island, was built by Sullivan Dorr on land originally held by Roger Williams. Dorr, a successful Providence merchant engaged in the China trade, was at one time consular agent in Canton. The wall paintings described by Mary were executed by Michele Felice Cornè, a Neapolitan artist who also decorated rooms in Salem and Boston and whose Newport home is still standing. The Dorr paintings were some years ago restored to their original brilliance by the Providence Preservation Society, which then owned the house.

26. Mary H. Parsons to Mrs. Abiel Holmes, November 20, 1822, HUCC. *The Rhode Island American & General Advertiser* (Providence) of November 19 and 22, 1822 reported the famous case of Tracy vs. Wood. This was a civil suit to recover a large sum of cash purloined from a trusted emissary hand-carrying it by steamer from New York to Providence. Presiding in the case in the United States District in Providence was Justice Story as Circuit Judge for New England. The brilliant Daniel Webster, now practicing law in Massachusetts and retained as counsel by the plaintiff, put on an eloquent and showy performance. Mary and her female neighbors avidly attended all of the sessions, *en masse.*

27. Mary H. Parsons to Mrs. Abiel Holmes, December 22, 1822, HUCC.

28. Solomon Drowne had studied locally with Doctor William Bowen of Providence and received his M.D. degree at the University of Pennsylvania. Following an extensive and highly regarded service as a surgeon in the Revolution, he returned to Providence to practice. He later sailed for Europe where he assiduously attended lectures and visited hospitals in London and in Paris, and where he became an intimate of both Thomas Jefferson and Benjamin Franklin. When he returned to Rhode

Island, he bought an estate in Foster in the western part of the state, built a spacious residence in a sylvan setting, to which he gave the name of Mount Hygeia, and developed there the first botanical garden in Rhode Island. His extensive collection acquired fame and attracted visitors from great distances. He was a delegate to the first pharmacopoeial convention in 1819. A very popular lecturer, he helped his students develop their own botanical garden on the college grounds.

29. William Ingalls, although less colorful than Drowne, was a prepossessing figure. A graduate of Harvard College and Harvard Medical School, he spent his whole professional life in Boston, where he gained considerable prominence because of his surgical skill and his opposition to bleeding. He kept a private room for the study of anatomy and an anatomical museum on School Street in Boston and also a lecture room on Market Street. After his appointment at Brown in 1811, he lectured in Providence regularly until 1815, when he resigned, feeling that the meager financial rewards did not warrant his trips to Providence. For some time, students were permitted to attend his lectures in Boston and receive course credit. To help fill the gap, Doctor John Mathewson Eddy, a physician of considerable promise and a founder of the Rhode Island Medical Society, was appointed adjunct professor, but he died prematurely barely two years later.

30. Doctor William Corlis Bowen, the remaining member of the original faculty triumvirate, was an only son of the eminent Providence physician, Doctor William Bowen. After attending Brown, he graduated from Union College and studied medicine with his uncle, Doctor Pardon Bowen. He received an M.D. degree at Edinburgh and then studied in Paris and London, where he was a private pupil of Sir Astley Cooper. He was a young man of brilliant attainments and yet was kind and endearing to his patients. As a diversion from his medical preoccupations, he experimented extensively with bleaching solutions, which activity laid the foundation for the thriving bleaching industry, an integral part of Rhode Island's textile empire. He died prematurely of tuberculosis in his thirtieth year, thought to have been aggravated by prolonged exposure to chlorine vapor. "Rhode Island," wrote Usher Parsons, "lost its brightest ornament of the medical profession."

31. Levi Wheaton graduated from Brown University, gained medical experience in the military hospital in Providence during the early Revolutionary War period, and then studied medicine with Doctor Joshua Babcock of Westerly, Rhode Island and Doctor William Bowen of Providence. He then served as surgeon aboard a privateer, but was taken prisoner by the British, who placed him in charge of a prison hospital ship. After the war he practiced for ten years in Hudson, New York, a community settled by emigrés from Rhode Island, practiced in New York City for two years, and then settled in Providence. Brown University awarded him an honorary M.D. degree in 1812. He was considered to be a man of erudition, a sound practical physician, and a

creditable lecturer. He was the author of papers on yellow fever and the use of calomel in Asiatic cholera. Unlike Ingalls, he was an enthusiastic proponent of phlebotomy. He served for many years as physician to the Marine Hospital at the port of Providence.

32. Doctor John DeWolf, Jr., after studying at Brown University, obtained his chemical education with Doctor Robert Hare of Philadelphia, who later became the eminent professor of chemistry at the University of Pennsylvania. Considered to be a brilliant lecturer and experimenter, DeWolf served as professor of chemistry at the University—college and medical school—for twenty years. Since the chemical apparatus belonging to the college was "hardly worthy of the name," he brought his own equipment to the lectures. He was admired for his sparkling wit and polished rhetoric.

33. Its most distinguished graduates were Alden March (1820) and Elisha Bartlett (1826). March, an eminent surgeon of Albany, New York, founded Albany Medical College and became president of the American Medical Association. Bartlett, a native of Smithfield, Rhode Island, after further study in Paris, taught in a total of nine medical schools. His career reached its culmination in 1852 when he was appointed to the chair of Materia Medica and Medical Jurisprudence at the Columbia College of Physicians and Surgeons in New York. His essays on the fevers and the philosophy of medical science became classics. William Osler described him as "a Rhode Island Philosopher," and Donald Fleming, the historian, considered him "sufficient justification of medical education at Brown." Cf. William Osler, "A Rhode Island Philosopher (Elisha Bartlett)," *Transactions of the Rhode Island Medical Society*, 6: 15–46, 1899, and Donald Fleming, *Science and Technology in Providence, 1760 to 1915* (Providence, Brown University, 1952). For histories of Brown's medical school, see Charles W. Parsons, *The Medical School Formerly Existing in Brown University, Its Professors and Graduates* (Providence, S. S. Rider, 1881, Rhode Island Historical Tracts, No. 12) and S. J. Goldowsky, "The Beginnings of Medical Education in Rhode Island," *Rhode Island Medical Journal*, 38:496–515, 555–593, 632–661, 1955. This account contains an extensive bibliography on the Brown University Medical School.

34. This episode is described in a letter from Mary H. Parsons to her mother, Mrs. Abiel Holmes of August 9, 1823, HUCC. Samuel Eddy (1769–1839) was later Chief Justice of the Rhode Island Supreme Court; Nicholas Brown (1769–1841) was of the famed Brown family; Stephen Hopkins Smith was a businessman; and Henry Edes was pastor of the First Baptist Church. Asa Messer (1769–1836) was President of the University from 1804 to 1826.

35. Charles W. Parsons, *The Medical School Formerly Existing in Brown University*, p. 31–32.

36. Samuel Brenton Shaw, "College and Town in 1819," in *Memories of Brown, Traditions and Recollections Gathered from Many Sources* (Providence, Brown Alumni Monthly Magazine Co., 1909), p. 38.

37. Brown University Medical Association. "Constitution, Bylaws, and Minutes," Brown University Archives.

38. Charles W. Parsons, *The Medical School Formerly Existing in Brown University*, p. 54.

39. *Ibid.*, p. 39.

40. *Ibid.*, pp. 38–39.

41. Usher Parsons to Abiel Holmes, January 1, 1823, private collection of Dr. Lawrence D. Longo, Loma Linda, California.

42. Mary H. Parsons to Mrs. Abiel Holmes, January 8, 1823, HUCC.

43. Mary H. Parsons to Mrs. Abiel Holmes, January 23, 1823, HUCC.

44. Mary H. Parsons to Rev. and Mrs. Abiel Holmes, March 2, 1823, HUCC.

45. Mary H. Parsons to Mrs. Abiel Holmes, March 23, 1823, HUCC.

46. *Natural Theology; or Evidences of the Existence and Attributes of the Deity* by William Paley (1743–1805), the English theologian, was a very popular work at that time. It was first published in 1802.

47. Mary H. Parsons to Rev. and Mrs. Abiel Holmes, March 2, 1823, HUCC.

48. Abiel Holmes to Usher Parsons, April 7, 1823, DPC.

49. "Minutes" of the Rhode Island Historical Society, Providence.

50. Usher Parsons's service record, WRDNA.

51. Mary H. Parsons to Mrs. Abiel Holmes, April 13, 1823, HUCC. Clark Collection.

52. Mary H. Parsons to Mrs. Abiel Holmes, May 9, 1823, HUCC.

53. *Rhode Island American and General Advertiser*, May 13 and 27, 1823.

54. Members of the senior class, unhappy about commencement plans, had committed "violent excesses." Fifty were expelled, but rumors of cancellation of the commencement were denied.

55. Amelia Leavitt to Mary H. Parsons, May 11, 1823, HUCC.

56. Mary H. Parsons to Amelia Leavitt, May 16, 1823, typed copy, DPC.

57. C. W. Parsons *Memoir*, p. 37.

58. Brown University Medical Association. "Constitution, Bylaws, and Minutes," Brown University Archives.

59. C. W. Parsons *Memoir*, p. 27.

60. Usher Parsons, "Statistics of Large Surgical Operations," *American Journal of the Medical Sciences*, 15:359–365, April, 1848.

61. Charles W. Parsons, *The Medical School Formerly Existing in Brown University*, p. 34.

62. *Ibid.*, p. 35.

63. Mary H. Parsons to Charles Upham, undated, HUCC.

64. Mary H. Parsons to Ann Holmes, May 25, 1823, HUCC.

65. Rev. and Mrs. Abiel Holmes to Mary H. Parsons, July 3, 1823, Houghton Library, Harvard University.

66. The artist, Francis Alexander, a native of Killingly, Connecticut, near the Rhode Island border, was then twenty-three years of age. Years later, now a prominent portraitist and lithographer of Boston, he recalled that the first painted pictures he had ever seen were trade signs on a trip to Providence as a youth. While Alexander was working in Providence, the *R.I. American and General Advertiser* (May 16, 1823) observed: "The encouragement which this gentleman is receiving is no small evidence of the taste of our citizens. He is a pupil of Trumbull [more accurately he was a Trumbull copyist], and bids fair to arrive at eminence in his profession. There can be no surer criterion of the state of society in a country, than the estimation in which the arts are held; they invariably follow the march of civilization and refinement. It has been remarked that our country, though in its infancy, has given birth to several painters. The productions of West, Copley, Stuart, Trumbull, Allston, Malbone . . . , and others, have already convinced our brethren across the Atlantick, that Americans possess genius, and that too of the highest order"—a judgment which has stood the test of time.

67. Mary H. Parsons and Ann Holmes to Mrs. Abiel Holmes, July 17, 1823, HUCC.

68. *Ibid.* See also Ann Holmes to Mrs. Abiel Holmes, July 10, 1823; Ann Holmes to Mrs. Abiel Holmes, July 23, 1823; Mary H. Parsons to Mrs. Abiel Holmes, August 9, 1823, all in HUCC.

69. The *Manufacturers and Farmers Journal, and Providence and Pawtucket Advertiser* of July 21, 1823 reported the wedding, "At the Friends' Meetinghouse in Cranston (R.I.) on Thursday morning, Mr. William Jenkins to Miss Anne Almy, only daughter of William Almy." William Almy was the son-in-law and business associate of Moses Brown in the firm of Almy, Brown and Slater.

70. Mary H. Parsons to Mrs. Abiel Holmes, August 20, 1823, HUCC. For Erasmus Darwin's anticipation of evolutionary principles, see *The Columbia Encyclopedia*, 2nd Edition (New York, Columbia University Press, 1950).

71. Mary H. Parsons to Mrs. Abiel Holmes, August 25, 1823, HUCC.

72. Mary H. Parsons to Mrs. Abiel Holmes, August 31, 1823, HUCC.

73. Such events are detailed in letters Mary wrote to Mrs. Abiel Holmes on August 9, 1823, HUCC; to Amelia Leavitt on August 12, 1823, typed copy, DPC; and to Mrs. Abiel Holmes on August 28, 1823, HUCC.

74. Mary H. Parsons to Ann Holmes and Mrs. Abiel Holmes, September 1, 1823, HUCC.

75. *Ibid.*

76. *Ibid.*

77. Mary H. Parsons to Mrs. Abiel Holmes, August 23, 1823, HUCC.

78. Mary H. Parsons to Mrs. Abiel Holmes, August 28 (incorrectly dated August 29), 1823, HUCC.

79. Mary H. Parsons to Amelia Leavitt, August 24, 1823, HUCC.

80. *Ibid.* Mary's observations provide insights into the mores of Cambridge-style courtship at that time:

> I know the Cambridge style of love-affairs—a year . . . to get sufficiently familiar with a lady's appearance to speak to her. Another year to talk on [only] the weather & literary subjects. Another to hint the attachment. . . . Another . . . in the formal declaration—which is really a formidable business . . .—then two . . . in making up the engagement, & 6 additional ones in . . . courtship. . . . I love Cambridge as much as anybody, I suspect, but I do think they are unconscionably slow about marrying.

81. Mary H. Parsons to Mrs. Abiel Holmes, January 10, 1824, HUCC.

82. *Historical Catalogue of Brown University, 1764–1904* (Providence, Brown University, 1905), p. 136.

83. *Manufacturers and Farmers Journal, and Providence and Pawtucket Advertiser*, September 4, 1823.

84. "Minutes of the Corporation of Brown University," Brown University Archives.

CHAPTER NINE

Proud Father—Bereaved Spouse

On the very next day Mary Parsons's maternal expectations were fulfilled, a week or two earlier than she, or at least Usher, had reckoned. In the late afternoon or evening of September 6, 1823,[1] Mary gave birth to a son, their only child and Usher's sole heir. Many years later it was written of this signal event:[2]"The birth of this boy was hailed with joy by a wide circle of relatives and friends." On Sunday, September 22, General Leighton noted in his diary, "afternoon went to Father Parsons," no doubt to share with him the happy tidings.[3]

Mary was more than commonly exhausted by the rigors of her confinement and labor, and she required the better part of two months to recuperate due to her precarious health. During much of this period either Ann or her mother were in attendance.

On October 10, Mary wrote to her mother,[4] who had just returned to Cambridge:

I have only passed a few hours without you; yet . . . I must tell you how nicely I am. Dr. was away. . . . When he came in, I told him my wish . . . [to go] riding, and in a few minutes a good nice cosy hackney was at the door. Dr. went with me, took the nicest care of me—gave me some bark[5] before I went and was attentive to all the little particulars. . . . I rode more than a mile, bore it perfectly well—felt finely when I got home, tended baby a great deal & now feel very well & have not laid down yet. . . . I am afraid to write more now. . . .

Amidst these events, Usher found time to prepare a medical paper, which was published in the October issue of the *American Medical Recorder*. Titled "On the Use of Alcohol in the disease produced by the bite of the Rattlesnake," it reported three cases with survival. Although attributed to "William Mayrant, Esq. formerly Member of Congress", it was "Communicated by Professor Parsons."[6] This ancient cure is now discredited.

Late in October Usher brought Mary and the baby to Cambridge. They remained through the Thanksgiving and Christmas holidays. Usher was pleased that the visit proved beneficial to Mary's health.[7] She reported fully to Amelia in a letter of two installments, widely separated in time, "Baby was christened by Father yesterday. His name is Charles William after Mr. Upham & Dr.'s Father. He is very healthy and grows finely."[8]

By January 3, 1824 Mary and Charles were back home, for on that date Mary wrote to her mother: "I found everything most kindly ordered for my reception by my kind husband, who had ordered a nice fire in my chamber & the nurse ready to take the baby." What proved to be a chronic problem with domestic help, however, surfaced at an inopportune time: "I found next day that she was not the woman to suit me & immediately dismissed her. . . . She was a weak delicate thing who required more attention than I did myself." Mary was thankful for Annie Bell's assistance during this troublesome crisis. She thanked her father "a thousand times for his good letter to Doctor . . . most affectionate and delightful."[9]

A week later, Mary wrote to her mother[10] expressing concern over unpaid bills. Usher had paid off some of the debts "in the way of his practice partly [i.e. in kind] & partly by money." Usher was "so industrious" practicing and trying to collect unpaid bills that, despite his fondness for his thriving son, "he only plays with baby ten minutes or so." Mary added, gently: "If you can send me some money, I shall like it." She concluded: "Come and see me when you can. We shall not always live in this three storied inconvenient house."

The correspondence suggests that Usher and Mary were given financial help by her parents, possibly in the guise of a dowry. Despite Mary's brave reference to his busy practice, Usher seems to have had a hard time in these early years due, probably, to the difficulty of collecting his fees. A permanent home of his own proved to be an elusive goal. Later,[11] Mary expressed pleasure at acquiring a new nurse, "good, kind & tender—more particular than I should be." Despite an abundance of parties and balls, she spent most evenings at home, mending Usher's wardrobe ("almost in tatters"), while he read to her Gibbon's *Decline and Fall of the Roman Empire*. Usher himself was "more fond of home than I ever saw him before," but on a Sunday—while Mary stayed home minding Charlie—he attended a sermon on the Greek cause, to which he was especially devoted since his Mediterranean travels.

Charles was thriving. "Baby has grown very much since I came home," wrote Mary,[12] ". . . and Dr. spends many a half hour playing with him. He is at present hardy & I wish to keep him so." "Dr.," she added, "inoculated him and Annie this morning." Mary, presumably, was referring to smallpox vaccination, the only inoculation then in use. The strain used in Providence was descended by direct arm-to-arm transfer from virus matter used by the eminent Benjamin Waterhouse of Cambridge and sent to him in 1801 by the celebrated Edward Jenner himself, the British discoverer of vaccination with cowpox matter.[13]

Mary described[14] a cold supper party at which Usher entertained William Hunter of Newport and Charles Sigourney of Hartford. Hunter, former United States Senator, was a noted classical scholar, while Sigourney, also a man of culture, was the husband of poet and author, Lydia Sigourney. The affair "went off very well," Hunter's "brilliant & witty conversation" contributing to the success of the evening. As Mary reported, Usher further demonstrated his active interest in the Greek cause by serving as chairman of the executive committee of the local organization, and as a member of the arrangements committee, together with Zachariah Allen, Jr. and other prominent citizens, for a ball which raised $200, a respectable amount for the time. Another exciting event was the arrival in town of the "much admired" novelist, James Fenimore Cooper.

The first intimation of Usher's long-term interest in Thomas W. Dorr, then a youth of nineteen recently graduated from Harvard, appeared in a letter of introduction to Joseph Blunt,[15] a relative of Usher's living in New York. Usher asked for Blunt's assistance in securing for Dorr a place as a law student with Chancellor William Kent, Justice of the State Court of Chancery of New York. He lavishly praised Dorr as modest and gentlemanly, of excellent talents and principles, and among the very best scholars in his class at Cambridge. Dorr's family and connections, he assured, were "of the first respectability both in Providence & Boston."

In a letter to his father-in-law in January,[16] Usher apprised him of his current activities. The unusually mild winter had been especially conducive to good health, and there was less sickness in Providence than any townsfolk could remember. It gave Usher the opportunity to prepare many lectures in advance, which he would soon start delivering to a class of some fifty students, continuing twice daily for three months. Each student paid fifteen or twenty dollars. Usher was so busy with his academic duties and "reckoning with our employees, since we have been connected in business," that he had little time for the Greek cause, although his interest remained high and he hoped with his friends to raise five hundred or a thousand dollars for "that oppressed people." The nature of his "business connection" was obscure at this time, but would come to light later in a newspaper advertisement. Mary later wrote[18] that Doctor Wheaton had been absent for a few days, so that "Dr. has been running all the time." She had translated six pages of French text for him that day and had also copied in all some fifty or a hundred pages of English. That he used this material in his lectures is evident, but how is not clear. Mary in her spare time was reading *The Pilot* by James Fenimore Cooper and Conyers Middleton's *Life of Cicero*,[18] a gift from her father. Usher, characteristically, put his oar in: "Dr. says he has been at Archimedes' tomb which Cicero discovered by the sphere & cylinders upon it."

In February Usher received an intriguing letter from his old friend John Holmes of Alfred.[19] Maine had achieved statehood in 1820 by separation from Massachusetts, and Holmes was elected United States senator. Throughout his life Usher maintained a lively interest in politics, and it was a measure of his shrewdness that Holmes, a seasoned politician, sought his views on a delicate issue.

The Republicans (i.e. the Democrats) had held a caucus, boycotted by many members of the party, and nominated William Harris Crawford for the presidency and Albert Gallatin for the vice presidency, but the division of the party and the number of candidates, Holmes feared, would inevitably throw the election into the House of Representatives. "Write me," asked Holmes, "what is to be expected from [all] this." If Usher communicated his impressions to Holmes, they remain undiscovered. Holmes himself quite accurately predicted the eventual outcome. Crawford suffered a stroke during the campaign and finished third to Andrew Jackson and John Quincy Adams. Since none of the candidates received an Electoral College majority, the election was thrown into the House of Representatives. Henry Clay, who ran fourth, delivered his support to

Adams, ensuring Adams's election to the presidency and his own appointment as Secretary of State.

During the winter and spring several meetings of the Brown University Medical Association were held in which Usher took a very active part.[20] On February 21 he was appointed to a committee "to procure books for the association." The committee acquired "Hunter on the Blood, Paris' Pharmacologia, Bartlett's Synopsis, Heberden's Commentaries, and Bell's Anatomy," all for the sum of $19.12-½. On March 5 the society accepted with thanks some two dozen mineral specimens, ten of which had been donated by Professor Parsons, and a copy of the *Sailor's Physician*, donated by the author. On March 13 "the room offered by Professor Parsons for a place of deposit of all donations of the association & their library" was accepted "for which the Society tendered their thanks." The Association met again on April 10 "at the usual time & place—Dr. Parsons in the chair." The discussions for the day were on burns and on the cause of animal heat. Usher's comments[21] on the latter subject were not too far from the mark:

> The President agreed substantially in the theory of respiration being the source of heat. . . . The heat of inflammation (he observed) might be explained by an increased flow of blood to the part affected—as might the heat of fever. The heat during digestion might (he said) be owing to the blood being first concentrated in the digestive organs and then sent back with increased violence to the surface [also, of course, to the specific dynamic effect of protein.]

At a later meeting on February 19, 1825,[22] it was concluded quite correctly that animal heat was "produced by a chemical process"; respired oxygen of course is essential to the process. Surface heat, Usher also had correctly reasoned, is proportionate to the local blood flow. At the meeting of April 1824 it was voted to present "Alexander Ramsay, M.D. of Edinburgh, now resident in New Hampshire, a distinguished teacher of Anatomy . . . with an honorary diploma from this association." Usher's old friend and teacher died in obscurity not long thereafter on November 24, 1824, in Parsonsfield, Maine.

The family correspondence rambled on,[23] revealing a lively and intimate picture of the little domestic circle. Mary reported to her mother that baby was "playful and amusing" and giving them all great joy. She was having chronic servant problems, but Annie Bell Leighton was a great help minding Charlie and "learning how to do everything in the kitchen." Her last maid had left the kitchen in execrable order and a "fortnight's washing untouched." Her present girl was fine so far—"she is *white*," and she was "determined not to have any more blacks—they are such creatures here." A gala Washington's birthday celebration—with cannon, guns, flags, processions, an oration, an ode (no less!), and a ball in the evening— would glorify the Greek cause, killing two birds with one shot. Mary, at long last, thought she would attend: "Dr. says it is well to go to one, & I think it is—not to forget how to behave in a ball." Two Boston boys, she reported, John Dix Fisher and Jeremiah Fisher Ames, recent Brown graduates and students of Usher's, had been visitors. Both in due course received their medical degrees at Harvard. Fisher, founder of the Perkins Institute for the Blind and a visiting physician at the Massachusetts General Hospital,[24] later recalled his visits to the Parsons home with great pleasure.[25]

Usher had been carrying on a running correspondence with Samuel Eddy, Democratic Congressman from Rhode Island (he later became Chief Justice of the Rhode Island Supreme Court). Eddy, in a salty letter from Washington,[26] commented that he was glad to hear that wealthy widower Ebenezer Knight Dexter (the "Marshall," he called him) was recovering from a recent illness under Usher's care. "What would become of all his money, poor man," he wondered, "were he to die without issue? I hope he will take to himself some damsel, not too old." (Dexter died some months later, and his money ultimately funded the erection of an almshouse in Providence, which would be known as the Dexter Asylum.)[27] He was much obliged to Usher for mentioning the Marshall, as otherwise he would have been puzzled to receive a letter without a single mention of either "the tariff or the caucus," two burning issues— the protective tariff particularly vital in industrial New England, and the presidential caucus discredited in the recent election.

During April Mary wrote to her mother that "Dr. has had a good deal of surgical practice lately & is this afternoon visiting one of his patients in Pawtuxet [about five miles south of Providence]." "Last night," she continued, "he left his bed to go to an accouchement & I never knew it till he told me this morning." Usher was looking for a new home and hoped they might be able to move by the following October.[28]

Later that month Usher traveled to Alfred, one purpose being to find a country girl for a maid—Mary having by this time fired five.[29] On the return trip he stopped at Cambridge to pick up Ann and Mary Hedge, daughter of Harvard philosophy professor Levi Hedge.[30] Arriving on May 6, Ann Holmes reported[31] a safe and pleasant ride. Mary, the doctor, and Anna Bell Leighton were all quite well and in fine spirits. "As for Charley boy," she wrote, "he is decidedly the most beautiful baby that I ever saw, & the sweetest little being in the world. He sits up at table beautifully secured by a handkerchief, & *eats & drinks* to perfection!" The next evening doctor, Mary Hedge, Anna, and Ann had a merry time dancing a figure-of-eight reel, while Mary played a "hopping tune" on her beloved piano. The next day the girls "sallied forth & shopped." "It is really 'mazing," reported Ann,[32] "how money taketh wings!" Perhaps her folks could send along a little extra folding money, as Mr. Russell's shop had some sparkling new merchandise from New York. Incidentally, she reported, "Doctor brought a good woman, Mrs. Ham, from Alfred"—a widow with "two children *up country*." Mary added: "I am sorry & perhaps afraid you will not like my sending back a 10$ bill which is a counterfeit. Counterfeit money was never so plenty this way."

They learned later that Father Holmes had recovered his ten dollars. Usher too had been caught off guard by a "very sharp old lady," but he also had retrieved his money. "Dr.," Mary wrote, "is a very good manager with these sharpers—I wish now and then Father would cut ... up ... such characters." Whereupon she revealed an important new development in Usher's professional career:[33]

> Dr. [i.e. Usher] & Dr. Wheaton are *amicably* thinking of dissolving. It is for their mutual interest. Dr. W's health is returning which renders it inexpedient for him to retain Dr. & Dr. W. has many political enemies, whom my Dr. would make friends in case of dissolving. They are good friends still. But Dr. will, I fancy, manage better for himself now. Do not say anything about this. . . .

Ann and Mary Hedge returned to Cambridge by stagecoach on May 25.[34] Arriving in their place was nephew Joseph Usher Parsons, fourteen-year-old son of brother Joseph and Charlotte Parsons of Francesville, Maine. Young "Usher," leading an "unsteady life" for the past three years (most likely at sea), had not been seen by his parents for some time. While he matriculated at Brown University, he did not graduate. During June Mrs. Holmes also made a short visit to Providence, traveling the whole distance by chaise.[35] Later Mary informed her[36] that "Dr. dissolved partnership about a fortnight since, most amicably, with Dr. W—& most advantageously for both. I have just now returned from Mrs. Wheaton. She was pleasant as ever."

Usher was acquiring a taste for local history, which grew with the years. On June 19, 1824 he wrote[37] to Walter R. Danforth, newspaper publisher and Cabinet Keeper of the recently organized Rhode Island Historical Society:

In the Rhode Island Register for 1823, published by yourself, I find in . . . a sketch of the history of this state, mention . . . of the word "*watcheer*" as being an Indian word for addressing people, and answering to '*how d'ye do*', and I have heard several persons give the same opinion of its origin. But in this I apprehend there is a mistake, for the word in question *watcheer*, or more properly *what-cheer* is English, and is contained in some of our old English Dictionaries, and defined "how d'ye do." It would seem then that the Indians who received Roger Williams and others at the what-cheer rock, on their arrival from Seekonk, attempted to address them in English, and not in Indian, with the word what cheer, or how d'ye do, which they had previously learned from the English. Roger Williams in his Key to the Narragansett language . . . speaking of the word, *netop*, an Indian word for friend or crony, says that "*What cheer netop* is the general salutation of all English towards the Indians." The expression doubtless arose in English from, "What have you to cheer you" or "how cheerful are you?"

If you agree with me . . . that there is some mistake . . . in regard to the origin and consequent orthography of this word or expression, you are at liberty to make this communication known to your Society which I understand meets this day [it actually met on July 19].

Either Usher had dated his letter incorrectly or was mistaken as to the date of the meeting of the Society. The "communication from Dr. Usher Parsons relative to the meaning of 'What Cheer'" was received and placed "on file." At the annual meeting in 1825 Usher was elected to membership together with Robert H. Ives, Nicholas

Brown, Jr., John Carter Brown, and Dr. Solomon Drowne, a distinguished group.[38]

The Boston Medical Intelligencer for July 13, 1824 reported:

> We had the pleasure of being very politely invited into Professor Parsons' lecture room (while on a visit to Providence last winter) and we must do him the justice to say that his Italian models of anatomy are done in superior style.
>
> A stranger would at first suppose the Professor of Anatomy a dull, inelegant teacher, who dealt altogether in dry realities; but, on subsequent observation, he could not but admire his increasing labour to benefit the class, by his anatomical knowledge, as well as practical experience. There is a kind of sprightliness required in a public teacher and if he neglects, or physically wants it, his hearers will most certainly fall below zero, and all his efforts will fail of exciting anything like a warm admiration of his talents or learning. . . .

Did Professor Parsons lack this sprightliness? The observer chose not to comment, but reminiscences of another contemporary, theologian Edward Amasa Park, add insight:

> I remember very well the impression made by the advent of Dr. Usher Parsons to the Professorship of Anatomy in Brown University. The fact of his having been a surgeon in the United States navy, and at the battle of Lake Erie, gave him great *éclat* as he assumed the Professorship. I heard him deliver two lectures. He read them from his manuscript. His manner was not animated. I was only fifteen years of age when I heard him, and could not understand him, for he was speaking to post-graduates.[39]

The *Intelligencer* of August 10 carried a curious little item bearing on another of Usher's activities: "Dr. Usher Parsons, Professor of Surgery at Brown University has recently established an infirmary in Providence for diseases of the eye." No other information about this obscure enterprise has come to light.

As the summer advanced, Mary was planning a visit to Cambridge.[40] Usher, meanwhile, engaged in correspondence which led to a sustained and zealous interest in his genealogy. On August 11 he received a long letter from his cousin Sarah Parsons Pitkin of East Hartford, Connecticut,[41] to whom he had sent information regarding mutual Parsons ancestors. She thanked him for his "very valuable letter" and continued: "I have been wishing to obtain a copy of the inscription on the gravestone of our oldest ancestor [i.e. Cornet Joseph Parsons]. . . . I thank you [meanwhile] for sending me the inscription on our great grandfather's tombstone. . . ." She had been told that "our grandfather" (i.e. the Reverend Joseph Parsons of Bradford, Massachusetts, Harvard 1720) was highly regarded by his contemporaries and "when he preached in Boston the house would be filled to overflowing." After disposing of three generations of Parsons antecedents, she turned to Mary's:

> You will permit me at this time to congratulate you on the connexion you have formed. Hope it will be prosperous and happy. Hope I shall have the pleasure of becoming acquainted with your lady, and may I not say I feel in the happiness of you both quite interested. Was your wife a descendent of Judge Wendell of Boston? [Correct.] If so I was acquainted with her grandmother, & also with her mother when she was very young. . . .

Sarah concluded on this wistful note: "I have traced on my mother's side my ancestors Mather [her mother was a granddaughter of Cotton Mather] & Williams back as far as 556 [!]. I wish I could do so by the Parsons's. . . ."

Mary planned to spend most of August in Cambridge with Charlie, remaining through the Harvard Commencement on August 25. The Commencement, Mary learned from her Cambridge friend Elizabeth McKean,[42] would be a brilliant one. The Phi Beta Kappa exercises featuring poet James Gates Percival and orator Edward Everett would be the best ever. While Mary was in Cambridge, Ariana Smith wrote that she would be unable to visit the Parsonses during Brown Commencement week. Mary expressed disappointment[43] that they would miss the gay times together. She had recently been quite ill, but was "now allowed to go out considerably & feel all the spirits of Mary Holmes." "I deferred answering [your letters]," she added, ". . . till I should reach here & then was too ill to think of writing [even to] my dear *doctor* for a week or ten days; & . . . he . . . was entitled to the first letter. All I shall say of my husband, after being married two years, is that my wish . . . is that you may have as superlatively kind & good a companion. . . ." The Reverend Holmes and Ann had driven to Providence on their way to New Haven and planned to participate in the colorful festivities attending the Brown Commencement.

As the time drew near, an air of excitement pervaded the town, which was filled with visitors, and the doctor's house was close to the very center of activity. On the eve of Commencement Day, the College Edifice, recently renamed University Hall, was brightly illuminated with tallow candles. The whole town gathered to witness the colorful ceremony.

The Holmes and Parsons families surely were in the throng. On Wednesday morning Usher marched in the academic procession that formed in front of University Hall at ten o'clock, dressed in his academic cap and gown decorated with the colors appropriate to his degree in medicine from Harvard. The marchers, some with gowns and some without, "arranged according to rank, wealth, and condition," ostentatiously paraded down the hill to the strains of martial music, led by the High Sheriff of Providence County wearing his top hat and sword, and the First Light Infantry in dress uniform, Captain Rathbone commanding. They entered the Baptist Meeting House ("built for the publick worship of Almighty God, and also for holding Commencement in"), where the Commencement was initiated by "an appropriate prayer by the Rev. President Messer."[44] That afternoon Mary entertained her family and guests at tea.[45]

In September, Judge Lyman invited Usher to a private dinner of the Society of the Cincinnati, an organization of Revolutionary War officers, several of the veterans (including the judge himself) being on hand. Usher enjoyed himself immensely, flattered by the invitation and by mention of his Lake Erie exploits.[46] During October[47] and November[48] Usher himself entertained at home with a pair of supper parties, welcoming to each a dozen or so of the first gentlemen of Providence, bearing such familiar Rhode Island names as Goddard, Whipple, Hoppin, and Dyer. Mary labored hard to make the little affairs enjoyable, although in the midst of recurrent servant problems ("I had to fly 'round pretty briskly—particularly as my nurse . . . took this opportunity . . . to walk off!"). In the medical realm, Usher received a gift from William Clift of London of "two beautifully printed medical affairs," as Mary described them, "short accounts of cases." And then, Anna Bell Leighton had returned to her folks in Maine in September, having spent a year in Providence.

As the season progressed, Ann begged Mary to come to Cambridge for Thanksgiving[49] and stay for the ordination of her fiancé, Charles W. Upham, as associate pastor of the First Church (Unitarian) of Salem. Usher, Mary, and Charles made the trip to Cambridge in

Usher's chaise. They spent Thanksgiving with the Holmes brood in the gambrel-roofed house, but they returned to Providence on Saturday, December 4 before the ordination occurred.[50]

On Christmas Day Mary wrote to her mother: "We have been making enquiries for a better house—but there is no prospect of getting one any better than this ... till next July at least. So we must stay."[51] She suggested to her father some recent publications that might be useful sources for his second edition of his *Annals of America,* surely surmising that he would make flattering reference to Usher (as indeed he did) and borrow freely from Usher's accounts of the great battle.

Early in the New Year Mary reported to Cambridge that Usher had gone to Attleboro, Massachusetts on a surgical case, had bought a "nice" cow, and had prospects of acquiring Doctor Wheaton's house in the summer or autumn. It was a most desirable place for them on many accounts, and the landlord, Nicholas Brown, would be willing to paint and repair it beforehand. Usher currently had several students to help him in his practice and to provide extra income. Doctor, she added, was now taking the *Review* "& I find it delightful."[52]

On the 17th of January, her twenty-third birthday, Mary noted in a letter to Ann[53] the following venture of Usher's: "Dr. I hope will do very well in his medicine manufacture. It will be useful to him in a variety of ways—particularly in not obliging him to buy medicines & in showing his students the different processes." It was common in an earlier period for doctors to prepare their own medicines, but now, especially in the cities, the practice was giving way to apothecaries. "He is coming on too in his practice, slowly, but surely," she added, "—had a new family & a very good one added to-day to his lists." Usher was very busy, giving two lectures a day and spending the rest of the time in the laboratory. His practice had recently taken him to North Providence, Smithfield, and Pawtucket, and to Seekonk in Massachusetts.

Still another venture of Usher's, "Doctor's vitriolic scheme," as Mary termed it, was coming on bravely. "It is the first of the kind in Providence," Mary wrote, "& he says there is enough Vitriol wanted in Providence to give constant employment to one & perhaps two such establishments. At present they import all their Vitriol & are much pleased with the opportunity of saving importation. The machinery, or rather construction of the rooms is quite interesting." Blue vitriol (copper sulphate) was of considerable importance in the dyeing and calico-printing processes, so vital to Rhode Island's rapidly expanding textile industry. "Doctor," Mary concluded, "has the offer of two more private students. He has four now, & his practice is gradually extending itself." Usher's curious flyer in business was reported in the local press. The *Rhode Island American* of March 1 carried the following item:

> *New Establishment.* Doctor Usher Parsons, associated with several capitalists, has recently established at the north end of this town a laboratory for the manufacture on an extensive scale of such gases and acids as are generally required for the use of a manufacturing community. The scientific attachments of Dr. P. amply qualify him for discharging in an efficient manner the duties devolving on the superintendant of this establishment.

The fate of this interesting venture is obscure.

Lectures, other duties at the Medical School, and his private students occupied much of Usher's time. After a lapse of several months the Brown University Medical Association met on February 19, 1825. Further meetings were held on March 21 and 28 with Usher presiding.[54] The debate then was on the proposition, "In which country France or England has the Medical Science attained the highest degree of eminence?" The minutes note, "Question decided in favor of the French. During the discussion in which Professor Parsons participated much historical learning & many ingenious observations were made by the disputants." The society hopefully "adjourned to the first Saturday Eve. in the next course;" but fate decreed that it would never meet again.

The *Boston Medical Intelligencer* continued to carry correspondence concerning the Medical School. On April 12 a correspondent, styling himself "The Compiler," described the school as "susceptible of much improvement," although on the whole better than it had been. The course in Anatomy, Surgery and Physiology, however, had "merit, character, and *force.*" On May 3 "Amici Veritatis" replied:

> Respecting the lectures, we can say the present course here has been perfectly satisfactory; and, so far as we are capable of judging, the professors are men of the first respectability in point of character and talent, and eminently qualified to fill their respective stations. Relative to the professor of anatomy and surgery . . . ,

we . . . confidently assert that his lectures have given the utmost satisfaction.

As Mary and Usher continued to participate merrily in the rounds of gay parties, Mary, daughter of a Calvinist minister, felt twinges of conscience for indulging herself. The existence of so much misery and want aroused conflicting emotions which she confided to her mother:[55] "I do not think the assembly gave me any more pleasure (much as . . . I love a pleasant dance . . .) than . . . being able to-day to send some coal & milk & wood & bread to a destitute widow close by us."

Usher was planning to go to New York on business for a few days on March 20, and Mary was looking forward to accompanying him. He had generously offered to have Ann "join our small party," and Mary thought it would be pleasant for both her sister and herself to be together once more before Ann Holmes became Ann Upham. "Write me about your sentiments upon my plan," wrote Mary, "or rather my kind husband's, for he makes all the plans for the family." They would go by way of Newport and return through Connecticut. Mary was uncertain when they could move from Cheapside, so that she might "board out in some countryhouse most of the warm weather."[56]

Ann arrived on March 17, carrying newsy letters form Cambridge. However, she decided not to join Mary and Usher on the trip, but rather would stay at home with nephew Charlie. She reported to her mother:[57] "Doctor & Mary expect to go in a day or two, & will get home probably the end of next week. . . . Two very good girls are here, & I think with *my superintendance* the family will do finely! Doctor's laboratory comes on grandly."

Usher and Mary left Providence for New York about March 25 and returned on April 1, apparently visiting Philadelphia in addition to New York. If indeed they went by way of Newport, they would have continued to New York by overnight steamer. Completion of the long journey in eight days was thus quite feasible. Ann promptly returned to Cambridge, having accomplished her mission of caring for Charles. She was anxious, no doubt, to rejoin her own Charles.

The Parsons family, obliged to vacate its home in Cheapside about May 1, took furnished lodgings, being unable to buy or rent a suitable place in time. There is no mention of the location or nature of their new residence, but the change must have been disappointing to Mary after a pleasant year in her own attractive, willow-shaded home. She was careful, however, not to betray any disappointment to her family. Besides, she planned to spend the summer on a farm in the country after a visit to Cambridge. Mary had at first considered not having Charles with her in Cambridge. She had hesitated, she wrote, to separate Charlie from his doting father and had thought, but only for a moment, that it might relieve her of his care during the visit. However, her family would not hear of Mary visiting Cambridge without him.[58]

Around the 21st of May Usher and Mary drove to Cambridge in the chaise with their precious Charlie between them. As they set out on their journey, Mary appeared to be in excellent health and spirits, anticipating an extended visit with her family. There is good reason to believe that she was happily expecting another baby. Athough she was greatly fatigued by the journey, Usher was not sufficiently alarmed to postpone his brief visit to Alfred. General Leighton noted in his diary that Usher set out for his return to Providence on the 24th of May.[59]

Unexpectedly, on June 15, 1825 the following notice appeared in the *Boston Centinel*:

> Died. In Cambridge yesterday morning, after a short illness, Mrs. Mary Jackson Parsons, wife of Dr. Usher P. of Providence, and oldest daughter of Rev. Dr. Holmes, aged 23. The funeral will be at her father's house tomorrow [Thursday] at 4 o'clock P.M. Relations and friends invited to attend.

Harvard tutor George Otis, one of Mary's many former admirers, wrote in his diary: "Attended the funeral of Mrs. Parsons. M. H. was after all an enchanting vision; connected in my memory with everything sparkling and joyous."[60] Mary was buried in the family plot in Cambridge, next to her little sister Sarah Lathrop Holmes, who had died thirteen years before at the age of seven.

We know very little of Mary's final illness. Years later Ann made a notation on a letter which Mary had sent to her mother on April 2, 1825:[61] "Mary went to New York & Philadelphia—home to Providence and rested a week or two, & then came on in chaise with Dr. & Charlie between them to Cambridge. In May—too much fatigue brot on—from which for a while she seemed to have recovered—then violent headache set in—the convulsions & on the 13th [sic] June she died at her father's house." Ann's recollection of the clinical manifestations of the illness is significant. Whether it was primarily cardiac, renal, or pulmonary—or a pre-eclampsia associated with pregnancy— is speculative. That Mary's health had long been a matter of concern is abundantly clear.

There is no positive indication that Usher was present at the burial, but it appears most likely that he was. The obituaries that appeared in the Providence and Boston newspapers were lavish in their praise of Mary's charm and culture, and George Otis wrote a lyric recollection in his diary. But not a line is written of Usher's reaction to his crushing loss. Left alone with an infant son, it is inevitable that he was devastated and lonely. As a bereaved widower with a growing medical practice, the problems of raising a child were almost insurmountable.

Arrangements were made for little Charles to live in Cambridge with his elderly grandparents, and he spent most of his boyhood and youth in this warm and cultured atmosphere, virtually a younger brother to his bright and sprightly Uncle Wendell. Usher moved to the boarding house of Samuel McClellan at 75 Benefit Street, where he lived for the next six years.[62]

NOTES

1. On the letter which Mary sent to her mother on August 31, 1823, cited in footnote 72 of the preceding chapter, Ann Holmes Upham many years later wrote: "C. W. Parsons was born 6th Septr./23, Saturday afternoon or evening."

2. Perry Amos, "Charles Parsons," *New England Historical and Genealogical Register*, 48:475, 1894.

3. "Diary of Gen. Samuel Leighton, 1818–1848."

4. Mary H. Parsons to Mrs. Abiel Holmes, October 10, 1823, private collection of Dr. Lawrence D. Longo, Loma Linda, California.

5. The "bark," cinchona, which contains quinine, was probably given to Mary as a tonic or less probably as a specific against a fever. For the medical uses of the drug at that time see James Thacher's *American New Dispensatory*, 4th ed. (Boston, T. B. Wait, 1821), pp. 176–184.

6. Mayrant, William, "On the Use of Alcohol in the Disease Produced by the Bite of the Rattlesnake, Communicated by Professor Parsons," *American Medical Recorder*, 6:619–621, October, 1823.

7. Mrs. Jasper Adams (signed "P. Adams") to Mary H. Parsons, November 1, 1823, HUCC. Mrs. Adams, wife of Prof. Adams of Brown University, wrote: "I am much pleased ... to learn from the Doctor that your health is much improved by your visit to Cambridge."

8. Mary H. Parsons to Amelia Leavitt, November 30 and December 22, 1823 (dated at Cambridge), typed copy, DPC.

9. Mary H. Parsons to Mrs. Abiel Holmes, January 3, 1824, private collection of Dr. Lawrence D. Longo, Loma Linda, California.

10. Mary H. Parsons to Mrs. Abiel Holmes, January 10, 1824, HUCC.

11. Mary H. Parsons to Mrs. Abiel Holmes, January 17 and 18, 1824, HUCC.

12. Mary H. Parsons to Rev. and Mrs. Abiel Holmes, January 24, 1824, HUCC.

13. James H. Cassedy, *Charles V. Chapin and the Public Health Movement* (Cambridge, Harvard University Press, 1962), p. 64.

14. Mary H. Parsons to Rev. and Mrs. Abiel Holmes, January 24, 1824, HUCC.

15. Usher Parsons to Joseph Blunt, January 25, 1824, DPC.

16. Usher Parsons, Mary H. Parsons and Mrs. Abiel Holmes to Abiel Holmes, January 26, 1824, HUCC. In this letter Mary mentions in casual gossip "a Mr. Mann," boarding nearby. This was Horace Mann (1796–1859), Brown A.B. 1819, then a Brown tutor and librarian, later lawyer and famed educator.

17. Mary H. Parsons to Mrs. Abiel Holmes, February 5, 1824, HUCC.

18. James Fenimore Cooper's novel *The Pilot* was published in 1823, and Conyers Middleton's (1683–1750) *Life of Cicero* in 1741.

19. John Holmes to Usher Parsons, February 16, 1824, The Charles Roberts Autograph Collection, Haverford College Library.

20. Brown University Medical Association. "Constitution, Bylaws, and Minutes," Brown University Archives.

21. *Ibid.* Antoine Laurent Lavoisier (1743–1794), French chemist and physicist, explained the role of oxygen in human respiration and in the combustion of ingested food in papers published in 1777 ("Expériences de la Respiration des Animaux") and 1793 ("Prémier Mémoirs sur la Respiration des Animaux").

22. *Ibid.*

23. Mary H. Parsons to Mrs. Abiel Holmes, undated, but c. February 10, 1824, HUCC; Mary H. Parsons to Mrs. Abiel Holmes, February 19–20, 1824, HUCC.

24. John Dix Fisher (1797–1850), Brown A.B. 1820 and Harvard M.D. 1825, in 1829 wrote a treatise on vaccination. Jeremiah Fisher Ames (1802–1829) received A.B. and A.M. degrees from Brown in 1822 and an M.D. from both Brown and the Harvard Medical School in 1827.

25. John Dix Fisher to Usher Parsons, September 10, 1825, HUCC.

26. Samuel Eddy to Usher Parsons, March 8, 1824, DPC.

27. The improvement in the infirmaties of "Marshall" Ebenezer Knight Dexter proved transient, and he died childless on August 10, 1824 in his fifty-second year. Early in life he had accumulated a handsome

fortune in "mercantile pursuits" and was for many years United States Marshall for the District of Rhode Island. How he handled the "painful task" of disposing of his substantial estate is revealed in the *Rhode Island American* of August 20, 1824:

> The forty acre farm in Providence neck, a part of his liberal bequest [along with other holdings], is given [to the town] on the condition that the town shall erect thereon, within five years an almshouse, which is to be enclosed with an extensive and permanent wall within twenty years, and we hope ere long to see a Dexter Asylum rearing its walls in these pleasant and productive fields.

On November 22 the Freemen in town meeting voted to accept the "princely" gift and directed that it be known henceforth as the Dexter Donation. A building committee was appointed, and the Dexter Asylum was completed in 1830 at a cost of $43,000. The building was taken down in 1960 after acquisition of the property by Brown University. The massive wall still stands.

28. Mary H. Parsons to Mrs. Abiel Holmes, April 21, 1824, HUCC.

29. *Ibid.* Also, Ann Holmes to Mary H. Parsons, April 13, 1824; Mary H. Parsons to Mrs. Abiel Holmes, April 17, 1824; and Mary H. Parsons to Mrs. Abiel Holmes, April 28–29, 1824, all in HUCC.

30. Levi Hedge (1762–1844) was Professor of Logic and Metaphysics at Harvard University, and later Alfred Professor of Natural Religion, Moral Philosophy and Civil Polity. Mary's brother, Frederic Henry Hedge, later became a professor at the Harvard Divinity School.

31. Ann Holmes to Mrs. Abiel Holmes, May 7, 1824, HUCC.

32. Ann Holmes and Mary H. Parsons to Mrs. Abiel Holmes, May 10, 1824, HUCC.

33. Mary H. Parsons to Mrs. Abiel Holmes, May 20, 1824, HUCC.

34. Ann Holmes and Mrs. Abiel Holmes to Mary H. Parsons, May 26, 1824, HUCC.

35. *Ibid.*

36. Mary H. Parsons to Mrs. Abiel Holmes, July 11, 1824, HUCC.

37. Usher Parsons to Walter R. Danforth, June 19, 1824, RIHS.

38. Rhode Island Historical Society, "Minutes."

39. Charles W. Parsons, *The Medical School Formerly Existing in Brown University*, p. 32.

40. Mary H. Parsons to Mrs. Abiel Holmes, July 17, 1824, HUCC.

41. Sarah Pitkin to Usher Parsons, August 11, 1824, HUCC.

42. Amy Elizabeth McKean to Mary H. Parsons, July 20, 1824, HUCC. She was the daughter of the late Rev. Joseph McKean (1776–1818), Boylston Professor of Rhetoric and Oratory at Harvard College. She later married Joseph Worcester, a lexicographer. The McKean home many years later became "Fay House," now a part of Radcliffe College.

43. Mary H. Parsons to Ariana Smith, August 22, 1824, HUCC.

44. *The Rhode Island American*, September 9, 1825.

45. Among the guests was George Otis, who later accompanied Ann and the Rev. Abiel Holmes to New Haven for the Yale Commencement. Diary of George Otis (1824–1825). Microfilm in Harvard College Archives (code no. HUG 1660) of the original Ms. in the Library of Congress. George Otis (b. 1797), later an Episcopal clergyman of Cambridge, Massachusetts, was the son of U.S. Senator Harrison Gray Otis (1765–1849) of Massachusetts.

46. Mary H. Parsons to Mrs. Abiel Holmes, September 4, 1824, HUCC.

47. Mary H. Holmes to Mrs. Abiel Holmes, October 10, 1824, HUCC.

48. Mary H. Parsons to Rev. and Mrs. Abiel Holmes, November 3 (incorrectly dated October 3), 1824, HUCC.

49. Ann Holmes to Mary H. Parsons, November 25, 1824, Houghton Library, Harvard University.

50. Mary H. Parsons to Mrs. Abiel Holmes, December 6–7, 1824, HUCC.

51. Mary H. Parsons to Rev. and Mrs. Abiel Holmes, December 25, 1824, HUCC.

52. Mary H. Parsons to Rev. and Mrs. Abiel Holmes, January 1, 4, and 5, 1825, HUCC.

53. Mary H. Parsons to Ann Holmes, January 17, 1825, HUCC.

54. Brown University Medical Association. "Constitution, Bylaws, and Minutes," Brown University Archives.

55. Mary H. Parsons to Mrs. Abiel Holmes, January 23, 1825, HUCC.

56. Mary H. Parsons to Ann Holmes, March 4 and 6, 1825, HUCC.

57. Ann Holmes to Mrs. Abiel Holmes, March 24, 1825, HUCC.

58. Mary H. Parsons to Mrs. Abiel Holmes, May 11, 1825, HUCC.

59. "Diary of Gen. Samuel Leighton, 1818–1848."

60. Diary of George Otis. See note 45. When sitting for a portrait being painted by Edwin T. Billings in 1889, Oliver Wendell Holmes discussed with the artist's wife Mary's tragic death sixty-four years earlier. Mrs. Billings reported some of the conversation she had with Dr. Holmes during these sittings. In one of them, she related, "he reverted often to his early life—told of a sister who had died when he was a very young man. They had been very dear to each other; and Dr. Holmes said the best in him, the most he had reached, was owing to her." Mrs. Billings's rememberance, and the rememberances of others of Holmes at the time the Billings's portrait was presented to the Boston Medical Library Association in 1894, were printed in the *Boston Medical and Surgical Journal*, 131:584–590, December 13, 1894.

61. This is in HUCC.

62. C. W. Parsons *Memoir*, p. 26.

CHAPTER TEN

Medical School Dissolves

In the aftermath of Mary's untimely and unforeseen death, Usher resumed his practice and his teaching career at Brown. A glimpse into one aspect of his practice is afforded by an article he published in *The New England Journal of Medicine and Surgery* for October 1826, which dealt with the use of galvanism in the treatment of a case of epilepsy.[1] This was accomplished by the application of a zinc plate to a factitious sore on the neck joined by copper wires to a silver plate applied at the knee. In a male of 25 years "not a single paroxysm of epilepsy . . . occurred from the day of the application to the present time, being more than two years," and the patient was able to discontinue the apparatus after six months. He theorized that the "animal electric matter" which motivated the muscles had accumulated in the brain in too great quantity and could thus be drawn off. He concluded, "Of this theory I offer no opinion; but in the efficacy of the remedy I feel the greatest confidence, . . . and recommend it to the profession for further trial." While the theory is primitive in concept, it anticipates discovery of the electrical activity of brain and muscle.

Usher's academic activities at Brown were not confined to his medical school lectures; he gave a course in anatomy for upper classmen of the college as well. The *Manufacturers & Farmers Journal* of Providence reported in its October 5, 1826 issue: "Professor Parsons has just commenced his popular course of Lectures on Anatomy, Physiology and Natural Theology; and it deserves to be mentioned, as an honorable indication of zeal in the acquisition of useful science, that these Lectures are attended by nearly all the upper classes, for whose benefit they are especially designed."

In connection with his undergraduate course, Usher prepared an essay titled *The Importance of the Sciences of Anatomy and Physiology as a Branch of General Education; being an Introduction to a Course of Lectures to the Upper Classes in Brown University.*[2] His progressive views have validity in the twentieth century: "In commencing a course of public lectures, it has been customary to offer some remarks on the nature and importance of the science to be lectured upon; and in treating of anatomy and physiology, such remarks have usually been confined to the consideration of the value of these sciences to the practitioner of physick and surgery. I shall deviate from this course, on the present occasion, by indicating some of the advantages of anatomy and physiology, as a branch of general education." This conformed to the progressive spirit engendered at Brown, where Benjamin Waterhouse, appointed Professor of Natural History in 1784, had delivered a systematic course of lectures on natural history as early as 1786 and 1787, which, he claimed, were the first to have been offered anywhere in America (two years before they were commenced at Cambridge).

Usher seized the opportunity provided by the lectures to speak out on two subjects about which he had strong feelings: the "natural bone setters" and negro slavery. Regarding the bonesetters, he ridiculed the supposedly hereditary powers of these quacks who perpetuated "as great a burlesque on common sense as it is on the healing art." As for slavery, Usher, fully thirty-five years before the Civil War, applied anthropological arguments to attack slavery advocates, who, he asserted, used the "peculiarity of features and complexion" of suffering Africans to vindicate the "right to drag them from home and kindred, and down them to perpetual slavery in far distant regions."

The Boston Medical Intelligencer took note of this lecture series in its issue of December 12, 1826: "In delivering these lectures Dr. Parsons has been engaged in the good work of diffusing a knowledge of the structure and economy of the human body, as a part of that information which is necessary to its preservation and improvement. . . . Dr. Parsons' discourse is clear and intelligible, and gives good evidence that he is well qualified to accomplish the task he has undertaken."

Usher's academic career, although an important phase of his life, was relatively brief. It lasted only as long as Brown University's medical school, which came to a rather abrupt end in an odd way during the years 1827–1828.

At a special meeting of the Corporation on December 13, 1826, the resignation of President Asa Messer was announced. The Reverend Francis Wayland, Jr. of Boston was unanimously elected to replace him. About the state of the college at this time Reuben Guild wrote:[3] "The circumstances in which [Wayland] found the College were by no means favorable. . . . The last two or three years of Dr. Messer's administration had been marked by idleness and dissipation on the part of the students. Influence beyond the reach of the President rendered salutary discipline almost impossible, and the results were disastrous alike to the moral and intellectual character of the men under his care."

This was the conventional view of the situation. Professor Walter C. Bronson, University historian, writes:[4] "President Wayland's first work was to tighten the reins of moral and mental discipline which in the last few years had been somewhat relaxed." Yet the tradition persisted that there was a more than casual relationship between the affair of the barrel of bones and the peculiar severity with which the impending blows fell upon the medical school.

At any rate, Doctor Wayland, wrote Charles Parsons,[5] "brought with him very definite views as to college discipline, and a profound conviction of its importance." In pursuit of his objectives he revived an old rule requiring instructors to visit students' rooms. Imposing a residency requirement on members of the medical faculty was peculiarly frustrating, since, as was the custom elsewhere, the medical students lived or roomed off-campus.

At a special meeting of the Corporation on March 15, 1827, a resolution sponsored by the President was adopted:[6]

WHEREAS, it is deemed essential to an efficient course of instruction, and to the administration of discipline in this University, that all its officers be actual residents within the walls of the Colleges; therefore, RESOLVED, that no salary or other compensation be paid to any Professor, Tutor or other officer, who shall not during the course of each and every term occupy a room in one of the colleges (to be designated by the President), and assiduously devote himself to the preservation of order and the instruction of the students, or the performance of such other duty as may belong to his station.

The secretary was directed to send copies to the non-resident professors. This action was implemented at the next regular meeting in the following manner. Salaries of present and future faculty members were approved only on condition that they "devote themselves during term-time exclusively to the instruction and discipline of this institution, occupy rooms in college during study hours, and attend in their several departments such recitations as the President may direct, not exceeding three recitations of one hour in every day."[7]

The course of medical lectures beginning in late February of 1827 and terminating in May proved to be the last. The names of the members of the medical faculty (Doctors Drowne, Wheaton, DeWolfe, and Parsons) appeared as usual in the University catalogue of 1827–28. The ensuing five years, however, produced a significant series of changes. The catalogue of 1828–29 presented the full medical faculty, but to each of the names was affixed an asterisk with the following explanatory footnote: "The gentlemen to whose names the asterisk is prefixed, are not of the immediate government; and do not, at present, give any instruction in the University." In the following year the same footnote appeared, but Wheaton's name was missing. In the catalogue for the academic year 1830–31 a more definitive statement appeared: "The gentlemen to whose names the asterisk is prefixed, give no instruction in the University, and have no concern in its government." Usher dropped out in 1831–32, leaving only Drowne and DeWolf. No medical faculty was listed in the catalogue of 1832–33.

President Wayland's motives for sacrificing the medical school are not entirely clear. He himself, following graduation from Union College, had studied medicine for three years with preceptors in Troy, New York and attended medical lectures in New York City.[8] Charles Parsons was of the opinion that Wayland had no hostile feeling toward the school.[9] Professor Theodore R. Crane, a Wayland authority, on the other hand has stated[10] that Wayland had little enthusiasm for medicine and that "he never showed much interest in medicine as a progressive science." It was suggested in later years (1859) "that the proximity of medical schools in Boston, New Haven and Pittsfield, which were provided with ample accommodations, would always prevent the growth and success of one in Rhode Island and the school ws therefore abandoned." Although no contemporary document supports this judgment, its validity is not readily discounted, as it was written by Doctor Usher Parsons.[11]

The weight of evidence and opinion, however, favors the view that dissolution of the promising school was, in fact, incidental to otherwise commendable and successful academic reforms. President Wayland himself provided a sturdy example of the moral and intellectual austerity which he sought to impose upon students and faculty alike. He doubtless knew what effect these measures would have upon the medical professors and apparently was ready to accept the inevitable in the face of what he considered to be the greater good of the college. At any rate, it soon became clear that men in active practice, receiving as compensation for teaching only the lecture fees paid by their students but otherwise dependent for a livelihood on their daily practice, could not long continue.[12]

Charles clearly associated his father's resignation with the new situation: "The policy of President Wayland, requiring the officers of instruction to be also officers of discipline and give their whole time to collegiate duties, necessarily severed his connection with the University."[13] When the community learned that a number of eminent professors had been released, a running controversy appeared in the local press. Much of the feeling seems to have been generated by the dismissal of Tristam Burges from the chair of Oratory and Belles-lettres. A United States representative from Rhode Island, prominent lawyer, orator and politician, he was a very popular figure locally. Yet he was subject to the same code and suffered the same fate. An editorial of 1830 stated:[14] "Some of the most able professors that formerly graced this institution have been dismissed, almost with insult, and nearly the entire course of lectures in different branches of science, which alone formed any pretense for denominating the institution a University, have been dispensed with, without an effort on the part of the Corporation to preserve these advantages to the students." Charles[15] weighed the gains in closer teacher-pupil relationship and in the moral and mental development against the advantages of welcoming "men of distinction and power . . . engaged in . . . active pursuits outside the college, who bring with them a breath from the conflicts of mature life." He concluded: "In drawing the reins up so suddenly and turning so sharp a corner, it was not strange that something should be jolted out, and the medical school had the loosest hold." Professor Frederick C. Waite observed, "This may be considered the first attempt to install full-time medical teachers [in an American medical school]."[16]

During its brief history the medical school made a substantial contribution to medical education. While a complete roster of students is not available, it appears that the number in attendance fluctuated between twenty-five and fifty. The hometown origins of the medical graduates is not a matter of record, but the Brown University catalogue of 1824 provides this information for the 38 students then taking a medical course (20 in the first course and 18 in the second). Only five were from the town of Providence, the remainder being scattered as follows: Rhode Island outside of Providence 9, Massachusetts 13, Maine 3 (two of whom were from Alfred!), New Hampshire 2, and Vermont 1—all from New England.[17] A variable number of graduates has been attributed to the school, but Charles Parsons identifies eighty-eight and lists them by name. Twenty of these had previously received an A.B. degree, nineteen from Brown and one from Dartmouth. Between 1804 and 1828 an additional thirty-one honorary M.D. degrees were awarded. A roster of those receiving honorary M.D.'s is a medical *Who's Who* of the period.[18]

Evidence has come to light which indicates that President Wayland might have permitted the Medical School to resume its activities under suitable circumstances, but he was anxious that it be an institution of high standards. In June of 1827, he sent the following communication to Usher:[19]

> Being informed that you are about to visit Northampton and expect to be present at the Meeting of the proposed Medical Convention at that place I take this opportunity through you to state to the gentlemen who may attend that the operations of the medical department in this University are at present, suspended. Whenever however they are resumed I am well assured that any regulations which the Gentlemen of the faculty generally shall deem expedient for the good of the profession to adopt will be rigidly observed, and that no degrees will be conferred but upon the exhibition of such acquirements as are considered sufficient to entitle a candidate to similar standing in the most elevated schools in our country.

In 1825 the Medical Society of the State of Vermont had sent a circular letter to the medical societies and institutions of New Hampshire, Maine, Massachusetts, Rhode Island, Connecticut, and New York, containing proposals to raise the requirements for medical degrees and licensure and to establish uniform standards for admission to practice. A conference was convened at the suggestion of the Massachusetts Medical Society and met in the courthouse at Northampton, Massachusetts on June 20 and 21, 1827. Usher was the only delegate from Rhode Island, accredited to the "Medical Institution of Brown College"; the Rhode Island Medical Society was not represented. The standards adopted were an important milestone in the sporadic efforts to raise the level of medical education in America.[20] They, however, had slight impact on the quality of such education at that time, as it was in fact actually beginning to decline. More to the point, they had no effect whatever on the fading prospects of Brown University's "Medical Institution."

Usher's convictions were accurately reflected in the proposals made at the convention. These suggested that each candidate hold a B.A. degree from a respectable college, or, alternatively, show proof of a good education in English, Latin, geometry, and natural philosophy (chemistry and physics). It was further proposed that candidates with college degrees shall have studied medicine with a licenced practitioner for three years after graduation or four years for those who lacked formal college education. Attendance would be required at two courses of lectures at an incorporated medical institution in anatomy and physiology, surgery, theory and practice of medicine, materia medica, chemistry and midwifery, with satisfactory examinations in each subject. Finally, in addition to meeting minimal age requirements, candidates must read and defend a medical dissertation and show proof of good moral character. These standards represented the unrealized dreams of American medical reformers from the time of John Morgan's *Discourse Upon the Institution of Medical Schools in America* (1765)[21] until the beginning of modern medical reforms in the last third of the nineteenth century.

Usher was busy preparing dissertations for the Boylston Prize competition at Harvard. The prize was established in 1803 by Ward Nicholas Boylston, "an opulent merchant in Boston," as Usher described him (actually a merchant of London), and grandnephew of Zabdiel Boylston, who "introduced the practice of inoculating for small pox into America in 1721." The cash prizes were awarded for the best essay on announced "medical, anatomical, physiological and chymical subjects," usually two years after the initial announcement. The prize amounted to "$50, or a gold medal suitably inscribed of that value, or, if the author prefer it, a piece of plate with an inscription."

Usher won on his first try in 1827 with a well-written dissertation "On Inflammation of the Periosteum [bony envelope], both Acute and Chronic." He opted for the medal. The essay follows the classical form, proceeding from pathological and clinical classification to treatment. The text is based largely on the work of European authorities, although significantly it contains an account of experiments which he himself had performed. It was published in the October 1827 issue of the *New England Medical Review and Journal*[22] and gave rise to a bitter controversy which will be described later. He was also successful on his second Boylston try in 1828 with a dissertation on eneuresis irritata, responding to the question of 1826 which was "On the disease called an Irritable state of the Urinary Bladder; its nature and treatment." While a well-written review of the literature, it reflected no personal experience. Although he had been invited by Doctor James Webster[23] of Philadelphia to submit it for publication in the *American Medical Recorder* of that city, it appeared more appropriately in the *Boston Medical and Surgical Journal* for 1828, formerly *The New England Medical Review and Journal.*[24] Usher won the prize twice more, in 1830[25] and 1835,[26] and on a fifth occasion commendation, but no prize.[27]

Usher, however, in 1828 did publish in the *American Medical Recorder* yet another paper titled "On the Administration of Medicines by the Veins; Being a Brief Inquiry into its Safety and Utility."[28] This described interesting experiments which he had performed employing animals (sheep) as subjects and a variety of pharmacotherapeutic materials (including arsenic). Although the results were discouraging, it anticipated by almost one hundred years Ehrlich's concept of *therapia magna sterilisans* by arsenicals (1910). Usher affirmed dogmatically "that the introduction of medicine by the veins can never be practiced with utility or safety, even in the few cases where, from obstructed deglutition, or other causes, they are inadmissible by the stomach," which prediction, of course, was very wide of the mark.

On December 12, 1825 General Leighton had written to Usher of his father's failing health and recorded in his diary,[29] ". . . afternoon went and shaved father Parsons." Desirous of seeing his aging father once more, Usher undertook the long trip to Alfred despite the difficulties of winter travel. On Friday, January 27, 1826 the General noted, ". . . very cold still morning. . . . Doctr. Parsons came in town from Portland. Mrs. Leighton & I spent the evening at her fathers with the Dr." On the next day the General "wrote a Deed from Dr. Parsons of the Mill, a Gore [a triangular tract of land], &c. in Newfield [15 miles from Alfred], & he signed & executed it. . . ." The old man's imminent departure induced Usher to settle his affairs in Alfred. On Sunday, the 29th, "a fine and clear morning," the General set out at daylight, and "carried Dr. Parsons to Doutis falls [Doughty's Falls, North Berwick, Maine] to Col. Hobbs & got there by past 8 o'clock & took the stage at 9 for Boston." This was the last time that Usher would see his father alive. We can be sure that he visited Charlie in Cambridge on his way home.

Usher continually promoted the sale of his handbook *Physician for Ships*, usually with genuinely unselfish motives. In a letter to his old friend Senator John Holmes,[30] however, he indicates that some financial benefit would not be unwelcome, and suggests a procedure that might accomplish this:

> I cannot withold an expression of gratitude to you for aiding my wishes in trying to bring into use a book, the writing of which I can truly say was dictated more by a wish to relieve suffering seamen, than by any expectation of pecuniary reward. The second edition has drawn a heavy expense upon me, which together with various losses and disasters recently sustained has placed me in a situation to feel very sensibly any relief that may come from the sale of it as proposed in your bill. There is but one opinion prevailing in this quarter as to the necessity of correcting abuses in putting up medicine chests; and the bill introduced by you is considered a very ample and appropriate remedy. . . .
>
> I would barely suggest whether it would not be advisable for me on hearing that the bill has passed to distribute a suitable number of copies with the custom-house officers where merchants or masters of vessels can always find them at hand, free from the exorbitant commissions charged by retailing booksellers, and thus obtain the book at a very low price. After the bill has passed you will favour me with a little advice on the subject.

The expected news regarding Usher's father was not long in coming. General Leighton's diary tells the story:[31]

> 31st July 1826 . . . father Parsons grows more sick & weak. I wrote a letter to Br. Usher informing him of the facts. 1st Augt. 1826 . . . got in some oats & hay, peas, &c., then I went & shaved father Parsons, he being very likely to die. . . .

4th Augt. 1826 Friday, fine day. Father Parsons died about 1/2 past 7 o'clock this morning without a struggle. Capt. G. W. Rogers & Capt. Sands layed him out. Mr. J. Holmes is to conduct the funeral. . . . I wrote to Br. Usher Parsons informing him of the fact & put it into the mail.

The sadness of this summer would soon be lightened, however, as little Charlie, now approaching his third birthday, made his first trip to Providence since entering the warm surroundings of Grandfather Holmes's ménage.[32] Also, later in the fall, Usher welcomed another of the visiting nephews from Maine, Usher P., the sixteen year old son of General and Mrs. Leighton, who had walked all the way from Portsmouth, New Hampshire—108 miles! Young Usher eventually became a physician.

During the ensuing year Usher endured two more emotional episodes. Commodore Perry, following his death from yellow fever contracted in Venezuela in 1819, had been buried in Trinidad. On November 30, 1826 the sloop of war *Lexington* arrived at Newport with his remains for reinterment in that city.[33] On Monday, December 4, the steamboat *Washington* left Providence with local military units and "a very numerous collection of officers and citizens." The *Rhode Island American & Providence Gazette* for December 5 reported that "of the survivors of the glorious battle of Lake Erie, there were present Dr. Usher Parsons of this place, Surgeon of the fleet; Capt. D. Turner, Lieut. W. V. Taylor, and Thomas Breeze, Purser, all of Newport, and now of the Navy." This reunion with his old comrades must have been a poignant experience for Usher. The *Washington* returned to Providence that evening. A later account quoted Commodore Perry's letter to the Navy Department describing Usher's surgical exploits in the battle and explained that his rank at the time had actually been Surgeon's Mate and not Surgeon of the fleet.

Earlier, in the summer of 1825, Usher had dispatched several letters to old comrades-in-arms, with the object of establishing in the official record the nature of his services at Lake Erie. Dan Turner, who had been captain of the brig *Calendonia* on Lake Erie, wrote[34] glowingly of Usher's surgical successes in that campaign and concluded, "Commodore Perry has often stated your services to others in my hearing, the same as I have here done and told me he had done the same to the Department, together with your high standing as a gentleman." From his residence, Perry Cabin in St.

Michael's, Maryland, Purser Sam Hambleton wrote:[35] "I had the pleasure, a short time ago, of receiving your letter on the subject of your service on Lake Erie. No person has a higher opinion of them than myself. . . . I have forwarded your letter, with Captain Turner's, to Mr. Goldsborough, with such notes as I thought might be useful—& I hope such notice will be taken of you in the Register as may be satisfactory."[36]

An important function of the Rhode Island Medical Society was the policing of medical ethics. On March 14, 1827 the society's Censors for the Northern District of Rhode Island adopted the following resolution: "Charges of unprofessional conduct, respecting the Laws of Consultation in the 7th Section of the 1st Chapter of the By-Laws, having been presented the Censors against Usher Parsons, M.D. of Providence, and having been sufficiently substantiated, are therefore referred to the consideration of the Society." Chapter 7 of the Society's By-Laws prohibited a fellow of the Society from consulting with or advising any person commencing the practice of medicine or surgery until he had been examined and approved by the Censors of the Society, with the penalty being disqualification from voting at the Society's meetings, censure, reprimand, and even expulsion. Further information regarding this accusation has not come to light as detailed minutes of the proceedings were not recorded, but the charges were examined.

At the annual meeting of the Society at Redwood Library (Peter Harrison's architectural gem) in Newport on June 27, 1827, barely a week after Usher had attended the convention on Medical Education at Northampton, the corresponding secretary was "directed to inform Dr. Usher Parsons that charges have been presented against him by the Censors of the Northern District—For unprofessional conduct in violation of the laws of consultation," as specified in Section 7, but never clearly defined.[37] The matter dragged on for a year until finally, at the annual meeting in Providence on June 25, 1828, it was voted "that Dr. Parsons has at this time made good his defence against the charges," and nothing further was heard of the affair.[38]

At the same session the report of the Northampton meeting was received, but because of the "short period which had elapsed since receiving said Proceedings," it was considered "expedient to postpone the consideration thereof until their next annual meeting [1829]." No further action was ever taken.

During August Usher traveled in New York State. He passed through Newport on August 10 and New York City on the 13th, and sailed up the Hudson to Albany. Fortified with an ample supply of letters of introduction, Usher visited with prominent lay and medical figures at the various stops, journeying as far west as Auburn where he inspected the prison.[39] He had returned to Providence by September 1.[40]

That fall Usher prepared a circular which indicated a resolve to continue undergraduate medical education in Providence despite the recent failure at Brown. The announcement read as follows:

> A Medical School will be opened at Providence on the 1st of October 1827, under the direction of Usher Parsons, Professor of Anatomy and Surgery, associated with two other medical gentlemen, for the purpose of educating students of Medicine and Surgery.[41]

The course was to last three full years, each year to be divided into three terms of three to four months with lectures in the conventional subjects. The second and third years would be devoted to repetition and review of the same subjects. The second year provided additional instruction in the performance of "Surgical Operations and [in] applying various kinds of dressings and medical treatment of Surgical cases," and the student would "be prepared to pass a close examination in Anatomy, and to perform every Surgical operation with facility and neatness." During each of the three years examinations would be given once or twice every week. The three-year course, one year longer than was customary at the time, was a deterrent to prospective students, while the weekly or semi-weekly examinations were downright threatening.

Further attractions were described in glowing terms:

> The means of instruction already prepared, are—a very rich Anatomical Museum—all the Surgical Instruments now in use—a Botanical Garden—a suitable Chemical Apparatus, with tests, &c.—suitable rooms for Dissections—valuable Plates, such as Cloquet's, Bell's, Demour's, Scarpa's, Cooper's, Monroe's—and a well selected Library of about 1000 volumes, containing all the standard English and French authors. The above form a set of materials and facilities for Medical Education as complete as is ordinarily to be found in the Medical Schools of the United States, and far greater than individual libraries generally afford.

The proposed plan of study is uniform and systematic, instead of leaving the student to explore, unassisted, the great mass of medical authorities. The attentions and superintendance of several medical gentlemen will be, it is confidently hoped, so united, as to render the studies of the pupil precise and definite.

Conditions will be for lectures, instruction, room, fuel, lights, use of Museum and Library, Apparatus and Garden, $60 for the first year—$50 for the second year—and $40 for the third year. Board may be had in the vicinity at $1.75 per week.

The yearly tuition, which was all-inclusive, purportedly covering all expenses except board, would be commensurate with costs incurred at other schools.

This was an excellent and progressive plan for its day, proposing a three-year integrated course of study. Clearly influenced by the recommendations of the Northampton meeting, it exceeded them in several respects. Despite its superiority the course, probably over-ambitious, was never given.

The project, moreover, would have faced other considerable obstacles. Medical schools were now beginning to proliferate more rapidly than the population. Many of the new establishments would be proprietary, and, further, there would be serious competition from a variety of medical sects, health cultists, uneducated practitioners, and quacks. All of this would make it very difficult to maintain, much less improve standards.

The problem of suitable hospital facilities in Providence occupied Usher's thoughts during these times, as it would for many years. In March of 1825 the following item appeared in the *Boston Medical Intelligencer*:[42] "A hospital and quarantine establishment are in contemplation at Providence, R.I., and a lot on Field's Point has been selected for its location." A smallpox hospital was established at Field's Point some three miles from the head of the bay, and a sentinel was kept there for many years to flag down ships as they entered the harbor. Mrs. Anne Royall, a visitor to Providence in 1826, observed:[43]

Providence is a very romantic town, lying partly on two hills and partly on a narrow plain about wide enough for two streets. . . . It contains 14 houses for public worship, a college, a jail, a theater, a market-house, 8 banks, an alms-house, part of which is a hospital, and 12,800 inhabitants. The churches are very splendid, and the jail is tolerable, but the poor-house does not deserve the name, and the hospital [the older Marine Hospital] is a wretched abode, disgraceful to the town. . . . The poor-house is an old building in the most unwholesome part of the town. There were about twenty paupers in it, the dirtiest set of beings I ever saw. I found five maniacs in the hospital, lying on straw upon the floor, which looked as though it had not been swept or washed for years. The citizens, however, are engaged in measures to render these establishments more comfortable.

One such measure, of which Mrs. Royall may have heard, was the opening in 1830 of the Dexter Asylum. In 1828, even before its completion, it had taken in sixty-four paupers. For some twenty years, until the opening of Butler Hospital in 1844, it provided shelter not only for the poor, but also for the insane, who amounted to one quarter of its inmates. These facilities, however, provided no general hospital beds. Usher was further distressed by the lay confusion between quarantine or isolation and hospitalization in the modern sense. Characteristically, his interests were colored by personal motives. Writing in 1827 to U.S. Representative Tristam Burges, he observed:[44]

> Respecting a place for the Hospital that is to be erected here, I beg leave to mention . . . a lot . . . as suitable for the purpose as the one already appropriated by the town, and is one mile nearer, and accessible by open roads. . . . the place at Field's Point is too far from town, . . . there will be [difficulty] in supplying an hospital daily, four miles distant from the market, and through five fences, saying nothing of the risk and additional expense of moving patients to & from, and the additional pay that must be allowed to the surgeon who attends the hospital. . . . their decision in favour of Field's Point was founded on a mistaken idea that a quarrentine [sic] hospital and a lazarette might be established on the same ground in connexion with a marine hospital.
>
> I beg leave to repeat what I have already made known to you, my extreme desire to obtain the surgeoncy of said hospital which must be my apology for troubling you at this time with my views on the subject of its location.

After the closing of the Medical School at Brown, Usher's academic activities were not completely neglected. In *The Rhode Island American and Gazette* of December 25, 1827 appeared the following item: "A popular course of Anatomical Lectures illustrated by wax specimens [the ones from Italy, no doubt], will be

The Rev. Abiel Holmes as a young man. Wash drawing, artist unidentified. Countway Library, Harvard Medical School.

"The Gambrel Roof House," residence of the Rev. and Mrs. Abiel Holmes in Cambridge, Mass. Birthplace of Mary Jackson Holmes Parsons and Oliver Wendell Holmes. Charles William Parsons, son of Usher and Mary Parsons, spent most of his formative years here with the Holmes family. Late 19th century photograph, Countway Library, Harvard Medical School.

Levi Wheaton, M.D., Professor of the Theory and Practice of Physic in the Brown University Medical School, 1815–1828. Painting by George Peter Alexander Healy (1846) in the Brown University collections.

Rev. Francis Wayland (1796–1865), President of Brown University 1827–1865. From a painting in the First Baptist Church, Boston, where he served as pastor from 1821 to 1826. From a photograph in the Brown University Archives.

Left: "The Cabinet," former quarters of the Rhode Island Historical Society, on Waterman St., Providence. Usher Parsons was for many years an active participant in its discussions. The building is now in the possession of Brown University. From a photograph in the Rhode Island Historical Society.

Right: Brick school house at the corner of College and Prospect Streets, Providence, built as a grammar school and used as an "anatomical building" during most of the existence of the Brown University Medical School. Photograph, c. 1870, Brown University Archives.

BROWN UNIVERSITY.

Lectures

ON

ANATOMY AND SURGERY,

BY

USHER PARSONS, M. D.

Admit *Mr Morril Robinson*

BROWN UNIVERSITY.

Lectures

ON

THEORY & PRACTICE OF PHYSIC

BY

LEVI WHEATON, M. D.

Admit *Morrill Robinson*

Tickets to the lectures of Drs. Usher Parsons and Levi Wheaton at the Brown University Medical School in the 1822–1827 period. Brown University Archives.

First Baptist Meeting House, Providence, 1870. Built "for the publick worship of Almighty God, and also for holding Commencement in" [Brown University]. Usher Parsons for many years lived within sight of this church and often attended services here. From a photo album in the Rhode Island Historical Society.

Nos. 10 and 11 Thomas St., Providence (left and center). In 1822 when Usher Parsons started practice in Providence, he was associated with and lived in the home of Dr. Levi Wheaton at No. 10. Both houses had been built by clockmaker Seril Dodge for himself, first No. 10 and then No. 11. Photographed in 1906. Rhode Island Historical Society.

The Levi Wheaton-Seril Dodge House, No. 10 Thomas St., photographed by the author in 1985. After 1906, it was raised a story over a store. It was bought by the Providence Art Club in 1919 and joined to No. 11 by an arch seen on the right. The Providence Art Club still occupies both buildings.

The Providence Athenaeum, Benefit St., Providence., c. 1870. An avid reader and user of the Athenaeum library, Usher Parsons always lived within a block or two of its site and at one time directly across the street. From a stereoscopic photo by Manchester Brothers in the Rhode Island Historical Society.

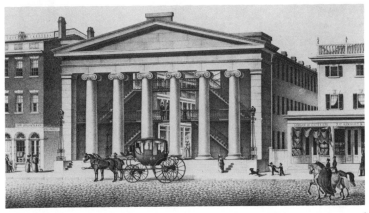

The Arcade, Westminster St., Providence. Built in 1828, it was one of the earliest shopping gallerias in America. Reproduced from an early lithograph in the Rhode Island Historical Society.

Exterior of Sullivan Dorr House on Benefit St., Providence, where Usher and Mary Parsons were entertained and Thomas Wilson Dorr of Dorr's Rebellion fame grew up. Photograph, 1907, Rhode Island Historical Society.

Drawing room of Sullivan Dorr House, showing wall paintings by artist Michele Felice Cornè of the Bay of Naples and Vesuvius. Photograph, 1877, Rhode Island Historical Society.

Oil paintings of Mary Jackson Holmes Parsons and Usher Parsons, rendered in Providence in 1823 by Francis Alexander. The painting of Mary is in the possession of Hugh Upham Clark of Arlington, Virginia, a descendant of Mary's younger sister. That of Usher is in the Brown University collections.

St. John's Church (Episcopal), North Main St., Providence. Both Mary and Usher Parsons often attended this church. Detail of a painting in the Genealogical Manuscript of the Allen family in the Rhode Island Historical Society.

Usher Parsons as a young man. From a miniature by an unknown artist in the Dwight-Parsons Collection, Brown University Archives.

commenced in this town on the 29th inst. by Dr. U. Parsons. Dr. P. is an excellent lecturer in this science, and attendance on his course will give one a correct and interesting knowledge of the wonderful structure of the human frame." The next day the *Literary Cadet and Rhode Island Statesman* outlined the course of nine lectures in considerable detail. The item continued: "The above subjects we think the most interesting of any that could have been selected from the whole range of Natural History, and from the lecturer's thorough acquaintance with Physiology, we may hope they will prove highly interesting and entertaining. A similar course given by Drs. Ware and Bradford to the ladies and gentlemen of Boston . . . attracted a very numerous audience." The lectures would be "illustrated by a variety of drawings and models." The first lecture was scheduled for Saturday the 29th, others following on succeeding Mondays and Saturdays. Single tickets were priced at $2, gentleman and lady $3 for the pair, and children attending with parents $1 each.

According to the *Providence Patriot and Columbian Phenix* of January 2, 1828 "the lectures of Doct. Parsons are attended by numerous and literary audiences, who have been not more pleased with the subjects, than with his happy manner of lecturing." The writer added: "His last lecture was upon the circulation of the blood, and upon the heart. The Doctor mentioned one fact with regards to the component parts of the blood [which is] truly astonishing, that is, its iron ingredients. He observed that it had been ascertained by fair experiment that there was enough in the blood of forty men to make a common plough share. We have often heard of the *'iron-hearted'*, but never knew exactly how to account for the expression."

In December of 1828 Usher became involved in a public controversy which agitated him deeply. Characterized by wordy and vituperous exchanges in the daily press, it extended over a period of nearly a month. Usher himself seems to have been responsible for this washing of dirty linen in public. On December 23, 1828 a public notice signed by Usher appeared in *The Rhode Island American and Providence Gazette*:

A medical dissertation which obtained the Boylston premium last year has been represented as made up of plagiarisms. I traced the report . . . to Dr [Joseph] Mauran,[45] who . . . has from time to

time spoken of it in this light. I called upon him through a friend
for a denial . . . or an apology. He returned for answer, thro' my
friend, Mr. Samuel Ames, Jr.,[46] that he would say in writing that
he had never asserted or thought that I had obtained the premium
unfairly, provided I would engage not to publish it. To this I
assented. Two days afterward he wrote me that he should decline
making any such statement in writing, and has added to the
former injury by saying there was ample foundation for what he
had asserted in the dissertation [itself]. I then wrote to Dr. [John]
Ware, one of the most learned physicians in New England (whom
the Boylston Committee entrusted with the preparation of it for
the press) for his opinion as to my claims to originality in the
Dissertation.

Usher quoted Ware's reply[47] at length in which Ware affirmed
that Usher had not indeed made greater "use of the writings of
Bichat or any other medical author than is fair and allowable."
Marie F. X. Bichat (1771–1802), famous French anatomist, had written several works which were frequently and freely quoted. Usher
concluded with the charge that "Mauran has been guilty of prevarication and of falsehood, all of which I am prepared to substantiate."
On December 26 the statement also appeared on the front page
of *Microcosm,* another Providence newspaper. Usher would have
been better advised not to air the messy business in the press, but
he was prompted to do so by the prominence of Mauran and the
vigor of his attack.
Mauran's long and bitter reply, which appeared in the *Rhode
Island American and Providence Gazette* on December 30 (and the
Microcosm on January 2), stated that, after reading Dr. Parsons's
dissertation on the "Inflammation of the Periosteum," he had found
its first pages enriched with familiar passages from Bichat and other
authors, which he compared with original French editions in his
library. Whereupon, he told some of his medical friends that portions of the dissertation had been borrowed verbatim from French
authors. The affair was further aggravated by a series of events in
which Mauran first wrote a denial that he had made an accusation,
and then retracted the denial. This caused Usher to threaten,
through his lawyer Ames, to take action, after which Mauran published in the *American* a score of parallel quotations, purporting to
show the close similarity between Usher's text and the original
Bichat or George Hayward's English translation of it. While raising

some justifiable questions, Mauran revealed the personal resentment, if not jealousy, which had motivated his attempt to undermine Usher's reputation:

> The Dr. well knows that I have not, for many years, professed
> for him any extravagant friendship. . . . A man exhibiting himself
> annually, yea semiannually, as a mammoth in *science* must ex-
> pect . . . to be . . . critically investigated. . . . Did not Dr. P. while
> Professor of Anatomy in Brown University take written schedules
> of Lectures of a young gentleman then reading Anatomy in his
> office . . . and receive private explanations sufficient to enable
> him to lecture to a class . . . ? Also while lecturing has he not
> read . . . as original the works of reputed authors. . . . , excepting
> the occasional introduction of cases from his celebrated 'Erie
> Battle', with . . . which the public has been annually surfeited?
> Did he not advertise in the New England Journal for 1826 that
> 'Dr. Parsons of Providence, R.I. has in preparation a new trans-
> lation of the Surgical works of Celsus [Roman physician, 25 A.D.],
> which has never appeared . . . ?[48]

Mauran concluded self-righteously, "Yet I flatter myself [that] it
will not be less objectionable to my friends and the public that my
defence has not been embellished with the abuse and scurrility
which characterizes the writings of that individual."

In the *American* of January 2, 1829 Usher attempted a reply. The
accusations relating to the work on Celsus, he suggested, were
irrelevant, but he would discuss them anyway. He had given up the
translation project three years earlier on advice that the work would
not have a sufficient sale. Entirely at his own expense and to satisfy
his curiosity, he had engaged a "French master [named Hinkley]
who pretended to an extraordinary knowledge of Latin." The latter
abandoned the task after a week, "complaining that several lines
were inexplicable." Hinkley sent a bill for eight dollars, but he
proved "willing to take five." Usher obtained a signed statement
from Doctor Richmond Brownell, who had originally spread the
Hinkley story, that he was now "satisfied that Joseph Hinkley told
me a lie." Regarding the charge that he had used the lectures of a
student as his own, Usher explained that he had "employed one of
his students, who had himself lectured on optics, to draw me some
diagrams of the eye." He did not need this help, and it was in fact
"well known" to my medical pupils that nine out of ten of these
lectures were extemporaneous."

Usher concluded in noble prose: "And now having brushed away the dirt strewn by Dr. Mauran . . . , I leave him with the infamy of being proved guilty of slander, of prevarication, and of falsehood." Ames, embarrassed and unhappily spattered in the mud-slinging, plaintively vowed in a note published in the same issue that his motives were purely altruistic, that legal remedies had never been proposed, and that he had indeed acted out of friendship for Usher.

The *American* of January 6 carried letters written in support of Mauran by Doctors David B. Slack and Joseph W. Fearing of Providence and Edward W. Greene of New Bedford, which tended to substantiate Mauran's accusations of plagiarism in Usher's medical lectures going back to the years 1823 and 1824. Feeling the need for more authoritative support, Usher wrote to his teacher of Harvard days, Doctor John C. Warren of Boston. His letter was the clue that led to discovery of the controversy, buried in dusty family papers for more than one-hundred-and-thirty years. It was the single most important factor in Usher's final vindication. Dated January 7 (the year was incorrectly given as 1828), Usher's letter read in part:[49]

> I am involved in a difficulty with an enemy, and appeal for a candid opinion in my behalf, and for any advice or aid you may be pleased to afford me. The accompanying newspaper will unfold the subject. You will perceive that . . . the Boylston Committee is assailed by the unfounded accusations against me. . . . I understand now that the Boylston Committee are [also] assailed in the Massachusetts Journal. . . . If you can find the time to review . . . my Dissertation you will be convinced that I could have had no intention of purloining from Bichat. A word from some of the Committee . . . may save me from ruin.

On January 9 Usher announced[50] that to "satisfy the public of the importance of the diagrams and notes [on the eye], for which Dr. Slack assumes so much credit, I have left them at the office of the *American*, where ['these slight materials'] can be inspected."

Slack re-entered the scene on January 12 with a wordy rebuttal of his own.[51] After ridiculing Usher as "this man of certificates," he asked, does one "go to North Providence and Pawtucket for certificates that he knows Greek, Latin, French, and Italian . . . ?" The disclosures which followed must have been embarrassing to

Usher, even though their bearing was on a minor, rather than major phase of the controversy:

> I read anatomy with Dr. Parsons, . . . he was glad of my assistance, and I should have thought nothing of it, but for a plunder which he afterwards committed upon me, and one other, of experiments upon Comstock's spring water, and published them as his own. [He also asked] me the solution of some of the most common experiments in chemistry. I knew him then to be perfectly ignorant of science. . . . Whether his memory was somehow or other shot away in the *Battle of Erie* or over charged 'by his fourteen years study in Europe and America' (being half that time on the water and the rest in close quarters in Providence), I cannot say. . . . You may say what you please about diagrams and notes. [I nevertheless] spent three successive evenings in your own rooms to explain to you [those] principles and phenomena, [and] afterwards drew the diagrams and wrote the notes and voluntarily offered them to you: you took them and lectured to the class and repeated the illustrations.

Nevertheless, on January 20 Usher confidently concluded:[52] "If further proof is wanted . . . , it is exhibited in the following . . . letters written under a full knowledge of the controversy by two members of the [Boylston] Committee." One member of the committee had written, "We are of the opinion that the use of extracts of a descriptive nature . . . is not unusual nor improper. The Committee were not misled by them." Another stated, "I conceive the anatomical facts, such as may be found in different, elementary works on anatomy [such as Bichat, may be used without] . . . the imputation of plagiarism." "The original of these letters," wrote Usher, "are open to the inspection of my friends. The letter containing the first extract has been forwarded from Boston to Dr. M., who still withholds . . . any apology due for the injury he has endeavoured to inflict by slanderous reports."

This final barb settled the matter so far as the Providence newspapers were concerned. The citizens of Providence had seen the sordid business laid before them in full detail. The wisdom of exposing this private feud to public view was very doubtful despite the provocation. Mauran's attempt to injure him was of course motivated more by jealousy or dislike than by any actual grievances.

Usher's final vindication, attributable to his letter to Warren, came a week later in the *Massachusetts Journal* of Boston, a citadel of respectability and culture: "Some weeks ago we noticed a professional controversy between two gentlemen in relation to the Boylston Medical prize Dissertation of 1827. . . . We are satisfied from Dr. Parsons' character, from the learning and care of the Committee who awarded the prize, and from the opinion of some of the distinguished members of the medical profession in this city that . . . the Committee were not deceived, and that there was no intention to deceive them."

In the long run Usher has come off somewhat better than his detractors. Such public disputes, however, were working insidiously to undermine the public's confidence in "regular" (orthodox) physicians just at a time when they were coming under attack by sectarians and cultists—Thomsonians, homeopaths, herb doctors, and faith healers.

On Washington's birthday in 1828 Usher began his long correspondence[53] with son Charles. The first letters were carefully printed for a child. If it appears unlikely that a four-and-a-half year old could read, Charles, noticeably bright and already attending school, in fact was rapidly acquiring that skill. Usher sent him children's books, and a copy book and pencil "to make marks in," spurring him on to read and write. In the fall, Usher, learning that Charles had come down with some childhood illness, traveled briefly to Cambridge to appraise the situation. Soon after his return to Providence, Usher was informed by Charlie's young uncle, John Holmes, that Charlie had quite recovered and was "a tremendous reader, and requires very attentive listeners."[54]

Charles Henry Holmes, seventeen-year-old son of Senator John Holmes of Alfred, who himself had graduated from Brown in 1796, had become ill early in his junior year at the college in the fall of 1827. Usher had cared for him until his parents could take him home. The Senator later wrote to Usher expressing his deep gratitude for Usher's solicitous care.[55] Two other Alfred boys, nephew William Lewis (son of sister Abigail Parsons and Colonel Dan Lewis) and Cyrus K. Conant, had studied medicine at Brown from 1822 to 1824, although neither received a degree.[56]

During September of 1828[57] Usher had traveled to Philadelphia in quest of an academic appointment there. The trip produced no immediate results, but he tried again later with a different outcome. At the close of the year he grasped an opportunity to address an old

Erie friend, the Reverend Robert Reid:[58] "Permit me . . . to introduce my particular friend Mr. T. Wilson Dorr [then twenty-three years old and the future instigator of the Dorr Rebellion], . . . , attorney . . . [and] scholar . . . [who] is on a tour of pleasure to the West." "I avail myself," he added "of the opportunity . . . of renewing our acquaintance . . . so agreeable to me while residing in your village." His nostalgia for the old navy days was never far from the surface.

NOTES

1. Usher Parsons, "Case of Epilepsy," *The New-England Journal of Medicine and Surgery*, 15:355–357, 1826. This actually dealt with his treatment of one Michael Hogan in early 1823, but included follow-up of more than two-and-a-half years.

2. Usher Parsons, *The Importance of the Sciences of Anatomy and Physiology as a Branch of General Education; Being an Introduction to a Course of Lectures to the Upper Classes at Brown University* (Cambridge, Mass., Hilliard and Metcalf, 1826).

3. Reuben A. Guild, *History of Brown University* (Providence, Brown University, 1867), pp. 31–32.

4. Walter C. Bronson, *History of Brown University, 1764–1914* (Providence, Brown University, 1914), p. 206. See also pp. 159–165 and 211–212 *passim*.

5. Charles W. Parsons, *The Medical School Formerly Existing in Brown University*, p. 46–50 *passim*.

6. *Ibid.*

7. *Ibid.*

8. Theodore Rawson Crane, "Francis Wayland and Brown University, 1796–1841" (Doctoral dissertation, Harvard University, 1959), pp. 41–43. See also Theodore R. Crane, "Francis Wayland: Political Economist as Educator," *Rhode Island History*, 21:65–90, 1962.

9. Charles W. Parsons, *The Medical School Formerly Existing in Brown University*.

10. Theodore R. Crane, "Francis Wayland and Brown University, 1796–1841."

11. Usher Parsons, "Sketches of Rhode Island Physicians Deceased Prior to 1850," *Transactions of the Rhode Island Medical Society*, 1:1–64, 1859. See p. 56.

12. Charles W. Parsons, *The Medical School Formerly Existing in Brown University*.

13. C. W. Parsons, *Memoir*, p. 26.

14. Charles W. Parsons, *The Medical School Formerly Existing in Brown University*.

15. *Ibid.*

16. Frederick C. Waite, "The Third Medical College in New England, That of Brown University (1811–1828), *New England Journal of Medicine,* 207:30–33, 1932.

17. *Catalog of the Officers and Students of Brown University, March, 1824,* (Providence, Brown University, 1824).

18. Charles W. Parsons, *The Medical School Formerly Existing in Brown University,* pp. 39–45, 56–59. Several regular graduates became prominent in the profession locally, while a few attained eminence elsewhere. Jerome V. C. Smith, Class of 1818, served as port physician of Boston for twenty-three years, taught at Berkshire Medical College, made numerous contributions to the medical literature, and edited the *Boston Medical and Surgical Journal* for twenty-eight years. He was elected mayor of Boston in 1854. Alden March, Class of 1820, founded Albany Medical College, serving as president and professor of surgery. Distinguished as a surgeon in Albany, he attained national recognition by election to the presidency of the American Medical Association. Most distinguished of all was Elisha Bartlett, a graduate of 1826, whose career is outlined in footnote 33 of Chapter 8.

19. Francis Wayland to Usher Parsons, June 27, 1827, New York Public Library.

20. *Proceedings of a Convention of Medical Delegates, Held at Northampton, in the State of Massachusetts, on the 20th Day of June, 1827* (Boston, Wells and Lilly, 1827).

21. John Morgan, *A Discourse Upon the Institution of Medical Schools in America* (Philadelphia, William Bradford, 1765). Morgan's policies for requiring a liberal education for medical students and the separation of medicine, surgery and pharmacology into distinct disciplines met with wide opposition from colonial physicians and failed to gain acceptance.

22. Usher Parsons, "Dissertation on Inflammation of the Periosteum, Both Acute and Chronic, Which Obtained the Boylston Premium for 1827," *The New-England Medical Review and Journal,* 1:376–408, 1827.

23. James Webster to Usher Parsons, December 1, 1828, DPC.

24. Usher Parsons, "A Dissertation on the Disease Called an Irritable State of the Urinary Bladder; Its Causes and Treatment," *The Boston Medical and Surgical Journal,* 1:705–712, 721–728, 737–745.

25. Usher's essay appeared under the title "On the Connexion Between Cutaneous Diseases Which Are Not Contagious, and the Internal Organs" in the *Boston Medical and Surgical Journal,* 3:425–441, 1830.

26. This essay also appeared in the *Boston Medical and Surgical Journal,* 13:69–90, 1835, under the title "A Dissertation on Cancer, Which Obtained the Boylston Prize for the Present Year, 'What Are the Diagnostic Marks of Cancer of the Breast; and is this Disease Curable?'."

27. His essay on this occasion, "On the Comparative Influence of Malaria,

As a Cause of Fever," was later published, as the fifth and final essay, in a gathering of all of his Boylston Prize essays in a volume titled *Boylston Prize Dissertations on 1. Inflammation of the Periosteum. 2. Eneuresis Irritata. 3. Cutaneous Diseases. 4. Cancer of the Breast. Also, Remarks on Malaria. By Usher Parsons, M.D. . . .* (Boston, Charles C. Little and James Brown, 1839). This cumulation appeared in a second edition, printed by B. T. Albro at Providence, in 1849.

28. Usher Parsons, "On the Administration of Medicines by the Veins, Being a Brief Inquiry into Its Safety and Utility," *The American Medical Recorder*, 14:353–365, 1828.

29. "Diary of Gen. Samuel Leighton, 1818–1848."

30. Usher Parsons to John Holmes, April 10, 1826, Maine Historical Society.

31. "Diary of Gen. Samuel Leighton, 1818–1848."

32. Abiel Holmes to Usher Parsons, August 15, 1826, Boston Public Library.

33. News and details of this event appeared in the *Rhode Island American & Providence Gazette*, issues of November 30, December 5, and December 8, 1826.

34. Daniel Turner to Usher Parsons, July 3, 1825, DPC.

35. Samuel Hambleton to Usher Parsons, August 11, 1825, DPC.

36. Charles Goldsborough was a civilian administrative officer in the Navy Department and a naval historian.

37. Rhode Island Medical Society, "Minutes."

38. *Ibid.*

39. The Dwight-Parsons Collection at Brown contains letters of introduction for Usher written by Dutee J. Pearce to William L. Marcy, John W. Taylor (of Ballston Springs, N.Y.) and Henry B. Storrs (of Whitestown) dated August 10, 1827, and to Professor McNaughton and to unknown persons in Utica and Auburn, the latter three being dated August 13, 1827. Pearce was U.S. Representative from Newport, Rhode Island.

40. John Holmes to Usher Parsons, September 2, 1827, HUCC.

41. This commences, "Circular - A medical school will be opened at Providence on the 1st of October, 1827 under the direction of Usher Parsons." A copy of this flyer is in the Massachusetts Historical Society. The other two gentlemen referred to in it remain unidentified.

42. *Boston Medical Intelligencer*, 2:188, March 29, 1825.

43. Anne Royall, *Sketches of History, Life, and Manners in the United States* (New Haven, The Author, 1826). The above account was reprinted in Gertrude S. Kimball's *Pictures of Rhode Island in the Past, by Various Authors* (Providence, Preston and Rounds, 1900), pp. 170–173.

44. Usher Parsons to Tristam Burges, December 17, 1827, Historical Society of Pennsylvania.

45. Joseph Mauran, thirty-three years old, was the son of a French immigrant seaman who had held a command in the American Navy during the Revolutionary War. He graduated from Brown in 1816. After studying medicine with Doctor Pardon Bowen, he received an M.D. from the College of Physicians and Surgeons in New York and entered practice in 1819 as Bowen's assistant. Prominent in alumni affairs at Brown, he was a member of the Board of Censors of the Rhode Island Medical Society. In this capacity he had earlier participated in the action against Usher.

46. Samuel Ames, Jr. (1806–1865), was then a young Providence lawyer. He later became Chief Justice of the Rhode Island Supreme Court.

47. John Ware, a respected Boston physician, whose support in the controversy was very important to Parsons, was an editor of the *New England Journal of Medicine and Surgery* and later (1836–1858) Hersey Professor of the Theory and Practice of Physic at the Harvard Medical School. Ware's letter contained interesting unsolicited comments regarding the original experiments performed by Usher, but Ware in editing the paper for publication unfortunately and incorrectly attributed them by the addition of quotation marks to the famous English surgeon, Sir Astley Cooper. The experiment on rabbits sought to locate the site of bone regeneration after experimental fracture. These studies were undoubtedly carried out by and were original to Usher, and do not, in fact, appear in Cooper's experimental work. Yet, ironically, in two later reprintings of the dissertation (see footnote 27), the quotation marks were still not deleted.

48. Usher had indeed. On page 335 of the July, 1826 issue of the *New-England Journal*, appeared under "Works in Preparation" the following curt announcement: "Dr. Parsons, of Providence, (R.I.) has in preparation, a new translation of the Surgical Writings of Celsus."

49. Usher Parsons to John C. Warren, January 7, 1829, Massachusetts Historical Society. Because the letter was incorrectly dated "1828," a long and frustrating search ensued before the newspaper stories of this episode were uncovered.

50. *Rhode Island American and Providence Gazette*, January 9, 1829.

51. *Manufacturers & Farmers Journal and Providence and Pawtucket Advertiser*, January 12, 1829.

52. *Rhode Island American and Providence Gazette*, January 20, 1829.

53. Usher Parsons to Charles W. Parsons, February 22, 1828, DPC.

54. News of young Charles at this time appears in the following letters, which are preserved in HUCC: John Holmes and Abiel Holmes to Usher Parsons, March 23, 1828; Usher Parsons to John Holmes, March 25, 1828; John Holmes and Abiel Holmes to Usher Parsons, April 22, 1828; Usher Parsons to Charles Parsons, no date, but April, 1828; John Holmes and Abiel Holmes to Usher Parsons, May 11 and 12, 1828;

John Holmes and Abiel Holmes to Usher Parsons, November 8, 1828; John Holmes and Abiel Holmes to Usher Parsons, November 22, 1828; Usher Parsons to Charles W. Parsons, December 11, 1828.

55. Senator John Holmes to Usher Parsons, December 9, 1827, DPC: Senator John Holmes to Usher Parsons, February 13, 1828, Haverford College Library.

56. *Brown University Historical Catalogue, 1764–1904*, p. 132; also *Catalogue of the Officers and Students of Brown University, March, 1824*, p. 5.

57. Dutee J. Pearce to J. Barnes, September 8, 1828, DPC. Pearce informed Barnes that Usher Parsons was "desirous of an introduction to some of the following gentlemen in your city" (Philadelphia), naming seven individuals including three clergymen and a general. "As there is no person here" he wrote, "within his or my knowledge, who is personally acquainted with them, I am induced by a desire to oblige him, to ask the favour of you to introduce him to such of them as he may wish to be made acquainted with."

58. Usher Parsons to Robert Reid ("Rev. Reed"), December 2, 1828, DPC.

CHAPTER ELEVEN

The Middle Years

In the Spring of 1830, following a trip to Cambridge to visit Charles and to see Ann and her family, Usher took to the road in quest of a more promising academic opportunity, stopping first in New Haven, Connecticut. While in Cambridge he had obtained a letter of introduction from John White Webster, Professor of Chemistry at the Harvard Medical School (and many years later notorious for the murder of Doctor George Parkman), to Professor Benjamin Silliman of Yale.[1] Usher's first meeting with Silliman was the beginning of a useful relationship which continued in the ensuing years. Professor Romeo Elton of Brown University had provided letters to Denison Olmstead, Professor of Mathematics and Natural History at Yale, and to Henry E. Dwight, principal of the High School ("Gymnasium") there.[2]

From New Haven Usher went on to New York, arriving about May 29 and remaining through June 1. By June 3, he had reached Philadelphia, where he visited his kinsman John Frost, principal of Central High School. Frost gave him letters for use in New York on his return trip, describing Usher as "one of my oldest & most valued friends."[3] Usher's inquiries did not produce immediate results, but probably opened doors which led to a teaching venture in Philadelphia the next year.

In June of 1830 the annual meeting of the Rhode Island Medical Society was held in Providence in the Senate Chamber of the County Courthouse. Usher was appointed to a committee, with Doctors Waring and Eldredge, "to revise lists of books recommended to be read by Students of Medicine in this state," a commission for which Usher with his academic background was well suited.[4]

Sometime in October Usher learned that Colonel Dan Lewis,

husband of his sister Abigail, had suffered a stroke. A letter to his nephew, Doctor William Lewis, who had studied at Brown and now practiced in Shapleigh near Alfred, offered professional advice and provides a revealing glimpse of the prevailing therapeutics:[5]

> This afternoon I have received your letter conveying the melancholy information of your father's illness. It is a very serious case and from the nature of his constitution I should pronounce it Sanguineous apoplexy. You was right in opening the temporal artery, and after this I should rely on counter irritants as the next most important remedy. With energetic treatment such patients sometimes quite recover. An embrocation of Tartar Emetic ointment that will produce a crop of pustules along the spine of the neck has sometimes proved beneficial. Of the two remedies I should prefer the latter. They may be applied one every day for a week, mostly on the diseased side, half an inch or an inch from each other. A slight mercurial course may help to promote absorption of extravasated blood in the brain. The bowels should be kept gently free. If bleeding should be carried too far there is danger of converting the disease into serious apoplexy [whatever that is]. Rubefacients along the affected limbs as pearl ash water, volatile linament, pepper sauce, &c., &c.—are worth a trial.

The Colonel survived this treatment two-and-a-half years.

During the years 1829 and 1830 Usher was busily engaged in the preparation and publication of medical papers, while simultaneously carrying on an active correspondence with Charles and the Holmes family in Cambridge. The _Boston Medical and Surgical Journal_ of August 10, 1830 announced that a premium of fifty dollars ("or a Gold Medal of that value") had been awarded on August 4 to "Usher Parsons, M.D., Professor of Anatomy, &c. in Brown University, Providence, R.I." for a dissertation "On the connexion between cutaneous diseases which are not contagious, and the internal organs." The winning of this prestigious award for the third time was no mean accomplishment. The essay, published in the August 17 issue,[6] introduced the concept (now generally accepted) that a cutaneous disease is often the local manifestation of a systemic disorder rather than a purely local phenomenon. Although many of Usher's classifications and concepts are archaic, his generalizations remain valid and have a classic simplicity:

> The laws of vitality that preside over organized bodies preserve a mutual dependence and a reciprocal influence between their sev-

eral component parts. The more perfect and complicated the organization is, the more numerous are its ties of connexion and relation. Not only the several organs are thus held in mutual dependence, but each tissue is so modified that the exercise of any one of them, whether healthy or morbid, is felt and responded to by all the others.

He cited as an example the train of events set up by the "cognizance of savory foods" which culminates in its digestion and absorption. He concluded: "If healthy actions are thus mutually extended from part to part, so also are morbid ones."

The September 7 issue of the *New-England Journal* carried a letter critical of the essay. The author of the letter, a resident of Newport, styled himself "Medicus." Although he approved in general of the concepts expounded, he correctly questioned phraseology which implied transfer of blood *away* from, rather than *to* the stomach and intestine during digestion. Usher's testy rejoinder (issue of October 12) displayed an acute sensitivity, probably stemming from the trauma of the Mauran controversy:

> The word *from* . . . should have been printed *upon* [i.e. to]. I think you will find it so in the manuscript; for, on discovering the mistake, when the Journal first reached me, I turned to the first rough sketch of the dissertation, and found the words [as indicated]. . . . The criticism of 'Medicus' is just, and you learn from it, Mr. Editor, that it was not without cause that I protested so strongly to the publisher against the course pursued with my dissertations of publishing them without giving me an opportunity to examine the proof sheets, or even the least intimation that they were to be printed at all, until they were actually struck off.

The editor replied that the prize essays were submitted directly by the Boylston Committee, and in turn rebuked Usher:

> When any of our friends favor us with a communication for the Journal without any special request to send them a proof for revision, it is our custom to have it so revised [to conform] . . . verbatim . . . [with] the written copy. . . . Had we attempted to send [a proof] . . . to Providence and wait Dr. Parson's amendments, fleeter horses would have been required than we have ever yet heard of. . . . We conceive no man justified in offering for this prize any production which he considers not in a fit state to appear before the public.

In the October 26 issue of the same journal Usher published a little paper on the "Effects of Large Doses of Tartar Emetic."[7] He theorized that antimony tartrate (tartar emetic) may be less fatal than certain other poisons because it "causes its own expulsion" by exciting emesis or purging before it can produce any deleterious effect. To illustrate his point he described an incident from his naval experience:

> In 1813, while attached to the U.S. squadron on Lake Erie, I suffered, in common with the crews, with a slight bilious remittent, and, while convalescent, drank daily of *cremor tartari punch*, as I called it,—made by dissolving a tablespoonful of cremor tartari in sweetened water and adding a tablespoonful of brandy. On my return one afternoon, after an . . . absence from the ship, I found our three ward-room servants missing, and after some searching discovered them in a remote part of the ship, unable to stand, and scarcely able to speak.

After relating that the servants confessed that they had taken a large dose of undiluted cream of tartar from the medicine chest, mistaking it for his "punch," Usher went on to prove his point:

> The lads were from sixteen to twenty years of age, and had enjoyed good health. I ordered them demulcent drinks and chamomile tea, and they recovered the next day, so as to return to duty. . . . They had contracted a fondness for ardent spirit, but the *punch* cured them of it entirely. It had all the effects in this case of Chamber's medicine with the additional one of keeping their fingers out of the medicine chest.[8]

Another article of Usher's, titled "On the Comparative Influence of Vegetable and Animal Decomposition as a Cause of Fever," appeared in the November 1830 issue of *The American Journal of the Medical Sciences*.[9] This closely reasoned essay attempts to prove that decaying animal matter, as well as decaying vegetable matter, could be a cause of fever, a concept eventually rendered meaningless by the germ theory of disease.

During 1830 Boylston prizes were awarded for both of the questions advertised by the committee that year. The prize for the second question on cutaneous diseases was the one won by Usher. The first question was "Whether Fever is produced by the decomposition of animal and vegetable substances, and if by both, their comparative influence?" The similarity between the phraseology of the question and the title of Usher's paper is not a coincidence. The prize on this question was won by Doctor Charles Caldwell of Transylvania University in Lexington, Kentucky, with "Thoughts of Febrile Miasms," published in *The Boston Medical and Surgical Journal.* The committee's announcement mentioned "other Dissertations" on the first question, one of which, it stated, was of outstanding quality. Usher had, in fact, entered dissertations on both questions that year, and he himself later wrote that the one on fever "had received respectful commendation from the Boylston Committee, accompanied with a wish that it might be published, and its author's name known."

Despite the praise of the Boylston Committee, Usher's paper did not pass without criticism. The eminent Doctor James Jackson of Boston, in a letter to the editor of the *Boston Medical and Surgical Journal,*[10] remarked that butchers and people living near cemeteries were no more prone to fevers than other mortals, casting doubt upon the importance of decaying animal tissues in causing fevers. Usher's reply was somewhat inconclusive.[11] He admitted that butchers enjoy good health, but thought this "less owing to the sanative or salubrious qualities of the air . . . than to the active and regular employment, and to the abundance of wholesome animal food they always have at hand." Jackson retorted:[12] "I trust it will not be concluded . . . that I think putrid fish, &c. are not a nuisance in a city or village. . . . If they do not produce fever, they may produce other diseases." He concluded: "I . . . did not state . . . that the occupation of a butcher is peculiarly salubrious, but that . . . This opinion would not be entertained if it were remarkably otherwise." Usher, certainly with the historic yellow fever epidemics of Providence in mind, replied in a letter dated December 28:[13] "Concerning city interments, . . . I am not inclined to give an opinion . . . different from [his] . . . ; but I do believe that putrid fish or hides, in stores or ships at the wharf, during the greatest heats of summer, may become prolific causes of fever." Louis Pasteur was then eight years old.

The controversy reached the shores of England. *The Lancet,*[14] in a lengthy review, commented: "There is, perhaps, no dogma more generally and implicitly subscribed to than that of the dangerous effects of putrid exhalations. . . . We have now completed our analysis of Dr. Parsons's Memoire," the author of which was described as "the American professor" and "learned and ingenious."

The editor concluded with admirable clairvoyance: "The innocuous character of putrid animal exhalations [remains unshaken]."

Meanwhile, Usher was working on his second book, published in 1831. It was a textbook of 316 pages on *Directions for Making Anatomical Preparations. Formed on the Basis of Pole, Marjolin and Breschet, and Including the New Method of Mr. Swan.*[15] He affected the title "Professor of Anatomy and Surgery," although he did not now have a formal university appointment. The book, which he dedicated to Doctor William E. Horner, Professor of Anatomy at the University of Pennsylvania, was essentially a manual of techniques. The preface is graced with this classical period: "That a minute knowledge of anatomy is essential to success in the practice of physic and surgery, is an opinion so generally prevalent, that the assertion of it at the present day wears the air of a truism." Because of the great difficulty of procuring cadavers for dissection, Usher deemed the techniques of making permanent anatomical preparations a desirable accomplishment and a practical necessity; "for, with the exception of Massachusetts, whose legislature has nobly [and recently] raised its voice in favour of practical anatomy, prejudice and legal impediments . . . will long exist . . . throughout the union." The text was clear and practical and quite up-to-date for the period. A review in a contemporary medical journal was favorable:[16] "We . . . recommend it to the student and practitioner as the best exposé of the present state of the art of making anatomical preparations, and hope it will be found in every dissecting room, and in the hands of everyone engaged in post mortem examinations. . . . descriptions are for the most part clear, concise, and intelligible."

Usher continued to seek new academic affiliations. Among his papers are several letters of recommendation solicited from his friends and associates to various individuals in Albany, New York, and Philadelphia, some dated as early as 1827 and 1828.[17] It was not unusual in those days for a competent lecturer to give courses in several medical schools within a single year.

Since Usher now had no medical school affiliation, he welcomed any opportunity to participate in medical education, even if it involved considerable inconvenience. At last, in the spring of 1831, he received from Doctor George McClellan of Philadelphia an offer of an appointment as Professor of Obstetrics at Jefferson Medical College. Jefferson had been founded in 1825 through the exertions of McClellan, a noted surgeon and brilliant practitioner, and, incidentally, the father of Civil War General George Brinton McClellan. McClellan's offer was attractive indeed and provides some insight into Usher's intentions at the time:[18]

> I determined that I would not write you . . . till I had done the best I could. . . . we had the chairs of *Theory & Practice*, of *Materia Medica*, and of *Obstetrics* left vacant. The Trustees kindly consulted me, and I recommended three of *my friends* for these chairs. . . . This eveg. the board of Trustees have . . . unanimously appointed Dr. Wm. Rush [the son of Benjamin Rush] Professor of Theory & Practice, Dr. Samuel Calhoun of Materia Medica, and *Dr. Usher Parsons* of *Obstetrics* & adjunct Prof. of Surgery. . . .
>
> I shall . . . want you to give about 16 or 18 lectures for me on inflammation & military surgery, as connected with wounds, fractures, &c. The course of Obstetrics will not require more than three lectures a week for the whole session. Your ticket will be $15. All the expense you will have . . . will be for your proportion of the Rent of the College edifice—about 215, or 220 dols. . . .

McClellan pointed out to Usher that this surely would not make his fortune, but it would give him independent support until he went housekeeping again, and it would serve to introduce him into good family practice. Nor was he required to move to Philadelphia permanently unless he wished to. His letter concluded:

> No chair does so much towards introducing its occupant into practice as the Obstetrical. . . . the adjunctship to my Surgery will make your station as important as any in the school.
>
> . . . I am a bold fellow to presume . . . your acceptance of this offer. But I was confident from the tenor of your conversations & from Joseph Howard's statements to me since his return from R. Island. We shall announce your name accordingly at the Commencement on Wednesday next. You will find yourself in excellent company among kind and liberal friends. You need not come here before fall unless you prefer to do so. But write me immediately. . . . Do not on any account demur. If you should it would mortify me exceedingly, at the same time it would impair my influence with the board of Trustees. . . .

Subsequent correspondence indicates that Usher replied favorably. On June 10, 1831 McClellan wrote[19] that he had "visited all the principal towns in the interior of our state & of Jersey," presumably to recruit students, and found "all interested in our favour." He concluded, "Mr. Frost has just engaged a very desirable situation in Arch St. just above the Theatre & will reserve the office for you."

Usher attended the annual meeting of the Rhode Island Medical Society, held that year in the Redwood Library in Newport on June 28, a lovely season for a trip down Narragansett Bay. At the meeting, George McClellan of Philadelphia and Sir William Clift, curator of the Hunterian Museum in London, were elected honorary members of the Society,[20] at the instance no doubt of Doctor Usher Parsons of Providence. Usher at his best could be a subtle and effective medical politician.

Usher, meanwhile, collected more letters of introduction[21] and prepared for his move to Philadelphia. Samuel Calhoun wrote to him about further developments concerning the Jefferson faculty:[22]

> ... it is thought expedient by some of the faculty to consult you on ... being here as early as possible, not only [to] make arrangements on the subject of the course but to assist in giving efficiency to your obstetrical operations connected with the Dispensary. There are already 7 patients on the list for delivery & the young men are very active. I have no doubt that ... you will be able to give a case or two to each of the graduating pupils.

Calhoun (1787–1841), a graduate of Princeton, who received his M.D. degree at the University of Pennsylvania, had accepted the chair of Materia Medica and Medical Jurisprudence. He reported that Granville Sharp Pattison (1792–1851) would be professor of anatomy and that William Sweetser would briefly fill the chair of theory and practice of physic, to be followed by John Revere (1787–1847).[23] "The energy of Pattison," he wrote, "is beyond everything." (Pattison, it will be remembered, had served briefly at the University of Maryland.) "Dr. Physick [Philip Syng Physick] has resigned in the old School [the University of Pennsylvania], so that the pupils have no reason to prefer that institution. . . . if you could . . . come at once it would be for the advantage of the School." In late October Usher left for Philadelphia, stopping briefly in New York, where he had a hurried meeting with young Thomas W. Dorr,[24] the future Rhode Island governor, who was visiting there in the familiar surroundings of his law-student days with Chancellor Kent.

An appraisal of Usher's professional experiences in Philadelphia is difficult. He did not find it expedient to settle there, nor, in fact, did he ever lecture there again. McClellan wrote of him:[25] "The Doctor finds that we cannot hold out encouragement enough to induce him to remain permanently with us. He is a very kind friend [to our institution], however, and will continue to do all in his power to promote our interests." In describing this phase of his father's life, Charles felt that "The subject was one for which his experience had not particularly qualified him," and observed, "He did not afterward accept any appointment which would require him to reside away from Providence."[26]

Before returning to Providence, Usher visited Baltimore and Washington, the former for academic and social reasons. His trip to Washington involved business, and he had been preparing for it by collecting letters of support.[27] While the nature of the business is not revealed, it was likely connected with the knee injury he had sustained at sea. Charles later wrote that as a result "he many years afterwards received a pension."[28] One of Usher's visitors soon after he returned to Providence was his brother-in-law, Oliver Wendell Holmes, now a medical student at Harvard. Wendell apparently assisted with a dissection.[29]

In the summer of 1832 Usher was again in trouble with the medical society. Most state medical societies at the time were little more than nominal organizations, scarcely functioning, with only a small proportion of the profession as members. The Rhode Island Medical Society, however, was somewhat exceptional in that it had adopted the strong position of the Massachusetts Medical Society, by which it was undoubtedly influenced, rather than the weak position prevailing elsewhere.[30] The Censors, zealous as always, had received information[31] on June 27, 1832 "that Usher Parsons has in violation of the By-Laws consulted with Mowry T. Peckham, a member of the Central Medical Society," and voted to report this violation to the Society. The Central Medical Society was set up by a group of dissidents who felt themselves excluded from the counsels of the Rhode Island Medical Society. The existence of a competing chartered organization, which would dilute its policing authority, was very disturbing to the elder establishment. Usher was notified of the Censors' action, but disposition was deferred until the next annual meeting, at which he apparently satisfactorily answered the charges. The problem of the competing medical society persisted for several years.

In the spring of 1832 Usher had received a letter from Doctor

Timothy L. Jennison of Cambridge describing in great detail a new dressing for applying fomentations, enumerating conditions in which it might be useful, and expressing hope that Usher would "cause one of them to be made . . . and then favour me with your opinion of its future utility, as also any improvement upon it."[32] It is surprising that commercial packaging of compresses, to be available for sale in apothecary shops and for use in hospitals, was conceived 150 years ago. Usher expressed[33] "favourable views" of this "novelty," suggested additional situations where it might be useful, and offered advice as to its marketing and production. In July Jennison[34] notified Usher that he had applied for a patent and reported: "I know I have an overwhelming majority of the nurses in my favour." (Nurses even then were not averse to labor-saving devices.) He continued with a calculated appeal to Usher: "If it prove useful and necessary in a Hospital, so also must it prove in a Ship of war. And what owner of a large merchant vessel, who regards the comfort of his sailors, would hesitate to pay ten dollars to add to his medicine chest such an auxiliary as I propose." Jennison closed his letter with a comment on the cholera epidemic which had recently reached the eastern seaboard from Europe. It was very much on the minds (and in the correspondence) of New Englanders.[35]

In the spring of 1833 Usher became involved in an exercise in forensic medicine. Rhode Island was titillated by a scandalous murder case called "The Terrible Haystack Murder". The *Providence Daily Journal* of Christmas Day 1832 carried what for those days was a scare headline: "Outrage and Murder". "We learn very direct," it continued, "that a murder, attended by the most aggravated circumstances has been committed in the town of Tiverton [Rhode Island] near Fall River [Massachusetts]. A young [Fall River] woman [then] residing in Bristol, was some time since seduced by a minister of the Methodist denomination stationed at Bristol." On December 21 the body of a young pregnant factory girl had been found hanged by the neck in a haystack. Letters implicating the parson were found secreted in the poor girl's bandbox. Postmortem examination of the body strongly indicated that she had died a violent death. The charge was that the Reverend Ephraim K. Avery had strangled her and then hung up the body by the neck on a haystack to simulate suicide. The Reverend was indicted for murder. The sensational trial opened at a special term of the Rhode Island Supreme Court in Newport on May 6, 1833. It lasted for twenty-seven-and-a-half days.

Many witnesses, including nine physicians, were called. The prosecution called two physicians who had viewed the body after the murder and then several days later performed an autopsy on the exhumed body. Usher was among a half dozen physicians called by the defense as expert witnesses. He was identified as having "delivered lectures in anatomy connected with the College in Rhode Island, and also in Philadelphia." He testified on two matters: whether bruises on the corpus had been inflicted before death or were postmortem changes in a person who had died from hanging (they could be the latter), and on the age of the fetus found in the womb as estimated from its length. Much hinged on the date of conception. Usher admitted that he "had not had extensive practice in obstetrics," but had "examined on this point twelve French, English, and American writers." He estimated the fetus to be about three months and twenty days old, long enough for the victim to have known she was pregnant. The judge had ordered the reporters not to release any information until the trial was over. One reporter violated the pledge and was barred from the court. The dam, however, then broke, and many columns of the four-page *Journal* were devoted to the lurid proceedings. The terms "intercourse" and "pregnant" were bandied about freely in the graphic reports—four years before Victoria ascended the British throne and made prudishness establishment policy. At noon on Sunday, June 2, the jury after deliberating sixteen hours brought in a verdict of acquittal. Most people, probably including Usher,[36] had believed the minister to be guilty, but his testimony for the defense in this celebrated trial contributed to this unexpected result.[37]

In September 1833 Usher was invited[38] to accept the chair of anatomy and physiology at the Medical College of South Carolina. This would have required his lecturing there for a period of about four months beginning in the middle of November. That he declined this flattering offer is certain, for with his growing practice in Providence he never again found it advantageous to accept academic responsibility away from home. Toward the end of 1833 Usher looked into opportunities for founding or editing a medical journal. On January 12, 1834 he wrote to an unidentified colleague in New York[39] seeking his opinion. In those days technical journals were often conducted by individuals as a source of income. Some New

York publisher, Usher thought, might be willing to undertake the project, and he was not especially concerned with being named editor—provided he could share in the receipts. Nothing ever came of this project.

Usher's practice was growing, and he was held in increasing respect and affection in the community, as a note from the Reverend Robert Edward Pattison of Providence indicates:[40] "I enclose the sum of $50. I do not send it as a compensation for your services in my family, for I am aware it has no proper comparison with them ... but as a simple acknowledgement of my obligations & as an expression of my confidence & interest in you as my physician." In spite of this, and for reasons which are not clear, Usher felt insecure in Providence. On September 21 he wrote to George Mason of Newport[41] about extending his practice to that city. Usher was hesitant, however, lest he displease Doctor Waring. Edmund T. Waring, a native of South Carolina and a founding member of the Rhode Island Medical Society, had an extensive and successful practice in Newport, but his health was then known to be poor. In his letter to Mason, Usher asked about the status of Doctor Waring's health and whether Waring intended to go south that autumn. He also inquired about his chances of success in getting business in Newport and obtaining the good will of its citizens. Usher later wrote[42] that Waring had indeed gone to South Carolina for his health and died there in January 1835. Despite the opportunity provided by this sad event, Usher remained in Providence.

The Boston Medical and Surgical Journal of August 12, 1835 carried the announcement that the Boylston Committee of Harvard University had awarded its premium for that year to Usher Parsons of Providence, Rhode Island. This was the fourth time that Usher had won the Boylston medal, and in doing so he had surpassed his previous achievements. The prize question (No. 2 for 1835) was "What are the diagnostic marks of Cancer of the Breast; and is this disease curable?" Although his total operative experience in the disease was then but five cases, his paper was the most competent he had yet written. It was published by the prize committee in the September 16 issue of the journal.[43]

Although there has been much progress in breast surgery, x-radiation, and chemotherapy, many of Usher's observations have retained validity over the years: "No medicine has been hitherto discovered, either of general or local application, or both combined, that can disperse a scirrho-cancerous tumor, even in the incipient or scirrhous state. . . ." He called attention to the significance of size, fixation, speed of growth, and axillary spread. He wrote: "It has become a maxim with all good surgeons, that the longer extirpation is delayed, other things being equal, the greater is the liability to a return of the disease. . . . Extirpation . . . with the knife . . . is the chief if not the only measure that promises to effect a cure. . . . Fortunately, the operation is not dangerous nor difficult, and the wound appears to heal kindly, and it is not one in five hundred die of the operation, and it is most usual for the wound to wear a healthy appearance for some time after. But alas! our cherished hopes are often cut off by the recurrence of cancer, either in the cicatrix, or in some other part of the body, and it is commonly more rapid in its progress, than it was in the first instance." Concerning re-operation he stated: "It may be further remarked that a cancer which has broken out a second or even a third time may yet be a fit subject for an operation." His conclusions have not been altered by time: "1. That the extirpation of a scirrhous tumor whether indolent or painful, large or small, recent or of long standing, is no positive security against its reappearance . . . ; 2. That the danger of a return is greatly increased when the disease has been of long standing, or if ulcerated, and especially if it has affected the axillary glands, or adheres to the subjacent muscles; 3. That there is but little hope of preventing a return, by operating after the constitution exhibits marks of cancerous cachexy."

Usher's professional activities produced no outstanding event during 1836. He performed three of his lifetime total of sixteen breast amputations for cancer, one case surviving eleven years.[44] Also during that year he published two medical papers in *The Naval Magazine*, a new periodical of the United States Naval Lyceum, founded by officers at the Brooklyn Navy Yard "to elevate and adorn the character of our Navy." Although a well-edited journal, it survived only one year. The January and March issues carried a reprinting of Usher's paper on malaria and animal putrefaction.[45] The author was identified as "Professor of Anatomy and Surgery, Providence, R.I., late surgeon in U.S. Navy and Corresponding Member of the U.S. Naval Lyceum."

An original contribution appeared in the May and July issues[46] titled "Remarks on Quarantine Systems." It was probably not a coincidence that one of the Boylston questions for 1834 (Number

2) read "Are restrictions on the entrance of vessels into port, called Quarantine Laws, useful? If so, in what cases should they be applied." The cholera epidemic of 1832 had undoubtedly suggested the subject to the committee, cognizant of the skepticism aroused by the movement for more stringent quarantine regulations. Shortly after the announcement of the Boylston prize questions in the *Boston Medical and Surgical Journal* of October 2, 1833, Usher wrote two letters aimed at eliciting facts on the subject, one to the United States Secretary of State,[47] the other to Doctor Isaac Hays, the prominent Philadelphia physician.[48]

The Boylston number 1 question for 1834 was "What is the true nature of Polypus in the nostrils, and in what manner may the disease be best treated?" While it appears that Usher had considered firing both barrels in the competition, he did not, in fact, leave to posterity a work on nasal polypus. His essay on quarantines, however, had considerable merit, although it did not win the prize. Usher argued sensibly that quarantine of a ship had no virtue unless there was actual sickness aboard. He discussed the application of quarantine in four separate diseases: plague, cholera, smallpox, and yellow fever. He observed that plague had not appeared in America for two centuries. Smallpox was endemic in most cities despite quarantine and was unlikely in any case to be imported if there were quarantines in practically every nation in the western world. He believed correctly that yellow fever was not contagious at all within the usual meaning of the term, anticipating Walter Reed by sixty-four years.

Usher had become increasingly active in the affairs of the Rhode Island Historical Society. On October 25, 1830 he was appointed chairman of a committee whose purpose was to bring to America for the use of future scholars copies of colonial records now available only in England.[49] Since the Society had no permanent quarters and was planning to build a "cabinet," it was granted permission by the Rhode Island General Assembly to conduct a lottery for this purpose.[50] The lottery was not held immediately, and Usher served as chairman of a later committee which successfully petitioned for an extension.[51] He clearly did not have the same scruples about lotteries as did another prominent member of the Society, President Francis Wayland of Brown University, who a little later resigned from membership because of it.[52] The "Cabinet," completed in 1844, was sold to Brown University in 1942.

As he grew older, Usher showed evidence of increasing versatility. In 1830 he submitted to the *American Journal of Science and Arts* a review[53] of a book on mechanics by Zachariah Allen of Providence titled *The Science of Mechanics as applied to the present improvements in the useful arts in Europe and in the United States: adapted as a Manual for Mechanics and Manufacturers*.[54] Usher's critique of this practical little handbook was systematic and intelligent. He noted with evident satisfaction: "This is the first work of the kind, of domestic origin, that has been put into the hands of our practical mechanics and manufacturers." The Editor and founder of the journal, Professor Benjamin Silliman of Yale, its first professor of chemistry, remitted a modest stipend ($6), which Usher credited toward a subscription to the journal. When Zachariah Allen published his second little book, based on a tour of Europe and titled *The Practical Tourist, or Sketches of the Useful Arts, and of Society, Scenery, &c., &c., in Great Britain, France, and Holland*,[55] Usher again wrote a review, which he submitted to the *American Monthly Review*. When this was returned because another author had already been assigned the chore, Usher sent his review to Benjamin Silliman, who accepted it for the *American Journal of Science and Arts* after making some editorial suggestions. This time Doctor Silliman credited Usher's account at $1 per printed page.

Another of Usher's outside interests was his work on behalf of temperance. On May 27 of 1831 Usher delivered an address on this subject before the Temperance Society in Providence. Although directed to a lay audience, Usher's essay[56] was objective and quite advanced in concept, for he viewed alcoholism as a malady rather than a moral vice. He described a surging epidemic of drunkenness (375,000 "drunkards") and an annual consumption of seventy million gallons of spirits. The problem in the United States was in fact truly alarming, and Usher's figures were not too far afield.[57] The following excerpts from his address reveal its medical orientation:

> I am unable on any other supposition than that of hereditary tendency, to account for the fact that intemperance so often runs in families. Besides hereditary tendency, the acquisition of intemperate habits is facilitated by peculiarity of temperament. Some are constitutionally phlegmatic and unyielding to temptation—others of a sanguine temperament are more accommodating in their disposition, [and] are easily led astray by the example of their associates. . . . [Intemperate habits] act as an exciting cause

to all diseases to which a predisposition whether hereditary or acquired previously existed. . . . The free use of ardent spirits hastens a premature old age with all its attending infirmities. . . .

Usher outlined the damage that the abuse of intoxicating liquors inflicted on the liver, the stomach, the skin and the brain, attributing to it a trembling hand, a flagging of strength, stiffness of the joints, and mental imbecility. The catalog of diseases that result from alcoholism, he observed, included jaundice, gout, rheumatism, dropsy, palsy, epilepsy, apoplexy, and dyspepsia. Usher's address brought out a large crowd of townfolk. The Board of Managers of the Providence Association for the Promotion of Temperance requested permission to publish it, to which Usher agreed. Responding to invitations to lecture in Newport[58] and Pawtucket,[59] he continued to speak out during the next couple of years on the pernicious effects of alcohol.

Usher also dabbled in phrenology, but he left no papers or notes on the subject except for a brief discussion published in the local periodical, *The Literary Journal and Weekly Register of Science and the Arts*.[60] Concerning this episode in Usher's life Charles later wrote:[61]

> Dr. Parsons had too active a mind to rest satisfied with the knowledge required for every-day medical practice. He investigated many subjects more or less connected with his professional studies. When the doctrine called Phrenology was presented in Boston, graced by the zeal and eloquence of Spurzheim [one of its German co-inventors], Dr. Parsons gave much attention to it.

This empiric "science," which determined the mind and character from the shape of the skull, was much in vogue in medical circles in Boston and elsewhere in the early 1830s. Phrenology gradually faded from the national scene, to be embraced by quacks and disreputable characters who practiced it and preached it for many decades afterwards.

More fruitful was Usher's preoccupation with genealogy, and he appears to have infected Charles with the same curiosity. Charles later wrote:[62]

> From an early age, he was interested in tracing the history and genealogy of his family. Till the year 1834, he did not correctly follow up the line beyond his great grandfather, Rev. Joseph Parsons, of Salisbury. In that year, he carried on a lively correspon-

dence with the eminent antiquary of Northampton [Massachu-
setts], Sylvester Judd, Esq. Mr. Judd's valuable letters are now
before me. They helped him to connect Joseph Parsons, of Salis-
bury, with the first Joseph, of Springfield, and the second Joseph,
of Northampton. He explored old graveyards, records and all written sources of genealogical lore. He visited the towns where his
ancestors had lived, talked with the old men of those places, and
treasured up the knowledge he had learned from their trembling
lips. A manuscript book is still preserved, in which he wrote out
the history of the families of Parsons, Frost, Usher, &c., with
sketches of the lives of individuals, and preserved autographs of
many. In 1838, he printed on a sheet an outline of the "Genealogy
of the Family of Joseph Parsons."

On February 5, 1834, Usher's old friend and colleague at the
Medical School, Solomon Drowne, died in his eighty-first year after
a brief illness. He was buried at Mount Hygeia in Foster, wrote
Usher, "on an eminence near his residence, overlooking the orchard
and garden grounds, and under the shade of his favorite robinias."[63]
Usher composed a charming sketch of Drowne, which appeared in
May in *The Literary Journal and Weekly Register of Science and
the Arts.*[64] He wrote of his gentle spirit, his love of nature, and his
passion for the English poets and the ancient classics.

Toward the end of the summer of 1835 Usher wrote to Sir William
Clift, Curator of the Hunterian Museum in London, with whom he
had carried on a long and cordial correspondence.[65] He told Clift
that he was growing indolent and indifferent to medical science,
having recently refused two professorships in the western country
from sheer laziness. "I know nothing," he said, "that would be so
likely to revive my zeal and interest as a visit to your medical
schools and particularly to the Hunterian Museum." He told Doctor
Clift that he hoped to visit him in a year or two and, knowing of
Clift's interest in anthropological matters, reported the following:

> I have just returned from seeing Joice Heath [Heth] . . . exhibited
> in a publick hall as a rare curiosity on account of her great age,
> . . . 161 years, and . . . the fact that she was the nurse of our great
> Washington, was owned as a slave by his father, and was the first
> person that dressed the unconscious infant who was in after days
> to lead our fathers to glory and independence. She relates many
> accounts of him that seem to bring us into an intimate acquain-
> tance with his boyhood. She was baptized by immersion and

joined the baptist church in 1720. . . . Her frame was once large, but is now reduced to the weight of 46 pounds, and her appearance is that of a living Mummy. Yet [although blind] her general health is perfectly good, her pulse ranging from 60 to 65, full strong, and perfectly regular. . . . Her intellect is bright, hearing perfect, voice strong, so that she sings psalms and hymns that she learned more than a hundred & forty five years since. . . . Her diet consists of a little weak tea and corn bread with rare cooked eggs, which she takes three or four times a day. . . . Her greatest temporal enjoyment is her pipe and tobacco, which she has used constantly for 120 years. She has never taken any medicine. . . . She is constantly in a recumbent posture. I have been thus particular because I have no other subject of equal interest to write upon. . . .

Usher appears to have harbored no doubt about the authenticity of her story. The exhibition Usher mentioned was promoted by one Phineas Taylor Barnum, aged 25, and the successful carrying-out of this hoax was the beginning of his celebrated career as a showman.[66]

About this time Usher contemplated writing a biography of Oliver Hazard Perry, and during the closing days of 1835 made preliminary inquiries among the Perry family and his former naval comrades.[67] Although eventually he gave up the plan, Usher was able to give valuable assistance to Alexander Slidell Mackenzie, who a few years later wrote the definitive work. While on Navy matters, Usher also sought to have his pension increased, but with no immediate results.[68]

During the summers of 1830 and 1831 Usher had visited Alfred.[69] Charles wrote in his *Memoir* regarding such visits:[70]

A sketch of Dr. Parsons's career would be very incomplete if it did not allude to the tenacity with which he clung to early attachments, and the pleasure he took during his mature and declining years, in revisiting the scenes of his boyhood and youth. Almost every summer, after he had gained an established position in Providence, he went to his native place and the neighboring towns, where he had struggled with poverty and youthful ambitions. No recreation gave him greater pleasure. He kept up intimate intercourse and correspondence with relatives who still lived there.[71]

Shortly after arriving in Philadelphia in the fall of 1831, Usher received word from attorney Nathan Dane Appleton[72] of Alfred concerning some family real estate to which Usher held title and which he was apparently trying to sell. The parcel lay directly across the street from the courthouse, and Usher's brother-in-law, General Leighton, wanted to buy the buildings and an acre of land for a tavern. Leighton offered $600, but the attorney had "uniformly asked $900.00 for this part of the real estate, as you directed." Despite an absence of other prospective buyers, Usher was not above driving a hard bargain with his brother-in-law. The correspondence dragged on for several months. They finally settled for $800, the General possibly capitulating because he hoped to be in business by the time of the next court session.[73] The inn was known for many years as the Alfred House. It eventually burned to the ground.

Usher in 1831 was still living at McClellan's, where he had boarded since Mary's death, but in 1832 he constructed a one-story office of three rooms on President Street (now lower Waterman Street), in a block since occupied by the Rhode Island School of Design. Charles wrote:[74] "This he afterward enlarged, and occupied till his death. Until the marriage of his son [i.e. Charles], in 1853, he had no home establishment, but took his meals at hotels or boarding-houses, and generally slept in his office. He liked the freedom of this way of living."

In October of 1832 Usher brought Charles to Providence for a stay of several months. After seven years in the Holmes household, he was acutely missed, particularly by his Uncle John, to whom the bright, well-behaved youngster seemed like a little brother. Charles kept up his studies, at which he had already proved gifted and precocious, with a private tutor.[75] He stayed on until the next summer.

The following June Usher accompanied Charles back to Cambridge for a visit, although he was uncertain about his son's future schooling. In a letter to both John and Charles on June 21 after returning to Providence, he wrote to nephew John Holmes:[76]

> I arrived here safely Wednesday evening and of course in time to witness the entry of the President [Andrew Jackson] yesterday morning. He rode through the city again in the afternoon and started for Boston this morning at 6 o'clock. I suppose and hope you will make your obeisance to the old general when he visits Cambridge. His appearance is very imposing, dignified, and appropriate. I wish you to take Charles along with you when he receives the salutations of the people of Cambridge. His manner

is very pleasant to children and I have a particular desire that Charles should have it in his power to say he has shaken hands with Old Hickory. The form is to pass by him and shake hands without stopping; let Charles follow next to you and follow your motions. . . .[77]

I have thought much upon the proposal of your parents to have Charles attend Mr. Wells' school and conclude that it will be decidedly better for him to continue with his private tutor for some time to come. Besides I have contracted with said tutor until next October. After that time I should think more favourably of his going to Cambridge than I do at present.

Unfortunately, when President Jackson visited Cambridge, Charles was sick and unable to participate in that historic event.[78]

Usher had other directions for Charles's education, which he expressed in his letter of June 21 to his son:

I shall not advise you to study much while you are in Cambridge because I consider it rather as a vacation to you. Still, however, it will be desirable to gain as much information as you can at the Botanic Garden. Your uncle John will furnish you with a little change if what I left you should give out before you have done visiting the garden. If you can collect a leaf from each plant and write the name of it, you would be more likely to recognize the plant afterwards. I particularly want that you should increase your knowledge of the external characters or appearances of plants so as to be able to pronounce the names whenever you meet with such again. This will be quite different from the dry study of Books.

In fostering his son's interest in botany, Usher hoped to arouse enthusiasm for scientific pursuits, and possibly for medicine.

In the summer of 1834 Usher again visited Alfred, staying a night with the Leightons.[79] In the late fall Charles reported on his academic progress and some other matters:[80]

Homer is yet very hard. But [a] little easier than at first. I shall get through it before a great while, I hope. It is not very easy or interesting to read about Jupiter telling the Gods, that if they interfere with the Greeks or Trojans, he would "hurl them to the lowest Hades." We received a letter from Uncle Wendell [now in Europe] today, dated 22 October. He sent his love to you, but had not received a letter from you. We should be very glad to see you here. . . . My arms remain small, and I want dumbbells. Give my love to all my friends at Providence. . . .

Wendell, after two years at the Harvard Medical School, had decided to pursue studies in Paris before taking his M.D. degree (which he received from Harvard in 1836).

On February 4, 1835 Usher attended the dedication of the new Manning Hall at Brown University, a Greek revival gem which still dominates the old college row. He wrote to a friend:[81] "President Wayland's dedicating address at the new chapel was considered to be his happiest performance."

In March Usher sent for Charles, offering some fatherly advice:[82]

Inclosed is some needful to bring you to Providence. Tell the driver in Boston that you are eleven years old, as this will reduce your stage fare one half, that is if under 12 years. . . .

I have got through some writing that has employed me for some time past and shall now take hold of my Botany again—and you and my students can Botanize together.

Usher's suggestion regarding the stage fare was really quite in order, with Charles's twelfth birthday still almost six months away. Charles spent the month of April in Providence, "botanizing" and visiting old friends.

Shortly after the annual meeting of the Rhode Island Medical Society in Newport in June, Usher set out on a sentimental journey to Lake Erie, his first visit there since his naval service. He was accompanied by Captain Daniel Turner, who had commanded the *Calendonia* in the battle. They were joined at Buffalo by Captain Stephen Champlin, who had commanded the *Scorpion*. The three visited the *Queen Charlotte*, which had been captured by the British and later sunk. Usher wrote: "A company of merchants lately bought the ships, and have raised the *Queen* and refitted her. The captain received us politely, and gave us some pieces of oak from her to make walking canes. Captains Turner and Champlin and myself made out an inscription to be put on a gilded cannon ball that is to be slung in her cabin. Said ball was taken from among her timbers; and, as we stated, was fired by the *Tigris*."[83]

Usher continued to pursue his claims for a pension, based on the injury to his knee in 1816 during the Atlantic crossing in the *Java*. Thrown between decks while aiding injured seamen during a storm, he broke "his right knee-pan," as Charles recounts it.[84] In a letter[85] describing his claim to U.S. Congressman Dutee J. Pearce of Rhode Island, Usher states that "The injury at the time was apparently so slight that I did not suspect a fracture of the knee pan for some days, when the continuance of lameness induced me to examine it more thoroughly." He goes on to say: "My disability is permanent in its nature and interferes with my gaining a livelihood, besides occasioning me no small degree of pain."

The authorization for payment[86] of the pension dated August 5, 1835 is preserved in Navy Department files. The certificate had originally carried the date of inception as "7 of February 1816," but this was struck out. It offered a monthly pension of $12.50, not a very munificent sum even for those simpler days. This, however, was not the end of the matter, as Usher would try once more for a better result.

Charles entered Harvard in the fall of 1836 at the age of thirteen, the youngest member of his class. A member of the senior class at that time recalled many years later[87] that "he was then a youth of fine, though delicate features, and was pointed out to the writer . . . as possessed of unusual attainments and as being the youngest and one of the most promising members of his class."

In the late summer of 1836 Usher had become interested in a new enterprise called the Smithfield [Rhode Island] Western Emigrating Association, organized for land speculation and emigration to the west. Emigration fever was running high, and land speculation was rife. The newspapers carried notices of many emigrating schemes, including another based in Rhode Island called the Pawtucket Western Emigrating Company. The great migration was a potent force in the growth of America, but was not an unmixed blessing to the folks back home. The *Providence Daily Journal* of September 5 commented editorially:

> Almost everybody is talking of going west, and settling down in Illinois, Michigan, &c. We regret it, not on their account, because they will be quite likely to better their condition, but because it is taking away some of the best part of our population. They long for a wider sphere, more enterprise and activity. The truth is, that every article of domestic consumption is so extravagantly high, with no prospect of diminution in price, and moreover the business here being so limited, some find it absolutely necessary to seek employment elsewhere. New England has seen her best days. The tide of population and enterprise is in another

direction, and it is making large draughts upon our cities and towns, and it will be some time before it will cease. The West is the land of promise and abundance, and there all meet a full return for labor and capital. . . . We know of several of our most valuable citizens, who have determined to emigrate with their families the present year. . . . It is a consolation to know . . . that they will contribute much to the character and prosperity of their settlement.

On September 4 Usher wrote:[88] "About three weeks since I caught the western land fever for speculation, which has ever since occupied my thoughts. Two weeks yesterday I attended a meeting at Scott's pond, and bought four shares. I was chosen [a] member of the purchasing committee, to have my expenses paid." He set out for the west by way of New York City on September 16, keeping a journal which, unfortunately, has not survived. Charles later reported[89] that Usher was absent for seven weeks, traveling as far as Chicago, part of the way on horseback, buying land, then and later, in various parts of the west. Some of the investments, after entailing a continual burden of taxes and other expenses, in fact became profitable many years later. On setting out, Usher wrote to Charles:[90] "If any accident befalls me, my affairs can be ascertained from Mr. T. W. Dorr with whom I leave my papers."

He kept Charles apprised of his progress in a series of letters.[91] After traveling overnight to New York City, he sailed up the Hudson River in the steamer *DeWitt Clinton,* recalling his very first trip up the river in a sloop. From Albany he proceeded to Utica by rail ("I took the carrs"). "This railroad," he wrote, "now takes all passengers from Albany to the west . . . a great relief to the canal . . . now crowded with freight boats." From Utica he traveled by canal boat to Buffalo, impressed by the beautiful and varied scenery and reminiscing about the old navy days. Buffalo, now an "elegant city" of twenty or thirty thousand souls, had but half a dozen houses in 1814. He stayed at a hotel run by a Mr. Hodges (formerly proprietor of the Franklin House in Providence), "superior in size and richness . . . to the Tremont in Boston."

From Buffalo Usher proceeded to Maumee, Erie (stopping only a few minutes), Cleveland, "a place called Toledo" (where he bought a horse), Fort Wayne, and Chicago. "Thence," he wrote, "I shall go to the land office at Galena . . . [in] Illinois, where are lead mines." From there he sailed down the Mississippi by steamboat to St. Louis and eastward overland to Philadelphia, where he arrived on November 3. He was entertained lavishly in Philadelphia.[92] He returned to Providence on the 6th and reported to Charles that he had been "absent seven weeks and traveled 3000 miles—700 of them on horseback." His expenses were $311.25. His health was much improved, "perhaps it was never so good as at present." Reverting to family matters, he inquired of Charles's health and progress in college.[93] "Write me," he added, "when your uncle's [Wendell's] poems are to be offered for sale."[94]

On December 4 Usher admonished Charles [95] for not acknowledging receipt of expense money mailed several days before. Had the letter miscarried, or was Charles ill? He would send some further funds to settle college and other bills, but expected Charles to reply promptly. With this stern parental reproach the record for 1836 closes.

NOTES

1. John White Webster to Benjamin Silliman, April 18, 1830, DPC.

2. Romeo Elton to Denison Olmstead, April 13, 1830 and Romeo Elton to Henry E. Dwight, June 3, 1830, both in DPC.

3. John Frost to William J. Adams and John Frost to an unknown person, both dated June 3, 1830; DPC.

4. Rhode Island Medical Society, "Minutes."

5. Usher Parsons to William Lewis, October 26, 1830, private collection of the late Georgia H. Stearns, Alfred, Maine. Miss Stearns was a granddaughter of Dr. William Lewis, and a great-granddaughter of Colonel Lewis. In 1960 she recalled that her mother, born in 1846, remembered great uncle Usher very well and was thus aged twenty-two when he died. She always spoke of him with affection and had memories of his great interest in all members of his family. "The family gatherings," she observed, "must have been funereal. I remember some!" Personal communication from Miss Stearns to the author.

6. See notes 25 and 27 of Chapter Ten.

7. Usher Parsons, "Effects of Large Doses of Tartar Emetic," *Boston Medical and Surgical Journal*, 3:592–594, 1830.

8. The active principle of Chamber's nostrum, contrived to discourage drunkenness and chronic alcoholism, was tartar emetic.

9. Usher Parsons, "On the Comparative Influence of Vegetable and Animal Decomposition as a Cause of Fever," *The American Journal of the Medical Sciences*, 7:80–113, 1830.

10. James Jackson, "Whether Animal Decomposition Is Productive of Fever?" *Boston Medical and Surgical Journal,* 3:674–677, 1830.

11. Usher Parsons, "Whether Animal Decomposition Is Productive of Fever?" *Boston Medical and Surgical Journal,* 3:688–690, 1830.

12. James Jackson, "Whether Animal Decomposition Is Productive of Fever?" *Boston Medical and Surgical Journal,* 3:704–706, 1830.

13. Usher Parsons, "Whether Animal Decomposition Is Productive of Fever?" *Boston Medical and Surgical Journal,* 3:769–771, 1830.

14. *Lancet,* 2:321–326, 353–362, June 11 and June 18, 1831. This was essentially what today would be known as a review article, covering Usher's paper as well as Parent du Chatelet's works, "Récherches, Jusqu'à Quel Point les Emanations Putrides Provenant de la Décomposition des Matières Animales . . . ," published in the French journal *Annales d'Hygiène Publique et de Médecine Légale,* in January, 1831, and the article by that same author and Doctor D'Arcet, "De l'Influence at de l'Assainissement des Salles de Dissection," published in the same journal in the following April. The second part, on pp. 353–362, is given over mainly to Usher's article.

15. Usher Parsons, *Directions for Making Anatomical Preparations, Formed on the Basis of Pole, Marjolin and Breschet, and Including the New Method of Mr. Swan* (Philadelphia, Carey & Lea, 1831). This was the largest work Usher ever published, amounting to 316 pages and containing 4 plates.

16. *American Journal of the Medical Sciences,* 9:143, 1831.

17. See notes 1–3, 5 and notes 39 and 57 of Chapter Ten. Also, Joseph Howard to A. McIntyre, June 1, 1830; Benjamin T. Onderdonk to Rt. Rev. Henry M. Onderdonk (of Philadelphia), May 29, 1830; Benjamin T. Onderdonk to William H. DeLancey, May 29, 1830; Romeo Elton "to Whom Concerned," August 1830; Alexis Caswell "to Whom Concerned," August 30, 1830; and Tristam Burges to Ezekiel F. Chambers, September, 1830. All of the above letters are in DPC.

18. George McClellan to Usher Parsons, March 5, 1831, DPC.

19. George McClellan to Usher Parsons, June 10, 1831, DPC.

20. Rhode Island Medical Society, "Minutes."

21. Thomas W. Fessenden (of Worcester) to Usher Parsons, September 27, 1831; Thomas W. Fessenden to Samuel B. Fales, September 27, 1831; Romeo Elton to Rev. Cushman (of Philadelphia), September 27, 1831, all in DPC.

22. Samuel Calhoun to Usher Parsons, October 18, 1831, DPC.

23. Revere, son of Paul Revere and a graduate of Harvard College, had studied with James Jackson in Boston and had received his M.D. degree at Edinburgh.

24. Thomas W. Dorr to Usher Parsons, November 2, 1831, Historical Society of Pennsylvania.

25. George McClellan to J. B. Sutherland, January 10, 1832, DPC.

26. C. W. Parsons *Memoir*, p. 32.

27. William Sweetser to Nathan R. Smith, February 3, 1832; George McClellan to (U.S. Representative) J. B. Sutherland, January 10, 1832; Samuel Calhoun to (U.S. Representative) Thomas A. Crawford, January 3, 1832; Sarah Perry (mother of Oliver Hazard Perry) to Usher Parsons, March 31, 1829, all in DPC. In Mrs. Perry's letter was enclosed a letter from Captain George Washington Rodgers to John Rodgers, President of the Board of Naval Commissioners.

28. C. W. Parsons *Memoir*, p. 13.

29. John T. Morse, Jr., *Life and Letters of Oliver Wendell Holmes* (2 v., Boston, Houghton, Mifflin, 1896), v. 1, p. 73.

30. *The History of the Rhode Island Medical Society and Its Component Societies, 1812–1962* (Providence, Roger Williams Press, 1966), pp. 3–9.

31. Rhode Island Medical Society, "Minutes."

32. Timothy Jennison to Usher Parsons, April 6, 1832, DPC.

33. Timothy Jennison to Usher Parsons, July 9, 1832, DPC.

34. *Ibid.*

35. For example, it was the subject of a letter which Thomas B. Parsons wrote to Usher on August 28 or 29 (the year is not given, but it was probably 1832), DPC. Cousin Tom had been "afflicted with the disease 12 days ago" and it had "caused considerable excitement" in Portland, Maine. He wanted to know whether the disease was "appedemick" and asked for advice.

36. Personal communication from Professor William G. McLoughlin of Brown University to the author.

37. Reports of the case and trial appeared in the *Providence Daily Journal* between December, 1832 and June, 1833, but especially on December 25, 1832, and May 9, 10 and 27, and June 3, 1833. The trial was reported by Benjamin F. Hallett in a pamphlet titled *Trial of Mr. Avery. A Full Report of the Trial of Ephraim K. Avery, Charged with the Murder of Sarah M. Cornell, Before the Supreme Court of Rhode Island, at a Special Term in Newport, Held in May, 1833, with the Arguments of the Counsel* (Boston, Published at the Offices of the *Daily Commercial Gazette* and the *Boston Advocate*, 1833).

38. J. B. Whitridge to Usher Parsons, September 6, 1833, DPC.

39. Usher Parsons to an unidentified person, January 12, 1834, DPC. The letter is incomplete.

40. Robert E. Pattison to Usher Parsons, April 7, 1834, DPC.

41. Usher Parsons to George Mason, September 21, 1834, RIHS.

42. Usher Parsons, "Sketches of Rhode Island Physicians Deceased Prior to 1850," p. 47–49.

43. See notes 26 and 27 of Chapter Ten.

44. Usher Parsons, "Statistics of Large Surgical Operations," *American Journal of the Medical Sciences*, 15:359–365, 1848.

45. Usher Parsons, "Malaria Produced by Vegetable and Animal Putrefaction, as a Cause of Fever," *Naval Magazine*, 1:66–79, 148–172, 1836.

46. Usher Parsons, "Remarks on Quarantine Systems," *Naval Magazine*, 1:244–259, 356–367, 1836.

47. Usher Parsons to Secretary of State, October 22, 1833, draft, DPC.

48. Usher Parsons to Isaac Hays, November 5, 1833, DPC.

49. Rhode Island Historical Society, "Minutes."

50. Printed circular letter from Usher Parsons, W. R. Staples, and Thomas W. Webb, committee, to Rhode Island Members of Congress, November 1, 1830. A copy is in DPC.

51. The manuscript report, signed by Usher Parsons and W. R. Staples, is in RIHS.

52. Francis Wayland to the President of the Rhode Island Historical Society, January 3, 1831, RIHS.

53. *American Journal of Science and Arts*, 17:338, 1830.

54. Providence, Hutchens & Cory, 1829.

55. Boston, Richardson, Lord, Holbrook, etc., 1832. Usher's letter to Silliman on this matter, dated October 22, 1831, is in the Yale University Library.

56. Usher Parsons, *Address Delivered Before the Providence Association for the Promotion of Temperance, May 27, 1831* (Providence, Weeden and Knowles, 1831).

57. In 1810 the annual national consumption was 20.5 million gallons of absolute alcohol equivalent (or twice that figure for "ardent spirits", which were about 45 per cent alcohol). This amounted to a per capita consumption of seven gallons of absolute alcohol (or 14 gallons of spirits). In 1829, in Albany, New York, it had reached a lofty per capita average of ten gallons (or an incredible 20 gallons of "ardent spirits"— i.e. liquor!). The comparable figure for 1850, after a generation of temperance agitation, was 2.1 gallons of absolute alcohol (4.2 gallons of spirits), which highlights the effectiveness of the early Temperance Movement. The per capita figure for 1970 was 2.61 of absolute alcohol (5.2 gallons of liquor). See Norman H. Clark, *Deliver Us From Evil: An Interpretation of American Prohibition* (New York, W. W. Norton, 1976), pp. 19–20.

58. Benjamin Hazard to Usher Parsons, July 6, 1833, inviting him to lecture at the recently consolidated First and Second Congregational Churches in Newport on the effects of alcohol, DPC.

59. Johnson Gardner to Usher Parsons, August 31, 1833, thanking him for his talk before the Pawtucket Temperance Society, DPC.

60. Usher Parsons, "Phrenology," *The Literary Journal and Weekly Register of Science and the Arts*, 1:125, 1833.

61. C. W. Parsons *Memoir*, p. 35.

62. *Ibid.*, p. 41.

63. Usher Parsons, "Sketches of Rhode Island Physicians Deceased Prior to 1850," p. 33.

64. Usher Parsons, "Sketch of the Life of Solomon Drowne, M.D., Late Professor of Materia Medica and Botany in Brown University," *Literary Journal and Weekly Register of Science and the Arts*, 1:39, 1834.

65. Usher Parsons to William Clift, August 31, 1835, DPC.

66. This well-known incident is recited in all biographies of Phineas Taylor Barnum, as well as in accounts of him in the *Dictionary of American Biography*, the *Columbia Encyclopedia*, the *Encyclopedia Britannica*, etc. As the *DAB* article worded it, "It was Joice Heth who pointed the way to fortune, and led Barnum to it. . . ."

67. Sarah Wallace Perry (O. H. Perry's sister) to Usher Parsons, December 15, 1835; Stephen Champlin to Usher Parsons, December 15, 1835; Sarah Wallace Perry to Usher Parsons, December 19, 1835, all of the foregoing in DPC. Also, a manuscript, undated and unsigned, directed to "My Dear Doctor," in RIHS. This appears to have been written by Sarah Wallace Perry; it contains a long sketch of O. H. Perry's life, but has little useful information.

68. Usher traveled to Washington, possibly twice, but certainly in late March or April 1836. The following were letters of introduction pursuant to the trip: John Whipple to Virgil Maxcy, March 28, 1836 and John Whipple to Henry Clay, March 28, 1836, both in DPC. The letter to Maxcy, lawyer and diplomat, Brown class of 1804, requested introductions "to such senators as he may desire." Clay, of course, was the unsuccessful candidate for the American presidency, having been defeated by Andrew Jackson in 1828 and 1832.

69. "Diary of Gen. Samuel Leighton, 1818–1848."

70. C. W. Parsons *Memoir*, p. 51.

71. Usher's interest in Alfred, while certainly an emotional one, was not entirely devoid of material concerns. His father, not a wealthy man in terms of realizable assets, nevertheless was a large landholder in Alfred, owning up to several hundred acres. Usher and brothers Joseph and John each was bequeathed a one-third interest in the large tract of land on the northeast side of what is now Kennebunk Road, where the "Mansion House" (as the family farmhouse was designated in the will, including the farm) was located, and also fifty acres of land near the courthouse in Alfred village. Usher also received "all my books in the Latin and Greek languages" and a one-quarter interest in "notes on hand", amounting to $530. Usher's three sisters received most of the household furniture, while William was bequeathed all residual real and personal properties. This information comes from the will of William Parsons on file in the courthouse in Alfred, Maine.

72. N. D. Appleton to Usher Parsons, November 14, 1831, DPC.

73. Samuel Leighton to Usher Parsons, November 28, 1831; Samuel Leighton to Usher Parsons, January 16, 1832; N. D. Appleton to Usher Parsons, February 1, 1832; Samuel Leighton to Usher Parsons, February 20, 1832; N. D. Appleton to Usher Parsons, March 21, 1832, DPC.

74. C. W. Parsons *Memoir*, p.26.

75. Abiel Holmes to Usher Parsons, October 11, 1832; John Holmes to Usher Parsons, November 16, 1832; John Holmes to Usher Parsons, December 19, 1832, HUCC. See also Thomas Wentworth Higginson, *Cheerful Yesterdays* (Boston, Houghton, Mifflin, 1898), pp. 13, 24, 30–35, 39–41, and Anna Mary Wells, *Dear Preceptor: The Life and Times of Thomas Wentworth Higginson* (Boston, Houghton, Mifflin, 1962), pp. 9–10, 24–25. At that time Higginson, Charles's playmate aged 7, wrote his very first letter to Charles. He later described Charles as a "prim, grave little boy," who "was called 'old fashioned'," but "was very precocious."

76. Usher Parsons to John Holmes and Charles W. Parsons, June 21, 1833, DPC.

77. According to the *Manufacturers and Farmers Journal* of June 24, 1833, President Jackson arrived in Providence by steamer from Newport on June 20th. He was welcomed at Fox Point by a throng of people and escorted by dignitaries and the Marine Artillery. After a procession through the streets, he settled at the City Hall, where he appeared on the balcony and received the "individual addresses [handshakes, no doubt] of a great majority of the unnumbered throng." Following an elegant dinner he rode through the streets on a white palfrey and then visited the mansion of Thomas P. Ives, Brown University, the Arcade, and other sights. He left Providence early on Friday.

78. Charles W. Parsons, John Holmes and Abiel Holmes to Usher Parsons, June 24, 1833, DPC.

79. "Diary of Gen. Samuel Leighton, 1818–1848," entry for August 3, 1834.

80. John Holmes and Abiel Holmes to Usher Parsons, June 24, 1833, DPC.

81. Usher Parsons to an unidentified person, fragment of a letter, undated, Historical Society of Pennsylvania.

82. Charles W. Parsons to Usher Parsons, March 28, 1835, DPC.

83. C. W. Parsons *Memoir*, pp. 51–52.

84. *Ibid.*, p. 13.

85. Usher Parsons to Dutee J. Pierce [i.e. Pearce], Navy Invalid File 1–176, WRDNA.

86. Manuscript authorization, dated July 29, 1816, Navy Invalid File 1–176, WRDNA.

87. Amos Perry, "Charles William Parsons," *New England Historical and Genealogical Register*, 48:475, 1894.

88. C. W. Parsons *Memoir*, p. 52–53.

89. *Ibid.*, p. 53.

90. Usher Parsons to Charles W. Parsons, September 16, 1836, DPC.

91. Usher Parsons to Charles W. Parsons, September 20 and 23, 1836, DPC.

92. Manuscript invitation from the Misses Rawls to Dr. Calhoun, November 3 (no year given), affirming that "They will be very happy to see his friend Dr. Parsons." Mrs. James Rush to Usher Parsons, November 4, 1836. This was an invitation from the wealthy Mrs. Rush, wife of Dr. James Rush, who was the son of Benjamin Rush. Robert Hare to Usher Parsons, November 5, 1836. This was an invitation to attend a "Wistar party" at the home of the eminent chemist. DPC.

93. Usher Parsons to Charles W. Parsons, November 8, 1836, DPC.

94. C. W. Parsons *Memoir*, p.53.

95. Usher Parsons to Charles W. Parsons, December 4, 1836, DPC.

CHAPTER TWELVE

Reunions and Reminiscenses

At the annual meeting of the Rhode Island Medical Society held in
June 1837 at the Redwood Library in Newport, Usher was honored
by election to the presidency, an office he held for three years.[1] As
Charles pointed out in his *Memoir,* Usher had bypassed the customary term as vice president—an appropriate reward for his faithful
attendance at meetings and his eminence in the profession. The
following June the annual meeting of the Society was held in Providence, and now for the first time Usher attended as presiding
officer. According to the record, "The president read a physiological
address, and Drs. [Lewis L.] Miller & [Isaac] Hartshorn, of Providence, were appointed to a committee to thank him for his very
able and ingenious discourse."[2] The paper was never published.

From time to time Usher obliged his friends and former pupils
with medical consultations by mail. A letter he wrote to Doctor
Milton Bradford of Woodstock, Connecticut (Brown 1828 and Harvard Medical School 1831) in July of 1838 provides a vivid example
of his therapeutics:[3]

> I have this moment returned from a tour west after an absence
> of two or three weeks and find your letter dated 18th instant.
> The case you describe is a serious one. I have found [effective]
> the caustic pile made with ¼ of a grain of Lunar caustic [silver
> nitrate] & given three times in 24 hours increasing the dose
> gradually. I have also found old rum agrees better with such
> patients than any other cordial. It may be mixed with sugar and
> water and given often and a little at a time. The greatest attention
> to diet is indispensible—weak chicken tea thickened with Rice
> flour and arrow root, &c. are as much as the disordered stomach

and bowels will bear. An occasional emetic with Sulphate of Lime may be indicated.

Often consulted by colleages in and around Providence, Usher was not himself averse to seeking counsel when confronted by a difficult clinical problem. Late that fall he sent a case of suspected tuberculosis to his friend and teacher, James Jackson, recently retired as Hersey Professor of the Theory and Practice of Physic at Harvard. Before the days of x-ray, the diagnosis of pulmonary phthisis was not always easy. Jackson reported on December 4:[4]

> After reading your letter & learning from Miss Newcomb the history of her case I examined her chest; and did it under strong prejudice that I should find tubercles there. But I found no signs of them. This was at my house before dinner. This afternoon I called on her & had all her thick clothing removed and examined the whole chest. But I have not found any physical signs of tubercles in any part, neither by percussion, nor by auscultation. Her chills, flushes & sweats with her cough and occasional hemoptysis tell another story. . . .

He suggested a regime of nourishing food, fresh air, and mild exercise, concluding, "I cannot see any call for medicine." In a day of purging and puking, this was indeed a progressive view.

In the fall of 1838 Usher visited New York and Philadelphia. He wrote to Charles from New York:[5] "I have passed the day thus far at the Medical College, Historical Society, and Hospital. Saw a very interesting operation at the latter, the excision of the elbow joint, which required half an hour. . . . I have relinquished the Charleston trip. Shall go to Philadelphia tomorrow."

The 1839 annual meeting of the Rhode Island Medical Society was again held in Newport at Redwood Library with Usher Parsons presiding. James Jackson and Jacob Bigelow, professors at Harvard and former teachers of the president, were elected to honorary fellowship in the society. Usher and Theophilus C. Dunn of Newport were "elected delegates to the decennial convention of Physicians, for revising the Pharmacopoeia of the United States, to be held in the City of Washington in January next."

During 1839 Usher's collected *Boylston Prize Dissertations* was published in Boston by Little and Brown.[6] The volume contained his four prize-winning medical essays, and a fifth which had received honorable mention from the Committee, all but the fifth previously published in medical journals. In the preface Usher gave an historical sketch of the origin of the prize and listed all questions and prize winners to date. He also added a three-page appendix, in which after a hiatus of eight years he again belabored the controversy with *Lancet* of London over animal versus vegetable decomposition in the causation of malaria. He gracefully dedicated the little work to his distinguished friend: "To William Clift, F.R.S., Conservator of the Museum of the Royal College of Surgeons in London: as a Testimonial of Respect for his Untiring Zeal in Physiological Researches, and of Esteem for the Private Virtues, This Volume is Inscribed, by his often Obliged and Grateful Friend, The Author." The book received favorable notice in the *Boston Medical and Surgical Journal.*[7]

At about this time Usher began to delve into the early medical history of Rhode Island. He was not a pioneer in the field, as the venerable and noted Benjamin Waterhouse fifteen years earlier had produced a delightful essay titled "Medical Literature of Rhode-Island, With a Sketch of Some of Her Most Eminent Men,"[8] certainly familiar to Usher. There was still much spadework to be done, however, and Usher set about the task.

He induced friends and acquaintances in various parts of the state to make inquiries and to talk to old-time doctors. "My much esteemed friend, Henry Bull, Esq.," wrote Usher, ". . . has furnished me with the materials relating to the south part of the State." Bull was the scion of a distinguished family of Newport lawyers and a prominent Newport businessman. Usher also interested T. Wilkins Updike of Kingston, Rhode Island, an eminent lawyer, member of the General Assembly for many years, and a local historian in his own right. Updike wrote to Usher:[9] "I have seen Dr. Anthony since I came from Providence & mentioned to him that you had written him. . . . I have also seen Dr. Aldrich who lives on this Hill, [is] old, & has given up practice. He has lived in Westerly & Hopkinton & practiced in both places besides a long practice here." He listed other doctors, as far as the memory of living residents could recall them, who had practiced in Exeter, Westerly, Richmond, Charlestown, Hopkinton, North Kingstown, and South Kingstown—a vague and sparsely populated area then and now known unofficially and popularly as South County. Despite possible discrepancies, he hoped that what he offered would be useful. The fruit of this endeavor was a sketch titled "A Brief Account of the Early Physicians and of the Medical Society of Rhode Island," which appeared in the February 1840 issue of *The American Quarterly Register.*[10]

Usher's original notes are still preserved, containing listings of early doctors in the scattered communities of the state. His story of the Bowen family of physicians accounted for no less than nine of that name dating back to 1680, although there were then "No physicians of the name and family . . . now left in the State." He sketched the history of the Rhode Island Medical Society and its bylaws and listed its officers, honorary members, and orators from its origin. A section on Medical Education contained paragraphs on the "Medical School . . . opened at Providence in connection with Brown University," mainly of interest because of its bearing on the reasons for the school's failure. He modestly concluded his own history thus: "Three medical books only have been published, viz: *Advice to Seafaring People*, a work on the *Art of Making Anatomical Preparations*, and a volume of *Boylston Prize Essays*—and these by the same individual."

At the annual meeting of the Rhode Island Medical Society of 1840 held in the courthouse in Providence, Usher retired from the presidency after serving for three years. The minutes noted a "donation of books . . . to the Society by Usher Parsons of Providence." A report was received from Theophilus C. Dunn regarding the decennial convention on the Pharmacopoeia held in Philadelphia the previous January. Usher had been delegated to attend, but his name did not appear among the participants.[11]

On Tuesday, August 18, 1840 the American Institute of Instruction gathered in Providence for its eleventh annual meeting. Providence was not a little proud of the honor, this being the first meeting of that august body held "without the bounds of Massachusetts." The members, "scattered over the Union . . . came up annually from the remotest parts of it to attend these meetings." As a public school system had just been established in Providence, the *Providence Daily Journal*[12] "deemed it particularly fortunate that this city has been selected as the place for the meeting of the Institute." The public were invited to attend the meetings and to participate in the discussions. After opening exercises in the First Baptist Meeting House, subsequent sessions were held in Franklin Hall. President Wayland of Brown University and the distinguished Horace Mann, Massachusetts educator and Brown alumnus, each read papers. The *Journal* reported: "The lectures and discussions have been generally attended, and they have been of a character which well repaid attendance. Some of the discussions were spirited, and were participated in by many gentlemen."

The final lecture of the series delivered by Usher Parsons on Friday morning was titled *On the Connexion and Reciprocal Influence between the Brain and Stomach*.[13] One newspaper[14] described it as "an able discourse" and commented: "As he proceeded in his instructive remarks, we were more than ever desirous that instruction in animal physiology might form a part of every teacher's education. Much good might be done, much evil prevented by judicious teachers well informed on this subject." If one reads "psychology" for "physiology," this was a prophetic judgment. "The lecture being ended," the account continued, "resolutions were passed expressive of the gratification felt by the members of the Institution with their visit to Providence. This courtesy was returned. . . ."

Usher's excellent treatise was perhaps the best medical paper he wrote in his lifetime. It was strongly influenced by the monumental experiments in gastric physiology of William Beaumont, the American army surgeon, as reported in historic papers[15] published between 1825 and 1833. Usher's well-chosen words, written thirty years before Walter B. Cannon, the famed American physiologist of Harvard, was born[16] and almost a century before the terms "psychosomatic" and "stress" had entered the language, have a strikingly modern sound:

> The nervous and dyspeptic complaints incident to adult persons, whose brain or instrument of the mind is constantly overexcited by emulation, ambition, anxiety, tribulation, and a thousand other causes, are constantly multiplying in frequency and intensity, with the increase of population and with the march of intellect and refinement. The fury of politics, the jealousies, envyings and rivalries of professions, the struggles for office, the contentions of trade, the excitements of speculation, and the anxieties of commerce, the privations, discontents, and despair of poverty, and various other causes of mental perturbation, induce, directly or indirectly, a large proportion of the diseases to which we have referred.

He concluded his essay with a quotation in Latin from Cicero's *De Senectute*, his own graceful translation of which deserves repetition: "Attention must be paid to health; moderate exercise should be used, food and drink sufficient to refresh, not to load the powers; nor should the body alone be regarded, but also the mind, since this also unless you feed it as you would a lamp with oil, dies out with old age."

During this period Usher was busy with his practice. He received a note from Newport dated September 14, 1840 and signed "Chas. Collins":[17] "Dr. [Enoch] Hazard informs me that he had some conversation with you in Boston respecting my diseased eye, and that he coincides with you in opinion that (the weather being much cooler) no time should be lost in operating on it. If you will write me, and let me know what day you will come here, I will be prepared to attend to the business."

The sixty-six year old Collins, addressed by Usher as "Gov. Collins," had actually served for several years as lieutenant governor. While we do not know whether in fact Usher operated upon him that summer, he did so two years later. This was the only "extirpation of the eye" he performed in his lifetime:[18]

> [He] had long been affected with fungus hematodes [bleeding fungating malignant tumor] of the eyeball, which projected nearly an inch beyond the lids. I cleared out the whole socket. He recovered to all appearance perfectly, and remained well for more than two years, when the fungus grew again from the socket, and was beginning to project through the lids. I operated again in May 1844, but found the socket filled with bony, as well as soft material. He died a few months after.

The year 1840 also saw other significant surgical achievements.[19] Among them was his first successful trephine operation for depressed fracture of the skull. The patient was a ten-year-old boy in whom, as he described it, "five pieces of bone, making a surface of one inch square [was] driven in by the kick of a horse." He was "trepanned" and "recovered." That year he also performed his first major amputation for arteriosclerotic gangrene—only two for this condition out of a total of twenty-four major amputations performed during his lifetime. This was an above-knee procedure in a sixty-three-year-old man. His accurate and graphic description of the process as "dry gangrene from ossification and obstruction of arteries by calcareous deposit" leaves no doubt as to its nature. He, however, did not use the term arteriosclerosis, if indeed he had ever heard it. These traumatic procedures were, of course, carried out without benefit of anesthesia.

In a New Year's Day (1837) letter to Charlie,[20] Usher had proposed that on Charlie's next vacation they might work together on an historical project which Usher had had on his mind. He had recently been elected a corresponding member of the Massachusetts Historical Society and desired to acknowledge the honor by presenting to the Society a map of the lower Blackstone River showing Roger Williams's crossing into Providence. "I will," he wrote, "mark the supposed residence of R. Williams in Seekonk [Massachusetts] before he crossed it into Providence, trace the course of his canoe to Watcheer Rock, from thence round the south end of the town and up the cove to St. John's Church within three or four rods of which it is known that he lived, and also the place where he was buried, which was in Mr. Dorr's garden [on Benefit Street]. . . . I think the Society will attach some value to it. . . ."

On January 12, 1837 it was announced in the *Providence Daily Journal* that an organizational meeting of the recently chartered Rhode Island Society of Natural History would be held that evening at the office of Doctor Usher Parsons, who headed the list of incorporators. Another incorporator of note was Alexis Caswell, D.D., professor of mathematics and later of astronomy at Brown and president of the University from 1868 to 1872.

At this first meeting in Usher's office, the charter was accepted,[21] and a draft of bylaws presented by the chairman was adopted "with some trifling amendments." The original membership was sixty-four, although only twenty-eight actually signed the bylaws. It included some medical colleagues, such as George Capron, Christopher G. Perry (Oliver Hazard Perry's son), Theophilus C. Dunn of Newport, and Ezekiel Fowler of Smithfield, and a number of citizens with distinguished Rhode Island family names, such as T. W. Dorr, Crawford Nightingale, Rowland G. Hazard, E. Carrington Hoppin, Richard Steere, William Manton, and Joseph Bridgham.[22] The membership roll was generously increased at subsequent monthly meetings, which were held through May of 1837. Several of Usher's friends were elected "corresponding members," among them Doctor Walter Channing, dean of the Harvard Medical School; George B. Emerson, founder of the Boston Society of Natural History; Doctor J. B. Whitridge of Charleston, South Carolina; Doctor D. Humphreys Storer,[23] teacher at the Harvard Medical School and naturalist; and finally Usher's brother-in-law, Oliver Wendell Holmes. Navy friends Alexander Slidell (Mackenzie), Charles O. Handy, and Thomas Breese became corresponding members. The society honored itself by electing several honorary members, among them Benjamin Silliman of Yale, and its brightest star, Sir William Clift. The curators were directed "to get up a course of lectures, and a committee, of which Usher was a member, was appointed at the May meeting "to select a room and to make preparations for the Lectures." Corresponding members were invited to participate in the series, and Wendell's name was mentioned in this connection.

Thereafter the society languished. Charles wrote of the enterprise: ". . . the Rhode Island Natural History Society, of which . . . [my father] was chosen the first President . . . held several meetings, and made some collections, but never attained the position of a working scientific society." Usher, continued Charles, "kept up the practice of collecting specimens . . . and read the geological works of Buckland, Hitchcock and others. He had some knowledge of field botany, and occasionally gave private courses of botanical lectures to classes of young ladies."[24]

In the meantime in 1835 Usher's young brother-in-law Oliver Wendell Holmes was awarded his medical degree at Harvard and was elected to the Massachusetts Medical Society. He gained some merited attention by winning the Boylston Prize for 1836. The Boylston questions for the following year were "1. To what extent, and in what places had Intermittent Fever been indigenous in New England?" and "2. What is the nature of Neuralgia, and what is the best mode of treating it?" Wendell ambitiously set out to win both prizes for that year. In connection with the first question he sought some assistance from Usher, who went to considerable trouble to oblige.

Usher learned from local old-timers of sporadic outbreaks of intermittent tertian fever over the past eighty years. They appeared during summer flooding along the Moshassuck River north of Providence and in Cranston along the Pawtuxet River. Three cases in Cranston many years before had "yielded to treatment with Bark" (*i.e.* cinchona bark, the source of quinine, a malarial specific first recognized by Europeans in the seventeenth century). His old friend, Doctor Abiel Hall of Alfred, informed him that there had never been a case in York County in Maine in thirty years.[25] Usher also inquired of Doctor Samuel Emerson[26] of Kennebunk, Maine, who wrote a long historical account of the intermittent fever in that area. This, too, Usher forwarded to Wendell. The discovery of the malarial parasite was then still a half century away, and the role of the mosquito as vector ten years beyond that. Wendell found much of the information helpful, quoted at length from Usher's letters, and gave him full credit. Wendell won both prizes in 1837.[27] By winning the competition three times, he equaled in two years the impressive feat of his prominent relative in Providence.

Soon thereafter, Usher learned that Wendell had received an appointment familiar to Usher himself:

> I have just had official notice of my appointment as Professor of Anatomy in Dartmouth College.[28] Mussey and Oliver quit after this course. Mussey's office is divided—I have anatomy—a N. Hampshire man—Crosby I believe, has surgery, and Bartlett of Lowell has Physiology &c. in Oliver's place. Of course I am not obliged to reside there except during lectures. I think this is a very agreeable appointment, and as I do not lecture until next August, I shall have plenty of time to get ready.

In the fall of 1837 Usher finished an ambitious reading project which he had set for himself six years before. Charles described the wide range of his father's literary tastes:[29]

> His reading on subjects not connected with physical science was mostly in works of history and travel. He took little interest in purely imaginative literature. He read few of the classical novels. A special interest in the remains of Pompeii, which he had carefully examined when cruising on the Mediterranean, led him to buy and read Bulwer's "Last Days of Pompeii." In poetry, his favorites were [James] Thomson and [Edward] Young. He often read through the "Seasons," as the seasons came round; and was equally familiar with the "Night Thoughts" [respectively works of those authors]. He selected the opening lines of this poem, for his son to speak at a school declamation when less than ten years old; and it will be readily believed that they were not very intelligently or impressively uttered.

Charles noted that his father was a regular reader of the Bible. Beside certain favorite parts, especially of the Psalms, he went through the Bible, with probably some omissions, four times in the last thirty years of his life. Charles mentioned that Usher wrote in his notebook in November 1837:

> I have this day finished the Old Testament, which I began in June, 1831. I cannot but think that the Christian religion would gain by excluding some of the books. Two-thirds of what follows the first chapter of Jeremiah might be omitted, and all of Solomon's Song. These writings of the Prophets might be transferred to the Apocrypha, or incorporated into a separate division of the Bible, and considered as elegies on the woes prepared by Divine Power to bring upon this ill-fated people the Jews. The Bible, after such exclusion, would be read more generally, intelligibly and thoroughly than it is while encumbered with such a mass of matter so irrelevant to subsequent ages of the world. As a rule of life, and a history of God's government and the plan of salvation, an abridged volume might be formed for general circulation, which would embrace all that is essential. I shall now commence reading Tyndall's New Testament with notes.

Early in July of 1838, Usher again traveled west to Erie for his first real visit there since his military service almost a quarter of a century ago. Charles recorded the incidents of this trip in his *Memoir* (p. 53). Cayuga Lake was the only place en route to Buffalo which Usher could recognize. He arrived in Erie on the 5th, and on the 6th visited the courthouse, which had served as his hospital. Few of the persons with whom he had been acquainted recognized him at first, but then expressed great joy on meeting him again. In the burying-ground he sought out the graves of Claxton, who had died of a wound received in battle, and of other naval comrades. He called on Captain Dobbins, a sailing-master in the war and now commander of a revenue cutter, and went with him to the Peninsula (Presqu'isle). There he trod once more the deck of the *Lawrence*, now a hulk resting about a quarter of a mile from the old blockhouse, where she had recently been raised from the deep. Her timbers, they were pleased to learn, were perfectly sound. "Took some pieces from her to make canes of," wrote Usher. He also visited James Miles, whose arm he had amputated the day after the battle. "He did not recollect me," Usher recalled, "but on learning who I was, shed tears of joy." "This visit to Erie," concluded Usher, "gave me indescribable pleasure."

In the summer of 1840 Mackenzie's biography of Perry was taking its final form. On June 17 Mackenzie asked Usher[30] "to send me all the anecdotes you can remember or collect respecting him as soon as possible." He continued:

> You thought you would be able to send me some anecdotes relative to his boyhood and early life. They would be particularly acceptable. Any information you can give me about the lake service, the difficulties in creating a squadron in that remote inland sea, the effect of climate or nature on the crews, and the condition particularly of Perry's health, about the circumstances attending the difficulty with commodore Chauncey about rum; remarks of wounded during battle as they came down; you must of course have listened to their reports with intense interest. Picturesque appearance of the squadron before and after the battle, when you last saw them and then first saw them again; whatever in short has made an impression on your mind will be of interest and use to me. If you recollect any of the events of our cruise to the Mediterranean in the *Java* they would also be useful. I was too young at the time to have retained any distinct impression of what occurred. Handy destroyed his journal some years ago much to my present regret. If you should have kept one and retain it, a perusal of it would be of great service to me, and it would be used with whatever restriction you might impose.

Mackenzie's *The Life of Commodore Oliver Hazard Perry* appeared later that year. His preface contained this acknowledgment: "To Doctor Usher Parsons of Providence . . . the writer has to acknowledge himself under great obligations for a variety of facts, and just and intelligent opinions with regard to the character, manners, and acquirements of Perry." Mackenzie later in the book described an interesting episode aboard the *Java* in which Usher played an important role. Before arriving at Gibraltar on the eastward passage, Lieutenant Dulany Forrest fell overboard "booted and buttoned to the chin." He was fished out of the water, apparently lifeless, "but the skilful applications of the surgeon quickly restored him."[31]

As fall of 1840 approached, interest in the political campaign reached a lively pitch. William Henry Harrison, hero of the War of 1812, and John Tyler were running on the Whig ticket. This was the year of "Log Cabin and Hard Cider" and "Tippecanoe and Tyler too." The newspapers were full of political gossip and rhetoric, and a log cabin was built on the "town house lot" in Providence to serve as Whig headquarters. For a special reason Usher became interested in the campaign and participated vigorously. As Charles described it:[32]

> He seldom took an active part in politics. He voted with the Whig party in the day of it. The nomination of General Harrison for President awakened a special interest in him, on account of the general's connection with Commodore Perry and the service on Lake Erie. Dr. Parsons wrote several newspaper articles in favor of Harrison, which were widely reprinted, and spoke on the same subject in the old town house [corner of College and Benefit Streets], October 19, 1840. He was appointed messenger to carry the electoral vote of Rhode Island to Washington, and handed the package of votes to Vice President Richard M. Johnson.

On September 22 a long open letter dated the 19th and addressed to Asher Robbins, former Democratic United States Senator from Rhode Island, appeared in the *Providence Daily Journal*. The Democrats argued incorrectly that Harrison's military exploits were overrated and that it was Secretary of War John Armstrong who had recommended the creation of a fleet on Lake Erie, and not Harrison as claimed by the Whigs. Usher's vigorous refutation exploded in purple prose:

> And cheering must it be to every true patriot to behold such a redeeming spirit, and to witness the total failure of demagogues and hirelings to asperse the illustrious General's hard earned fame. Public opinion armed with the truth, as with the spear of Ithuriel, has touched their foul machinations, disclosing to the startled sense of the universal people their odious and portentous deformity, and from the north and south, the east and west, thronging multitudes have arisen in the majesty of their strength, and girding up to the combat, are resolved to redress a hero's wrongs, and to cheer the evening of his days with the highest honors that a great people can bestow.

On Usher's address of October 19 the Whig press reported:[33]

> The address of Dr. Parsons before the Tippecanoe Club last Monday evening was an excellent one. It was chiefly historical, and the more interesting on that account. He took up the life and services of Gen. Harrison, and dwelt particularly on the Battle of Lake Erie, in which Dr. Parsons was concerned. It was listened

to with great attention. We wish this address might be repeated in different parts of the State.

The Whigs carried Rhode Island and won the national election as well. The four Whig electors, headed by Nicholas Brown, met in Bristol on December 2 to cast their ballots. It was the custom to dispatch two copies of the official ballot to the president of the United States Senate, one by mail and one by special messenger. They would be opened and counted in the presence of both houses of Congress on the first Wednesday in January. This was obviously a good way to get a free trip to Washington. How Usher came to be selected is explained in a news item of December 3:[34] "As usual there were a great number of applications from candidates to carry the electoral votes to Washington. The College, not being able to agree upon their respective merits, the names of the candidates of the several electors were put in a hat, and one drawn therefrom; which happened to be that of Dr. Usher Parsons of Providence, and he therefore accordingly was appointed."

Throughout his active years Usher delved into the anthropology of the local Indians. In reference to this Charles wrote:[35]

In his rides extending many miles around Providence, he examined the Indian burying-grounds, and gradually made a collection of bones and various utensils, such as hatchets, arrow-heads, pots of soapstone, &c. He recorded the Indian names of localities, with the meanings that had been assigned them by tradition or by guess. In 1840, he furnished a barrel-full of skulls, from an aboriginal burying-place in Washington county, to Dr. Samuel G. Morton, of Philadelphia, author of "Crania Americana."

That handsome work, the subtitle of which was *A Comparative View of the Skulls of Various Aboriginal Nations of North and South America*,[36] had already appeared in 1838 before the grizzly cargo had arrived. It doubtless startled the learned professor, who never mentioned any indebtedness to his medical colleague in Providence, if indeed there were any.

Before the year ended, a literary contribution of Usher's appeared in *The Knickerbocker* (or *New York Monthly Magazine*) for December 1840. It was an anecdote in the form of a short story, bearing the romantic title "The Avenger of Blood: A Reminiscence of a Scene on Board a Ship of War."[37] The little tale recalling an incident during Usher's navy years tells the story of a crewman aboard the

Guerrière, once a pirate, but since pardoned by President Monroe, who was involved in an incident of melodramatic proportions. The opening sentences vividly evoke the ambiance of a man-o'-war at sea:

> 'Twas in a dark, tempestuous night, that the frigate *Guerrière* ploughed her way through the Gulf of Finland, rolling and plunging at the sport of every billow, as it dashed its spray over her deck. The incessant creaking and groaning of the ship's joints at every surge, were occasionally interrupted by the hoarse sound of the officer's trumpet, or the shrill pipe of the boatswain, and the tramp of men running with the halyards.

Late in January of 1837 Thomas Breese, Usher's old shipmate, wrote to ex-Senator John Holmes of Alfred,[38] reviewing in detail Usher's naval career and his later accomplishments. "His native state," he concluded, "has abundant reason to feel proud to rank him among its sons." Although Usher's disability sustained aboard the *Java* is not mentioned in this letter, it is clear that Usher had reopened the pension issue and was seeking support from any useful source. His Navy pension file in Washington contains a petition[39] indicating that he sought a pension of one-hundred-and-fifty dollars per year from the date of the accident in 1815 with payment of arrearages to July 1835 or "such other relief as shall appear reasonable." In March he wrote to Commodore Charles Morris,[40] one of three Naval Commissioners in Washington. He claimed that his pension had by mistake been set at $12.50 instead of $25.00, as he had lately ascertained, and furthermore that a recent act of Congress allowed payment of arrearages from the time of disability to the time of being placed on the pension list. He reminded Commodore Morris that "You knew me in the Navy" and that "my pay during the ten years was but . . . half of what is now allowed to surgeons" and was paid in treasury notes discounted 15 per cent at that!

Navy Surgeon B. Tickner in 1835 had certified to a fracture of the right patella (kneepan), rated at about fifty per cent disability for the affected limb. There were also certificates from Doctors George Capron and Lloyd B. Brayton of Providence indicating pain and lameness. These were proffered since there were no naval surgeons in easy reach of the city. Apart from the latter certificates, the naval summary concluded, "other papers in the case furnish no proof respecting the propriety of increasing the amount of the pension."[41] Secretary of the Navy Mahlon Dickerson submitted for review the entire file to Navy Surgeon Samuel Jackson. His finding read:[42]

> . . . I then gave it as my opinion that he could not, by any view of the circumstances of his case, be considered as totally disabled. . . . and I distinctly informed him that I thought no Surgeon could certify to a greater disability in his case, than one half. My opinion then was that Dr. Tickner's certificate was just and correct, and I have no reason to alter it now. I am well informed that the Doctor has, since he left the Service, been employed in an extensive practice. . . .

Thus ended the pension case.

Usher's correspondence with Charles through the spring of 1837[43] concerned such mundane matters as Charles's apparel and his progress in his studies. Usher had presented to his housekeeper, Mrs. Carpenter, in Charlie's name, a copy of Uncle Wendell's poems, as "she has done you many kindnesses." Mrs. Carpenter was "very much pleased." Charles wrote that he was "getting along very well" in Latin and Greek, but was "lower in mathematics than anything else." He added: "I have been chosen into two different college societies, the Institute of 1770 and the I.O.H., both of them lecturing and debating."[44] Usher replied: "The truth is, I feel ambitious to have you chosen into the Phi-Beta [Kappa] Society and this I know you will be sure of if only you sustain yourself through this term!" He scolded Charles, as he did on several other occasions, for not writing promptly and regularly. In May[45] Usher reported to Charles that he was adding a new room to his office and dwelling ("being No. 5 in a row"). "The walls," he wrote, "will . . . be covered with shelves for specimens in Natural History, which had collected so abundantly in my study as to incommode me very much." He added: "I have three students in [room] No. 1."

John Holmes reported[46] that Grandfather Holmes's health was failing and that, sadly, he had suffered a stroke: "Wendell thinks that the case amounts to apoplexy. . . . He has consulted Dr. Jackson." The Reverend Abiel Holmes died on June 4, 1837. In an obituary in the June 9th issue of the *Morning Courier and General Advertizer* (Providence), he was described as "one of the ablest and most distinguished Divines of our Country. . . . His American

Annals are a monument to his discriminating judgment and patient industry."

In July Charles, on vacation in Providence, described in great detail to his friend Wentworth Higginson (whom he addressed whimsically as "Hon. Thomas W. Higginson, Esq.") his busy times in Rhode Island and his teeming quarters in the Parsons abode. Higginson, then a mere fourteen years old, would someday be eminent as a cleric, abolitionist, author, biographer, and editor. The wide range of Charles's mind and his myriad activities reveal his avid curiosity:[47]

> Next morning we [Charles and Usher] . . . read & surveyed till about IX, when entered chaise. Rode by Pawtucket (where Sam Patch [a Yankee daredevil][48] began to stretch his legs), Lonsdale, Smithfield, &c., &c., &c. to Cumberland, R.I.[49] . . . visited grave &c. of [Rev. William] Blackstone, who formerly owned all Boston, & sold it for £40, I believe. We saw his grave, cellar, well, & 'Study Hill,' where he wrote sermons. . . ."[50]

They returned to Providence on Sunday morning, loaded with shells, stones, chain-cables, worms, alligators' scales, whales' teeth and other objects. Charles's letter continued:

> Attended St. John's church (Episcopal), where I wore out my legs as usual standing up. . . . Evening went to grave-yard[51] about 3 miles square, where read some 50,000 epitaphs, saw boys playing . . . on the tombs, & ret'd without supper. This forenoon have been arranging, labelling &c. said things. . . . Also, reading very old letters to my father, which are stuffed with Noah, Solomon, Socrates, &c., &c. wisdom. This afternoon am going to Dighton rock,[52] then on to Plymouth, &c., &c. So much for adventures . . . in this renowned & irascible city.
>
> The office I am in you have heard somewhat described in my former correspondence. Suffice it to say that 2 rooms have been added . . . & one of these contains the beetle bugs mentioned twice before together with a larger collection of similar materials—mostly dried skeletons of monkeys, bats, dragons, griffins, turtles, & ducks. Also several minerals, which may be of value, also a mug of coins, which I shall transport to Cambridge. There are, moreover, a few pots & kettles from Herculaneum, on one of which the name L. FABRICIUS is distinctly legible. The other room has a set of tools with which I try to make cracker boxes. . . .

By September Charles had returned to Cambridge. In an exchange of letters in October, Usher, again disturbed by Charlie's failure to write regularly, affected the role of stern parent:[53] "On the 6th of October I forwarded you $50.00 per mail to pay your board and other expenses. It is now 10 days and I have received no answer. . . . I hope you have some reasonable answer, as I shall otherwise on your omitting again to write me on Saturday feel it is my duty to remove you to this College [i.e. Brown]." Charles, chastened, replied:[54] "I beg most humbly & sincerely that I may, through your mercy, be pardoned. If, however, this may not be, & I must be removed to another College, I can only say that the keenest pain will be excited in me." He described how the money had been spent, and ended: "Mathematics quite good." Usher responded:[55] "I am alone this evening and know not how to pass a solitary hour with so much satisfaction as in writing to my dear Charles. . . . It is a subject of heartfelt pleasure to me to see you maintain your rank so well in College—particularly . . . in mathematics." Charles, of course, remained at Harvard.

Charles, still boarding with his widowed grandmother, yearned to be on his own and sought permission to transfer to the college dormitory. Usher's response was somewhat qualified:[56] "I think it had better be deferred till Commencement. Your fuel is laid in for the season and had best not be moved to the College. Besides I think your kind grandmother would prefer your remaining where you are for the present. We will talk over the matter . . . when you visit me next month."

On October 16, 1838 Charles read a "part" in the fall "Exhibition" of Harvard College, as the public exercises were called. It was a Latin version of a Phi Beta Kappa address by Joseph Story, Dane Professor of Law at Harvard and a Justice of the United States Supreme Court, whom Usher and Mary had met many years before in Providence. It bore the impressive title "Orationis Josephi Story apud Societatem P.B.K. habitae pars."[57] Usher's attendance is not a matter of record.

At a dinner held in Boston at the Pavilion Thursday evening, November 8, 1838 the Boston Medical Association honored Harvard professors James Jackson and John Collins Warren, recently returned from an extended tour of Europe and the British Isles.[58] Usher attended this important affair. While he did not have time to visit Charles in Cambridge, he purchased a present for him in Boston, and in a subsequent letter he expressed concern about Charlie's wardrobe:[59]

> I write partly for the purpose of reminding you of the dumbbells bought for you and which you will find at Brewer's Apothecary's store [in Boston] between old State house and Little's Bookstore. . . . I wish you would use them often and actively every day.
>
> When you come on I wish you to pack up your old clothes which you do not expect to wear again and bring them with you. I can do a great deal of good with them. . . . Get you a snug bodied coat having a slight, very slight mix. . . . Ask for a very strong cloth worth about $ pr. yard.[60] I hope that . . . your frock coat is repaired . . . for an everyday coat till May next. I shall have a black woolen vest ready for you. . . . A pair of stout shoes will be lighter for you to run in than boots and will save you some expense. If you need winter gloves, I have some here to give you. You must have your account of expenses of all kinds ready to bring on with you.

This letter was addressed to "Charles W. Parsons, Collegian, Cambridge." Usher was both father and mother to his only child.

In the spring of 1839 Charles was enjoying a second term of relative independence, now boarding away from his grandmother's house. The freedom did not affect his continued academic achievement. In March he wrote his father:[61] "I am as comfortably situated as last term . . . & we have as much fun as ever. I however study a good deal. . . . I am almost every day at grandmother's." He complained about his clothes, particularly the frock coat Usher had advised him to use for everyday wear: "My old frock-coat will not do to wear at all. . . . It is the shabbiest coat in college, everybody says. I have to wear my best therefore, some."

Charles dutifully kept his father informed of his academic progress, but was not boastful. Usher for his part held his ear close to the ground concerning his son's activities, as he revealed in a letter to Charles of June 13:[62]

> . . . I was pleased to learn from your tutor in elocution . . . that you spoke greatly to the satisfaction of Professor Channing. I think he said you had the highest mark. . . . You must therefore have underrated your performance, which speaks well for your modesty. . . . I would urge . . . you to improve every opportunity to declaim . . . cultivate your conversational powers, which can only be done by practice. You are naturally [so] taciturn . . . as to

prevent your succeeding well in life, in any profession—and the fashion of Cambridge is . . . rather unfavourable to your overcoming the impediment. The style of speaking [there] is elsewhere considered tame. . . . Dr. Johnson inculcated the precept that no opportunity should be lost . . . for expressing . . . opinions and thoughts whether in publick or in conversation. It is better to acquire this faculty even at the expense of being sometimes considered garrulous or obtrusive. . . .

In the fall, on October 15, 1839, Charles again participated in the Harvard College Exhibition, debating the question "Whether voting by Ballot should be introduced into all Elective and Legislative Proceedings?", apparently arguing the negative.[63] It is not clear whether Usher was able to attend, but it can be assumed that the Holmes clan was there.

This was Charles's senior year. He was busy with lectures and recitations, which gave him little of moment to write to his father. He found the lectures in botany by Professor Thaddeus William Harris to be the most interesting, but those by Professor Henry Wadsworth Longfellow on Dante were also worthwhile. In age-old student fashion, he complained about the food: "This week it got rather too bad, and I concluded to emigrate [for board] to my chum's place,"[64] where it was better and cost no more. He tried to be conscientious about writing in his diary every day, recording what he could remember of his lectures. His growing interest in physiology was evidenced by a lecture on "Respiration: The Chemical Changes and Operations Connected with Breathing," which he delivered before the Davy Club,[65] named after Sir Humphrey Davy, the great English chemist. His inclination toward botany, physiology, and natural history foreshadowed his choice of medicine as a career.

Yet Usher was disappointed in his son's mediocre marks in natural history, particularly in light of Charles's expressed interest in it. The implications were clear when Usher observed that "success in this is after all the most important whether viewed in relation to your College rank or *to future utility*" [his Italics]. "Botany," he affirmed, "I certainly wish you to pursue, as it will place you on a footing with my students, who will soon engage in it and will render your summer vacation very pleasant."[66]

The Harvard Commencement that year, held on August 26, 1840, was of more than passing interest, as Charles, eleven days shy of his seventeenth birthday, was to graduate. As his "commencement part" he read a dissertation with the pretentious title "The Sacrifice of Principle to Expediency."[67] Usher and the Holmes family proudly looked on as Charles, the youngest member of his class, received his well-deserved diploma.

NOTES

1. Rhode Island Medical Society, "Minutes."
2. *Ibid.*
3. Usher Parsons to Milton Bradford, July 26, 1838, DPC.
4. James Jackson to Usher Parsons, December 4, 1838, DPC.
5. Usher Parsons to Charles W. Parsons, November 2, 1838 (incorrectly dated November 3), DPC.
6. See footnote 27 of Chapter Ten.
7. *Boston Medical and Surgical Journal*, 19:432, 1839.
8. Benjamin Waterhouse, "Medical Literature of Rhode-Island, With a Sketch of Some of Her Most Eminent Men," *Boston Medical Intelligencer*, 2:49–50, 1824.
9. T. Wilkins Updike to Usher Parsons, November 24 and November 29, 1839, RIHS. The novelist John Updike is a member of this prominent Rhode Island family.
10. Usher Parsons, "A Brief Account of the Early Physicians and of the Medical Society of Rhode Island," *American Quarterly Register*, 12:254–260, 1840.
11. Rhode Island Medical Society, "Minutes."
12. *Providence Daily Journal*, August 18, 22 and 24, 1840.
13. Usher Parsons, *A Lecture on the Connexion and Reciprocal Influences, Between the Brain and Stomach* (Providence, B. Cranston, 1841).
14. *Manufacturers & Farmers Journal and Providence and Pawtucket Advertiser*, August 20, 1840.
15. William Beaumont, "A Case of Wounded Stomach," *The American Medical Recorder*, 8:14–19, 1825 (his report was erroneously attributed to Joseph Lovell), and *Experiments and Observations on the Gastric Juice and Physiology of Digestion* (Plattsburgh, F. P. Allan, 1833; 2d ed., Boston, 1834). The gunshot accident to the famed voyageur Alexis St. Martin, which resulted in a stomach fistula, allowing Beaumont to study the stomach and its actions by direct observation, occurred on Mackinac Island, a spot fixed in Usher's memory.
16. Cannon's early and pioneering study by x-ray of deglutition and the motility of the stomach and intestine led to his later studies on the influence of the emotions and the autonomic nervous system on the digestive system.

17. Charles Collins to Usher Parsons, September 14, 1840, RIHS.
18. Usher Parsons, "Statistics of Large Surgical Operation."
19. *Ibid.*
20. Usher Parsons to Charles W. Parsons, January 1, 1837, DPC.
21. Rhode Island Society of Natural History, "Minutes," Rhode Island Historical Society.
22. Thomas Wilson Dorr, later the principal protagonist in the Dorr War; Crawford Nightingale (1816–1892), Brown A.B. and A.M. 1830, and Harvard Divinity School, 1838, Unitarian minister; Rowland G. Hazard (1801–1888), manufacturer, politician, writer, and Brown University trustee; E. Carrington Hoppin (1812–1879), Brown A.B. 1834, son of Benjamin Hoppin, studied medicine in Philadelphia and Paris, but apparently did not practice; Richard Steere, of a very large Rhode Island family, was prominent in Smithfield, R.I.; William Manton attended Brown, class of 1835, but did not graduate; Joseph Bridgham (1815–1865), Brown A.B. and A.M. 1834, practiced law in New York, where he became a U.S. Commissioner.
23. David Humphreys Storer (1804–1891), M.D. Harvard 1825, an obstetrician and gynecologist, was Dean of the Harvard Medical School 1855–1864, and on the staffs of the Massachusetts General and Boston Lying-in Hospitals. He was also a founder of the Boston Society of Natural History and a noted ichthyologist.
24. C. W. Parsons *Memoir*, p. 36.
25. Usher Parsons to Oliver Wendell Holmes, January 10 and January 27, 1837, Houghton Library, Harvard University.
26. Samuel Emerson to Usher Parsons, February 11, 1837, Houghton Library, Harvard University.
27. The question (No. 1) for which Wendell won the prize in 1836 was, "How far are the external means of exploring the condition of the internal organs, to be considered useful and important in medical practice?" This was published, along with the essays of Robert W. Haxall and Luther V. Bell, in Volume 7 of the Massachusetts Medical Society's *Library of Practical Medicine* (Boston, Perkins & Marvin, 1836). His two prizes in 1837 answered the questions, 1, "To what extent, and in what places, has intermittent fever been indigenous in New England?" and, 2, "What is the nature of Neuralgia, and what is the best mode of treating it?" Wendell had all three essays published in a monograph titled *Boylston Prize Dissertations for the Years 1836 and 1837*, which was issued in Boston by Charles C. Little and James Brown in 1838.
28. Oliver Wendell Holmes to Usher Parsons, August 7, 1838, HUCC.
29. C. W. Parsons *Memoir*, p. 36.
30. Alexander Slidell Mackenzie to Usher Parsons, June 17, 1840, DPC.
31. Alexander Slidell Mackenzie, *The Life of Commodore Oliver Hazard Perry*, v. 2, p. 137.
32. C. W. Parsons *Memoir*, p. 30.

33. *Manufacturers & Farmers Journal and Providence and Pawtucket Advertiser,* October 22, 1840.

34. *Providence Daily Journal,* November 30, December 2, and December 3, 1840.

35. C. W. Parsons *Memoir,* p. 45.

36. Samuel G. Morton, *Crania Americana, A Comparative View of the Skulls of Various Aboriginal Nations of North and South America* (Philadelphia, J. Dobson, 1838). Morton's collection of 1,000 skulls still resides in the Philadelphia Academy of Natural Science.

37. Usher Parsons, "The Avenger of Blood," *The Knickerbocker, or New-York Monthly Magazine,* 16:531–533, 1840. The incident described in the sketch occurred during September 1818 aboard the U.S. frigate *Guerrière* while crossing the Gulf of Finland from Copenhagen to Kronstadt in Russia. A Russian pilot had boarded at Copenhagen to take the ship through Russian waters. A member of the crew, a pardoned pirate, was regaling the officers about his exploits on a Saturday evening over hot whiskey punch in the ward-room. He told of how his pirate ship had captured a Russian vessel in the Gulf of Mexico, murdered the captain and crew, plundered the ship, and then scuttled her. "My God!" said the pilot in his thick Russian accent, "that was my brother Nicholas." The ex-pirate thereafter had to be kept under wraps to prevent his murder by the outraged Russian. The Russian authorities at Kronstadt attempted to take the culprit off, but the *Guerrière* saved him by claiming immunity as an armed vessel. The unhappy crewman, whose story had been revealed for the first time, eventually jumped ship in Sicily. "The whole [story]," wrote Usher, "savors so much of fiction, that the writer stated that he was [the] surgeon [aboard] at the time, and knows the material factors to be as . . . here related. . . ."

38. Thomas Breese to John Holmes, January 28, 1837, DPC.

39. Manuscript petition, dated January 11, 1837, signed "Usher Parsons" by his attorney, D. A. A. Buck, Navy Invalid File 1–176, WRDNA.

40. Usher Parsons to Charles Morris, March 16, 1837, Navy Invalid File 1–176, WRDNA.

41. Manuscript document, dated April 3, 1837, unsigned, Navy Invalid File 1–176, WRDNA.

42. Samuel Jackson to Mahlon Dickerson, April 6, 1837, Navy Invalid File 1–176, WRDNA.

43. Charles W. Parsons to Usher Parsons, February 4, 1837; Usher Parsons to Charles W. Parsons, February 10, 1837; Charles W. Parsons to Usher Parsons, March 4, 1837; Usher Parsons to Charles W. Parsons, March 20, 1837; Charles W. Parsons to Usher Parsons, April 19, 1837; Usher Parsons to Charles W. Parsons, April 21, 1837. DPC.

44. In his *Three Centuries of Harvard* (Cambridge, Harvard University Press, 1936, pp. 202–203), Samuel Eliot Morison described the Harvard clubs of the period thus: "Clubs fairly pullulated. The Speaking Club

... in 1825 ... combined with two rivals ... as the Institute of 1770; but its character was unchanged: lectures and debates at fortnightly meetings. In 1848 the Institute absorbed another club of like nature, the I.O.H. with its library. ... It is difficult to see how any student of this period, unless invincibly unsocial in temperament and tastes, could have been wholly unclubbed. Lack of money or social background was no bar."

45. Usher Parsons to Charles W. Parsons, May 13, 1837, DPC.

46. John Holmes to Usher Parsons, May 26, 1837, HUCC.

47. Charles W. Parsons to Thomas W. Higginson, July 25, 1837, DPC.

48. Sam Patch (1807–1829), a native of Pawtucket, Rhode Island, was a daredevil exhibitionist who attracted wide attention by jumping from great heights. He lost his life in a jump of 125 feet at Genesee Falls at Rochester, New York.

49. These northern Rhode Island towns are strung along the Blackstone River Valley.

50. The Reverend William Blackstone, a graduate of Cambridge University and an Episcopal minister, is reputed to have lived at the present site of the Massachusetts State House in Boston. Finding "the Lord Brethren" of Boston fully as objectionable as "the Lord Bishops" of England, he removed to Lonsdale, six miles north of Providence on the river eventually named after him, in 1634 or 1635, several months before Roger Williams reached Providence (1636).

51. The North Burial Ground in Providence.

52. Dighton Rock near Taunton, Massachusetts, on the Taunton River, a tributary of Narragansett Bay, carries inscriptions believed then to be of Indian origin. More recently the late Professor Edmund B. Delabarre (1863–1945) of Brown University established that they were placed there early in the sixteenth century by Miguel Corte-Real, Portuguese explorer and navigator, and possibly the first European to reside on the North American Continent.

53. Usher Parsons to Charles W. Parsons, October 16, 1837, DPC.

54. Charles W. Parsons to Usher Parsons, October 17, 1837, DPC.

55. Usher Parsons to Charles W. Parsons, October 18, 1837, DPC.

56. Usher Parsons to Charles W. Parsons, March 11, 1838, DPC.

57. Harvard University Archives, Pusey Library, Cambridge, Massachusetts.

58. The event was reported in the *Boston Medical and Surgical Journal*, 19:293–301, 1838.

59. Usher Parsons to Charles W. Parsons, November 12, 1838, DPC.

60. His cotton shirts were sewn in Providence.

61. Charles W. Parsons to Usher Parsons, March 8, 1839, DPC.

62. Usher Parsons to Charles W. Parsons, June 13, 1839, DPC.

63. Harvard University Archives, Pusey Library, Cambridge, Massachusetts.

64. Charles W. Parsons to Usher Parsons, March 21, 1840, DPC.

65. According to Samuel Eliot Morison, "A Humphrey Davy Society for amateur chemists flourished for several years." (*Three Centuries of Harvard*).

66. Usher Parsons to Charles W. Parsons, April 12, 1840, DPC.

67. Harvard University Archives, Pusey Library, Cambridge, Massachusetts.

CHAPTER THIRTEEN

The Dorr War

Following his graduation from Harvard, Charles returned to Providence and for a while studied medicine with his father. He kept up an active correspondence with the Holmes family. Early in 1841 he reported to his grandmother:[1] "Father is well and busy as usual. He talked of going on to Washington, to Gen'l [William Henry] Harrison's Inauguration, which takes place next Thursday [March 4], and I had some idea of accompanying him. But he has given it up, I believe, concluding he would rather stay at home and attend to his practice. Lots however have gone from this city and state."

Later, Charles wrote to his college chum, Wentworth Higginson, that he still hoped to visit Washington with his father:[2] "In case of the contemplated Extra Session of Congress being actually held, I think it highly probable I may honor the illustrious city with a visit. If father's professional business will allow him, I believe he means to go on & see Gen'l.,—I beg his pardon, President Harrison, and I shall try to accompany him." Usher had strong sentimental reasons for wishing to see his old comrade-in-arms, who had commanded ground forces during the Erie campaign.

Meanwhile, the untimely death of President Harrison a mere month after his inauguration had changed Usher's plans. Charlie's hopes of traveling to Washington with his father in June were thus dashed. "Father," he wrote to Higginson,[3]

was desirous of paying his personal respects to the late President of the U.S., but alas! he is numbered with the dead, & the project is abandoned. . . . There is something very solemn to my mind in this event—following right on the heels of exultation & party tumult & Tippecanoe songs. . . . Tomorrow I believe the big funeral procession comes off in Boston. . . . They talk of getting up a eulogy &c. here, I believe. The day the news arrived, shops were hung with black silk (a fine chance of showing their stuffs, especially the arcade, a long building of stores, three stories high, with opposite galleries from which the drapery was hanging in rich & sombre folds).[4]

"To change the topic," he continued later,[5] "I got shaved on the 12th of June, ay, shaved by a barber, and came out smooth faced like a babe. It forms a great era, a turning-point in my life. . . . I remember [from school days] longing to be a man, & turning incredulously away from Uncle Wendell, who told me he would rather be a boy than a man." Charles tried his hand at poetry and wrote a romantic piece titled "Song of the Crusaders," which appeared in the *Providence Daily Journal* of July 29 under the pseudonym, "Y.Z."

While Usher's practice went on as usual, Charles was busily engaged in apprentice chores, such as preparing, bottling, labeling, and corking some seven "junk bottles" (as he called them) of senna, made up pills and decoctions, and read two books on physiology. His father's practice was too limited in scope to give him much experience, but he had many opportunities for study.[6]

At this time, Charles also wrote the following to Uncle John:[7]

> I will also mention that a very smart little man, Dr. Okie, of our city is writing a review of Uncle Wendell's lecture on Homoeopathy. Dr. O. is a Homoeopathic physician, not recognized by any of the faculty. My father alone has shown him civility, and he [is] a man of education and sense.

Charles made occasional visits to Cambridge by train during the spring and summer of 1841, but for the most part stayed pretty close to his father's office. In the fall he went to Boston to begin a course of medical lectures at the Harvard Medical School. In signing the matriculation book he listed his sponsor and instructor as "U. Parsons, M.D." and gave his residence as Providence, R.I.[8]

The course began on November 4 and lasted into March. It had recently been extended from three to four months and included the standard lectures on Midwifery and Medical Jurisprudence, Anatomy, Materia Medica, Surgery, and the Theory and Practice of Physic.[9] While Charles later received his medical degree at Harvard, this was his only attendance at the Medical School. No surviving correspondence indicates where he lived, but he likely boarded at

No. 8 Montgomery Place in Boston with Uncle Wendell and his bride, the former Amelia Jackson. It was convenient both to the Harvard Medical School on Mason Street and to the new Tremont Medical School, where Wendell was then lecturing.[10] Charles probably attended the fall lectures at the Tremont School in September and October, which many Harvard students found profitable. These lectures supplemented the course at the senior institution and offered generally superior instruction. Charles was back in Providence by early May, when his correspondence with Cambridge resumed.

During May and June of 1842, a serious constitutional crisis over universal suffrage erupted in Rhode Island, culminating in the comic opera rebellion known in history as The Dorr War. Thomas Wilson Dorr,[11] a liberal in the modern sense and in advance of his times, believed in universal suffrage, reserved under the ancient provincial charter solely to landowners. His party held a convention, adopted a new constitution, and elected him governor. This rump government was declared by the State Supreme Court to be unlawful and revolutionary. The lawful governor, Samuel Ward King, convened a special session of the General Assembly on April 25, which passed a precautionary act to "prevent riots and tumultuous assemblages," and on May 4 declared that a state of insurrection existed.

President Tyler declined to intervene before the outbreak of hostilities, and then only if duly constituted state authorities were unable to put down an insurrection. In the meantime, the political pot was boiling. On May 18 Dorr established his headquarters in Burrington Anthony's house on Broadway in the Federal Hill area of Providence and then marched on the State Arsenal at the nearby Dexter Training Ground. The state Adjutant General, Elisha Dyer, Jr., published orders directing all chartered companies of Providence to report to headquarters armed and equipped, whence they proceeded to Federal Hill to meet the insurrection.[12]

Charles reported to Uncle John Holmes on the afternoon of May 18:[13]

> ... at 6 this morning the Mayor issued a notice urging all citizens to lay aside their business & arm. This morning they formed, with the independent companies, & two or three companies from the south of the state, and marched up towards Dorr's quarters. Father and myself walked in the ranks as surgeons. On the appearance of the troops there was a great scattering. The

Govr. went to search the house, was long denied; but after the cannon and forces were arrayed in front, he was allowed, and found not Dorr, thus making sure what was before rumor [that Dorr had escaped]. The scattering of what forces were left, after the desertions of this morning, was gradual, but after some 3 hours, there were only 30 or 40 men left, guarding those cannon which were obtained [stolen] yesterday. They said, if the companies attacked them, they would fire the guns; if the companies would march back, they would bring down & surrender the cannon. The companies marched down; and this is now the state of things (2½ P.M.). I hear martial music, and am going down street.

8¾ P.M. I hasten to get this in the P.O. tonight. Since the above was written, the suffrage folks rallied, have thrown up a breast-work about the cannon, and refused to surrender them as they pledged themselves to do. The company who own them went up to demand them this afternoon, but were refused. The numbers over there amount to some 150 or 200, said to be pretty desperate men. Dorr went north. His uncle pledges himself that Dorr will never return to the state; many still will not believe he is out of it. . . . This will let you know I am safe, & that no bloodshed has yet taken place.

. . . For myself I have been under father's orders, & accompanied him to the scene of expected action this morning and also during the day. Had there been fighting today, I should probably have been in some danger; but I do not think there will be any more danger. This is the first day that the fuss has much interrupted my studies.

Dorr escaped to Connecticut. In later years it was written that Charles's "first public service, and his only military experience, was in 1842, when he, with his father, accompanied" the troops "on their march to Federal Hill, where Dorr's adherents had made a stand."[14] The picture of the grizzled veteran of the War of 1812 and his son, a callow youth of nineteen, bearing the staff of Aesculapius through the streets of Providence is an intriguing one. Charles gave this account of the business:[15]

When the suffrage troubles arose in Rhode Island, he [Usher] did not share in the attachment felt by many natives of this State, to the charter of 1663, and his sympathies were with the movement for enlarged suffrage. Mr. Thomas W. Dorr was his intimate friend. But when the affair took on a revolutionary character, he rallied to the support of the existing government. He acted as volunteer surgeon of the Marine Artillery.

The following day Governor King thanked the various units "for their steady courage and efficient action in executing the orders of yesterday while dislodging and dispersing the insurgents upon Federal Hill." The surgeons accompanying the troops had little work to do since, as the press reported, "the crowning part of the victory was that it was bloodless." While not directly reported by the press, the presence of medical officers with the state militia was implied: "A correspondent inquires if surgeons were brought on the ground by the insurgents when they attacked the Arsenal. We are not able to answer the question."[16]

Charles had had enough of military medicine. He later wrote to Uncle John:[17]

> The Marine Artillery have passed a vote of thanks "to Dr. Usher Parsons & son for their proffered professional services in the prospect of a sanguinary conflict with the troops of the insurgent, Thomas W. Dorr." If there is any more trouble, I shall shoulder the musket, as I believe I could do little good in the surgical way, and moreover it is poor satisfaction to run one's chance of being shot . . . without any chance of returning the compliment. . . .
>
> As the city grows calmer, we return more steadily to our studies in this office; and the past few days I have worked about as common, save as the hot weather has made me lazy. The war has interrupted my studying, and not, as yet, given any chance for seeing surgery—thank Heaven! . . . I have already begun professional visiting to some extent, and today, my father being out of town, went through the ceremony of a visit quite to my own satisfaction, taking care beforehand to have full directions from my father what to prescribe.

Dorr's efforts were not entirely in vain. Charles reported to Uncle John on June 24[18] that the legislature had called a convention to frame a Constitution. This would propose that all native citizens of three years residence vote for delegates, be they black or white, penniless or rich, and even foreigners who possessed some real estate. This move, he had heard, had drawn off a hundred of Dorr's adherents and altered the aspect of the situation. He continued:

> For myself I feel if called to fight that I am fighting in a good cause, in defence of my native city against a desperate invader, and a gang of rowdies and ruffians; I am astonished to find how the spirit of war rises with the prospect of some. I really think I am better prepared in my mind than *physically*. I am not strong;

and the fatigues of preparation have tired me so as to make me dread the fatigue of actual service. But I doubt not the greater occasion will bring with it strength. This aft'n (a very hot day) all the city troops are ordered out for review by the Governor and Gen. McNeal; every day this week but one we've drilled in the street or the hall; and then my turn comes occasionally for the nightly patrol; and all in all I am more afraid of fatigue than bullets. Father is surgeon of the Providence Marine Artillery, and carries the musket. . . .

For myself, I question whether there will be fighting yet, if ever. . . . I don't relish fighting myself, and should accept your invitation [to visit Cambridge], but you see how we regard things, and that it has become the duty of every citizen who is able to stand in defence of the city & state.

On the 25th, various militia units were posted on the western approaches to the city, and on the 27th the state was placed under martial law. On the morning of June 28 several units of the state militia, including the Marine Artillery, marched to Chepachet to confront Dorr.[19] We do not know whether Usher accompanied his unit. Charles continues the story in a letter to John Holmes a few days later:[20]

. . . Let me assure you, and all my relations & friends in other lands, that their fears [about my health and comfort] are without foundation. . . . I by no means do my share in the labors required of R. Island's citizens; and am now writing in full health and freshness, stronger probably than at any former period of my life. . . . If I wanted to retreat, I couldn't; as the City Guards are forbidden to leave the city—unless by orders. . . .

Our people have turned out truly nobly to defend the state, and have borne fatigue and met expected dangers in the true spirit. At the tavern we stopped at Monday night, the house was full, one regiment being quartered there, and the men had had no sleep many of them for 3 nights, and only pork & old bread to eat till we brought a supply. Within these 3 days they had been marched 35 miles to Providence [from South County], 16 from there, and next morning started when we did, for Chepachet, 12 miles. They were the true yeomanry, a rough tough looking set of men; I wish some of these "sympathizers" had seen them as specimens, and they were but average specimens, of the "silk stocking aristocracy" who were summoned to defend the state against the oppressed, the sovereign people.

The war I suppose to be over, and I hope soon to relapse into the quiet pill-maker.

Years later Charles wrote this sequel to the exciting events:[21]

> The subsequent imprisonment of Mr. Dorr was exceedingly distasteful to him [Usher]. He exerted himself to procure his release, by circulating petitions, &c.; but his course did not suit the uncompromising views of Mr. Dorr, and was unavailing. Immediately after the passage of the act of liberation, he visited Mr. Dorr as physician and friend.[22]

The Rhode Island Medical Society was scheduled to hold its annual meeting in Providence on June 29. Understandably amid the tumult, it met but briefly to reconvene on September 8,[23] which occasion proved to be an eventful one for Usher, as revealed in the following announcement:[24]

> At an adjourned meeting of the Rhode Island Medical Society held at Providence on the 8th day of September, 1842, the Trustees of the Fiske Fund announced that they had awarded to the author of the Dissertation bearing the motto, *"Vestrae petitioni respondeo diligenter"*, the premium of one hundred dollars by them offered for the best dissertation on the question, "What are the Causes, Character, and Nature of the Diseases of the Spine, both structural and functional; and what is the best mode of Treatment to be employed in each?"
> Upon breaking the seal of the accompanying packet, they ascertained its author to be Usher Parsons, M.D., of Providence.

The dissertation[25] was classical in form and rather lengthy, but reported no original observations. Although fairly well-written, it was a potpourri of disorders, ranging through curvature, hump-back, rickets, psoas abscess, injuries, osteomyelitis, spina bifida, and diseases of the spinal cord. He aired some of his own pet theories of treatment, which were not only old-fashioned, but also a little vague as well. He considered together such diverse disorders as meningitis, myelitis, epilepsy, abortion, and torticollis, even strangury and cross-eye ("spasmodic strabismus"). "Of all the remedies I have tried . . . ," he wrote, "cupping has been most beneficial." He considered "leeches [to be] nearly as valuable, but not as efficacious or convenient," and counter-irritation to be of some use. From "traveling and change of residence," he added, "I have always noticed marked good effect." The paper is of slight importance, but one cannot readily dismiss his lifetime accomplishment of winning five major prizes—the Boylston four times and the Fiske once.

Some interesting surgical cases occupied Usher during 1842.[26] He performed his second successful trephine upon an eight-year-old boy in whom "a portion of the frontal bone, near its junction with the temporal and parietal, [was] driven in nearly an inch by the kick of a horse." There was "abolition of sense, and the membranes of the brain were perforated." The boy was "trepanned the same day" and "recovered." Usher also performed a breast cancer operation. The patient, thirty-eight years old, died of "tubercular consumption about five years later; [there was] no reappearance of cancer." The conclusion, however, is suspect, since pulmonary spread of cancer could only be guessed in the days before the x-ray was discovered. During the year he also performed a second eye operation on Governor Collins.

The third edition of *Physician for Ships*,[27] rewritten and with new diseases added, appeared in 1842. A section on choice of climate for patients with pulmonary disorders was included. "The liberal patronage bestowed on the last edition of two thousand copies, now all sold," said the preface, "has induced the author to spare no pains to render this one as useful as its number of pages would permit." The *Boston Medical and Surgical Journal* of October 26[28] noted that it had "hitherto expressed the favorable impression made by this judicious compilation," which would "probably become as familiar to the intelligent mariner as . . . the quadrant." The reviewer gave the following horrible example of medical practice on board a merchant ship:

> If a man is taken sick, the first order of the captain is to give him a dose of salts, without much regard to symptoms. If word comes from the forecastle next morning that Jack is no better, then follows a huge paper of jalap and calomel; and after that, he is left to fate, much like a ship in a gale—the sails torn, bolt ropes gone, rudder twisted from the pintons, and, in a sinking condition, drifting at the mercy of the waves. It may be he lives to reach port—but, live or die, the whole crew would swear that nothing more could have been done for him, "as the captain gave Jack a plenty of physic."

"Our merchants," the reviewer concluded, "ought to put a copy on board every vessel leaving port."

During 1842 and 1843 Usher submitted two brief obituaries of Rhode Island physicians to the *Boston Medical and Surgical Journal*, there being then no local medical journal. The first memorialized Doctor Jeremiah Williams of Warren, Rhode Island, one of few surviving charter members of the Medical Society, "a bold and efficient" practitioner and a "close observer of nature as well as a reader of books. By industry and enterprise in mercantile and professional business, he acquired a large estate," which, unhappily, he did not live to enjoy. In the second he eulogized Doctor Niles Manchester of Pawtucket:[29] "In accurate diagnosis he met with few equals among physicians educated in his day, and his kind and soothing manner in a sick room rendered his visits peculiarly agreeable."

In the fall and winter of 1842 Charles attended medical lectures in Philadelphia, traveling south in the company of his father. Upon returning to Providence, Usher began a long, diary-like letter to Charles covering the period from November 19 to December 3.[30] John Holmes had spent a week of vacation in Usher's office during the latter's absence and planned to return at Christmas time. "Very few calls," Usher wrote, "have been made since my return, and I now wish I had remained a few days longer in Philadelphia." Much clinical information was included for the benefit of his medical student son—some recent and impending deaths of patients, a house call in rural West Greenwich, and several operations. Former President John Quincy Adams had given a lecture on the Constitution at the Fanklin Lyceum in Providence on November 25 before a large audience, which was "the more valuable" as it "was very anti-Dorric." "I came near going without a Thanksgiving dinner," Usher wrote, as "no one invited me," but at the last minute someone obliged and he was "glad to accept." The state constitution, he was sure, would "be adopted by a very large and respectable vote," which would, he hoped, "return peace to the state." Later he reported that this prediction was fulfilled by a wide margin. He urged Charles to take riding lessons on rainy Wednesdays and Saturdays ("six lessons will be sufficient"—three to learn the rudiments and the rest for practice). He also advised Charles to "visit the Penitentiary . . . and all other curiosities worthy of notice," and the Museum if possible. Horace Mann, always a sentimental favorite in Providence, delivered a Franklin Lyceum lecture, "the best we have yet heard, on the value and importance of school libraries." Usher found time to "run down" to Boston to examine proofs of his essays and while there "passed the evening with your uncle Wendell, who is busily engaged examining the structure of animal tissues with a powerful microscope."

This letter and others that followed reflected Usher's busy practice during his prime years. Charles became well acquainted with this practice, as he and his father shared the same roof for many years. Charles wrote of this period:[31]

> He rose gradually to a very prominent rank in his profession. Beside his varied opportunities, which brought him to the beginning of civil practice with more than usual experience and resources, he had many qualities of body and mind that fitted him for medical life. He was robust, with uncommon powers of endurance, and a frame strengthened by labor in early life. He was industrious, persevering, ambitious and social; faithful in attendance and considerate in his charges. His early training in naval service, and the predominance of the reflective powers, fitted him rather for the office of consulting physician, and for cases of exceptional difficulty, than for the ordinary run of daily medical practice. He had not that easy tact, that quickness of thought and command of language and features, which were conspicuous in some of his contemporaries. Yet in many families of refinement and education, his acquirements were appreciated, and his ready sympathies and sound judgement made him a trusted adviser and friend. As consulting physician and surgeon, he was very widely known in Rhode Island and neighboring parts of other states. For many years, a large part of his practice was out of Providence. He was a fast driver, and, before railroads were multiplied, his sulky was well known on the roads leading from Providence in all directions. [His forte was caution, not dexterity.]

Usher's letter to Charles of December 5 to 7[32] contained further local gossip—the wedding of a local damsel for whom Usher had stood as witness, the performances of a traveling dramatic company, and the trial of a leading Dorrite. "The fact is," he wrote, "Dorrism is done up and settled." Usher acquired a new boarder who "begins today in John's place, sleeps in the front room, makes fires and studies hard." "John" was nephew John Parsons, son of his brother William of Kennebunk. He had just graduated from Brown with the Class of 1842 and later studied for the ministry at Andover Theological Seminary.

An old student of Usher's, Doctor Thomas Mawney Potter, a naval surgeon and medical graduate of the University of Pennsylvania, was visiting in Philadelphia; "I hope," wrote Usher to Charles, "you will fall in with him." He went on:

> I like your description of the professors as it accords well with my own notions of them. I am particularly well pleased with your plan of going to the Hospital once a week and paying each time. This is far better than paying $10.00 for Blockley [The Philadelphia General Hospital]. Don't forget to take five or six lessons in riding; they will be very advantageous to your health, will come in grandly some stormy days, when you are prevented from walking.
>
> We have very little doing here in the way of practice, less than I almost ever knew. As soon as my Essay is finished I shall, for the purpose of employing my leisure moments, take up some subject for a Lyceum Lecture. I am just finishing Liebig's Organic Chemistry, and a capital book it is. I hope you will listen to all that Dr. Hare has to say, notwithstanding his heavy manner. You probably will never have another opportunity equal to it to see chemistry illustrated by rich and accurate experiments; and it is best to make the most of the opportunity. You have described Dr. Hare's manner to the life, but with a little reading I think you may turn his lectures to a good account. I wish you to apply the [obstetric] forceps to the mannikin while in Philadelphia. It is very important to learn the art. I believe the professors give each pupil an opportunity.

The lull in practice soon ended, however. Usher's patients and the gay holiday festivities occupied him fully (January 9, 1843):[33]

> Your two letters . . . came safe and afforded me a great deal of comfort and real pleasure. I hoped you would have received more invitations to visit during the Christmas pleasure days than you did and wish you had been here. I never knew Providence half so gay as it was during that and the succeeding week. Last week I was out every evening—and on Wednesday, Thursday & Friday nights so far renewed my youth as to dance till midnight, first at a hop at the Franklin house, then at a sleighing party at Jacob Dunnel's, and then at the Mansion house where Miss Estin gave a supper to her old boarders, and the young men of the house brought in a band at 9 o'clock and made a merry time of it.

Nowhere in the abundant correspondence available to us is there more than a bare suggestion of romance in Usher's life during his long years of widowhood. His letter to Charles continues:

Tomorrow evening there is to be a great ball at the Infantry Armory, which I shall not attend—having better business on hand, viz. a surgical case of a tumor of the face in Richmond to visit. Business in the way of surgery has been good of late—a broken arm at Horton's grove, a broken leg at Fiske's, two luxations of the humerus in the office, and last and best of all a case of umbilical hernia at Ezekiel Burr's, his wife aged 76 years, very corpulent. I was called to her just 48 hours since, and found she had been vomiting for 24 hours, with very great pain at the umbilicus, which presented a tumour a little larger than one's fist, which would not be reduced any how. I immediately proceeded to operate and made an incision from the middle of the tumour straight upward and dissected the fascia so as to expose the omentum, passed my finger over it, but could not enter it or probe even under the stricture: and the reason was an adhesion had long existed there between the parietes and the omentum, a piece of which I now learned for the first time had long protruded and had not been reduced. I then went back to the starting point in the incision and continued it downward to the lower side, and then passed the finger under the protruding omentum and could enter the point of it into the abdomen and could feel the stricture. I passed the probe-pointed bistoury along the finger flat wise, and having entered the abdomen, I turned it and cut the stricture, and then passed the omentum and bowel into the abdomen and put two stitches in the upper part, and adhesive straps over the middle and lower part, and a compress and bandage over all. Gave her a dose of Senna [a cathartic] & Manna [a mild aperient and cholegogue] and 50 drops of Laudanum [tincture of opium] at 2 o'clock. At 4 I found some chills and occasional violent pain by the rolling of the bowel that had been impacted. Bled her at 5, the pulse having risen. She slept part of the night—next day bled her again and gave injections of salt and water. There was occasional pain, most violent, and some vomiting. This morning I thought she would die of enteritis, but I now think, 12 o'clock, that she will recover. She has had several free discharges.

Usher added, "Besides the call to Richmond, I have another to Greenwich [some 30 and 15 miles respectively from his office], . . .

which I shall take in on my way to Richmond tomorrow and return next day . . . in the Carrs [*i.e.* by railroad]." Later he reported on the medical cases he treated ("in Richmond fungus hematodes under the eye [skin cancer] . . . in Greenwich orchitis" [inflammation of the testicle.] He advised Charles to subscribe to *Medical News and Library*, published in Philadelphia, and discussed new plans for Charles and other matters:

> I think seriously of opening an Infirmary for the treatment of spinal diseases, hernia and clubfoot, and diseases of the Eye. A part of my plan is to send you to Paris to gather up all such information respecting such matters as you can collect, and to add it to my own stock. I am invited to give a Lecture in Woonsocket before a Lyceum.

In a letter to Charles on January 22, 1843,[34] Usher reported that he had been unusually busy for the past two weeks, during which he made five visits to Bristol and several to other towns, and in addition "have had many calls at the office, so that I often wished you were here." After relaying news of the current lectures, hops, concerts, and parties, and mentioning the demise of the old pre-Dorr state charter, he continued with specific details from his practice:

> My patient with umbilical hernia was cured in ten days from the operation. I have an interesting case of Varioloid in the Jackson house, . . . —and I think it not unlikely that other cases will spring from it. Yesterday I had a case of fungus growth from the roots of a diseased tooth incisor. I extracted the tooth with forceps and then put the dissecting hook through it and extirpated it at the root with the knife. The bleeding was profuse and was stayed by a hot iron about the size of a pipestem; this was pressed against the bleeding vessel.
>
> They are all well at McClellan's except Jane, who ran the thorn of a house plant into the corner of the eye exactly in the axis of vision. The aqueous humor did not escape, the cornea not being perforated entirely through. Leeches have been perseveringly applied and inflammation is subdued.

Continuing his letter to Charles the next day, he ruminated further on his plans and added: "I now have more leisure and shall turn my attention to the Infirmary." He went on:

The physicians to whom I have mentioned my plan agree to assist me to patients, particularly in Warren, Bristol, Scituate, &c. I shall issue circulars far and wide proposing to receive patients labouring under chronic diseases, particularly of the eye and ear, and hernias, and deformities as clubfoot, curvature of the spine, and contracted joints.

I wish you would call on Dr. Chase and with my respects to him ask him if he would like to send me some of his trusses and other instruments to sell to my patients. I will receive them and take good care of them and return all that are unsold at the end of a year, and account for sale. . . .[35]

As you now know the nature of diseases that I intend to treat, I wish you would collect all the information you can respecting them in lectures and otherwise; and if there should appear to be any new invention respecting them or other surgical diseases, I wish you to inform me of it that I may provide myself with them. A knife for tenotomy will I think be requisite.

On February 2 Usher told Charles that he had been busy that day trying to influence physicians to support his infirmary.[36] He also reported that "Drs. Okie & Wells lost today a patient at Revd. Mr. Granger's, a lady aged 21 with erysipelas." This he thought would be "a heavy blow to homoeopathy, for they had fair chance to test its infallibility." On the general scene, he added: "I have been this afternoon listening to a warm debate in the General Assembly for the suppression of Lotteries. They are to exist no longer in the state after the present year." Rhode Island did, in fact, adopt a unique constitutional ban on lotteries. They remained outlawed until a state lottery was established more than a century and a quarter later (1974).

Writing on March 2, Usher acknowledged two "excellent" letters from Charles, discussed some financial matters relating to room and board, and continued:[37]

In respect to the future I object to your remaining more than one year in Paris at a time. A longer time denationalizes one's habits and feelings, and lessens his chance of success at home—witness Dr. O. W. Holmes, and Stephen Kean. Your uncle admitted as much to me not long since. One year is sufficient to learn what is essential; and after applying the knowledge acquired in that time and finding out your weak points, you can then go again and fortify them, at the same time that you glean up all new discoveries since your former year. Your uncle thinks that it would now benefit him very much to pass a year in Paris.

My wish is that you go to Paris in May and stay 12 to 15 months, when you can graduate at Cambridge [*i.e.* Harvard]. My further plan is for you to stay in Providence when you return from Phila. about a week and then to go to Boston, to the South Boston Infirmary[38] where you can see from 50 to 100 patients a day, and have charge of obstetrick cases at the same time, and also attend surgical operations at the Mass. Genl. Hospital, and bring up your reading. I prefer this to entering you as a student to hear lectures in Boston, believing as I do that you have heard lectures enough. Dr. [Charles Harrison] Stedman will inform me in a few days how you can be accommodated. Your stay there will of course be short if you go to Paris so soon—and you can in that time be engaged in brushing up your French. . . .

Still concerned about his city-bred son's horsemanship, Usher turned to the subject of riding lessons. He informed Charles that the Philadelphia anatomist Samuel G. Morton, the recipient of Usher's barrel of skulls, had sent his sons to an establishment near the head of Sansom Street, in the direction of Jefferson Medical College, and that three lessons would be enough. "I only want you to know," he explained, "how to hold a whip and reins, and to mount and dismount gracefully." He then reverted to his plans for Charles's medical career:

My object in sending you away so soon is to enable you to see practice immediately whilst principles are fresh on your mind, and also to remove you from the influences here of which you complain with good reason. You will moreover find it pleasant to visit Salem & Cambridge. It is possible you may succeed in getting a place in the Masstts. Genl. Hospital, and I should be well pleased to have you, but the practice of physick will be far more extensive and profitable in the South Boston [Infirmary], and the operations at the Masstts. will be in addition.

. . . Fletcher[39] has just called and says he shall go to Paris about midsummer. You may go with him. So that point is settled. He says you thought of going to Washington. If Congress were in session I would not object, but after the 4th instant there will be nothing there worth seeing.

I send you a few copies of my Fiske Fund Prize Essay of which I was able to purchase a few copies. Give one to the Academy of Natural Sciences, one to Dr. [J. K.] Mitchell, one to Dr. [Isaac]

Hays, editor of the Medical Journal [*American Journal of the Medical Sciences*], one to Dr. [Thomas Dent] Mütter, and one to whom you please, & one to the Philosophical Society, where I once carried you. Say presented by the author, written in fine hand and neatly.[40]

Usher's report to his son then turned to news of Cambridge, where he had spent the previous night and found everyone well:

Am glad you have written to your grandmother—she wants to hear from you. Your uncle is publishing an elaborate article in the *Boston Medical Quarterly* on the contagiousness of puerperal fever through the accoucheur. . . .[41] I have less practice for a few weeks past than usual. My circulars [on the Infirmary] are sent far and near, and [in addition] advertisements [have been placed] in newspapers. I have the promise of two or three clubfoot cases already and hope to have more. I send you a copy of my circular. . . .

We have some very interesting cases of phrenomesmerism and a successful exhibition in several persons of phrenological organic excitement.[42] Some of these I shall show you on your return. We have had capital sleighing and the gayest winter ever known in this city. Parties, balls, and every kind of dissipation.

Usher, with his growing interest in antiquarian pursuits and natural science, applied for membership in the American Antiquarian Society in Worcester, Massachusetts. He presented to the Society "two boxes of specimens in Natural History and some Indian trinkets.[43] The late Clarence S. Brigham, long-time Director of the Society, wrote in 1959:[44]

[Usher Parsons] was elected a member of this Society in 1843. . . . In 1841, before his election, he sent us two boxes of natural history specimens, minerals, and curiosities. They were contained in two large boxes and were listed carefully in our donation book under May 26, 1842. When we disbanded the Museum about sixty years ago, the Indian relics went to the Peabody Museum in Cambridge and local relics to the Worcester Historical Society. As I remember it, none of the items which he sent was of any consequence.

In midsummer Charles departed for Paris, and Usher followed on November 1, sailing from Boston.[45] At last he was able to renew memories of his youth and simultaneously to share these pleasures with his son. Charles wrote the following account of the trip:[46]

After becoming well established in practice, Dr. Parsons allowed himself more liberty in regard to absence from Providence, than is usual with equally busy physicians. In the autumn of 1843, he visited Europe for the third time, contemplating a journey to Egypt, but going no farther than Paris, where his son was studying medicine. He spent some days in London on his outward journey, renewing his acquaintance with Mr. Clift, and attending a meeting of the Geological Society, where he saw Dr. [William] Buckland, whose Bridgewater Treatise[47] he had read with great interest. In Paris, he frequented the hospitals, and took copious notes of surgical cases, as he had done twenty-four years earlier. A few extracts from his diary show the character of his observations:—

"There is to my mind an unaccountable aversion on the part of French surgeons to attempt uniting wounds after operations, by the first intention. To-day, the flaps made in the amputation might have been brought together, a depending opening left, and the whole or nearly all the wound closed; instead of which the old system in vogue twenty-three years ago is continued, of stuffing the wound with *charpie* or lint."

"There is in French surgeons an indifference to life that seems inhuman. They operate when they should not;—when they must know that the advantages to be gained are not to be compared with the risk of life, and the certain amount of severe pain that must be suffered from the operation."

He bought several valuable instruments and anatomical preparations in Paris. He also bought a copy of Josephus, printed by Schüssler at Augsburg, 1470;[48] and the "Annals of the World's History," printed by Walch at Venice, 1479, and adorned with wood-cuts representing the tower of Babel, Nineveh, Solomon's temple, &c. He was in Paris from November 19, 1843, till February 19, 1844, when he set out for London, where he received polite attentions from a number of luminaries. These included Mr. Richard Owen [joint conservator with his father-in-law, William Clift, of the Royal College of Surgeons],[49] Branby [Blake] Cooper [surgeon at Guy's Hospital], Mr. [Sir John Flint] South [surgeon at St. Thomas's Hospital and anatomist], Dr. John [Sir John] Forbes [Physician Extraordinary to the Prince Consort and Physician in Ordinary to Her Majesty's Household], other distinguished surgeons and men of science, visited the largest hospitals, and attended a meeting of the Royal Society [possibly as a guest of his friend, William Clift]. He left London, March 8, for Liverpool, Glasgow and Edinburgh. Returning to Liverpool, he there passed several days in the agreeable society of some old American friends, and sailed April 4, bearing dispatches from the minister, Mr. Everett.[50] He arrived in Providence, April 22, 1844.

NOTES

1. Charles W. Parsons to Mrs. Abiel Holmes, February 26, 1841, HUCC.

2. Charles W. Parsons to T. Wentworth Higginson, March 16, 1841, DPC.

3. Charles W. Parsons to T. Wentworth Higginson, April 19, 1841, DPC.

4. The Arcade, a fine Greek Revival edifice, still standing and recently restored, was a monumental business strucure, erected in downtown Providence in 1828. With six massive monolithic Ionic columns at either end, the largest monoliths in America at the time of erection, it was the first shopping galleria in America. The columns were quarried in Rhode Island.

5. Charles W. Parsons to T. Wentworth Higginson, June 25, 1841, DPC.

6. Charles W. Parsons to John Holmes, May 11, 1842, DPC. A medical bill among Usher's papers in the Dr. Wilfred Pickles Collection at the Rhode Island Hospital, submitted at this time to one Lemuel Vinton, hat maker, reveals something of the mode of practice and the medical economics of the times when a house call cost a dollar:

Sept. [1841]	Advice and meds. as per agreement for yourself & wife	15
Oct. 19	Advice [no charge?]	
20 & 21	2 visits & bleeding	2
24 & 31	4 visits & opening abscess	4
Nov. 8	1 vis. & meds	1
	Recd. payt. Usher Parsons	20

7. *Ibid.*

8. Harvard Medical School, "Matriculation Book, 1826–1860," Harvard Medical Archives, Countway Library of Medicine. Charles's entry is on p. 54.

9. Thomas Francis Harrington, *The Harvard Medical School*, pp. 483–486.

10. Eleanor W. Tilton, *Amiable Autocrat*, pp. 148–149.

11. Thomas Wilson Dorr (1805–1854), Harvard College 1823, was the son of Sullivan Dorr, insurance executive, and grandson of the Ebenezer Dorr who participated with Paul Revere in the famous ride.

12. *Providence Daily Journal*, May 18, 19, and 20, 1842.

13. Charles W. Parsons to John Holmes, May 18, 1842, HUCC.

14. "Obituary of Charles William Parsons, M.D.," *Transactions of the Rhode Island Medical Society*, 5:245–246, 1895.

15. C. W. Parsons *Memoir*, pp. 38–39.

16. *Providence Daily Journal*, May 20, 1842.

17. Charles W. Parsons to John Holmes, May 26, 1842, HUCC.

18. Charles W. Parsons to John Holmes, June 24, 1842, HUCC.

19. *Providence Daily Journal*, June 27 and 30, 1842.

20. Charles W. Parsons to John Holmes, June 30, 1842, HUCC.

21. C. W. Parsons *Memoir*, p. 39.

22. Dorr was tried for treason and in 1844 sentenced to life imprisonment, but he was released a year later.

23. Rhode Island Medical Society, "Minutes."

24. Usher included the announcement in the preface to his Fiske Fund Dissertation (see note 25). The motto "Vestrae petitioni respondeo diligenter" translates "I respond diligently to your request."

25. Usher Parsons, *Fiske Fund Prize Dissertation, No. VII. On Spinal Diseases, Both Structural and Functional, Their Causes and Treatment* (Boston, Thomas H. Webb, 1843).

26. Usher Parsons, "Statistics of Large Surgical Operations."

27. Usher Parsons, *Physician for Ships, Containing Medical Advice for Seamen and Other Persons at Sea . . .* (Boston, Charles C. Little and James Brown, 1842). This was the first edition under its new title.

28. *Boston Medical and Surgical Journal*, 27:207–208, 1842.

29. These appeared in the issues for January 19, 1842 and June 21, 1843, volume 25, page 385, and volume 28, page 420.

30. Usher Parsons to Charles W. Parsons, November 19–December 3, 1842, DPC.

31. C. W. Parsons *Memoir*, pp. 26–27.

32. Usher Parsons to Charles W. Parsons, December 5–7, 1842, DPC.

33. Usher Parsons to Charles W. Parsons, January 9, 1843, DPC.

34. Usher Parsons to Charles W. Parsons, January 22–23, 1843, DPC.

35. Doctor Heber Chase of Philadelphia wrote extensively on the use of the truss in the treatment of hernia.

36. Usher Parsons to Charles W. Parsons, January 29–February 2, 1843, DPC.

37. Usher Parsons to Charles W. Parsons, March 2, 1843, DPC.

38. In South Boston (part of the city of Boston) near Dorchester Heights and City Point, a complex of municipal buildings was erected, which included the Almshouse; an Infirmary; the Houses of Industry; Reformation and Correction; and a new Boston Lunatic Hospital (est. 1839). Charles Harrison Stedman (1805–1866), Harvard Medical School 1828, was appointed superintendent of the latter in 1842.

39. Probably Ezra Wood Fletcher of Providence, a Brown graduate who had just received his M.D. at Harvard.

40. John Kearsley Mitchell (1798–1858), practitioner, teacher and writer, was the father of the famed Doctor S. Weir Mitchell. Isaac Hays (1796–1879) was editor of the *American Journal of the Medical Sciences* for 53 years. Thomas Dent Mütter (1811–1859) was professor of surgery at Jefferson Medical College and a pioneering American orthopedic and plastic surgeon.

41. This actually appeared in April, 1843 in the initial volume of *The New England Quarterly Journal of Medicine and Surgery* and is now considered an important medical classic. Wendell was the first definitely to establish the contagious nature of the so-called childbed fever, predating Semmelweis's important report by about six years. Holmes's essay on the subject took a strong line against the opinions that then prevailed and stirred up a violent controversy and opposition among the obstetricians of Philadelphia.

42. Phrenomesmerism (also called phrenomagnetism) was the power of exciting the brain by mesmeric or magnetic (i.e. animal magnetic) influence. Both terms are part of the phrenological nonsense of the period.

43. Usher Parsons to Samuel F. Haven, April 20, 1842, American Antiquarian Society.

44. Clarence S. Brigham to Seebert J. Goldowsky, September 2, 1959, author's file.

45. Usher's departure date and port of embarkation are mentioned in a letter of introduction which John Pickering sent to Charles Pickering, dated November 1, 1843. John Pickering (1777–1846) was a legal authority, who also acquired fame in linguistics and philology. Charles Pickering (1805–1878) was a graduate of Harvard College (A.B. 1823) and Harvard Medical School in 1826 and a nephew of John. At this period he was traveling in the Middle East, pursuing anthropological studies. He gained his scientific reputation as a naturalist and was recognized in several scholarly societies. Usher also carried the following letters of introduction to persons in Egypt, which initially he hoped to visit: George R. Gliddon to John Gliddon, November 1, 1843, and George R. Gliddon to Alexander Todd, November 1, 1843. George Gliddon (1809–1857) spent many years in Egypt, where his father, John Gliddon, was a merchant and U.S. Consul, currently at Cairo. He explored the ancient ruins extensively and later published a scholarly archeological work based on his studies, titled *Ancient Egypt* (1850). He later succeeded his father as U.S. Consul. Todd, not otherwise identified, was acting U.S. Consul at Alexandria. All of the above letters of introduction can be found in DPC.

46. C. W. Parsons *Memoir*, pp. 28–29.

47. William Buckland (1784–1856), famed English geologist, also wrote on theological subjects. He became Dean of Westminster in 1845. Francis

Henry Egerton, eighth earl of Bridgewater (1756–1829), a clergyman, left in his will £8000 to whoever would write a treatise on the goodness of God as manifested in creation. Buckland was one of eight beneficiaries; the collected essays were the Bridgewater Treatises.

48. In his *Memoir*, Charles makes this reference (p. 29): "See *History of the Art of Printing*, by Noel Humphreys; London, 1868; page 102."

49. While in London Usher spent profitable moments with Clift and became acquainted with his son-in-law, Richard Owen. Upon his return home Usher commenced a long-lasting correspondence with Owen and his charming wife, Caroline Amelia, which proved to be both cordial and useful. A letter which Usher wrote to Owen on August 29, 1844 can be found in the American Antiquarian Society.

50. Edward Everett (1794–1865), Boston orator, minister, Harvard professor, and statesman, and later President of Harvard University, was currently U.S. minister to England.

CHAPTER FOURTEEN

Doctor Usher and Doctor Charles

Charles returned from Europe early in the spring of 1845 after a long rough voyage of forty-six days.[1] Having met all of the requirements, he now applied for his M.D. degree at the Harvard Medical School. In 1841 the specifications for graduation were "three years study of medicine, the attendance upon two full courses of lectures, [of not less than four months each]—one of these at least must have been attended at this school, the other in this or any other school which shall furnish equal opportunities." Examinations for degrees were held twice during the year, at the close of the winter term and just before commencement; a dissertation was required. Charles appears to have taken the summer examination and graduated with the Class of 1845. He received his diploma at Harvard Commencement on August 18. His doctoral thesis, no copy of which survives, was titled *Purulent Ophthalmia of Adults.*[2] It has been stated that he studied with Uncle Wendell, but the evidence is slight.[3]

In the fall Charles, somewhat run down in health, visited Washington to enjoy its milder climate and to take in the sights, a pleasure he had long anticipated. Usher wrote to him there in December:[4]

> . . . I have returned this morning from Middleboro [Massachusetts]. The case was one of Fungus Hematodes [a soft bleeding maglignant tumor] extending from the clavicle downward 8 inches & 7 inches broad, and weighing if extirpated three pounds. The patient [is] near 70 years old & very feeble. I of course advised doing nothing, there being no pain or suffering, and probably she will have some months' comfortable life if let alone, but would be likely to die from the effect of the operation if it were removed. Several physicians had assembled to witness the operation, but

all agreed that it was best to let it alone. From this house I was called to Bridgewater [Massachusetts] to a case of Femoral Hernia, a maiden lady of about forty-five. I here operated, and believe the case will do well. If I mistake not, this region will open a respectable business to me hereafter. This afternoon I go to Apponaug [Rhode Island] to visit a patient of Dr. James's.

I have one or two small operations in reserve for you. . . . Your cousin [Mary Leighton Burney] left here with her brother George [Leighton] on Tuesday eveng., he for N. Carolina & she for Philada. There is but little sickness in the city.

In 1846 Usher enjoyed a fairly active surgical practice. It included the only lithotomy performed during his lifetime.[5] The patient was a male of seventy-four. "The stone," he wrote, was "three inches in circumference. The operation was performed in July in very hot weather. The lateral operation was performed, with the *bistouri caché.*"[6] He listed the result as "Cured." Usher also performed his first and only carotid artery ligation, or "ligature" as he termed it. The patient was a nineteen-year-old young man, "Affected with intense headache, remittent in character. There was total blindness. After a very great variety of treatment, the disease having existed two years, he was advised by counsel in Boston, to have the carotid artery tied. There was great abatement of pain for some weeks; but it returned, and he died in a few months after." The symptons strongly suggest a brain tumor. Usher also recorded two femoral herniotomies for strangulation, both in females, seventy-six and forty-four years of age respectively. The older woman survived, but he lost the younger. These were among the last operations which he performed without benefit of ether. The historic demonstration of "anaesthesia" (a term suggested by O. W. Holmes) on October 16, 1846 at the Massachusetts General Hospital revolutionized the practice of surgery throughout the civilized world.

Usher continued to be preocuppied with problems other than surgical. Since famed Butler Hospital for the Insane in Providence did not receive its first patient until 1847, suitable shelter for the mentally disturbed was difficult to find, except in Dexter Asylum (the city poor farm not appropriate for the gentle classes). On June 8 Usher wrote to Doctor Luther V. Bell, superintendent of McLean Hospital, the noted psychiatric institution then located in Charlestown, Massachusetts:[7]

Mr. Dorrance [8] of this city, the bearer of this [he and lady among our most respected citizens], takes a patient to your asylum concerning whom I state [a] few particulars—

Miss Tiffany is bout 25 years of age, the only one of a numerous connexion that has ever been deranged. She became aversed to company some years since, has within a few months imbibed the notion that some of her family were her enemies, and willing to poison her. Within a few days her mania has been chiefly upon two or three subjects, religious terror and despondency being one—and the presence of a malign or sulphurous influence imparted by her family on approaching near her. . . . Her fits of mania seem to be quieted by exercise in riding and by walking. . . . I learn that 18 months since she fell at the doorsteps and struck the back of her head, and has often referred to it since that time, and applied cooling lotions to it. Also that fifteen years since she had the measles.

The head injury and the measles were irrelevant. The young lady obviously suffered from dementia praecox—paranoid schizophrenia.[9]

Usher at this time was asked to see an interesting patient in consultation, the young son of T. Wilkins Updike of Kingston, Rhode Island, who several years before had helped Usher with his research on early Rhode Island physicians. Updike described the circumstances in a letter to poetess Sarah Helen Whitman of Providence (whose unhappy love affair with Edgar Allen Poe has become part of our literary tradition):[10]

Our favorite, Daniel, was taken sick, so much as to require medical aid; the Doctor announced his disease dangerous, and in a few days after, the Physician, Daniel, & myself, went up to see Dr. Parsons & when he announced to me that his case was an incurable one in all probability, I thought my heart would break. He ordered some experiments made & . . . has come to the conclusion that it is not the same disease he thought it was, & . . . that it is not dangerous—which cheered us all. When I . . . announced the Doctor's [first] opinion I never saw a more mournful house, but we are now restored to our hope & cheerfulness. Can you believe it, that he told the Doctor that he had been in the habit of drinking from one to two pailfuls of water a day & nearer to two than one. This was unknown to us for a long time; he thought it was mere thirst & informed no one & none of the

family discovered this great excess of drinking. This course he
told Dr. Parsons he had indulged in . . . from about August or
September last according to his recollection. Myself & his sister
. . . watch him night & day, for his thirst . . . is so great that if he
can get water he will indulge himself in drinking against all our
arguments & remonstrations. You know, My Dear, that he is a
pet with us. . . . the Physican has requested him to be kept in a
warm room [to] produce a perspiration . . . but none has yet been
produced. [If we can] effect a reversion of action in the system,
. . . his danger will be over.

This was, of course, a classical case of childhood diabetes insipidus,
a pituitary gland disorder, possibly caused by a brain cyst or tumor
and at that time uniformly fatal. Usher's favorable prognosis is
incredible, implying that he had never heard of the disorder, which
had been described as early as 1800. Young Daniel died shortly
thereafter.

Charles had been elected a Fellow of the Rhode Island Medical
Society at its annual meeting in the courthouse in Providence on
June 26, 1846, and thus embarked on his professional career. He
was also chosen recording secretary, a post he held for the next
three years.[11] During the Society's semi-annual meeting on December 10, past president Theophilus C. Dunn of Newport, the only
Rhode Islander who had attended the "National Medical Convention" in May, read a belated report of its historic organizational
meeting. Dunn, Richmond Brownell, George Capron, and Usher
Parsons were chosen delegates to the next national convention to
be held in Philadelphia. On motion of Doctor Parsons, a Committee
of Publications was appointed to select papers from among those
read before the Society for publication. The committee, of which
Usher was chairman, eventually recommended establishment of a
medical journal.[12]

The next meeting of the National Medical Convention, known
thereafter as the American Medical Association, was held in Philadelphia on May 5 to 7, 1847 in the hall of the Academy of Natural
Sciences. Usher and Dunn were there, but not the others. Charles
wrote of this episode:[13]

. . . Dr. Parsons was present as delegate, and took an active part.
In writing of the receptions then held, he says: "It was gratifying
to me to find whenever I introduced myself to any stranger,—
which I did a dozen times this evening,—as Dr. Parsons of Rhode

Island, they all called me at once by my Christian name, having read of my writings through journals."

During June Usher visited Alfred, stopping to see his niece, Abigail Parsons Lewis, who was "very sick" according to General Leighton's diary. He returned to Providence for the June 30 annual meeting of the Rhode Island Medical Society, where he reported for the delegates to the National Medical Convention in Philadelphia.[14] During the spring and summer Usher traveled extensively in upper New York state and western Massachusetts, visiting Saratoga and the Berkshires.[15]

At the interim meeting of the Rhode Island Medical Society on December 29, 1847 invitations were read from superintendent Doctor Isaac Ray and the trustees of the new Butler Hospital for the Insane to visit the hospital. The doors of the handsome Tudor edifice, a model of its kind, had been opened on December 1. No doubt the ever-inquisitive Usher inspected this humane and progressive institution. The Society's "Minutes" record that Usher was once again elected delegate to the American Medical Association's next meeting to be held in Baltimore in the spring of 1848.

The minutes further contain this entry: "Dr. U. Parsons read parts of a paper giving the statistics of his capital operations in Surgery." Now approaching his sixtieth birthday and with a capable and well-trained son to take over, Usher was beginning to think of gradual retirement from practice—an opportune time to review his lifetime experience in surgery. The term "capital" would approximate "major" in modern usage. The unabridged report appeared in *The American Journal of the Medical Sciences* the following April. "The Medical profession," he wrote, "have occasionally been favoured with valuable reports from hospital surgeons, on the results of large surgical operations that have occurred in hospital practice," both in this country and in Europe. "It has occurred to me that similar reports from private practitioners [*i.e.* those without hospital affiliation] would possess some interest. I therefore present the following brief summary of cases that have come under my care during a practice of thirty-five years, hoping that other practitioners advanced in life will pursue a similar course."

Some of his cases have already been described. His largest series consisted of twenty-four major extremity amputations (or as he expressed it "of the large limbs"). In this group there were but three deaths. Two procedures were performed during 1847, the last year of record. The next largest series consisted of sixteen cases of "extirpation of Cancerous Breasts." There was no mortality in this group. This is possibly the first report in the world literature of long-term follow-up results in this condition. The series contains two apparent extended cures of eleven and six years, accomplished without benefit of radical surgery. About mastectomy he stated: "The patients all bore the operation well, giving no signs of syncope in a single instance." In one case he reported, with disdain, that a recurrent tumor was "afterward cauterized by a quack." There were fifteen strangulated hernias—ten scrotal, two umbilical, and three femoral. Only three patients of this group failed to survive. Further, there were four trephines for depressed skull fracture, with two survivals, and single cases of lithotomy and carotid artery ligation, and an extirpation of the eye already described. Of the latter Charles wrote, "He extirpated the eye-ball, with the lachrymal gland and much of the other textures in the orbit, as was then the practice, instead of the milder process of enucleation."

In summarizing his father's surgical career, Charles mentioned other surgical procedures with which Usher was familiar: "He operated frequently for cataract. He was at one time much interested in the surgical treatment of deformities, and performed tenotomy [cutting of tendon] often. He contrived and used with fair success an apparatus for securing union in cases of cleft palate"—still a difficult type of surgery.

Of two breast operations performed during 1847, Usher commented laconically, "In the last two cases, ether was employed." He was most certainly one of the first surgeons in Providence to use this important innovation, introduced at the Massachusetts General Hospital the previous year. Charles commented: "It was only in the latter part of his professional career that he enjoyed the advantages of etherization in surgery. He never became so fully at home with it as the later generation of surgeons. In the greater part of his operations, the only anaesthetics at his command were such as laudanum [tincture of opium] and brandy, and the words of encouragement and sympathy.,"

Over the years Usher had provided training for many medical students. "While in active practice," recalled Charles, "he gave a great deal of attention to private pupils in medicine, having often several at a time and more than fifty in all. He very commonly had private dissecting classes in the winter."

On January 31, 1848 several unnamed physicians met in the office of Doctor Henry Wheaton Rivers of Providence in order to establish a local medical society. A constitution and bylaws were adopted for a Providence Medical Association. The very first signature appended to the bylaws was that of Usher Parsons. Usher and Charles were faithful attendants at its regular monthly meetings.[16]

Later that year Usher departed early for the convention of the American Medical Association held in Baltimore from May 2–5, so that he would have time to stop off in Philadelphia and Washington on the way. He reported to Charles from Philadelphia on April 23:[17]

I arrived here on Friday evening [April 21]. Spent Saturday looking about, called on Drs. Norris, Hays, & Brewer,[18] and visited the Academy of Natural Sciences. At 10 o'clock this evening I shall leave for Baltimore—I learn that the profession in all directions are wide awake in reference to the National association and that the meeting bids fair to be very interesting. Much will be said in the Surgeon's report respecting Letheon [ether], Chloriform [sic] & the like, but collodeon [sic] will not be considered. I can account for this omission solely on the fact that it is a Boston invention.[19] The Philadelphia Surgeons were (probably for the same reason) slow to acknowledge the virtues of ether. In discoursing with some of them, I felt satisfied that a jealous spirit exists among them. . . . Horner and Leidy have gone to Germany to prosecute microscopic studies. . . .[20]

The trip of Horner and Leidy was an early manifestation of the growing influence of the German school on American medicine.

Usher participated actively in the deliberations in Baltimore. His old adversary Joseph Mauran, president of the Rhode Island Medical Society, was also present, but other delegates did not attend. Usher was apppointed to the Nominating Committee and to a committee to prepare a memorial to Congress on the falsification of drugs. He was also named to a committee of five to report at the next annual meeting on "The nature and extent of the sophistication and adulteration of drugs, as practised by the wholesale and retail druggists," and "The best means for the prevention of the evil in its various forms." Thus the A.M.A was deeply concerned from its beginning with the problem of purity and effectiveness of pharmaceutical preparations. According to the minutes, "Dr. Usher Parsons, from the select Committee on the Adulteration of Drugs, presented a draft of a Memorial to Congress relative to the subject, and, on motion, it was ordered that said Memorial be ... sent to the ... Chairman of the Special Committee appointed by Congress upon this subject." The historic document, written in Usher's lucid prose ("To the Honourable Senate and House of Representatives in Congress assembled") read as follows:[21]

> The memorial of the American Medical Association, consisting of delegates from the several states in the Union, at their annual meeting in Baltimore, assembled May 1848, respectfully represents:—
>
> That it has become notorious among druggists, apothecaries and physicians, that of late important drugs and medicines are specially adulterated in foreign countries, for sale in this country, and pass daily through the custom-house to be disseminated by ignorant and unprincipled dealers, to the great detriment of our citizens.
>
> That believing Congress possesses the power to enact laws to prevent the evils complained of, by subjecting all drugs and medicines to the inspection of persons duly qualified, whose duty it shall be to ascertain their real character and to keep such records as will guard the honest dealer against imposition—
>
> Your memorialists therefore ask of your honourable bodies that a law be enacted, embracing the appointment of a proper inspection at each port of entry, whose duty it shall be to examine all imported drugs and medicines, and to keep a record of such inspections, including the names of the parties, which shall be open for consultation to druggists and apothecaries and others concerned;—or to adopt such other measures as in your wisdom may seem best adapted to prevent the evils complained of.

At the annual meeting of the Rhode Island Medical Society on June 28,[22] President Mauran read "an eloquent and highly interesting ... account of the proceedings of the National Medical Association ... at Baltimore." Usher was disturbed by the failure of several Rhode Island delegates to attend, and it was voted upon his motion that delegates neglecting to attend after consenting to do so "shall pay the society six dollars unless excused by a unanimous vote of the Fellows."

Highly satisfying to Usher was the announcement that Charles had won the $50 Fiske Fund Prize for 1847. The question was, *"Vis Medicatrix Naturae*: How Far Should It Be Relied On In the Treatment of Diseases?" *Vis medicatrix naturae*—the healing power of nature—is a concept dating from Hippocrates and a noble phrase in Latin! The essay, in essence a defense of good therapeutics, later appeared in the *Boston Medical and Surgical Journal*.[23] There was a justifiably strong reaction against puking, purging, bleeding, and other harsh and drastic treatments; in some quarters the *vis* had "been made to stand for a sort of mythological personage, an angel of Hygeia, deputed to guard over the sick, and guide the events of disease by her intelligent watchfulness into favorable issues." We must, declared Charles, be sure before giving "Cathartics, diuretics, &c. . . . that we shall do good and not harm." "The *Vis Medicatrix Naturae* should not," he argued, "be left to itself, when a disease exists which we have specific remedies to control." Charles was then twenty-five years old.

At the September 1848 Brown University commencement Charles was awarded an honorary A.M. degree, a singular recognition for so young a man. Already well-endowed with degrees, Charles certainly had no need for another to establish his professional qualifications. Nor had he as yet taught at the college, his teaching career, in fact, being twenty years in the future.[24]

Later that fall Usher visited his young nephews in Savannah, Georgia, whose growing prosperity gave him great pleasure.[25] On December 20, at the interim meeting of the Rhode Island Medical Society, he read a paper on "abscesses of the iliac fossa."[26] He was again elected delegate to the American Medical Association and was appointed chairman of a committee on cholera, its purpose being to collect facts on the history of that disease. Charles was asked to be the Society's secretary. The revival of interest in cholera was inspired by a new American outbreak of the disease. Invading through New Orleans in 1848, it quickly spread up the Mississippi Valley, across the country to California, and to the east coast. An outbreak in Providence the following year reached epidemic proportions.

Before the annual meeting of the Providence Medical Association on March 5, 1849,[27] "Dr. C. W. Parsons exhibited . . . several specimens of Ascaris Lumbricoides [intestinal round worm]. Also a necrosed portion of the upper jaw. The necrosis was consequent upon severe Typhoid Fever. Dr. Parsons gave a very interesting history of this case." During the ensuing years both Usher and Charles participated actively in the scientific portion of the meetings, usually devoted to reports of interesting and unusual cases. Before the era of hospital staff meetings, this was a valuable educational medium and an important forum for communicating medical knowledge.

The next A.M.A. convention conveniently met in Boston May 1 to 4, 1849 in the hall of the Lowell Institute.[28] Usher, speaking for the select committee on adulteration and sophistication of drugs, reported much progress for the short period the committee had been in existence. Legislation adopted by Congress upon recommendation of the committee had already virtually halted the importation of spurious and worthless drugs. As a result of the operation of the new law, the New York Custom House alone had in the short space of five months condemned upon entry some thirty tons of adulterated or worthless drugs and preparations. The committee then sought to determine the extent of the problem of adulteration in the domestic market. Although it was not possible to "implicate all or any considerable portion of druggists in the charge of fraudulent dealing," there were enough individuals "ready to engage in such dishonest work on a large scale, and so great is the temptation ... that it will require the utmost vigilance of the Association and of the public." The committee urgently recommended a larger more sustained effort on the part of the Association, sound proposals for stringent and uniform legislation, and a program of public information. The report was historic, initiating a long vigorous campaign by the A.M.A. to assure pure and safe drugs. Prompted by the excellent report, the president appointed Usher chairman of the Committee on Medical Sciences to report at the convention of 1850.

In letters of May 8 and 9 Usher sent to John Collins Warren of Boston, the new A.M.A. president, a copy of his report on drugs and suggestions for members of the new committee. The list included Doctors George Capron and Charles W. Parsons of Rhode Island. He also wrote to Gilbert C. Greene, United States Senator from Rhode Island, urging him to support appropriate legislation.[29]

Usher's committee on the history of cholera in America presented its report, "portions of which were read by Dr. C. W. Parsons" at the annual meeting of the Rhode Island Medical Society, held in the State House in Providence on June 27, 1849.[30] The General Assembly, having under advisement legislation on the "important question of Registration of Births, deaths, & Marriages," appointed a conference committee to meet with the Society. In response to the legislation, the Society named a committee "to confer with the Legislative Committee, and report at the ensuing semiannual meeting of this Society." Usher was also appointed to this committee. He was then named one of three delegates "to the National Convention to be held at Philadelphia, to revise the Pharmacopoeia." He would be very busy indeed with Society affairs.

During July Usher again visited his down east home. Upon returning to Providence, he reported on his trip to his nephew, Doctor Usher Parsons Leighton, now practicing in Kenton, Ohio. It had been a deeply emotional experience for him. "It is not likely," he wrote,[31] "that I shall ever see so many of the family again." He noted that "this is our National Fast day [August 3] on account of Cholera. We have [had] about 25 deaths in about six weeks. The number is increasing." Although his young nephew was new in medical practice, he did not have the benefit of an M.D. degree. Usher advised him to take another course of lectures so that he could complete his doctorate: "You would feel better satisfied with yourself and would pursue practice the rest of your life with much more satisfaction than at present." He hoped to attend the National Medical Convention in Cincinnati the following May and urged young Usher to join him there: "The meeting will last about three days and is very improving."

At the semi-annual meeting of the Rhode Island Medical Society held in Franklin Hall, Providence, on December 19, 1849,[32] the committee on uniform registration of births, marriages, and deaths, of which Usher was a member, proposed statewide registration ordinances. Adopting the committee's recommendations, the General Assembly in 1852 enacted excellent progressive legislation which, with modifications, is still in effect. Usher was again appointed delegate to the A.M.A. convention for the May meeting in Cincinnati.

Charles read the final report of the committee on cholera, which the Publications Committee was requested to disseminate. Titled "Cholera in Rhode Island," it appeared in the *Boston Medical and Surgical Journal* of February 13, 1850.[33] "The readers of medical journals," wrote Usher, "have in general been surfeited with accounts of cholera prevailing in different cities and states during the past year. Such communications may, however, be serviceable . . .

to some future writer on cholera, who may wish to present a map of its rise and progress throughout the country." Following the appearance of the first case in Providence on May 27, 1849, which was fatal in eleven hours, the epidemic rose to a peak in August and burned out in October. Although the total number of cases could not be estimated, there were 156 deaths in Providence, 34 occurring in the first week of August. Most of these were in cases "unfavorably situated" and receiving city-poor care. In the same issue of the *Journal* appeared a short demographic study by Charles titled "Mortality of Providence, R.I.," a by-product of the report and of the statewide recording of vital statistics.[34] Since causes of death had now been accumulated in Providence for eight years, Charles deemed the system "well enough carried out to secure results worth posting up." It was as a direct result of a greater epidemic surge of cholera in 1854 that Providence's famed Health Department was established in 1856 with the able Doctor Edwin Miller Snow as Superintendent, predecessor of the renowned Doctor Charles Value Chapin.

The United States Navy, following British custom, long practiced flogging for punishment and discipline. Usher throughout his career loathed the practice as cruel and unnecessary and vigorously advocated its abolition. His views were gathering wider support, particularly after an unsavory episode in 1842 connected with a mutiny aboard the U.S. brig of war *Somers*. As a sequel to that peculiar incident, his old shipmate Alexander Slidell Mackenzie had been tried at court-martial. In January 1849 the Rhode Island General Assembly petitioned Congress[35] to abolish the "supply of ardent spirits as rations" and to prohibit "the use of the lash." The similarity of the phrasing to that in an unsigned article in the New York *Sunday Dispatch* of February 17 suggests its inspiration. We would not know the author's identity had it not been revealed by Charles:[36] "In 1850 [my father] helped to agitate the question of the abolition of flogging in the navy, and wrote a pungent article on the subject for a New York newspaper." The article, titled "Grog-Ration and Flogging in the Navy," read in part:

> . . . Government has made and continued in force such laws in respect to the rations allowed to crews as are known and admitted to have a direct tendency to induce habits of intoxication and consequent disorderly conduct. . . . Seven eighths of the flogging, Congress has been told again and again, results from drunkenness.

Is not that body then chargeable with the blame? . . . Prohibit the employment of foreigners, change the ration of grog into coffee, abandon that relict of barbarism the lash, and forthwith there would be a rush of our best seamen into public service. . . . Then our public ships would be changed from schools of vice and cruelty to nurseries of good order and sound morals. Then the sound of the lash and the shrieks of tortured victims would cease to reverberate in our ships.

Congress abolished flogging on September 28, 1850.

Usher was elected vice president of the Providence Medical Association at its annual meeting on March 4, 1850.[37] This led to the presidency a year later and heralded another significant period in his career. Usher had earlier been elected a delegate to the National Convention for revision of the Pharmacopoeia. It was obviously impossible for him to attend both that and the A.M.A. session, since they met almost simultaneously. Joseph Mauran, therefore, attended the Pharmacopoeia meetings in Washington and Philadelphia, while Usher proceeded to the A.M.A. in Cincinnati. On the way he visited familiar places along the southern shore of Lake Erie and arrived in Cincinnati a few days before the meetings. He had stopped very briefly at Erie and chatted with his old friend Captain Dobbins, who had commanded a vessel on the Lake during the campaign. He came away with a souvenir—a large cane made from a fragment of timber from the old flagship *Lawrence.* "This," he wrote, "I value very highly." In Cincinnati he put up at the Barnet House, "which is the most elegant hotel I ever saw."[38]

On May 8 Usher wrote to Charles:

. . . We met and organized yesterday. Dr. Warren made a long speech and made a fool of himself. Few heard him and nobody felt otherwise than mortified. After which a nominating committee was appointed. . . . The President and Vice President [were] all from the west excepting [George W.] Norris from Philadelphia. The room assembled [in] is worse to speak in than the Howard Hall [in Providence], as much so as that is worse than [the] Historical room. The transmitted reports are taken up first, and that on education is assigned for this morning. This will lead to a long discussion, and wishing to get clear of the task of reading my report in such a hall, I have sealed it up and handed it over to [Daniel] Drake and am going down the River to Louisville to return on Friday morning, and shall then go to Kenton [Ohio] with Usher Leighton, who is here with me. I shall try to be home by the 20th.

Not a civility of any kind has been shown any of us. Not a call has been made. [Reuben D.] Mussey is chosen President. The Profession here are all at variance. A miserable meeting. . . .[39]

"The Report of the Committee on Medical Sciences" appeared in the *Transactions of the American Medical Association.*[40] Serving on the committee with Usher, who drafted the report, were among others Jacob Bigelow, and J. B. S. Jackson of Boston and Harvard, and David King of Newport, Rhode Island. The report was a collective review of significant medical papers of the preceding year. One of the papers reviewed, titled "Contributions to Physiology," was the brainchild of Doctor Bennet Dowler of New Orleans, who Usher wished "had staid at home." This rather curious paper described the reflex behavior of the alligator after transection of the spinal cord and after decapitation. Dowler observed that an alligator whose "spinal marrow" had been cut across between the shoulders and the hips, "during a period of two hours, displayed complete intelligence, volition, and voluntary motion *in all divisions of the body.*" But the "ferocious separated head sprang up from the table with great force at me, passing very near my breast [and] alighted upon the floor, from six to eight feet distant from its original position!" Chairman Usher's report concluded tactfully, "Dr. Dowler is a bold experimenter and his laudable zeal and industry have already added many facts to medical science, and we doubt not his future labours will either strengthen or correct the opinions he has advanced."

The chairman explained that the committee was limited by its mandate to American scientific contributions and to certain specific categories of medical and allied progress. Yet he was eloquent concerning the great strides in American medicine and was optimistic about the future of the American Medical Association. "Who," he declaimed, "can contemplate the scene without a thrill of professional enthusiasm, or doubt for a moment that a rich harvest of American science will ere long be annually collected and diffused through the instrumentality of the Association?"

Arriving home earlier than anticipated, Usher promptly wrote to his sister Frances Leighton about her prospering brood:[41]

I returned yesterday from my tour Westward and on my way home passed Saturday and Sunday a week ago with Usher at

Kenton. He is very well situated and for that region is considered wealthy, the most so of any man in the county. What is still more agreeable, he is respected and beloved more than any man. He has several houses, two farms under good cultivation, two saw-mills, and perhaps a thousand acres of excellent land, besides house lots in the village. His practice is the best, and his house is well furnished. Oner [a younger sister of Usher Leighton, also living in Kenton and married to Doctor William Jones] is pleas-antly situated; but her husband not so prosperous though they make a good living. I dined with them and was pleased with appearances. I think that Usher, if he lives ten years, will be very wealthy. You did well in not going on with me, for the boats and cars are all hustle and speed, beyond what you could indure.

On August 26, 1845 Usher had requested assistance of his niece Frances in collecting information about their Frost ancestors for a sketch of Charles Frost.[42] He recalled one Frost "who lived I think near General Furnald's. Your father can tell. I have some faint recollection of a little old red faced man named Simon Frost who lived thereabouts 45 years ago. You see that I have marked out considerable work for you." He went on: "Have you heard what is the lowest price that the Alva Conant estate can be had for? Inquire. The price would be raised if I were to inquire, and let me know."

In the July 1849 issue of the *New England Historical and Genealogical Register* Usher finally published his excellent historical sketch, a "Memoir of Charles Frost," who was his maternal great-great-grandfather.[43] Born in Tiverton, England in 1632, Frost arrived at Piscataqua (i.e. the Piscataqua River at Portsmouth, New Hampshire) in 1635 or 1636. After describing Frost's civilian responsibil-ities, Usher explored his military exploits in some detail: "Being enrolled as a soldier at sixteen, he gradually rose, through successive grades, to be commander-in-chief of the militia of Maine." Most of his years were spent fighting Indians, and, appropriately, Frost met a violent death at their hands. On July 4, 1697, a Sabbath morning, while on the way home from church, Frost, his wife, and two sons were ambushed by a party of Indians hidden "by the wayside under a large log, in which they had stuck a row of green boughs." Frost was murdered, but his wife and sons escaped.

Early in the new year of 1850, Henry B. Dawson of New York addressed certain "queries" to Usher concerning details of the Battle of Lake Erie. Dawson, having already as a young man of thirty acquired a reputation as editor of the Federalist Papers, in future years became a distinguished American historian. He was now at work compiling his definitive *Battles of the United States by Sea and Land*. Usher furnished a complete tactical analysis of the battle and the positions of the ships at various stages.[44] "My own opinion on this subject," he stated, "is not so good as Mr. Champlin's and others. The last view I had of the squadrons before the fight, they were a mile apart. The next time was when the *Detroit* hauled down her flag. At that moment I leaped upon deck, and saw the *Detroit*'s flag down, and the *Niagara* discharging her last guns at them." "The blame attached to Elliott," he continued, "is not so much for being out of line . . . , as for holding back."

He sent along numerous documents and a diagram of the battle made by an officer who had participated. He requested its return since, although "the diagram is coarse . . . I value it." He would try to procure for Dawson through his connections in Providence documents relating to an earlier war: "Commodore Esek Hopkins has a granddaughter, Miss Angell, in Providence. Wm. B. Staples, formerly judge, has the custody of his papers, and if applied to directly and not through another would be likely to accommodate you." Usher's eyewitness accounts contributed importantly to Dawson's vivid description of the Battle of Lake Erie.

At the mid-winter meeting of the Rhode Island Medical Society in December,[45] Usher was again appointed a delegate to the forthcoming A.M.A. convention to be held in May in Charleston, South Carolina. Charles, who read a paper "On some of the Remote Effects of Injuries of Nerves," was complimented for "displaying much & patient research." The paper, published in the April 1851 issue of *The American Journal of the Medical Sciences*,[46] carried a footnote expressing the hope that "some peculiarities in its style may be excused . . . that it was intended to be read before a Society, and is published only" on request. A hodge-podge of unrelated cases taken from his private practice and from the literature, the paper has little scientific value. Charles's philosophical observations are more enduring: "The mode in which the system reacts against disturbing causes varies so much in different constitutions as to make [it] an inexhaustible subject for study. A little puncture [of the skin] aided by some peculiar impressibility [has been known to] produce speedy death. On the other hand, men have recovered after having the thorax skewed by the shaft of a chaise,[47] or a tamping-iron shot through the brains."[48] Charles reflected: "The public do not understand this uncertainty, which springs from the very nature of life. The physician, oftener the surgeon, is sometimes held answerable for a good result as if he were dealing with mere machinery, governed by the laws of lifeless matter alone." This is still a sore point in the modern debate over malpractice.

Nephew George Parsons, who had been in Providence for almost a year, departed for Maine in the late summer of 1845. After visiting his relations in Kennebunk, he set out for Savannah, Georgia to make his fortune. George, Charles, and Edwin Parsons were Usher's favorite nephews.[49] In later years they became successful and wealthy businessmen, while John, a fourth brother, was of a more scholarly bent. He was graduated from Andover Theological Seminary in 1845 and eventually became a prominent clergyman in the Boston area. Edwin, aged twenty-two, worked in the office of Carhart and Scott, cotton merchants of Savannah, Georgia, where George joined him. The following year the company moved to Macon. Edwin remained behind and established Edwin Parsons and Company. In 1857 he moved his operations to New York City. At the outbreak of the Civil War, George was also living in New York. In later years Edwin became Usher's confidant and traveling companion, described by Charles as "the Chosen Friend, Advisor, and Companion of [Usher's] Later Years."[50]

On February 19, 1846 seventeen-year-old William Henry Watson, a Providence lad and in later years an eminent physician of upstate New York, had sent George Parsons a vivid account of affairs in Providence:[51]

> Being at a Fair last evening I had the good fortune to see your Cousin Charles. . . . I presume that with you [in Savannah] there is no snow, but here we have it at present in great abundance, and the sleighs fly merrily, I assure you and Oh! I wish that you could be here to enjoy it for a day or two—the ladies are riding all the time as the weather is pleasant and it is fine sport to watch them and hear them laugh as they go bumping over the mounds of snow. . . . the Providence and Worcester Railroad Co. have petitioned the city council for leave to fill up a part of the cove, for a location for their depot, which has been granted much against the wishes of many of our citizens, who wished to have

it dug out and improved with walks around it for a Mall. Every way has been used to prevent their obtaining the petition, among which was the opinion of Dr. Wheaton, an old and distinguished physician, that it would be highly detrimental to the health of the citizens; in which Dr. Parsons agreed, but it was all to no purpose. The secret of their obtaining it was that all with one exception of the City Council are members of the Rail-road corporation, and were very willing to vote some thirty or forty acres of land in the midst of the city, and which is estimated to be worth about $200,000 into their own pockets. This has created quite an exasperated feeling among some of our citizens toward the Rail-road Co. and has made a considerable stir in the community. . . .

On March 16 Usher wrote to George,[52] reporting on family correspondence, the death of an "old rich Quaker [William Jenkins]," and the sudden demise of "Professor [William Giles] Goddard . . . in consequence of swallowing a piece of mutton which crowded into his wind pipe." He continued:

The office goes on about as formerly—no student at present, but I am expecting Mr. Lyon again. There is a very young man named Tripp in the office from Sanford [Maine], who does up the work in superior style. The boarders in the house and at McClellan's remain about the same as when you were here.

I wish you would give me some account of Savannah and of the condition of the slaves. . . . The Worcester R. Road it is decided shall pass along a few rods east of the catholic church and over the cove to Exchange Street and crossing Westminster, go through the east end of Weybosset down to the Stonington Depot. The cars will be drawn through the streets by horses. There is double the amount of building going on of any former year, in every part of the city. Grace church is near completed and inside is far superior to anything we have. Dorrism is on the decline.

The partial filling of the cove (somewhat analogous to Boston's Back Bay), the curving of the railroad tracks south of the cove into downtown Providence, and the construction of a large train depot[53] were events of sufficient moment to have been mentioned in several letters. Usher was obviously greatly impressed.

Usher's old friend and colleague, Professor Romeo Elton, had moved to Bath, England. Widowed in 1844, he was now wedded to a cultured English lady named Prothesia Goss. He retained his interest in Rhode Island lore and was writing *The Life of Roger Williams, the Earliest Legislator.* In a letter to Elton, Usher gave another lively picture of the local scene:[54]

> In respect to local news,—which I know by experience to be always acceptable to one in distant lands—I would say that our city continues to be active and prosperous. Great facility is afforded in traveling to and fro by the removal of the depot to the cove above the bridge. It is now only three minutes' walk from my office to the cars for Stonington, Worcester, and Boston; and the most elegant depot-houses are erected that I have ever seen. They are built on made land, and extend from the foot of Duncan's hill to near the bridge, and sweep round in the form of a crescent toward Carpenter's point, whence the Stonington train passes through Olneyville to the old Stonington railroad a few miles out.
>
> Our Historical Society, of which you were one of the presiding officers, continues its labors as formerly. . . . Two elegant portraits have been added, one of Commodore Perry, and the other a full length one of the President, John Howland. . . .
>
> Our presidential campaign, now opening, presents a novel aspect. Gen. Cass is the Loco candidate, but is not acceptable to the party in New York, who have nominated Martin Van Buren. It is not unlikely that the opposition of this gentleman to the extension of slavery will secure to him many of the votes of the free states. On the Whig side Gen. Taylor is the candidate; whose ranks will be thinned by abolition votes, so that there will probably be no choice by the people, and the election will devolve on the House, where I think Van Buren is most likely to succeed. [He was wrong.]

Usher and Charles had planned to visit Cambridge during Harvard commencement week. Uncle John wrote on August 23, 1847:[55]

> We received a note from Ann on Saturday telling us that her youngest child had died—it had been very sick with scarlet fever, and for some days not expected to recover. Ann begged Mother and me to come down and stay with them for a while, and we go tomorrow. This, however, must not hinder you from coming to Commencement—now your father and you will find yourself accommodated as well as if we were here. I hope you will come and have as good a time as the occasion can afford.

Usher and Charles later spent Thanksgiving Day in Salem with the Uphams, but once again missed seeing John and Grandmother Holmes.

During the summer of 1848 Usher had once more traveled to Alfred. His visit is recorded among the last entries in General Leighton's diary, kept daily without a single break for thirty years. Leighton noted that he gave Usher "my sword as gratuity for his extra kindness heretofore to me and my family, the same silver headed sword which I bought of Col. Saml. Ham of Portsmouth, N.H. 19th Sept. 1795 for thirty dollars . . . it being the same sword which was presented by Sir Peter Warren to Sir William Pepperrell, in England, when he conferred on him the honors of Baronet after the capture of Louisburg."

An unknown hand later noted in the diary that General Leighton "took cold" on October 2 and passed away on October 13, 1848.

NOTES

1. John Holmes to Charles W. Parsons, March 27, 1845, DPC.

2. George Parsons (nephew of Usher Parsons) to his mother, April 11, 1845, DPC. In the fall of 1844 George Parsons, eighteen-year-old son of Usher's brother William of Kennebunk, began a year of sojourn in Providence with his uncle to further his education. Unlike his brother John, who had graduated from the college two years earlier, George did not matriculate at Brown.

3. There is little to support this in O. W. Holmes manuscripts and papers in the Houghton Library of Harvard University, in the family correspondence, and in the Harvard Medical Archives in the Countway Library.

4. Usher Parsons to Charles W. Parsons, December 19, 1845, DPC.

5. Usher Parsons, "Statistics of Large Surgical Operations."

6. The bistoury was a long, narrow surgical knife, straight or curved, used for incising abscesses or opening sinuses and fistulas. The *bistouri caché* was a bistoury concealed in a cannula for introduction and made to protrude when incision was desired. Lithotomy, cutting for the bladder stone, had been performed since ancient times.

7. Usher Parsons to Luther V. Bell, June 8, 1846, Boston Public Library.

8. William Tully Dorrance (1809–1880) was a wealthy cotton manufacturer.

9. The term dementia praecox was introduced by Emil Kraepelin in 1896 and schizophrenia by Eugen Bleuler in 1911.

10. Wilkins Updike to Sarah Helen Whitman, January 5, 1847, RIHS.

11. Rhode Island Medical Society, "Minutes."

12. *Ibid.*

13. C. W. Parsons *Memoir*, pp. 30–31.

14. Rhode Island Medical Society, "Minutes."

15. Usher Parsons to Charles W. Parsons, July 11, 1847, DPC.

16. Providence Medical Association, "Minutes." These are now in the library of the Rhode Island Medical Society.

17. Usher Parsons to Charles W. Parsons, April 23, 1848, DPC.

18. George Washington Norris, M.D. (1808–1875), Clinical Professor of Surgery, Univ. of Penn. John Maitland Brewer, M.D. (1781–1859), Philadelphia physician. Isaac Hays, as previously noted, was editor of the *American Journal of the Medical Sciences.*

19. The ether preparation used in Boston was given the proprietary name Letheon. The use of collodion as a surgical adhesive was indeed a Boston, or at least a Dedham invention, having been introduced by Doctor John Parker Maynard of that town. See: John P. Maynard, "Discovery and application of the New Liquid Adhesive Plaster," *Boston Medical and Surgical Journal*, 38:178–183, 1848, and John P. Maynard, "The Original Application of a Solution of Cotton to Surgery," *Boston Medical and Surgical Journal*, 38:266–268, 1848.

20. William E. Horner, as previously noted, was professor of anatomy at the University of Penn. Joseph Leidy, M.D. (1823–1891), was an outstanding anatomist, chairman of the board of curators of the Academy of Natural Sciences at Philadelphia, and later professor at the University of Pennsylvania and Swarthmore.

21. American Medical Association, *Transactions*, 1:335, 1848.

22. Rhode Island Medical Society, "Minutes."

23. Charles W. Parsons, *"Vis Medicatrix Naturae*—How Far Should It Be Relied on in the Treatment of Diseases?" *Boston Medical and Surgical Journal*, 40:189–201, 1849.

24. Charles was professor of physiology at Brown 1874–1882.

25. R. J. Arnold to C. P. Richardson, October 28, 1848, DPC. Arnold, formerly of Providence, removed to Georgia in 1823. The letter states: "My particular friend and family physician, Dr. Usher Parsons, is about to sail for Savannah to pass a few days in your city. . . ." R. J. Arnold to Robert Haversham, October 28, 1849, DPC. The letter states: "Dr. Parsons has a nephew in Savannah & contemplates passing a few days there, & I shall feel highly gratified if . . . you make his time pass pleasantly. . . ."

26. Rhode Island Medical Society, "Minutes."

27. Providence Medical Association, "Minutes."

28. American Medical Association, *Transactions*, 2:655–661, 1849.

29. Usher Parsons to John Collins Warren, May 8 and May 9, 1849, Mas-

sachusetts Historical Society. Also, Usher Parsons to Albert C. Greene, May 10, 1845, RIHS.

30. Rhode Island Medical Society, "Minutes."

31. Usher Parsons to Usher Parsons Leighton, August 3, 1849, Parsons Memorial Library, Alfred, Maine.

32. Rhode Island Medical Society, "Minutes."

33. Usher Parsons, "Cholera in Rhode Island," *Boston Medical and Surgical Journal*, 42:29–33, 1850.

34. Charles W. Parsons, "Mortality of Providence, R.I.," *Boston Medical and Surgical Journal*, 42:31–35, 1850.

35. Schedules of the General Assembly of Rhode Island, session of January, 1849.

36. C. W. Parsons *Memoir*, p. 51.

37. Providence Medical Association, "Minutes."

38. Usher Parsons to Charles W. Parsons, May 5, 1850, DPC.

39. Usher Parsons to Charles W. Parsons, May 8, 1850, DPC. Perhaps Usher was a bit testy at the rousing ovation given to the illustrious home-town celebrity, Daniel Drake. The first volume of Drake's renowned *Diseases of the Interior Valley of North America*, his "crowning achievement," according to Ralph Major, had just recently appeared. The 200th anniversary of Drake's birth was observed in 1985.

40. American Medical Association, *Transactions*, 3:53–103, 1850. This was also reprinted as a separate at Philadelphia that same year by T. K. & P. G. Collins, printers to the Association.

41. Usher Parsons to Frances P. Leighton, May 19, 1850, Parsons Memorial Library, Alfred, Maine.

42. Usher Parsons to Frances P. Leighton, August 26, 1845, DPC.

43. Usher Parsons, "Memoir of Charles Frost," *New England Historical and Genealogical Register*, 3:249–262, 1849.

44. Usher Parsons to Henry B. Dawson, January 24, 1850, New York Historical Society.

45. Rhode Island Medical Society, "Minutes."

46. Charles W. Parsons, "On Some of the Remote Effects of Injuries of the Nerves," *The American Journal of the Medical Sciences*, n.s. 21:306–319, 1851.

47. Charles is here referring to one of the better-known cases of recovery from a traumatic injury, the driving of the shaft of a chaise through the thorax of a man when a horse bolted and moved the chaise forward. This incident is described in William Maiden's *An Account of a Case of Recovery, after an Extraordinary Accident, by Which the Shaft of a Chaise Had Been Forced Through the Thorax* (London, T. Bayley, 1812). A second edition appeared in 1824.

48. This refers to the renowned case of Phineas Gage of Cavendish, Vermont, whose skull was completely traversed by a heavy iron bar as a

result of a premature explosion while blasting. The strange story of this injury and survival had recently been reported by Doctor Jacob Bigelow in *The American Journal of the Medical Sciences* of July, 1850 (v. 20, April, 1851). Gage miraculously survived for a decade, dying in 1861, and his skull, showing the portals of entry and exit, has ever since been a prized exhibit in the Warren Anatomical Museum of the Harvard Medical School. See also A. T. Steegmann, "Dr. Harlow's Famous Case: The 'Impossible' Accident of Phineas P. Gage.," *Surgery*, 52:952–958, 1962.

49. George Parsons to Usher Parsons, December 13, 1845, DPC.

50. The dedication printed in Charles's *Memoir* of his father states that "This Memoir is Dedicated to Edwin Parsons, of New York, My Father's Nephew, and the Chosen Friend, Adviser, and Companion of his Later Years."

51. William Henry Watson to George Parsons, February 19, 1846, DPC. Watson (1829–1913) had a distinguished career as a physician in Utica, New York.

52. Usher Parsons to George Parsons, March 16, 1846, DPC.

53. An elegant Romanesque train station designed by Providence architect Thomas A. Tefft was opened in 1848. It was then the largest train station in America and it dominated Exchange Place (now Kennedy Plaza) for half a century. The oval cove was lined with stone and was encircled by a fashionable tree-lined promenade. In time, with increasing pollution, the cove became unbearably noisome and was filled in. The area was then used for freight yards. The station was demolished and replaced in 1896–1898 by a monumental pile which still stands, but no longer handles railroad traffic. After almost a century-and-a-half in this location, the tracks have been moved to the north of the cove lands as part of the sweeping Capital Center project, removing from the center of the city a barrier which had come to be known as the "Chinese Wall."

54. Usher Parsons to Romeo Elton, June 26, 1848, DPC.

55. John Holmes to Charles W. Parsons, August 23, 1847, HUCC.

CHAPTER FIFTEEN

Biographer of Pepperrell

In 1851 Usher at last embarked upon what would be his principal literary effort. According to Charles,[1]

> . . . the "Life of Sir William Pepperrell," sprang originally out of his genealogical studies. He began to prepare for his task in the year 1846, but suspended it on learning that Pepperrell's life would be written by others. The principal exploit of Pepperrell, in heading the attack on the French fortified town of Louisburg, in 1745, and reducing it after a siege of forty-eight days, had been fully described by [the Reverend Jeremy] Belknap[2] and other historians. But no extended memoir of Pepperrell had been published. Rev. Dr. Charles Burroughs,[3] of Portsmouth, New Hampshire, and Hon. Lorenzo Sabine,[4] of Framingham, Massachusetts, had both prepared sketches of his life. A connection of the family, Colonel George Sparhawk, of Kittery, where Pepperrell's mansion still stood [and still stands], had talked of writing his biography, and was known to have a great many of his papers, which had lain neglected in a shed or fish-house on the estate, till Colonel Sparhawk selected and arranged the more valuable documents. It was after correspondence with these gentlemen and many others, that Dr. Parsons determined to carry out the undertaking. He read the state and local histories bearing on his subject, examined the papers in the Massachusetts Historical Society and other public places of deposit, and procured documents from all available sources. The Sparhawk papers, after some negotiation, reached his hands in January, 1851, through the kind offices of Mr. John Blunt [a maternal relative of Usher's], of New York. For four years after that, he gave much of his leisure to this work.

Usher's interest in his famous ancestor is first revealed in a letter which he wrote to Colonel Sparhawk on December 1, 1847.[5] Having

learned of Sparhawk's interest in Pepperrell and his determination
to undertake a biography, Usher indicated his willingness to aid
him by turning over what he himself had collected. He informed
the Colonel that he had a letter written by Sir William's father to
his shipbuilder in Saco that was dated as early as 1690, copies of
the father's will as well as that of Sir William, some forty to fifty
letters on public matters from Pepperrell to Judge Hill of South
Berwick, the genealogy of the Frosts, and other materials. He also
directed Sparhawk to additional manuscript sources and to printed
histories that would aid him in this work. As Charles indicates, the
Colonel for unknown reasons appears to have abandoned the proposed biography. Usher then took over the project in 1851, devoting
much time and energy to it during the next several years.

Early in 1852, after he had become directly involved in the Pepperrell project, Usher received an invitation to deliver the annual
discourse of the Rhode Island Historical Society. He replied on
January 18 with fitting modesty:[6] "Believing it the duty of every
Fellow of the Society to perform any task assigned him, I have
concluded to comply with the request, though diffident of my ability to offer anything that will be acceptable." The meeting, held in
the Representatives' Chamber of the State House on February 16,
was a memorable one. Usher presented his excellent and definitive
account of the Battle of Lake Erie, the basis of several later versions.
He gave his reasons for selecting the subject:[7]

> I have made this choice, first, because this battle is a part of
> Rhode Island History, and therefore appropriate to the occasion;
> secondly, because I could speak of it from personal knowledge;
> and thirdly, because a very inaccurate and perverted account of
> it has been written and imposed upon the public by the late J.
> Fenimore Cooper, Esquire.[8] I am aware that this gentleman's
> mistakes and misrepresentations should have been noticed and
> corrected before his decease, and my apology for the delay is that
> I never saw the pamphlet containing them, nor knew of its ex-
> istence until within a few days past, and after commencing this
> discourse.

While Usher may not have actually remembered seeing Cooper's
pamphlet, it had indeed been vigorously brought to his attention
by Captain Stephen Champlin[9] many years before. With the lapse
of some seven years, however, it is possible that he might have
forgotten it. Usher continued:

My aim will be to give an account of the origin of the fleet or squadron on the lake; of its conflict with the British squadron, of the consequences, immediate and remote, and in conclusion to notice some of Mr. Cooper's erroneous positions and false inferences.

He followed with a graphic account of the now-familiar scene. Regarding Cooper's part in the Elliott-Perry controversy, he commented:

[Cooper] seems to have entered the controversy purely from love of it. He strives to save Elliott by disparaging Perry, and from his pen has flown more ink and bile than has been shed by all others. Much as Elliott's conduct deserves censure, Cooper's is more reprehensible. He enters the lists unnecessarily, and purely from love of paradox and thirst for notoriety, unless it were a prospect of gaining a medal. I am well aware that there is little honor gained by striking at a dead man, and therefore wish that Mr. Cooper were living to hear me.

His sketch of Perry was eloquent and polished:

A few remarks on the character of Commodore Perry must conclude this discourse, already too long. I have alluded to his being passionate under provocation, aside from which he was the most exemplary officer I ever knew. Possessed of high-toned moral feeling, he was above the low dissipation and sensuality that many officers of his day were prone to indulge in. His conversation was remarkably free from profanity and indelicacy, and in his domestic character he was a model of every domestic virtue and grace.[10] His acquirements were respectable. On the subjects of history and drama he was well read, and had formed opinions that evinced patient thought. He wrote with remarkable facility and in good taste. Trained under the experienced teachings of his father and Commodore [John] Rodgers, he could not fail of perfection in seamanship and naval discipline. Every germ of merit in his officers was sure to be discovered and encouraged by him and no opportunity was ever lost of advancing those who performed their duty with cheerfulness and fidelity. He was the most remarkable man I ever saw for success in inspiring his officers with a reverential awe in his presence, and with a dread of giving him offence. Generous to the full extent of his means, his elegant hospitality especially on ship-board in foreign ports, reflected great honor on our navy. Distinguished visitors ever found his ship in most perfect order, and left her with exalted opinions of his graceful and distinguished manners, and of the strict discipline prevailing among his officers and men.

He concluded on an emotional note:

> Nearly forty years have rolled away since Perry gained the memorable victory—the first one ever gained over a squadron by this country, and, with the lapse of time, have passed away most of those who were with him. Of the nine commanders of vessels, only one survives; and of the fifteen officers of the *Lawrence*, only Capt. Taylor and myself remain. The thought reminds me . . . that my own summons cannot be far distant. Entertaining the opinions I honestly do of the incidents and events of the battle, and of the chief actors in it—opinions which were formed on the spot at the time—and also of the controversy that long after ensued, I have for years felt it an imperative duty to present these opinions to the citizens of the State on some appropriate occasion. That duty . . . is now performed . . . and with it . . . a tribute of respect to the character of the illustrious son of Rhode Island. Ever may his memory remain enshrined in the hearts of the people of his native State, and of a grateful nation.

Samuel Greene Arnold, a contemporary student of Rhode Island history, deemed Usher's treatment of the Elliott-Cooper controversy incontrovertible, comprehensive, and complete.[11] Charles recalled his father's "fondness for written controversy." He observed that he "could handle the caustic pen as well as the scalpel or saw."[12]

More than a week elapsed before the *Providence Daily Journal* took note of the address (February 25): "We have refrained from noticing the discourse . . . in anticipation of an extended report, which we regret has not been made. The subject . . . was the Battle of Lake Erie, made essentially a part of Rhode Island History by the heavy contribution of officers and men from this State, and rendered particularly interesting . . . from the fact that the speaker was himself a participant in the scenes he so graphically described." It declared that no account of that bloody conflict ever gave so clear an idea of the order of battle and its progress, and concluded: "Dr. P. entered into . . . the Elliott difficulty, and in feeling language rescued the memory of Perry from the aspersions cast upon it by the modern naval historian."

At a special meeting of the Society on March 5, its thanks were "presented to Dr. Parsons for his interesting discourse," and a copy was requested for publication.[13] The first edition, numbering 250 copies, appeared in the summer of 1853.

For some months now Usher had been giving increasing time and thought to his work on Pepperrell. Wrote Charles, "Not satisfied with studying the details of Pepperrell's career in its written and printed records," he planned to visit and become familiar with "the harbor and ruins of Louisburg." Usher planned to travel with his favorite nephew, Edwin Parsons, who, as previously noted, became his father's "chosen friend and companion of later years." "They took the English steamer from Boston to Halifax," wrote Charles, "and then a small steamboat to Sydney [Nova Scotia], driving thence to Louisburg," where they arrived on August 22.[14] Usher kept a detailed diary of the journey.[15]

On their arrival at Sydney, Usher and Edwin dined at a private boarding house and set out for Louisburg in an open buggy, a trip of twenty-six miles over rough roads. On the way they passed not more than ten or a dozen run-down houses and log cabins. The land, forested and very rocky, reminded Usher of lower Maine, where he had grown up. The settlers were largely Irish and highland Scottish, with very few New Englanders among them.

They approached Louisburg at eight o'clock in the evening from the west, descending to the harbor near the royal battery, and skirted the shore until they crossed a bridge onto the old fortifications. After a good night's rest, they rose early and made a cursory survey of the area, which included island batteries, a lighthouse, some fifteen or twenty small dwellings, and a small Catholic church, the whole area having the appearance of the arena of an ampitheater. On a tongue of land projecting into the sea was the site of the ancient fortress. Its wall stretched from the west gate to the ocean. Close to the southeast terminus of the ancient wall and outside it was an immense rocky eminence forming a cliff overlooking the ocean. Much of the stone for the fortification had been quarried from this formation, and piles of the cut stone lay about near the cliff. The old drill-holes were still visible in the dark basalt-like rock. Toward the end of the tongue of land was the ancient burying ground, and the remains of some graves were still visible. Near the termination of the small peninsula and within a large battery was a glacis and trench.

After taking a swim in the cool waters, they walked toward the ancient city, over a grassy field to the old ruins of the hospital, chapel, and nunnery, the stone walls of which were leveled almost to the grassy ground. Further on they passed the site of the Governor's house and public offices. On one white facing stone of a public building Usher could clearly read the carved name "I. Gridley, 1745," probably done by Gridley's own hand. Isaac Gridley, Pepperrell's chief engineer, some thirty year's later planned the battery thrown up on Bunker Hill the night before that critical battle. Many barrels of old iron, hinges, spikes, horseshoes, bolts, kettles, and other odds and ends were strewn around, and half a dozen cannon were lying about the cliff. Further descriptive notes of the journey appear in the published version of *The Life of Sir William Pepperrell, Bart.*[16] The fortifications, governor's quarters, and about one third of the village have been restored authentically and with great care by the Canadian government and are now maintained as a National Park.

In further correspondence with Colonel Sparhawk,[17] Usher demonstrated his striving for historical accuracy even in regard to small details, such as documenting the gift to Pepperrell from King George of a snuffbox and the presentation by the City of London of a long table of solid silver covered with an extensive service of plate. He reported to Sparkhawk that

> I am delving away upon the Life of Sir Wm. & hope soon to have it finished. If you can gather anything traditional from the old people of Kittery Point, or Portsmouth, or Great Island in the way of anecdotes, &c., relating to old Sir William, I shall esteem it a great favor if you will transmit the same to me. I am meagre as to early facts tending to show how he passed through boyhood and early manhood, where his son Andrew fitted for college, &c., &c.

Perceiving an opportunity to save a few dollars in the preparation of his Pepperrell work, Usher in January 1853 wrote to George Bancroft, the American historian.[18] He informed Bancroft that for his projected Pepperrell biography he had visited Louisburg and surveyed its topography and had looked over various plans of the old city and fortifications. No map, he continued, "pleases my eye so well as the one . . . in your history. . . . It might be an advantage . . . to use your plate . . . and thus divide the expense of it between us. . . ." His own veneration of Sir William, he stressed, and several requests from others had led him to the undertaking, rather than any expectation of profit. In fact, he advised Bancroft that he expected to lose by it, "which makes me more calculating as to expense than I should otherwise be. If I can retrieve from oblivion some valuable manuscripts that are now time-worn and scarcely legible, I am satisfied for my labor. Please to think of the proposition. . . ." Bancroft's reaction to this suggestion is not a matter of record, but the fact is that his map was used in Usher's *Pepperrell.*

A few days later Usher acknowledged receipt of additional Pepperrell material from Sparhawk and continued pursuing the matter of the silver.[19] He expressed the opinion to Sparkhawk that it was doubtful that George II would have given a silver snuffbox to a military hero like Pepperrell as a token of respect for the important services he rendered. A sword, he thought, would have been more appropriate, and he asked Sparhawk to obtain a description of the sword. Usher was most certainly endeavoring to authenticate the sword attributed to Pepperrell, which General Leighton had given him before the General's death. He also requested Colonel Sparhawk's assistance in obtaining an account of Pepperrell's revolving library left to York and Kittery Parishes and also a suitable engraving of Pepperrell to illustrate the book.

The innumerable details connected with the publication of Usher's life of Pepperrell had required some two years of labor, but by early 1855 it was virtually completed. "At the beginning of the year," Charles wrote,[20] "his book . . . had been submitted to the friendly criticism of several historical scholars."[21] It was released in May. Charles continued: "It was favorably received by students of colonial history both in America and England, and was kindly noticed and somewhat copiously analyzed in the leading newspapers and magazines in this country, and in the London Athenaeum.[22] The subject being ante-revolutionary," much interest was aroused "in the mother country, where several descendants of Pepperrell still exist, and in America." Usher dedicated the small work to the Honorable Lorenzo Sabine, "whose sketches of the lives of 'American Loyalists' and other valuable publications entitle him to the gratitude of the public."

Most of the reviews, as Charles observed, were confined to an analysis of the book's contents. That published in the *Providence Daily Journal* on June 13, however, was somewhat more perceptive:

We notice, with pleasure this life of one who was in his day among the foremost men of New England. . . . His fame rests principally upon his heroic conduct at the siege and destruction of Louisburg. . . . Such books as the life of Pepperrell will correct our errors and prejudices. They will teach us that the honors of fame do not all belong to the heroes of the Revolution, and that the subject who was loyal to his King was not for that reason a traitor to his country. . . . Dr. Parsons has done a good work. He has written a book which will be read with pleasure and profit. Out of scant material he has arranged and constructed a biography—which is a valuable contribution to the history of our country, and has perpetuated the bright example of a wise statesman and an honest patriot. Few would have undertaken a task so difficult—fewer still would have accomplished it so well. We can find no fault with the publishers. They have executed their part of the business in a workmanlike manner. They have given us a good paper, good type, and a book of just the right size. We are tired of cheap things, and it is really refreshing to see a well-written book—printed in a fair round type on substantial paper.

A clipping of a pleasant review appearing in the *Maine Democrat* of Saco[23] is preserved among Usher's papers. Rhode Island historian Samuel G. Arnold, having the advantage of the perspective of time, about a decade-and-a-half later gave a favorable estimate of the work,[24] referring to it as "a very important contribution to our colonial history." At least one modern historian has not been as generous; Byron Fairchild, writing in 1954, stated:[25]

The real story of the Pepperrells lay in the papers that Parsons discarded as worthless. . . . Many of Parsons' generalizations relating to William's career in business in the earlier period are unsound. His account of the preparations made by William for organizing the frontier defences [are borrowed] without quotation or acknowledgement. . . . The remainder of Parsons' book consists almost entirely of letters and extracts. . . . Many cannot be found elsewhere . . . [and] must be used with caution, for Parsons made omissions and inserted words without warning, which in some cases has damaged the sense of the document.

It must be remembered, in all fairness, that as historians both Parsons and Fairchild are representative of their respective periods. Parsons, like most historians of his day, engaged in such work as an avocation. His endeavors reflected his era's concern with biography and genealogy, as well as political, military, and diplomatic history, and he emphasized or omitted material accordingly. Fairchild, a professionally trained historian of the modern day, expresses more the interests of today's generation in economic and social history. Things that seemed unimportant to Usher in the early 1850s are looked upon as most important today. Historians of Usher's era were more interested in proving the bestowal of honors through the gift of a snuffbox or a sword than in the statistics of shipbuilding in the colonial period or in analyzing the content and quality of American life at that time. While under the scrutiny of today's standards Usher's *Pepperell* undoubtedly has many defects, he nonetheless performed a valuable service to scholarship and to American historical lore in undertaking this work and especially by preserving valuable colonial documents which otherwise probably would have been lost to posterity. Had he not accomplished this, there might not be anything left for historians like Fairchild to use and to criticize.

Early in 1851 Usher received a request from William Edmonds Horner, the scholarly Philadelphia anatomist, to summarize his "experience on amputations of the limbs according to state of accident, time, constitution, the limb itself and the region of the limb."[26] Horner was preparing the eighth [and last] edition of his *Special Anatomy and Histology,*[27] the first, and highly successful American textbook on pathology. Usher, of course, was flattered to be consulted by so eminent an authority and complied. There is no evidence, however, that the material was ever used.

Usher was elected president of the Providence Medical Association on March 3, 1851.[28] On the 19th, at the Rhode Island Medical Society meeting in the Woonsocket Odd Fellows Hall,[29] "Dr. U. Parsons related three cases of rupture of the uterus," while on April 7, before the Providence Medical Association, "Dr. C. W. Parsons exhibited a uterine tumor removed by Dr. U. Parsons," the latter from a twenty-seven-year-old housewife whom Usher had seen in consultation. "There was a difference of opinion," he wrote later, "as to the nature of the [vaginal] tumor, whether it was an inverted uterus, a polypus of unusually firm texture, or a fibrous tumor." The tumor, removed without benefit of anesthesia, "was immersed in spirit and was first examined in [the] presence of the Providence Medical Association some days after the operation," where "it was found to be the body of the uterus inverted, but otherwise in a normal state, and exhibiting a portion of the Fallopian tubes." Unknowingly, he had performed a vaginal hysterectomy! "Mrs. F," whose case was later reported in the *Boston Medical and Surgical Journal*,[30] made an uneventful recovery, became "quite fleshy, and able to take charge of her house, and enjoys better health than at any time since her marriage." With Victorian delicacy Usher observed, "Her husband informs me *qu'elle reste sensible aux voluptés conjugales*."

In May Usher attended the annual convention of the A.M.A. in Charleston and was much involved, as usual, with committee work.[31] He did not miss the opportunity to visit his nephews and nieces in the south.[32] During the summer of 1851 he was very active in local medical affairs. On August 4 he reported to the Providence Medical Association "a case of a woman swallowing six teeth attached to a gold plate, which passed the bowels without difficulty."[33] On the 20th he and Charles made the pleasant sail down Narragansett Bay for a meeting of the Rhode Island Medical Society in Newport's Redwood Library.[34] Charles presented a paper on "Acute Inflammation, Involving the Psoas Magnus Muscle," which later appeared in the trusty *Boston Medical and Surgical Journal*.[35]

The October 6 meeting of the Providence Medical Association was devoted in part to a general discussion of a medical fee table recently adopted by the association.[36] Usher asserted, "I have to the best of my recollection, charged my patients $1 a visit according to the Fee Table, and have adhered to said Table in all other charges. It is my intention to continue to adhere to said Table in all future charges." A memorable action was taken at the meeting: "In accordance with a suggestion from the President, it was voted that a Committee of Seven be appointed to take into consideration the propriety of establishing a Hospital in this city & to take such measures for inquiry upon the subject as they may deem necessary & expedient thereto. In accordance with this vote, the following gentlemen were appointed that Committee to report at the next monthly meeting—Dr. Usher Parsons, Chairman, Dr. J. Mauran, Dr. L. L. Miller, Dr. R. Brownell, Dr. Geo. Capron, Dr. S. Augustus Arnold, & Dr. C. W. Fabyan."

They were an able and influential group, carefully selected to carry weight with the community, and certainly better educated than the run-of-the-mill physicians of their day.[37] Although the minutes of later meetings do not reflect it, the Committee of Seven did in fact take prompt action. On December 10, 1851, it issued an eloquent letter to the Taxpayers of the City of Providence, urging prompt recognition of the long-felt need for a general hospital. A prime example of Usher's vigorous prose, the letter commenced:[38]

> The Physicians of Providence have long since felt the want of a Hospital in the City for the reception of patients who require medical and surgical treatment, and who are not otherwise provided for. They meet with such patients in their professional walks daily, whilst to the public generally their great number rarely becomes known. To this fact is attributable the delay in making suitable provision for them in this city, where so much has been done in other respects to ameliorate the condition and promote the welfare of the people generally. They, therefore, feel it a duty to represent to the public the actual and pressing need of such an establishment which in other cities of the size of Providence has long since been provided. Accordingly the Medical Association have requested the undersigned as a Committee, to call the attention of individuals to the importance of the proposed measure, and with this view we present for your consideration some of the cases which call for hospital relief.

It is true, the petition continued, that some patients receive aid from the Dispensary, and still more from the gratuitous services of physicians, and some few are sent to the Dexter Asylum. However, it argued, there are others in need of medical help who remain badly lodged, often in garrets without light or ventilation, and open to the storms of winter. Many of these are destitute of food and fuel and are unable to obtain good nursing. Under such circumstances, the petition argued, a hospital for those who are suddenly overtaken with grave diseases or severe injuries would not only supply what is needed, but would actually preserve many lives.

"Again," the report went on,

> there are persons of good industrious habits who meet with sickness or injury just as they are entering into life, and who have not had time to prepare for such a calamity. These cases are constantly occurring among clerks, journeymen, mechanics and apprentices, whose accommodations in cheap boarding houses are barely sufficient in health. Such persons may fall from buildings, be wounded on railroads, or in attempts to extinguish fires in our City, who in other cities are conveyed to a good hospital

to receive the best medical or surgical aid, but in Providence are carried to a crowded garret or cellar, where they prefer suffering many privations during a lingering cure, and incurring heavy expenses to be paid for by future earnings, to being carried to the Dexter Asylum, to dwell with paupers and the victims of debauchery. The Asylum, however spacious and well-adapted it may have been years ago, is now crowded with the off scourings of Europe, and patients cannot receive proper treatment without such a change in its arrangements as would be incompatible with its ordinary or legitimate uses.

At the present day, many persons afflicted with chronic diseases, and requiring skillful operations and treatment, go from our City and State to the well-established hospitals of Boston or New York; and many others would avail themselves of that high privilege, but for want of means. These, certainly, ought to be provided for within our State.

Finally, there are a very large class of patients who can meet the ordinary expenses of board in a hospital, either personally, or by the aid of charitable societies with which they are associated, who are unable to pay for professional services and nursing. These should be provided for as they are in other cities; and they would assist largely in sustaining the current expenses of a hospital.

The above facts have been deeply impressed upon the minds of the physicians of Providence. In presenting them to your notice, they wish it to be distinctly understood that they are actuated by no selfish motives, collectively or individually. As an earnest of their readiness to aid in supporting a hospital, they engage to serve it gratuitously as physicians or surgeons, whenever they are required.

The petition went unheeded for twelve years. The role of the hospital in society has changed radically since Usher's day. Then, and well into this century in some places, the hospital was looked upon as a place for medical charity, to which one sent industrious working people to help them mend from diseases and disabling injuries. It was for these very purposes that the Massachusetts General Hospital had been opened in 1821.[39] The striking similarity in style and language between the Providence document and the circular letter sent by Doctors James Jackson and John C. Warren in 1810 "to several of our wealthiest and most influentual citizens," which led to the founding of the Massachusetts General Hospital, was doubtless more than coincidental. The establishment of hospitals was an infrequent occurrence and then mainly in larger cities, such as Philadelphia, New York, Boston, and Baltimore. The founding of a similar institution in Providence had to await the seventh decade of the nineteenth century for fulfillment. Until then, most medical care, including even operations and obstetrical deliveries, was provided at home. For those who had no homes, or had inadequate ones, places like the Dispensary and the Dexter Asylum were deemed sufficient or had to do.[40]

The problems that led to the founding of larger municipal hospitals grew out of the changing American population and social structure, which was caused mainly by immigration and industrialization. As Joseph E. Garland has noted,[41] Rhode Island had been undergoing a slow, wrenching shift in its economy from sea trade and agriculture to industry. By mid-century this trend, centered in Providence and its adjacent area, was remaking the character of the state. The city was swelled by immigrants ("off scourings"), whose sheer numbers, living habits, economic status, and threatening competition in the labor market aroused resentment, fear, and disdain among the established Yankees. A new class of mill owners, manufacturers, and other entrepreneurs, who were accumulating great fortunes, frankly exploited labor. Fast-growing Providence was a city in turmoil, ground down by the Industrial Revolution at its worst. This was poor soil for civic consciousness and responsibility. Indifference on the part of the wealthy, city officials, and the hard-pressed medical profession was compounded by ignorance. "That touchstone of social progress, leadership," Garland concluded, "had not yet arisen." The national ferment undoubtedly contributed to the delay, but in the end construction was started at the height of the Civil War.

Even as the circular letter was in preparation, the president found time to present yet another interesting case ("Neuralgia" of the spermatic cord due to tumor) before the Association on December 1. A further case record from the Parsons offices, prepared by Charles, appeared in the popular *Boston Medical and Surgical Journal* under the title "Aneurism of Commencement of Descending Aorta, Projecting Backward—Fatal by Bursting into Left Lung."[42] It was a sophisticated clinical-pathological analysis, revealing Charles's extensive and modern medical education. The clinical diagnosis was confirmed precisely by a carefully performed autopsy. Charles first saw this patient, a forty-year-old hack driver, "formerly intemperate," on February 12, 1851. After a careful and detailed physical examination, he made a diagnosis of "aneurism of the aorta, obstructing the left subclavian artery." "The diagnosis," he concluded correctly, "was perfectly clear, and treatment only palliative." Nevertheless "an advertising 'surgeon' of this city visited my patient, unasked by the family, during my absence, and proposed, if their consent was obtained, to have an operation performed by tying the vessel!" Death came suddenly, as is characteristic of this disorder, on June 6. "He had," Charles noted, "borne his sufferings with remarkable fortitude." The postmortem examination confirmed the nature and location of the lesion and revealed rupture into the left pleural cavity. It was clearly a classical syphilitic aortic aneurysm. The year 1851 was also marked by the publication of the fourth edition of *Physician for Ships*.[43] The office at 19 President Street had indeed been very productive.

Despite his growing prominence, Usher was again challenged by the Rhode Island Medical Society for a breach of professional ethics. On November 1 the *General Advertiser* of Providence carried an advertisement touting the professional qualifications of one "H. N. Mattison, Physician and Surgeon: Office 142 Westminster Street." It contained a curious reference signed by one P. H. Hard, M.D. "President of the Medical Society of the State of N.Y." Mattison, he affirmed, had studied in his office "4 successive years and . . . his industry and close application during the time is deserving much praise." What set off the storm was the testimonial of local residents to the effect that "We the undersigned, being personally acquainted with Dr. H. N. Mattison, believe him to be a temperate man in the most appropriate sense, and that his moral character and professional skill are undoubted." It was signed by seventeen physicians (including nine Fellows of the Rhode Island Medical Society) and by several clergymen and other prominent citizens. Heading the list of signatories were Lewis L. Miller, a past president of the Rhode Island Medical Society, and Usher Parsons. How so many prominent residents became involved in this chicanery is not clear.

The Censors of the Society on December 17[44] "recommended that Dr. U. Parsons, L. L. Miller & other Fellows of the R.I. Medical Society be requested to explain . . . why they suffered their signatures to be used in a very unprofessional advertisement." After some adroit testimony by the principals at the Society's semi-annual meeting, "it was voted that the explanation of Drs. Parsons & Miller be deemed sufficient; but that in [the] future all Fellows of the Society be requested to be cautious how they allow their names to be used."

The meetings of the American Medical Association in 1852 were held from May 4 to 7 in Richmond, Virginia in the sanctuary of the Second Presbyterian Church. Usher attended as delegate from the Providence Medical Association, of which he was then president. He participated in a committee report on prize essays and was appointed chairman of a committee on displacements of the uterus.

Concerned as always with the welfare of seamen on merchant vessels (and not unmindful of an opportunity to promote a new edition of his best seller), he offered a resolution to the convention requiring that a chest of medicine be furnished to every merchant ship, with suitable directions for its use; additionally, that a committee be appointed to prepare those directions. The proposition never saw the light of day. Upon motion of the shrewd Doctor Isaac Hays, savant of Philadelphia, the "preamble and resolution . . . were laid upon the table."[45]

Both Usher and Charles attended the A.M.A. convention in New York City from May 3 to 5, 1853 at the Bleecker Street Presbyterian Church. The assembly honored Usher for his diligent and conscientious committee work and regular attendance at meetings by electing him vice president.[46] On Friday, May 6, the day following adjournment, a disaster struck which only through the intercession of a kind fate spared both Usher and Charles. While Usher and Charles tarried in New York, an express train carrying many of the conventioneers back to their homes in New England was involved in a spectacular accident. The engineer failed to heed a lowered signal, traveling at full speed as he approached an open drawbridge over a creek near Norwalk, Connecticut. So great was the momentum, that the locomotive actually leaped the sixty-foot gap, striking the abutment on the opposite bank. It then slumped into the flood with the tender and several cars on top of it, and all sank in the mud. Forty-four people were killed or drowned, including seven members of the American Medical Association, mostly from New England, but none fortunately from Rhode Island. A special meeting was called in New York City to gather members still remaining there in order to appoint a committee to commemorate the disaster and to draft suitable resolutions to be sent to the bereaved families.

On June 30, at the annual meeting of the Rhode Island Medical

Society,[47] a committee was authorized "to collect information concerning all the members of this Society who have died since its formation, and cause the same to be recorded in a book procured for the purpose." The plan was not pursued at the time, but it led some years later to the publication of a more ambitious historical document for which Usher would be largely responsible.

At the November 7, 1853 meeting of the Providence Medical Assocation, the subject of a community hospital was again revived after two years of seeming inactivity. The minutes of the meeting read, "The subject of a City Hospital was discussed, and on motion of Dr. [Edwin M.] Snow it was voted that the committee appointed in October, 1851 be authorized and requested to take such measures as they may think expedient to further the object."

In April 1854 Usher set out for the St. Louis meetings of the A.M.A. to be held from May 2 to 4, which he alone from Rhode Island attended. As President Jonathan Knight of New Haven was seriously ill, Usher, as first vice president, presided at the sessions in Verandah Hall and delivered the presidential address.[48] Because of the unexpected circumstances, he put together some random thoughts "as an apology for a discourse." Yet it proved to be an inspiring and accurate forecast of the future. Among the most cogent of his eloquent remarks were the following:

> . . . Whoever glances at a map of the Mississippi valley, extending from the base of the Allegheny and Cumberland Mountains to the margin of the Rocky Mountains, from the highlands bordering on Lake Superior to the Gulf of Mexico, and contemplates the fertility of its soil, its adaptation for cereal productions, which are so necessary for human subsistence and increase, and who surveys the majestic Mississippi, navigable through this whole territory, with its numerous navigable tributaries pouring in their treasures on either side, and adds to this the vast mineral resources—lead, copper, iron, and coal, which are far more conducive to healthful opulence than the golden regions of California; whoever, I say, candidly surveys all these elements of future growth, expansion, and power and moved onward by the agency of steam on land and water, and in labor-saving mechanical and manufacturing operations, can arrive at no other conclusion than that this vast territory, the largest and most favored one by nature of any under the whole canopy of heaven, will, in time, be densely populated with scores of millions, and become the seat of empire of the western world; and that it is destined to be the grand

theater of human progress, in every department that is calculated to advance the dignity and promote the happiness of the human family.

And in no department of human affairs is progress here more sure than in medical knowledge. Our Atlantic States have inherited a reverence for European opinions, which, although commendable in our early medical history, is at the present day less favorable to American progress, and discovery in Medicine. We need to interrogate nature and experience more, and European opinions less. We need mental as well as political independence, a freer swing of thought and purpose that characterizes our brethren of the West, and which this Association is adapted to call into action.

There is much to encourage you in your recent discoveries and contributions, in the results of the vivisections of saurians, the half of which, if confirmed by future experiments, will shed new light on physiology; and again, in the discoveries made relating to the process of digestion by your late lamented [William] Beaumont, of St. Louis, who, for the theories and speculations before prevailing, has substituted ocular demonstration of the *modus operandi* of that wonderful process. . . .

Eloquently and with feeling he then recalled the "terrible catastrophe" that had befallen their colleagues in Norwalk a year before. After paying respects to their memory, he concluded his remarks with an appraisal of the A. M. A.'s progress during the eight years since its founding: ". . . The results of its labors have equaled the expectations of the friends of reform and progress in our profession. . . . There is every reason to hope that our future labors will . . . be crowned with . . . success."

On his way home, Charles relates in his *Memoir* (p. 54), Usher "journeyed to Chicago and St. Paul's [*sic*], visited the falls of St. Anthony, and returned by way of Buffalo, Montreal and Quebec." Although Usher left no record of this journey, a letter[49] some months later to Daniel Dobbins of Erie reflected his sentimental attachments to his old friends. He acknowledged receipt of half a barrel of whitefish, one of the more delectable reminders of his days on the Lakes, reported on a few surviving veterans in Rhode Island, and hoped that he might have the opportunity of showing Mrs. Dobbins a little of his own state. He returned to Providence in time for the annual meeting of the Rhode Island Medical Society on June 7, where he read a report of the St. Louis Meetings. Forty-six members, the largest attendance thus far, partook of a sumptuous dinner at which Doctors Henry J. Bigelow and D. Humphreys Storer of Boston were speakers. It is significant that all five newly elected fellows of the Society held diplomas from medical colleges.[50]

The Trustees of the Fiske Fund announced at the meeting that Charles W. Parsons had won a $50 premium for the best dissertation on *Neuralgia, Its History and Best Mode of Treatment*,[51] which was, in essence, a review of the current literature containing little personal experience. It was competently written, but not of great consequence. Uncle Wendell implied as much in a letter to the author:[52]

> I was gratified to hear that you have had the success which I anticipated for you in gaining the Prize of the Fiske Fund. I believe there is nothing more useful than to take a subject in this way, with some express motive and exhaust all the knowledge bearing upon it within our reach. No other mode of study has ever seemed to me to fix facts and principles so firmly in the memory.
>
> I think the second question for the next year would well repay you for examining it with reference to writing upon it. But I would not depend wholly on books—I would make extensive enquiries among those who have been to Cuba, Florida, Madeira, Georgia, etc. or among their friends and base my results on a statistical examination of the facts I could collect, as far as possible. Such a Dissertation would be of great use to yourself and to others. If I can help you in any way, it will give me the greatest pleasure to do so. I would not write on the other also—it is a *tour de force* to get both prizes which is well enough if you have nothing better to do, but it will be wiser to put your whole strength into the very important subject I have mentioned.

The Fiske Prize questions for 1854 to which Wendell referred were No. 1 on *Croup*, and No. 2 on *Effects of Climate on Tubercular Disease*. If in fact Charles entered the contest, he did not win a prize.

Both Usher and Charles were in Philadelphia for the A.M.A. meetings of May 1–5, 1855 in Musical Fund Hall.[53] Usher was honored by election to permanent membership in the House of Delegates. He and Charles attended a reception in Independence Hall on May 2 at noon. They joined a procession of some five hundred members, which marched through Independence Square and entered the Hall, where the ladies awaited their arrival. The crowded assembly was addressed by Doctor Isaac Hays, who referred in his remarks to Doctor Benjamin Rush, a signer of the Declaration of Independence and a member of the Continental Congress, and to General Joseph Warren, who, though a physician, had been killed at Bunker Hill while serving as a combat officer of the line.

On the 10th of September, 1853 a celebration had been held in Newport to commemorate the fortieth anniversary of the Battle of Lake Erie. The morning exercises were marred by a heavy downpour, dark skies, and a southeast wind. The procession nevertheless formed on the Parade and proceeded to Christ Church for the morning exercises. The invited guests (including Usher) rode in carriages behind the uniformed companies. With the galleries already occupied, the procession filled the sanctuary. The survivors of the battle had seats on an elevated platform in front of the pulpit, "a position, we doubt not," said the reporter, "more trying to the nerves than that assigned them forty years ago in front of the enemy cannon."[54] As the ceremony ended, the rain ceased and a brilliant sun broke through the clouds. The procession re-formed and proceeded to the Ocean House, which was decorated with flags, shields, and mottoes, and a collation was served.

Usher reported on the doings to his old friend Stephen Champlin:[55]

> You have heard of the Newport celebration of Perry's victory which you declined attending, and would like to know how it went off. Had there not been a very heavy rain during the forenoon, it would have gone off right well. There would have been at least a thousand more from Providence. Taylor, Brownell, and myself were placed on a high seat in front of the pulpit, and George Cornel on the right, and another sailor of the *Somers* on the left, making a row of five; and old Commodore Peckham occupied a pew in front of us. He being a ragged old sot was thought unworthy of a conspicuous place by the side of old Billy. The house notwithstanding the rain was filled. A prayer preceded the oration by Mr. Calvert of Newport. It was well got up and as full of glorification to the surviving officers as anyone could bear, without staggering. Honorable mention was made of Captain Champlin, of the *Scorpion*. Old Billy was in full rig on my right, and Brownell on my left had all the lace and buttons he could find a place for, and no one could doubt from their appearance that both of them were on perfectly good terms with themselves. Each of them reminded me of a peacock when exhibiting his

utmost dimensions. The storm subsided when the services closed, and the procession which was postponed from the forenoon now took place, consisting of several uniform companies and fire companies, the governor & aides, and then a barouche with the three officers, then the three men in another, then a cavalcade of generals and aides. We landed at the Ocean house after a march of a mile or two; with three splendid bands of music, one of them from the fort [Adams]. A splendid collation was prepared, after which all retired to their homes on the strength of coldwater. Not a speech was made at the table. I had prepared one, intending not to be caught napping, as I was at Buffalo, but I had to put this into pickle for some future occasion. About 1,000 dollars was raised by individual subscription in Newport to meet the expenses of the celebration.

Usher also reported that his oration before the Rhode Island Historical Society had been received with enthusiasm. Champlin replied[56] that he regretted having missed the opportunity to shake "the hands of those few remaining participants of that glorious battle, perhaps for the last time." He hoped, as Usher had suggested, that they might meet, perhaps in Illinois, as Usher proceeded to the A.M.A. convention in St. Louis in 1854, while Champlin journeyed from Buffalo to St. Paul to visit his children. We do not know whether they managed such a meeting, but it is likely that they did.

An important event took place on October 11, 1853 which most certainly gave great pleasure and satisfaction to Usher: Charles's marriage in Princeton, Massachusetts to twenty-four year old Mary Hallowell Boylston, daughter of John Lane and Sally Hallowell Boylston. The young couple were united by the Reverend Henry Wickes in a double wedding at which Mary's sister Louisa was wed to another Providence young blood, Edwin J. Nightingale, scion of a prominent mercantile family.[57] Charles's bride, the granddaughter of the opulent Ward Nicholas Boylston, benefactor of Harvard and donor of the Boylston Medical Prizes, was a great-great-great-grand-niece of Doctor Zabdiel Boylston, the renowned advocate of smallpox inoculation. The union brought together several Boston Brahmin blood lines—the Holmeses, the Hallowells, and the Boylstons—with the Parsons genes as catalyst. The Parsonses, both father and son, had indeed married well. Charles and Mary Parsons made their home at No. 3 George Street in Providence, where they welcomed Charles's widowed father. For the first time in twenty-eight years, since the death of his young wife, Usher could relish the luxury of a real home. "During the last fifteen years of his life," wrote Charles laconically, "he had a home with his son."[58]

On the following Thanksgiving Day Usher attended services at the Unitarian Church, deriving much satisfaction from the sermon. Charles wrote a vignette of this little episode and discussed Usher's religious preferences:[59]

> His ecclesiastical relations were peculiar. He was brought up in congregational worship and the faith of the Puritans. His grandfather, the minister of Bradford, was suspected of Arminianism. Whether any traditionary influence, inherited from him, softened the rigor of Calvinistic belief in the family of his son William, I do not know. Soon after his marriage, he was admitted to the Episcopal communion, at St. John's Church. In later years, he had a seat in one place of worship after another,—St. John's, the First Baptist, St. Stephen's (now Church of the Saviour) and the Central Congregational church. For the last twelve years of his life, the latter was his usual place of attendance on Sundays, and the only one where he owned a pew, though he frequently partook of the communion of the Episcopal Church. He often went to other churches, especially the Unitarian under the ministry of Dr. Edward B. Hall, whose preaching he much admired. After hearing him on Thanksgiving Day, 1853, he wrote in his note book: "I wish he and other Unitarians would follow after St. Paul's example, and preach a little more about Christ and him crucified. At the same time, I wish the Orthodox would preach more practical sermons, and not be forever harping on particular doctrines of the Calvinistic order." In his busiest years of practice, he was remarkably regular in attending church once or twice on Sunday.

In the summer of 1854 the newly married couple, with Usher in tow, visited Uncle Oliver Wendell Holmes at the Holmes's summer place in Pittsfield, Massachusetts. On the arduous journey home by carriage through the Berkshires and on a very hot day, Usher had been very ill throughout the trip. Charles feared a "serious congestion of the brain," but it proved to be "only a severe attack of indigestion."[60]

Soon after the New Year of 1855, Usher traveled to Washington, where he made his usual and familiar rounds and stayed at the home of sister-in-law Ann and husband Charles Wentworth Upham, who now was a United States Representative from Massachusetts.[61] Later, in February he wrote to Doctor John C. Warren of Boston acknowledging Warren's gift of his family's genealogy and expressing his continued interest in genealogical matters:[62]

> Your very elegant and highly valued present "the Genealogy of the Warrens" arrived during my absence at the South, or its receipt and grateful acceptance would have been sooner acknowledged. Aside from its great merit as the most beautiful specimen of typography and dress that has appeared in America, I esteem it invaluable as an enduring monument to the illustrious general who fell on Bunker's Hill, and to his brother your late venerated father, whom I ever regarded as the most elegant lecturer and accomplished gentleman I ever saw. The letters and memoranda are moreover a precious contribution to the history of times and scenes that tried men's souls, in which the two brothers sustained so conspicuous a part. . . .

Usher, although now approaching his allotted three score and ten years, maintained an active interest in medical affairs, the frustrating debate over a hospital, and his Erie connections.

NOTES

1. C. W. Parsons *Memoir*, p. 41.
2. Reverend Jeremy Belknap (1744–1798), a Harvard graduate of 1762 and later a resident of Dover, New Hampshire, and of Boston, wrote *American Biographies* (1794–1798) and a history of New Hampshire (1784–1792). Material on Pepperrell is included in both works.
3. The Reverend Charles Burroughs (1787–1868), Rector of St. John's Church in Portsmouth, New Hampshire, delivered on March 3 and 10, 1842, as part of a series of lectures at the Massachusetts Historical Society, two lectures on the "Life of Sir William Pepperrell, with an Account of the Siege of Louisburg in 1745." His lectures were not printed, and his manuscript has not been located at this time. It is possible that either Usher or Charles attended and heard these lectures.
4. Lorenzo Sabine (1803–1877), historian and author of *The American Loyalists or Biographical Sketches of Adherents to the British Crown in the War of the Revolution* (1847), had discussed Pepperrell in that work.
5. Usher Parsons to George Sparhawk, December 1, 1847, in the private collection of Joseph W. P. Frost, formerly of Kittery, Maine, and now of Eliot, Maine. Colonel Sparhawk was not a descendant of the Pep-

perrells, but was allied to them through the marriage of William Pepperrell's daughter, Elizabeth, to Colonel Nathaniel Sparhawk.

6. Usher Parsons to E. M. Stone, January 18, 1852, RIHS.

7. Usher Parsons. *The Battle of Lake Erie.*

8. James Fenimore Cooper, *Battle of Lake Erie, or Answers to Messrs.
   Burges, Duer & Mackenzie* (Cooperstown, H. & E. Phinney, 1843).

9. Stephen Champlin to Usher Parsons, July 11, 1843, DPC.

10. Perry's sterling qualities reflected his Quaker background, as was true
    of that other Rhode Island Quaker warrior, General Nathanael Greene.

11. Samuel Greene Arnold, *Green-Staples-Parsons. An Address Delivered
    Before the Rhode Island Historical Society on June 1, 1869* (Providence,
    Hammond, Angell & Co., 1869).

12. C. W. Parsons *Memoir*, p. 49.

13. Rhode Island Historical Society, "Minutes."

14. C. W. Parsons *Memoir*, p. 42. Also, Usher Parsons to Edwin Parsons,
    August 14, 1852, and Edwin Parsons to Usher Parsons, August 16,
    1852, DPC.

15. Part of the diary was printed by Charles in the memoir of his father.
    The original manuscript is not extant.

16. Usher Parsons, *The Life of Sir William Pepperrell, Bart., The Only
    Native of New England Who Was Created a Baronet During Our
    Connection with the Mother Country* (Boston, Little, Brown, 1855), p.
    330 *et seq.*

17. Usher Parsons to George Sparhawk, November 20, 1852, DPC; George
    Sparhawk to Usher Parsons, December 9, 1852, Collection of J. W. P.
    Frost, formerly of Kittery Point, Maine, now of Eliot, Maine. The
    Pepperrell silver consisting of a grace cup, a tray, and two salvers is
    now owned by Joseph William Pepperrell Frost of Eliot, Maine. It was
    displayed on March 11–13, 1966 at the 175th Anniversary celebration
    of Berwick Academy in South Berwick, Maine. The silver is described
    in a booklet issued for the exhibition. There was no snuffbox.

18. Usher Parsons to George Bancroft, January 18, 1853, Massachusetts
    Historical Society. Bancroft (1800–1891), Harvard 1817, wrote the mon-
    umental *History of the United States* in 10 volumes. Among his other
    offices was service as Secretary of the Navy and Minister to Great
    Britain.

19. Usher Parsons to George Sparhawk, January 20, 1853, collection of J.
    W. P. Frost, formerly of Kittery Point, Maine, now of Eliot, Maine.

20. C. W. Parsons *Memoir*, p. 42.

21. Lorenzo Sabine and John Wingate Thornton (1818–1878), Harvard Law
    School 1840, Boston lawyer and historian, whose writings on American
    history are extensive.

22. The *Athenaeum* article was reprinted in *Littell's Living Age* (Boston,
    v. 11, p. 753, Decmber 1855). The Athenaeum concluded that Usher's

biography "constitutes, as will have been seen from our analysis, a perfect little history in itself,—of equal interest on either side of the Atlantic."

23. *Maine Democrat,* June 19, 1855. This is preserved in DPC.

24. Samuel Green Arnold, *Green, Staples, Parsons.*

25. Byron Fairchild, *Messrs. William Pepperrell: Merchants at Piscataqua* (Ithaca, Cornell University Press, 1954), pp. 202–214. Fairchild also noted: "A few years later Parsons contributed a biographical sketch of Sir William to Freeman Hunt, ed., *Lives of American Merchants,* which consisted primarily of verbatim extracts from his previous work and in which the Louisbourg affair was reduced to a two-page complaint that the Army was deprived unfairly of sharing in the prizes taken by the naval forces. All later sketches . . . rely heavily on Parsons' work." Fairchild's reference is to *Hunt's Merchants Magazine and Commercial and American Review,* 39:27–41, 1858. The magazine was established by Freeman Hunt in 1839 and was published by George and John A. Wood in New York.

26. William E. Horner to Usher Parsons, January 5, 1851, DPC.

27. William Edmund Horner, *Special Anatomy and Histology* (8th ed., 2 vols., Philadelphia, Blanchard & Lea, 1851).

28. Providence Medical Association, "Minutes."

29. Rhode Island Medical Society, "Minutes."

30. Usher Parsons, "Amputation of the Uterus, After Partial Inversion," *Boston Medical and Surgical Journal,* 45:511–513, 1851.

31. American Medical Association, *Transactions,* 4:23, 1851. Usher received appointments to the Nominating Committee and to the Committee for Volunteer Communications.

32. George Parsons to his mother, April 30, 1851, DPC. George told her: "Uncle Usher arrived here [Savannah] last night and will spend a few days with us."

33. Providence Medical Association, "Minutes."

34. Rhode Island Medical Society, "Minutes."

35. Charles W. Parsons, "Acute Inflammation, Involving the Psoas Magnus Muscle," *Boston Medical and Surgical Journal,* 45:120–123, 1851.

36. Rhode Island Medical Society, "Minutes."

37. Joseph Mauran's early education has been reviewed in footnote 45 of Chapter 10. He was president of the Rhode Island Medical Society in 1849 and again in 1852 to 1855. He successfully promoted the registration of births, deaths, and marriages; in 1850 was a delegate to and vice president of the Convention on Revising the [National] Pharmacopoeia; and for many years was a delegate to the A.M.A. Lewis Leprelete Miller, the son of a busy surgeon, received A.B. and A.M. degrees from Brown University in 1817 and an M.D. from Brown University in 1820. He appears also to have attended lectures in Boston. After conducting a private hospital with his father in Franklin, Massachu-

setts from 1820 to 1827, be began a successful surgical practice in
Providence. He was president of the Rhode Island Medical Society in
1846–47. George Capron, after attending the Academy in Union Village
in Rhode Island, was a student of Doctor Levi Wheaton of Providence
for three years, attended lectures in Boston and at Brown, and received
his M.D. degree from Brown University in 1823. He acquired a large
practice, was physician to the United States Marine Hospital in Providence, and was elected president of the Rhode Island Medical Society
in 1850. Salmon Augustus Arnold received A.B. and A.M. degrees from
Brown University in 1816 and, after studying medicine in New York,
received an M.D. degree at the College of Physicians and Surgeons in
that city in 1821. He developed a large practice and was president of
the Rhode Island Medical Society in 1849–50. Charles Wesley Fabyan
studied in Maine with his brother, Doctor George Fabyan, and received
his M.D. degree from the Medical Department of Bowdoin College in
1837. After practicing in New Hampshire for a few years, he removed
to Providence, was elected treasurer of the Rhode Island Medical Society, and later became the first admitting physician of the new Rhode
Island Hospital. Richmond Brownell's education is not a matter of
record. He was, however, a successful physician and surgeon and served
as president of the Rhode Island Medical Society from 1840 to 1843.
In 1825 he had successfully ligated the femoral artery for popliteal
aneurysm. His obituary listed him as "Richmond Brownell, *M.D.*,"
probably significant, but not documented. Collectively they contributed a number of communications to the medical literature.

38. Rhode Island Medical Society, "Petition to the Providence City Coun-
     cil," December 10, 1851, RIHS. This is reprinted in Joseph E. Garland's
     To Meet These Wants: The Story of the Rhode Island Hospital (Prov-
     idence, Rhode Island Hospital, 1963).

39. See Nathaniel I. Bowditch's *History of the Massachusetts General
     Hospital* (Boston, J. Wilson, 1851), pp. 3–9.

40. The changing role of the hospital from a nineteenth century charitable
     institution to the institution that exists today is reviewed in Morris J.
     Vogel's *The Invention of the Modern Hospital: Boston, 1870–1930*
     (Chicago, University of Chicago Press, 1980).

41. Joseph E. Garland, *To Meet These Wants: The Story of the Rhode Island
     Hospital*, p. 8.

42. Charles W. Parsons, "Aneurism of Commencement of Descending
     Aorta, Projecting Backward—Fatal by Bursting into Left Lung," *Boston
     Medical and Surgical Journal*, 44:413–415, 1851.

43. See note 25 of Chapter 7.

44. Rhode Island Medical Society, "Minutes."

45. American Medical Association, *Transactions*, 5:34, 1852.

46. American Medical Association, *Transactions*, 6:30, 1853.

47. Rhode Island Medical Society, "Minutes."

48. American Medical Association, *Transactions*, 7:47–50, 1854.

49. Usher Parsons to Daniel Dobbins, October 7, 1854, Buffalo Historical Society.

50. Rhode Island Medical Society, "Minutes." While this was ostensibly evidence of progress in medical education, it may also have reflected, as pointed out by Professor Philip Cash, the burgeoning number of medical schools, many with low standards and negligible admission requirements.

51. Charles W. Parsons, *Neuralgia, Its History and Best Mode of Treatment* (Philadelphia, T. K. and P. G. Collins, 1854). This was reprinted from the *American Journal of the Medical Sciences*, n.s. 23:417–446, 1854.

52. Oliver Wendell Holmes to Charles W. Parsons, June 23, 1854, Houghton Library, Harvard University.

53. American Medical Association, *Transactions*, 8:9–62, 1855.

54. *Newport Mercury*, September 17, 1853.

55. Usher Parsons to Stephen Champlin, September 16, 1853, DPC.

56. Stephen Champlin to Usher Parsons, September 29, 1853, Historical Society of Pennsylvania.

57. *Manufacturers & Farmers Journal* (Providence), October 17, 1853.

58. C. W. Parsons *Memoir*, p. 26.

59. *Ibid.*, p. 37.

60. Mary H. Parsons to "My dear friends" (unidentified), January 29, 1855, Parsons Memorial Library, Alfred, Maine.

61. Charles W. Parsons to Charles W. Upham, January 15, 1855, HUCC.

62. Usher Parsons to John C. Warren, February 3, 1855, Massachusetts Historical Society.

CHAPTER SIXTEEN

Erie Celebration

Usher and his congenial nephew Edwin traveled together on a long jaunt to the west during the summer of 1855.[1] They explored the far reaches of Lake Superior, where Usher looked upon once familiar scenes not visited by him in over forty years. He recalled poignant memories of his youth spent in this far north country. "On his way," related Charles, "he rehearsed on the spot his adventures in the capture of Fort Erie in 1812. He stopped at Mackinac and Sault Ste. Marie and examined the copper mines at Lake Superior."[2] While at the Sault, Usher met one George Johnston, a prominent local businessman, who, Usher was happy to learn, was the younger brother of Lewis Saurin Johnston, a midshipman of the British *Lady Prevost* during the Erie battle. Having been wounded in the arm, Lewis was among a group of British officer prisoners retained for some months at Erie and cared for by Usher.[3]

In the summer of 1857 Usher received an interesting communication from New York City from one W. H. Powell, who related:[4] "I learned a few days since from Mr. Ward Cowing that you were now in Providence and had kindly expressed your readiness to furnish me with any information you possess relative to the Battle of Lake Erie. . . . I am extremely desirous of talking with you about this great event, which I am about to illustrate in painting for the rotunda of the State Capital of Ohio. . . ." The writer, William Henry Powell (1823–1879) of New York City, was a popular historical and portrait artist, who had painted the heroic *Discovery of the Mississippi River by DeSoto* for the Capital Rotunda in Washington. However, Usher and Powell did not meet that year, as plans for the Ohio painting were deferred for a couple of years.

374

As the summer of 1858 waned, Usher planned for a September trip to Sandusky and Put-in-Bay, site of the forty-fifth anniversary celebration of the historic battle fought in the nearby waters. (Usher had carried on a running correspondence pertaining to arrangements for this event during the previous year.) He was invited to be the guest of Doctor R. R. McMeens, a physician of Sandusky, but sent his regrets.[5] He had "previously engaged to visit my old companion in arms, Captain Champlin. [I] will be expected by the managers of the affair to accompany him to the bay. After the ceremonies are ended I shall be pleased to accompany you to your dwelling and pass a day or two there." He added:

> I wish it might occur to some of the managers that this would be a good time to lay the corner stone of a monument to Perry at Put-in-Bay, to be built and paid for in future years. It would give point and pith to the celebration, and need not exceed in expense more than five or ten dollars on the present occasion. This movement for a celebration reflects great honor on the patriotic citizens of the Lake shores.

The official account of the event evokes the air of excitement which pervaded the great occasion:[6]

> The celebration of the Battle of Lake Erie on the 10th of September, 1858, was one of the most imposing and thrilling spectacles, and interesting events, witnessed upon the waters of Lake Erie since the glorious day of the terrible conflict and brilliant victory itself. Large delegations, with vast crowds of citizens from most of the large cities and many of the smaller villages of the Lake, congregated upon the Island made memorable and immortal as the harbor of Perry's valiant fleet on the morning of the battle, and as the resting place of his illustrious dead, who fell in the action. The bay itself presented a most grand and gorgeous pageant, crowded with a fleet of magnificent steamers, sail vessels, and yachts, all decorated with gay colored banners, streamers, and pendants, while a battery of fourteen 'brazen mouthed' cannon waked the echoes of old Erie with a welcome that made the bold rocks of Gibraltar tremble with their reverberations.
> The morning of the day was ushered in with dark and threatening clouds, which, while the boats were on their way to the Island, discharged themselves of rain. But all failed to dampen the ardor of the thousands who had armed themselves with a

determination to spend the day in appropriate commemoration of the glorious victory with which it is identified. But most timely and unexpectedly the rain ceased, and the clouds disappeared as by magic, while the sun shone forth in the full effulgence of his glory, gladdening the hearts of all and causing the transparent surface of the Lake to sparkle far and wide in one glow of liquid light. By half past 12 o'clock all of the several delegations had reached the bay.

The number of excursioners was estimated to be "not less than" eight thousand. The formal ceremonies began at two o'clock with the Honorable Salmon P. Chase, Governor of Ohio, presiding. The exercises opened with a prayer followed by an address by Governor Chase. The Honorable Eleutheros Cooke of Sandusky officially welcomed the officers and survivors of the campaigns of 1813. Usher Parsons, introduced as "the only known living survivor of the flagship *Lawrence*," responded. He "gave a detailed and thrilling account of the engagement," which "was listened to with the most intense interest, and was frequently interrupted with cheers that made the welkin ring." These were his words:

> The survivors of the battle of Lake Erie here present have listened with intense interest to the eloquent address just delivered [Cooke's], and thank you most sincerely for the cordial reception you have given to its friendly and complimentary allusions to our services on the day we are now assembled to commemorate. Forty-five years ago, we were here as spectators, and participators in the battle, and now, in advanced years, are invited to join a vast number of patriotic citizens, gathered from the beautiful and flourishing cities bordering this Lake, to celebrate the victory then gained by our Squadron.
>
> We have come hither, my friends, to honor the memory of those who fell in that glorious conflict, and are sleeping under the soil near where we are now gathered. We have come also to pay a grateful tribute of respect to the memory of Commodore Perry and his associates in the battle, who have since passed away in the ordinary course of human life. And you, citizens of the Lake shore, have sought out and invited here a little remnant of survivors to bless our eyes with the evidences of your prosperity and happiness, and to warm our hearts with tokens of assurance that our toils and perils of life on that eventful day are not forgotten. Would to God that more had been spared to participate with us in these generous demonstrations of gratitude and respect. But

they have passed away; and in a very brief period of time, no spectator will be left to tell the story of Perry's Victory.

That victory derives a general interest from the fact that it was the first encounter of our infant navy, in fleet or squadron.

After recounting the familiar details of the battle scene, he concluded:

My friends, in the name and behalf of the citizens of Rhode Island, I tender you their grateful acknowledgements for the honor done that little State on this interesting occasion. She sent hither the commander of the squadron, and a majority of the officers and men. She glories in the victory gained, and regards the name and fame of her gallant son as one of her choicest jewels, and will ever cherish grateful sentiments towards those who respect and honor his memory. . . .

Old companions in the conflict, I rejoice to see you and once more to take you by the hand. . . . In the days of our youth we came to the rescue of this Lake, and to assist in restoring peace to the frontier. A kind Providence has bounteously prolonged our days beyond man's allotted period of existence, and now, after the lapse of nearly half a century, permits us to revisit the place where important scenes transpired in our early years, and to unite in celebrating the victory achieved by our much loved commander. We joyfully survey the wonderful changes and improvements that have occurred since the war of 1812. Buffalo was then a populous village, but soon after a heap of ashes. Erie contained but a score of dwellings. Cleveland was a cluster of log cabins, Sandusky the same, Toledo was nowhere, and Detroit in possession of the enemy, and not a single American vessel was left on the lakes, on which to hoist our stars and stripes.

And what do we behold now? A population increased a hundred fold; magnificent and prosperous cities, lofty spires and domes on temples of worship; colleges and seminaries of learning; extensive commerce; railroads diverging and intersecting in all directions; the white outspread wings of commerce gliding to and fro, and freighted with the exhaustless products of the North and North-west,—aye, and ploughing yon crystal waves, once shrouded in the smoke of our cannon, and crimsoned with the blood of our companions. . . .

Following the oration "nine hearty cheers" were raised. Poems and musical numbers completed the program. Doctor McMeens, secretary of the affair, read a poem titled *The Islands of Erie.* Captain

Stephen Champlin was introduced as the last surviving commander of the squadron and Lieutenant Thomas Brownell of Newport as second in command of the *Ariel*. The following anecdote is contained in the official account ("On Board the Steamer *Queen City*"):

> While the steamer was passing out of Sandusky Bay, with three of the survivors of the Battle on board, Dr. Usher Parsons recognized and pointed out the locality where the fleet had come to anchor, a few days before the engagement, and fired three guns, a signal previously agreed upon between Capt. Perry and Gen. Harrison. The next day the General and his suite came on board drenched with rain, among whom were the celebrated Gov. McArthur and Hon. Lewis Cass, and also a number of Indian chiefs. A day or two after their reception on board, the General and Staff were saluted with the usual number of guns. They stood during the time on the quarter deck of the *Lawrence* in full dress uniform, and the Doctor remarked that he has never since looked upon a nobler and more martial staff of officers. When the firing began, the "Indian Braves" dodged below in double quick time, and remained in the cabin until it ceased. Their ears were unused to such kind of thunder.

Charles wrote of the event:[7]

> In his more advanced life he became well known in the growing cities along the southern shore of Lake Erie. He often visited that region after his retirement from active practice. Those cities appreciated more and more the importance of Perry's victory, and commemorated its anniversary by yearly gatherings, and occasionally by special observances and various plans for erection of monuments. Dr. Parsons was the only surviving officer of the battle who had cultivated historical tastes and powers of writing and oratory. In 1858, the anniversary was celebrated at Put-In-Bay. . . . There was a very large assemblage, and a brilliant display of yachts and steamers. . . . Eloquent addresses were made. . . . Dr. Parsons read an elaborate narrative discourse. This was received with a great deal of interest by the large audience, and was afterward printed in all the principal newspapers of Buffalo, Sandusky, Cleveland, &c. He afterward wrote in his notebook, "this anniversary was among the most delightful of my life, as well as the most interesting."

In the summer of 1859 Powell, the New York artist, finally was ready to proceed with his painting for the Ohio State House and asked to meet with Usher regarding this: "As I have hitherto not been ready to use the valuable information it is in your power to give me, I have deferred my visit until the present . . . my interview with you should be the means of giving me higher inspiration than . . . the printed accounts." They met during August, either in Saratoga, where Usher was vacationing, or later in Providence.[8]

On August 23 a great celebration was held in Newport, called the Reunion of the Sons and Daughters of Newport.[9] It was really a general homecoming for natives of the city, scattered far and wide, making their fortunes elsewhere. Usher was invited to attend as a Lake Erie veteran. The city was lavishly decorated with flags, bunting, and streamers, and in the evening was brilliantly illuminated with colored lights, hundreds of Chinese lanterns, and fireworks. The steamer *Perry* brought two full boat-loads from Providence, including, presumably, the venerable Doctor Parsons. The morning procession formed at the Parade at 11:30 and slowly moved to a vast tent on a lot north of the Ocean House. The weather was fine and clear. One of the carriages reserved for invited guests carried Lt. Thomas Brownell and Doctor Usher Parsons, the only surviving commissioned officers of the Battle of Lake Erie. Brownell, we may presume, was again rigged out in his lace and buttons. They were seated at one of the three head tables placed on a large platform in the center of the tent. The principal address was given by the eminent Doctor Walter Channing of Boston, a native of Newport and a teacher of Usher's in his student days. Many toasts were raised, including one to "Our Old Doctors," to which Usher responded. He read a brief history of the doctors of Newport and concluded, "You have every reason to be proud, Sons and Daughters of Rhode Island, of your medical ancestry. . . . The memory of distinguished physicians of Rhode Island [i.e. the Island of Aquidneck] . . . have played their part in the drama of professional life." In the evening the ceremonies were resumed in the tent, now "brilliantly illuminated with Chinese lanterns and gas," piped in especially for the occasion. It was close to midnight when the festivities came to an end.[10]

As the year 1860 began, plans were evolving for a great Perry celebration in Cleveland in September. Since Usher was to have a leading role, much of his correspondence related to historical details of the battle. Several of the leading American historians of the period consulted him. Usher wrote to Henry Dawson on January

13,[11] ". . . In reply to the question 'did the Comre. take his battle flag with him?' So I have been told by those who rowed him. He left his broad pennant flying in the *Lawrence.* . . . and when he arrived on board the *Niagara,* it grieved him . . . to see it hauled down, though he approved its being done. The Commodore received the officers who surrendered on board the *Lawrence.* . . ." He added, "I hope you will not by haste make any mistakes. As your work will be a standard one, too much caution cannot be exercised."

On the 16th of January Usher wrote to Benson John Lossing, wood engraver and author of several popular illustrated histories:[12]

> In reply to your several inquiries . . . there is no locality within this state that was made memorable by any event of the war of 1812. All the battles of R. Islanders were fought on the water. . . . I have no sketches of battle grounds excepting of the fleet on the Lake. I have a fine portrait of Perry by Jarvis, and there are portraits of Turner, Taylor, Champlin, Holdup, & others in being. The above named officers were greatly distinguished in after life and are deserving of particular notice. . . . There is one spot worth sketching, and I wonder it has not employed the pencil of some artist. That is Put-in-Bay where a monument is to be erected.

The contractor for the Perry monument at Cleveland submitted for Usher's approval a photograph of a sketch of Perry. On February 4 Usher acknowledged receipt of "the elegant figure," deemed the "general form of the head perfect," and judged the whole to be "good, spirited and appropriate."[13] On the 6th he wrote to W. W. Dobbins of Sandusky:[14]

> That you should find the remains of Claxton, whose grave was marked 20 years after by guess, that you should find the very sponge I placed under his shoulder forty-seven years ago, and in a good state of preservation seems most remarkable. I wish you would preserve this sponge and place it in our historical society where many other relicts relating to Lake Erie are accumulated. I want the hair from Almy's skull to present to his maiden sister now of great age. The buttons too I want of Senat & Edwards who were both buried in uniform. The chair [made from timber from the *Lawrence*], if you can vouch for its genuineness, I should like to purchase to present to the R.I. Historical Society, provided it can be bought at a reasonable price. . . .
> I will write according to your suggestion to some of the leading men in Sandusky, to reduce the scale of the monument, or to

abandon it entirely. . . . My interest in the Put-in-Bay enterprise has much abated. I am invited to the inauguration of the statue at Cleveland next 10th of Septr. and shall expect to see you there. Some of our first people will go. The statue is to be 14 feet high, and I think will be a very successful piece of art. I hope old Erie will not be behind her sister city. She was benefited by the navy, and enjoys distinguished honor in having originated the fleet.

The authenticity of the chair was eventually established to Usher's satisfaction.

On April 3, 1860 Usher found time to read before the Rhode Island Historical Society "a list of men in this City [Providence] of 80 years of age and upwards."[15] On the 21st he reported to Dobbins:[16] "There will be a great turn-out from Rhode Island for [the] Cleveland celebration perhaps hundreds. The Governor and legislature and several generals, two companies of soldiers and many others."

Usher's correspondence concerning the Cleveland celebration continued. On June 9, 1860 he wrote to W. W. Dobbins, son of the Captain, to explain his apparent slight of the elder Dobbins in his lecture to the Rhode Island Historical Society:[17]

> I think you are here too sensitive. I was lecturing to a R. Island audience on the services she had rendered, and not to Pennsylvanians, or South Carolinians, or Kentuckians, whose officers of older warrant and commission than your father's, were at work on the vessels, whilst he . . . was engaged [in] . . . ever more important duties elsewhere. Had I been discussing the merits of the officers in those states, I should have placed S. Master Dobbins next to the commodore in Pa., and Holdup in S. Carolina, & Stout in Kentucky. . . . Now I beg you will write me soon whether this explanation is satisfactory, as, if not, I must despair of success in pleasing you. . . . If you wish for a more extended biography, I think you are the best person to write it, both as regards a wide range of facts, and skill in using them. . . .
>
> If you are not invited to the Cleveland celebration, please to consider yourself as invited by me . . . the son of my old friend shall not be omitted. I have invited the commodore's only son, and many others.

On August 11 Usher wrote to the committee on arrangements at Cleveland:[18]

I perceive by the programme . . . that a "Sham fight" is to come off on the 10th of September, probably to represent Perry's battle. . . . I venture to suggest that it might be well to consult someone who was in the fight. . . . There is such a person, who would be competent to inform the managers, and who could be consulted without trouble or expense. . . .

Hosea Sargeant is, I believe, the only survivor of the flag ship *Lawrence*, except myself. He escaped without injury in the battle, helped fire the last gun, and hauled down the Commodore's fighting flag, and passed it to him in the boat, which he carried with him on his shoulder to the *Niagara*. Sargeant has come to light within the last year. I well remember him in the *Lawrence*. Although an experienced sailor at the time, he enlisted in the army near Cincinnati for eighteen months as a sergeant. He was with Croghan in the defence of Fort Stephenson, and soon after volunteered . . . to serve on board the fleet. . . . He is perfectly reliable and truthful. The Presidents of the railroads, on my mentioning him, immediately offered him a full ticket to Cleveland and back.

The Perry celebration committee had sent out invitations as early as January 1860 to the Rhode Island official family and to other prominent citizens.[19] The Secretary of State sent a favorable reply for all concerned on June 5, 1860. Preparations for the mass movement to Cleveland were extensive. The large party included Governor William Sprague, his staff, two units of Rhode Island militia, the famous American Band, members of the General Assembly, the Mayor of Providence, various invited guests, and two survivors of the great battle—Captain Thomas Brownell of Newport and Usher Parsons.

On Wednesday evening, September 5, the gay and colorful throng gathered at the Providence railroad depot, the brilliantly attired military units attracting the major share of attention. As the party boarded the train for Stonington, Connecticut, crowds jammed Exchange Place (now Kennedy Plaza) and spilled out along the tracks. After some delay in boarding so large a party, the train moved slowly out of the station to the accompaniment of the peculiar staccato cheer of the military. Handkerchiefs were waved, and the warm evening air was pierced by shouts of good-bye, an obligato to the deep-throated puffing of the accelerating locomotive. The soldiers leaning out the windows waved their caps to the crowd. A passenger on board recalled: "The train quickened in its speed, the hurrahs of the ones we left behind grew fainter, the circle of lights around the cove dwindled away, and now we were fully *en route.*" The station platforms along the right of way were crowded by enthusiastic citizens cheering them on.

At Stonington the party was transferred to the Long Island Sound steamer *Commonwealth*, which sailed for New York late that night. Upon arriving in New York they "filed to the right and then to the right again" to board the ferry to the Erie Railroad terminus in Jersey. Excitement was heightened at Elmira, New York, when a car caught fire from an overheated journal. The fire was quickly extinguished and a replacement found. The party detrained briefly at Hornellsville (now Hornell), New York to be served late afternoon tea as guests of the local military. Ten miles west of Hornellsville the locomotive broke down; they waited three hours for another to be brought up. The itinerary called for a change at Dunkirk, New York for the Cleveland train. As a result of the delays they did not make Dunkirk until after the Cleveland train had left. Since the next train for Cleveland did not depart for six hours, everyone rushed to the only hotel in town, which could accommodate only a quarter of the passengers. Those fortunate enough to be taken in shared their small beds, while others rolled up in shawls or overcoats and slept on tables and chairs and even the floor. The remainder returned to the train to spend the few hours till daylight in the uncomfortable cars.

They arrived in Cleveland in a drenching rain on Saturday afternoon, September 8. They were received at the station by a military escort of the local Light Guards resplendent in Zouave uniforms. Governor Dennison of Ohio welcomed his guests, singling out Usher as "the Assistant Surgeon of the *Lawrence* . . . , whose humanity and skill in the discharge of duties, have honorably associated his name with that of his illustrious Captain." Governor Sprague acknowledged "the kind welcome" on behalf of the delegation and the "two veterans . . . Captain Brownell on my right, . . . and Dr. Usher Parsons, on my left, whose services . . . in ameliorating the sufferings of the wounded, have become historical. . . ." The Rhode Island militia marched to the Weddell House, while the official guests, including Usher and Captain Brownell, were driven in carriages to the Angier House. A formal reception, held later in the elegant drawing room of the Angier with officers in dress uniform and the ladies and gentlemen in their finest evening attire, was a sparkling affair.

Sunday morning was devoted to religious services at various churches. The Rhode Island party went on to Camp Perry for a special service led by Bishop Clark of Rhode Island. The camp was crowded most of the day with large numbers of spectators. Sunday dinner, announced by the sounding of a drum, was served to the large delegation at 12:30 p.m. followed by a formal military parade at four o'clock. Our heroes sat in the reviewing stand, with crusty old Captain Brownell decked out "in his full uniform of the old style" catching the eyes of the spectators.

"The Glorious Tenth," dawning clear and cool, was ushered in by the ringing of bells and the firing of cannon. Crowds gathered early, and martial strains from the numerous military bands filled the air. Hundreds of country teams (i.e. wagons and carriages) came to town, and packed excursion trains had been arriving during the past two or three days. The crowd was estimated at 100,000. The procession began to form at nine a.m. on Erie Street north of Euclid. It was a vast parade, taking forty minutes to pass a given point along the route. The Providence Light Infantry was the favorite unit, with its beautiful dress and martial bearing, marching in cadence to the strains of the renowned American Band. One parade division contained the survivors of the battle. The procession reached the park where the dedication was to be held at about 1:30 p.m. A large stand for the guests was located near the new statue of Perry, and up forward a smaller raised one for the speakers and survivors of the battle. Among the survivors was old Hosea Sargeant of Cambridge, who had actually "held the patients at many an operation" for the busy surgeon of the *Lawrence*. Suspended from the roof of the speaker's stand was an old lantern used in the Battle of Lake Erie.

The major address of the day was delivered by historian George Bancroft. At the end of his discourse he received an elegant cane made from the timbers of the *Lawrence*. Usher followed him on the program, opening his address with these words:[20]

> In responding to your flattering invitation to address this vast assemblage, vain would be any endeavor, after the rich banquet we have enjoyed, to entertain you with historic or classic allusions, or with the graces of a polished style. Mine, sir, is the more humble and appropriate task to describe briefly the battle of Lake Erie. A story so often told must fail to interest you, and I should decline repeating it, but for the expressed wish of many to hear

it from the lips of the last surviving commissioned officer of Perry's squadron.

In the midst of Usher's address a canny old fellow named Quinn from Pittsburgh climbed to the speaker's stand and announced himself as the very man who had made the cordage used in the rigging of the ships in Perry's squadron. He had with him the identical tools he had used almost fifty years before.

Following his vivid and historically accurate account, Usher expressed his admiration for "this beautiful specimen of native art," the Perry statue:

> The likeness of Perry, considering the limited sources of information available to the artist, is more accurate and striking than I expected to see. The conception of his attitude, his martial bearing and appropriate expression is highly successful. Of his drapery I have a word of explanation to offer. You see him in his usual official dress. But, in battle you must know that all official insignia are laid aside, and the dress of a common sailor is assumed, to avoid being a mark for the enemy's musketry in the tops. Perry wore in the fight a blue cotton round-jacket, which surrounded as brave a heart as ever beat in human frame, and here is the identical jacket!

Whereupon he waved the jacket over his head, arousing a burst of enthusiastic cheering. He concluded on a sentimental note: "Old companions in the conflict, a little remnant of us still live, and are permitted once more to take each other by the hand. . . . Old friends, I bid you an affectionate farewell."[21]

Following the formal exercises, the crowds moved to the lake shore to witness the much advertised mock battle. Every fence and house top was occupied, and the banks of the lake were lined with spectators in carriages and on foot. Although there was delay in getting the battle started, it finally went off smoothly with a great racket and quantities of smoke and fireworks. "Probably nothing so difficult of satisfactory execution," said the official account, "could have been placed upon the programme, but under the direction of the committee, guided by the charts of Dr. Parsons and Captain Champlin, as published in the *Cleveland Herald*, the real battle was faithfully represented in the mimic fray."

The evening reception of the governors at the Angier was a gala event. Soon after eight o'clock its spacious drawing rooms and halls were filled with "beautiful women and gallant men." At 8:30 the large dining hall was thrown open. The American Band, which "can have no superior," played appropriate music, and the Providence Light Infantry was impressive in its "elegant scarlet uniforms." After a two-hour reception, "the evening wound up with a hop" to "the entrancing strains of the American Band."[22]

While the crowds began to leave Cleveland that evening, a day of celebration lay ahead for the official guests, culminating in a full-dress military review at Camp Perry. Hardly was the parade over when the skies opened up, making a shambles of the trip back to town. The Rhode Islanders were entertained at a final five o'clock dinner party at the Angier, following which they marched to the station in pouring rain. The steamer trip from Cleveland to Buffalo was canceled because of a battering storm on the lake. They returned to Buffalo on the night train of the Lake Shore Railroad, which fortunately was equipped with comfortable sleeping cars. The men laid out the drenched uniforms or let them flutter from the windows. The long journey home was interrupted by a side trip to Niagara Falls. The party, on arriving at Providence Depot Saturday morning, September 15, was welcomed by enthusiastic crowds. Usher, however, was not among them, unhappily "detained a few days at Buffalo with a severe influenza." Soaked in the final deluge along with everyone else at the Cleveland celebration, it is not surprising that he caught cold.

In a letter of October 22, 1860 George Bancroft commended Usher for the excellence of his Cleveland address.[23] It was, he said, "too good to be lost," and he was grateful that it would be preserved in the press reports. The relics from the *Lawrence*, forwarded by Dobbins, finally arrived from Sandusky. Usher acknowledged them:[24] "The chair is in perfect order and looks better than I expected." He added, "There is to be within a few weeks an account of the celebration published. I shall by my own request furnish a page or two of the history and origin and final destruction of the vessels." To ensure historical accuracy, he inquired of Dobbins concerning the fate of several of the vessels in the battle and the identity of their commanders in later years.[25]

Of the chair, Benson Lossing wrote: "Pieces of the *Lawrence* have been sought for as relics by the curious, and many canes and other articles have been made of the wood. Captain Champlin and Dr.

Parsons . . . both have chairs made from the oak of the flagship." A "little engraving" of Champlin's chair by Lossing himself showed a neat upholstered armchair in the Victorian style.[26]

On November 10, Rhode Island Governor William Sprague wrote to Usher:[27] "I find on my desk a likeness of Com. O. H. Perry, taken from Jarvis's portrait, with a frame wrought from the timber of the flagship *Lawrence*, and presented to me by the last surviving commissioned officer of Perry's squadron. I thank you for your kind remembrance, and for this undeserved courtesy to me. . . . I shall prize it as the gift of one who has served his country faithfully & well. . . . my best wishes for your happiness in your declining years."

At the interim meeting of the Rhode Island Medical Society on December 19, 1860 Usher "read a paper on his surgical experiences connected with the battle of Lake Erie, and other actions, in the last war." It is probable that the impending Civil War had stirred among the members a renewed interest in military surgery, a likelihood in fact suggested by Charles in his *Memoir*.[28] Few then living could speak from personal experience with as much authority. It was a formal presentation to the Society, but it was titled a "Letter on Some Points of Military Surgery" when it appeared in the *Communications of the Rhode Island Medical Society* for 1861.[29]

Following the publication of *Pepperrell* in May of 1855, nothing further had issued from Usher's prolific pen until the appearance of its London edition late in 1856, published by Sampson Low, Son, & Co. In preparation for this event Usher had corresponded with Samuel F. Haven, librarian of the American Antiquarian Society in Worcester. Usher asked Haven for the loan of the Society's copy of an engraving of Sir William Pepperrell so that his engraver, W. W. Smith of Little & Brown, could make a new engraving from it. Haven graciously accommodated Usher, who sent the following acknowledgment:[30]

I return you the engraving of Sir W. Pepperrell with many thanks for the loan of it. It is copied from the full length portrait in the Salem Atheneum which was painted by Smybert while in this country. The portrait in the Portsmouth Atheneum was painted after his return to England in 1751. It is from the latter that my engraving was copied, of which I herewith send you a copy. In a few days I will send you a copy of my book containing the same likeness, as a present to the Antiquarian Library.

The Smith engraving served as a frontispiece for the London edition; the American edition had not contained a portrait of Pepperrell.

Edwin Parsons had recently severed his connections with the Savannah business and planned to enter a new partnership in New York in November of 1857. In the interim he traveled in Europe and the Middle East. Usher wrote to him in London on June 15 about affairs at home. Their mutual relatives to the eastward, he noted, appeared to be doing well. He reported at length to his business-oriented nephew[31] on the state of the economy both locally and nationally. Times were dull, Rhode Island having been hit particularly hard by the panic of 1857. "All New England has gone west," and the active New England farmers were emigrating to Kansas and Iowa in vast numbers, which was considered locally to be a calamity. Some half a million were trekking westward yearly. The hungry speculators, now less sanguine because of declining land values, were "returning and bringing their money" with them. Chicago, he wrote with canny insight, "as a thoroughfare between the eastern & middle states and the great west, that is now filling up so fast, must ever make it a place of rapid growth," likely to rival New York. Because of hard times in the East, such great numbers were flocking to the West that hotels in Detroit were lodging more on the floor than in beds—and at three dollars a day!

On the intellectual front, he reported that he had been preparing a sixty-page condensation of his *Pepperrell* for, as he called it, Hunt's Magazine (actually Hunt's *Merchants' Magazine and American Review*,[32] a business and financial monthly), where it was to be part of a series on eminent merchants. The unsigned article, titled "Mercantile Biography: Lieut. General Sir William Pepperrell, Baronet," was essentially a review of Usher's book, with emphasis on Pepperrell's business accomplishments. Hunt quoted at length a résumé by Usher of the vast Pepperrell holdings in Maine, seized from his great-grandsons after enactment of the Confiscation Act of 1778. "In preparing the foregoing," wrote the author, "much aid has been derived from this admirable work, abounding, as it does in letters and documents—it cannot fail to satisfy the most exacting lover of detail."

On the medical front he had spent ten days in May in Philadephia at a convention of delegates from the commercial cities seeking to adopt measures to lessen the burden of the current ship quarantine system. "It went off harmoniously," he told Edwin, "and will have the desired effect."

He mentioned the spectacular Atlantic cable, the high technology of his day, which was then being laid, "a stupendous enterprise," which would soon be in operation. In a couple of days (Bunker Hill Day on June 17) there would be a "grand celebration," culminating in the unveiling of a statue of the heroic General Joseph Warren. "It is possible," he surmised, "that it will be the greatest gathering ever witnessed in New England." General Winfield Scott and all of the New England governors would be present. Edwin Nightingale, "our kinsman and neighbor,"[33] would appear in full military uniform as the governor's aide. Charles's health had been poor, and he and Mary had that very day left for Princeton, Massachusetts, where they would visit for a while with Mary's folks. As the weather was fine and the countryside beautiful, they had elected to travel by chaise.

Usher hoped that Edwin's plans to "pitch" in New York would come to fruition, as "You seem like Joseph of old destined to bring up the rear of our tribe with flying colors." Edwin would indeed meet these expectations as he joined the New York contingent of Parsonses, who became the solidly affluent branch of the clan. Edwin, he hoped, might soon visit Providence, "as many young ladies are promised the pleasure of your acquaintance."

Pursuing his long-time interest in the Narragansett Indians, Usher had been delving into local Indian place names. At an afternoon meeting of the Rhode Island Historical Society on July 7, 1857[34] he read "a list of two pages of Indian names of places, persons, &c. in this State, with their significations, collected by him," and he suggested "the importance of obtaining a complete account of them." Later, on October 6, he presented a further list, commenting on "his views in forming the collection . . . now containing near 300 names," to which others were added by those present. Eventually the whole was published for the Society in pamphlet form.[35] At the same meeting a letter from Giles Sanford of Erie (dated August 31, 1857) was read, accompanying the latter's gift to the Society of the sternpost of the boat which conveyed Perry from the *Lawrence* to the *Niagara* at the Battle of Lake Erie. Usher doubtless had a part in this little matter. Finally, at the same meeting he read "a memorandum pointing out the location of the burying grounds of the Roger Williams family—one in the rear of Sullivan Dorr's residence in this city, another very near the junction of the old and new portions of the Stonington Rail Road [now the New Haven branch of Conrail] in Cranston, and the third a short distance west of the last named."[36]

Later, in February of 1858, Usher wrote to his old friend in England, Profesor Romeo Elton, recounting current events, local and national.[37] Brown University, he reported, was getting along finely under its recently elevated president, the Reverend Barnas Sears, and "has never before been in such general favor with the public." As in his letter to his nephew Edwin, he referred to the now relenting financial panic as the "sad reverse of fortune in the crash that has recently overtaken the commercial world." The national government was in a state of "high excitement" over whether Kansas would enter the Union free or slave. Usher was not optimistic that the "dough faces of the North" would resist the bribery of presidential patronage and "slave power," but this time he guessed wrong. Mexico, he wrote, was in a state of anarchy (Benito Juárez's War of the Reform), "will be soon knocking at our door for admission to the Union" (again he was wrong). And finally, he was happy to report that the best of feelings prevailed in America toward England in its struggle with India, and his own sympathies were strongly supportive. He also mentioned several favorable reviews of *Pepperrell* in British journals, one of which, indeed, had been written by Elton!

Another of Usher's genealogical studies was published in the spring of 1858—"The Descendants of Peter Hill of York County, Maine, with some Incidents Relating to the French and Indian Wars." It appeared in the April and July issues of the *New England Genealogical and Historical Register*.[38] "The foregoing account of the Hills," he wrote, "was gathered chiefly from manuscripts found in an old chest in the garret of Capt. Gerrish of S. Berwick, where they had been nailed up seventy years. All the commissions held by the Hills, both civil and military, were among them, and forty letters from Sir William Pepperrell, some of which were used in writing his life. I have also gathered some important facts from Folsom's history of Saco." Peter Hill, a planter, settled in New Biddeford near the mouth of the Saco River, probably prior to 1648. His son, Captain John Hill, married Mary Frost, the daughter of Major Charles Frost, the subject of Usher's earlier study. Major

Frost's son, John, married Mary Pepperrell, the sister of Sir William and Usher's great-grandmother. Thus were the families intertwined.

At the meeting of the Rhode Island Medical Society on June 16, 1858 held in the Redwood Library in Newport, a significant proposal was offered by the Committee on Publications: "that individuals of this Society be requested to prepare within the space of three months a brief sketch of the lives of distinguished members deceased belonging to this society."[39] Where relatives of the deceased able to assume the task were still alive, those individuals would be asked to do so. Quite logically Doctor Usher Parsons was appointed a committee of one to carry out the recommendations, which eventually came to fruition. Usher then offered a resolution "that a committee be appointed to confer with the Government of Brown University and ascertain if they will consent to receive the Library in one of the alcoves of its Library, and on what terms." The negotiations with Brown, led by Usher as chairman, failed, and other arrangements were made. A more recent move in the 1960s to merge the library collections of the Society and the University also failed because differences could not be reconciled over such matters as freedom of access to members of the Society, parking privileges for members, and clear identity of Society materials. In 1987, however, Brown University agreed to take over the substantial and valuable collections under an arrangement which preserves the identity of the materials and assures access to members.

On November 4, 1858 Usher displayed his eclectic interests at a meeting of the Rhode Island Historical Society. He first presented still another list of "Indian names in addition to those formerly presented, the whole now amt'g to between 4 and 500." He then read "a paper upon the revolutionary services of Com. Abraham Whipple of R.I.," and "a letter from Col. Meserve, Albany, 1756, giving an amusing account of the character of the troops at that time." Finally he exhibited an exotic item billed as "a specimen of Arabic manuscript written by a slave formerly belonging to Gen. Owen [of] Wilmington."[40]

At the semi-annual meeting of the Rhode Island Medical Society on December 15 in the courthouse in East Greenwich, the publication of the biographical sketches of Rhode Island doctors was finally authorized, thus launching the official journal of the Society. A new committee, consisting of Doctors Usher Parsons, Isaac Ray, and George L. Collins, was appointed "to publish such papers biographical or medical now in the archives of the society as might be considered worthy."[41]

During the fall of 1859, while Usher was busy preparing the biographical sketches of local physicians for the Rhode Island Medical Society, *The Providence Daily Journal* of October 14 carried an interesting little story titled "The Author of 'Sam Slick', History of Nova Scotia, &c.," signed simply "P", and apparently a by-product of Usher's biographical studies. The Sam Slick stories were among the earliest of American dialect writings. Usher clearly established the identity of the author of these stories as one Judge Thomas Chandler Haliburton, then a member of the Canadian Parliament. Usher's purpose in writing the essay was to dispel a prevalent misconception that they had been written by another Judge Haliburton who had Rhode Island connections, namely, Sir Brenton Haliburton, Chief Justice of Nova Scotia. The latter was in fact the son of Doctor John Haliburton, a Newport physician at the time of the Revolution. He had been the first preceptor of Benjamin Waterhouse, who considered him to be as well-educated and skillful a practitioner of physic and surgery as any in New York, Boston, or Philadelphia. Doctor Haliburton had come to Newport in 1750 as a surgeon aboard a British frigate, but resigned his commission and settled there. He became wealthy from his extensive practice and joined his fortune to that of his wife, who had been a Miss Brenton of Newport, "a lady of high family." During the Revolution, but after the British occupation of Newport had ended, Haliburton was suspected, and with good reason, of harboring loyalist sympathies. He fled for his life to British-occupied Manhattan and thence to a hospital surgeoncy in Halifax.[42] Doctor Haliburton's son Brenton, a Tory, later studied law in London and eventually entered law practice in Halifax. Like Thomas Chandler Haliburton, the writer of the Sam Slick stories, Brenton also became a judge, thus causing confusion as to the identity of the author of these stories. Their families were indeed unrelated. Brenton Haliburton, now advanced in years, still corresponded regularly with his Rhode Island cousin, Miss Elizabeth C. Brenton of South Kingstown, who, wrote Usher, was "an aged lady of high literary attainment . . . from whom the above particulars were chiefly derived."

Before the close of 1859, the useful and historically important little pamphlet *Sketches of Rhode Island Physicians Deceased Prior to 1850* had appeared.[43] Although a few of the thumbnail biographies were contributed by other members of the Society, the largest share of the work was done by Usher himself, who headed the committee appointed by the Society for this purpose. The first section consists of biographies, while the second, titled "Medical Education in Rhode Island," discusses briefly the medical school "in connection with Brown University." Few contributions from Rhode Island had appeared in the medical literature, Usher noted, although an occasional paper had been accepted for publication in Philadelphia, New York, or Boston. Other features were a complete listing of Fiske Fund Prize questions and winners from 1835 through 1858, some notes on the past activities of the Rhode Island Medical Society, and a list of all officers since incorporation. At the semi-annual meeting of the Society on December 21, 1860 in East Greenwich, Usher reported that his committee had published an edition of 300 copies, which were now ready for distribution.[44]

At a time when the question of providing a hospital for Providence had apparently been forgotten, the following tart comment appeared unheralded in the columns of *The Providence Daily Journal* of June 2, 1855:

> The need of a General Hospital still continues in our city, to the discredit of our philanthropy and to the inconvenience and suffering of many worthy people. It is strange that so large a city, with so great a mechanical interest and with so much wealth in the hands of so liberal men, should be destitute of one of the primary institutions of a well ordered society. It seems to us that the medical society ought to take measures to awaken public sentiment upon the subject, and to excite the benevolent and the liberal to a friendly interest in it. It is not for the poor only, it is not as a mere charity hospital that this is needed; it is needed by single men, by clerks and mechanics and others, whose homes are away, or who have not at their homes the conveniences for the comfortable care of the sick, and for the nursing and attendance which are even more necessary than medicine.

This was too much for Usher to bear. Considering his own urgent efforts to effect the creation of such an institution, he regarded the inference as eminently unfair. At the June 4 meeting of the Providence Medical Association[45] he "called up the subject of a City Hospital" referring "to a recent paragraph in the Provd. Journal, reflecting upon the tardiness of the medical faculty of this city in moving in this matter." Upon motion of Joseph Mauran "it was voted that Dr. U. Parsons, as being chairman of the Committee on Hospital be requested to take suitable notice of the subject, stating its whole history." To set the record straight, Usher sent a lengthy statement to the editor of the *Journal*:[46]

> A paragraph in your paper . . . calls the attention of our citizens to the importance of establishing a public hospital in this city. . . . The suggestion would seem to imply that we have been remiss in this matter. . . .
>
> In 1851, while President of the City Medical Association, I presented this subject at one of its regular meetings, and, after due discussion, a committee of seven of the senior physicians was appointed to consider what measures should be adopted in furtherance of the object. We reported that a circular should be prepared and sent to every tax-payer of more than one hundred dollars in the city. . . . This circular, so far as we can learn, awakened no interest whatever in the subject. In 1852, . . . advised to try a subscription paper, . . . I drew [one] up and handed a copy to each member of the committee to circulate among the citizens, but we could find no individual willing to head the list, and the plan was abandoned.
>
> Deeply impressed by the sight of suffering exhibited in their daily professional walks, the Association [then] directed me to draw up a petition to the city government, asking its aid and cooperation in the enterprise, and to hand it to individuals for signature. . . .
>
> The city government, on receiving the petition, with a request from the committee for permission to address them orally, invited me, with others, to appear before a committee of that body. After hearing us, they appointed a sub-committee to examine and decide upon the best location for a hospital on lands owned by the city. This sub-committee disagreed in their opinion . . . , and here the action of the city seems to have ended. The Association then concluded to proceed no further in the business . . . the new Mayor, in his inaugural address, mentions the subject of a hospital among those requiring the immediate attention and action of the city government. . . . We are ready to do everything in our power to further the contemplated laudable enterprise.

Doubtless sensing an opportunity to make political hay by contriving a popular issue, the new Mayor of Providence, James Y. Smith, in his inaugural address to the City Council on June 6 stated:[47] "I recommend the construction of a City Hospital, and trust that your early attention may be given to the subject. A system of free beds would enable our liberal citizens to participate in its construction." Characteristically self-righteous, the *Journal* commented, "We have repeatedly had occasion to refer to the necessity which exists in a city so large as this for a public hospital, and we hope to see the recommendation of the Mayor in relation to such an institution early carried into execution." Frustrated by the whole business and feeling that it was time for younger hands to take the reins, Usher resigned from the chairmanship of the Committee on a Hospital. His resignation was quietly accepted at the July 2 meeting of the Providence Medical Association. He could not in good conscience, however, withdraw completely from the pursuit of this desirable objective. But another eight years elapsed before the hospital became a reality, and thirteen years before it received its first patient.

Charles was the star performer at the annual meeting of the Rhode Island Medical Society in Mason's Hall in Providence on June 6, 1855.[48] He delivered the annual oration on the subject of *Oxaluria*. The discourse, said the *Rhode Island Country Journal*,[49] "manifested an intimate knowledge of the subject, the result of indefatigable research, and adds a fresh allure to the author's already well established reputation as a writer." Usher then reported on the A.M.A.'s doings in Philadelphia. The healthy state of the Society was duly noted by the *Journal*:[50] "A bountiful repast was furnished, and we believed, as a whole, it is the general feeling that the meeting was one of unusual interest, and augured well for the future of the Society." Charles, the day's orator, and Usher, as virtual past president of the American Medical Association, assuredly graced the head table.

The following year at the annual meeting of the Rhode Island Medical Society of June 4, 1856 Usher moved that a "committee be appointed to consider the necessary qualifications of physicians with whom the members of the Society may consult."[51] The proposal which was adopted was aimed at revising rules barring consultations with irregular, unethical, and poorly trained practitioners to bring them in line with the new A.M.A. Code of Ethics. Usher was appointed chairman of the committee. There is some irony in this in view of Usher's earlier brushes with the Society's Censors. Although the problem of consultations with "irregular" practitioners was not new, the increasing national attention paid to this perplexing question was undoubtedly prompted by the flourishing growth and mounting influence of the Eclectics, the Thomsonians, and especially the Homeopathic practitioners. During this era they were able to mount a serious challenge to regular physicians not only in the realm of theory and therapy, but—more poignantly— economically.[52]

At the interim meeting of the Society on December 17, 1856 Usher's committee on bylaws recommended the adoption, in lieu of the existing regulations on consultations, of "that part of the Code of Ethics of the American Medical Association relating to the 'Duties of Physicians to each other and to the Profession at Large'." This action reflected the growing influence of the A.M.A. in raising the standards of medical practice and conduct.

Once again at the semi-annual meeting of the Society in Providence on December 17, 1857 Usher was chosen delegate to the A.M.A. spring meeting in Washington.[53] After having absented himself from the national meetings for three years, he did indeed attend the annual convention of 1858 in Washington. The meetings of this vigorous and increasingly important organization were held from May 4 to 6 in the Lecture Room of the recently opened Smithsonian Institution building.[54] The capital city received the visitors with gracious hospitality. They were entertained both publicly and privately, and as time would allow they were taken by omnibus to various points of interest.

The following year, in December, Usher once again was chosen delegate to the A.M.A. meetings to be held in Louisville. By the spring of 1859, however, he had given up plans to attend or to travel to the west. At the December 21 meeting of the Society, Usher proposed the formation of a committee to engage quarters for a meeting place and library for the Society.[55] Having proposed the idea, Usher was, of course, appointed chairman. Despite his advancing years, he continued to devote his energies to the improvement of medical care and to the affairs of organized medicine in Rhode Island.

Early in June of 1860 Usher and Charles journeyed to New Haven to attend once again the annual gathering of the American Medical Association, held on June 5 through 7 in the Yale Chapel.[56] Usher was an elected delegate from Rhode Island and Charles president-elect of the state society.[57] On July 11 at Redwood Library in Newport, Charles became president of the Rhode Island Medical Society and would serve for two years.[58] It was a satisfying time for Usher, his long life having permitted him the opportunity to see his son attain prominence and recognition by his professional colleagues.

NOTES

1. George Parsons to mother, May 24, 1855, DPC.

2. C. W. Parsons *Memoir*, p. 55.

3. Lewis Johnston had died tragically as a young man many years before. Realizing belatedly that he had missed an opportunity to learn more about the war-time experiences of his late brother, George Johnston wrote to Usher asking him for his recollections of those meetings many years ago. Usher had pleasant memories of the young officer: "I had daily interviews with . . . [the British officers] and enjoyed their society very much, particularly Midshipman Johnston who I learned was from Sault Ste. Marie and was able to give me particular accounts of that region and of the Indian customs, character and condition. . . ." He remembered Johnston as a brave and faithful officer, and he told his brother that "his correct behaviour, candor and plain good sense and unpretending manner, had in high degree won my friendship and esteem. . . ." These and other facts in Usher's letter are recited in Majorie Cahn Brazer's "An Afterword to the Battle of Lake Erie," *Inland Seas*, 33:180–183, 1977. The original of Usher's letter to George Johnston, dated April 15, 1857, is in the Burton Historical Collection, Detroit Public Library. "How remarkable for George after all these years," wrote Brazer, "to encounter a man who had known his long dead brother during the one moment of glory in his short life."

4. William H. Powell to Usher Parsons, July 31, 1857, Historical Society of Pennsylvania. Ward Cowing, not identified, was probably related to Powell's mother, Mary Cowing Powell.

5. Usher Parsons to R. R. McMeens, August 6, 1858, Ohio Historical Society.

6. *An Account of the Organization & Proceedings of the Battle of Lake Erie Monument Association and Celebration of the 45th Anniversary of the Battle of Lake Erie at Put-in-Bay, on September Tenth, 1858* (Sandusky, Ohio, H. D. Cooke & Co.,1858).

7. C. W. Parsons *Memoir*, p. 49.

8. William H. Powell to Usher Parsons, August 12, 1859, DPC. William H. Powell to Usher Parsons, August 16, 1859, Historical Society of Pennsylvania.

9. *Newport Mercury*, August 27, 1859.

10. George C. Mason, *Re-Union of the Sons and Daughters of Newport, R.I., August 23, 1859, Compiled and Printed by Order of the General Committee of Arrangements* (Newport, F. A. Pratt & Co., 1859).

11. Usher Parsons to Henry B. Dawson, January 13, 1860, Henry E. Huntington Library. Henry Barton Dawson (1821–1889) was author of *Battles of the United States by Sea and Land, Embracing Those of the Revolutionary and Indian Wars, the War of 1812, and the Mexican Wars* (New York, Johnson, Fry, and Co., 1858).

12. Usher Parsons to Benson J. Lossing, January 16, 1860, Buffalo Historical Society. Benson John Lossing (1813–1891), historian and wood engraver, was author of *The Pictorial Field Book of the War of 1812; Illustrations, by Pen and Pencil, of the History, Biography, Scenery, Relics, and Traditions of the Last War for American Independence* (New York, Harper & Brothers, 1869). He also compiled similar works on the Revolutionary and Civil Wars.

13. Usher Parsons to Messrs. Jones & Sons, February 4, 1860, transcribed and published in George Bancroft, *Inauguration of the Perry Statue at Cleveland, on the Tenth of September, 1860, Including a History of the Battle of Lake Erie: Address and Other Proceedings, with a Sketch of William Walcutt, the Sculptor* (Cleveland, Fairbanks, Benedict & Co., 1861).

14. Usher Parsons to W. W. Dobbins, February 6, 1860, Buffalo Historical Society.

15. Rhode Island Historical Society, "Minutes."

16. Usher Parsons to W. W. Dobbins, April 21, 1860, Buffalo Historical Society.

17. Usher Parsons to W. W. Dobbins, 2d, June 9, 1860, Buffalo Historical Society.

18. Transcript of letter published in the official account of the proceedings cited in note 13.

19. This account is taken from the official proceedings (note 13) and from stories in Providence newspapers: *Providence Daily Journal*, September 8, 10, 11, 12, 13, 14, 15, and 17, 1860; and *Rhode Island Country Journal*, September 14, 1860.

20. Usher's address was printed in a number of press reports of the ceremonies. It was reprinted, along with several other of these addresses, in George Bancroft's *(Oliver Hazard Perry and the Battle of Lake Erie, Together with the addresses of Dr. Usher Parsons, Fleet Surgeon under Commodore Perry, and of Governor William Sprague of Rhode Island, Delivered in Cleveland Sept. 10, 1860, and Other Papers of Interest* (Newport, Mercury Publishing Co., 1912). This formed part of the Rhode Island Department of Education's Education Circulars, Historical Series VI.

21. In reporting the ceremonies, the *Providence Daily Journal* on September 14, 1860 related that "Dr. Parsons spoke with great clearness, force, and effect. He was listened to with the deepest interest by the many thousands in hearing of his voice."

22. The American Band, organized in 1837 as a unit of the First Light

Infantry (Rhode Island), acquired a national reputation under the famed band leader, D. W. Reeves. A successor American Band still exists.

23. George Bancroft to Usher Parsons, October 22, 1860, DPC.

24. Usher Parsons to W. W. Dobbins, October 27, 1860, Buffalo Historical Society.

25. Besides the several letters cited, the Buffalo Historical Society possesses a manuscript copy of Usher Parsons's diary; an unsigned plan in his hand of "Fort Erie and the American Camp and its defenses"; and an unsigned manuscript account of the surgical department of the Battle of Lake Erie written by Usher Parsons for Dr. C. G. Perry, son of O. H. Perry.

26. Benson John Lossing, *History of the War of 1812.*

27. William Sprague to Usher Parsons, November 10, 1860, DPC. Sprague (1830–1915), a Civil War-time governor of Rhode Island and a scion of great wealth made in textiles, married the beautiful, but tragic Kate Chase, daughter of U.S. Treasury Secretary Salmon P. Chase. The handsome Sprague mansion in Cranston, Rhode Island, has been preserved as an historic site.

28. Charles W. Parsons, in his *Memoir of Usher Parsons,* commented: "This paper would appear to have been suggested by the anticipation of civil war."

29. This appeared in volume 3, pp. 97–99, 1861.

30. Usher Parsons to Samuel F. Haven, September 27, 1856. He had made his original request of Haven on September 5. Both letters are in the American Antiquarian Society.

31. Usher Parsons to Edwin Parsons, June 15, 1857, DPC.

32. This appeared in *Hunt's Merchants' Magazine and Commercial and American Review,* 39:27–41, 1858. See note 25 of Chapter 15.

33. Nightingale was Charles's brother-in-law, having shared a double wedding with Charles and Mary.

34. Rhode Island Historical Society, "Minutes."

35. Usher Parsons, *Indian Names of Places in Rhode Island* (Providence, Knowles, Anthony & Co., 1861).

36. Rhode Island Historical Society, "Minutes." Only the day before he had made a field trip to prepare for his presentation. This memorandum written in his own hand and dated October 5, 1857, still exists in the collections of the Rhode Island Historical Society:

    I this day called on Frederick Williams who lives two miles up the Pawtuxet river from its entrance into the bay and on a farm descended to him from *Roger Williams,* his ancestor, of the 5th generation back. Half a mile west of him at the crossing of roads is an old red house owned by a Williams, another descendant of Roger; and not far from his is a family burying ground of the Williams family—descendants of Joseph, the son of Roger, whose grave stone has a long inscription. N. West from this, and near the foot or s. end of Marspaug [Mashapaug] pond, is a large white house owned by two aged maiden ladies [of the seventh generation]—who are owners of the farm, on which is the last mentioned burying ground of Joseph W. Thus there are ... farms still owned by three descended from Roger W. . . . They tell me that the only antiquaries who ever have called on them were Theodore Foster and a lady—but they have seen none of those who have written the life of R. Williams. . . .

The names of the two ladies are Rhoda and Betsey [Williams]. [Their farm is the present extensive and picturesque Roger Williams Park, deeded to the city by Betsey and containing the Betsey Williams Cottage Museum.] Their mother, they said, was [also] a descendant of Roger Williams, and of the sixth generation.

37. Usher Parsons to Romeo Elton, February 7, 1858, Brown University Library.

38. Volume twelve, pages 139–145 and 258–264, 1858. It was also reprinted as a separate by H. W. Dutton & Son, Boston that same year.

39. Rhode Island Medical Society, "Minutes."

40. Rhode Island Historical Society, "Minutes."

41. Rhode Island Medical Society, "Minutes."

42. Benjamin Waterhouse, "Medical Literature of Rhode Island, With a Sketch of Some of Her Most Eminent Men."

43. This was designated as Volume 1, Number 1 of the *Communications of the Rhode Island Medical Society*, which was the direct antecedant of *The Rhode Island Medical Journal*. The pamphlet was printed at Providence by Knowles, Anthony & Co., 1859. In 1878 the *Communications* became the *Transactions of the Rhode Island Medical Society*. The aspiration to prepare this compilation was, as pointed out by Professor Philip Cash, evidence of a rising sense of professional identity among Rhode Island physicians, characteristic of the period, or at least of a prominent segment of them.

44. Rhode Island Medical Society, "Minutes."

45. Providence Medical Association, "Minutes."

46. *Providence Daily Journal*, June 8, 1855.

47. *Manufacturers & Farmers Journal* (Providence), June 7, 1855.

48. Rhode Island Medical Society, "Minutes."

49. *Rhode Island Country Journal*, June 8, 1855.

50. *Ibid.*

51. Rhode Island Medical Society, "Minutes."

52. Paul Starr, *The Social Transformation of American Medicine* (New York, Basic Books, 1982), pp. 47–54.

53. Rhode Island Medical Society, "Minutes."

54. American Medical Association, *Transactions*, 11:9–51, 1858.

55. Rhode Island Medical Society, "Minutes."

56. American Medical Association, *Transactions*, 13:9–44, 1860.

57. Rhode Island Medical Society, "Minutes." Also, *Communications of the Rhode Island Medical Society*, v. 1, no. 2 [Second Part of its Proceedings], pp. 3–5, 1860.

58. Rhode Island Medical Society, "Minutes."

CHAPTER SEVENTEEN

The Final Act

Although Usher was now in his seventy-third year, his correspondence was active, his handwriting firm and youthful. Early in the new year, with Sumter still three months away, Usher wrote to W. W. Dobbins (January 22, 1861):[1]

> ... I fully endorse your remarks on the distracted state of our country. Nothing but an overruling power can save us from the vortex to which we are drifting. Another month I suppose will decide whether cotton and slavery are henceforth to rule our happy country. It may, however, be a step in progress towards emancipation, for slavery cannot exist much longer in this enlightened age. It is, however, a curious problem now before us what will be the fate of the border slave states. If they secede, then the laws will cease that now make us all negro catchers for the south, and those states will have to sell all their slaves south.

The diversity of Usher's interests was not diminished during his declining years. An association calling itself The Rhode Island Society for the Encouragment of Domestic Industry was currently very active in local affairs. Numbering eight hundred members, it was concerned with the promotion of "Horticulture, Manufactures, and the Mechanic Arts." Recently it had become involved in promoting the cultivation and processing of flax in Rhode Island. While not stated, this activity probably stemmed from concern that the impending war might cut off cotton supplies from the state's growing and important textile industry. The minutes of the January 23, 1861 meeting noted:[2] "Gov. [Elisha] Dyer presented a communication to the society, from Dr. Usher Parsons on flax culture and manufacture, which was received and ordered to be printed in the transactions of the Society."[3] Dyer was chairman of the Committee on Flax Culture. Although the motives for Usher's interest in the problem do not emerge, he was not deterred from expressing his views by any doubts about his qualifications in a field beyond his expertise.

Fort Sumter was bombarded on April 12, 1861. Despite his advanced years, Usher volunteered for military service. While it is not likely that his offer was taken seriously, a post of sorts was found for him. According to Charles,[4] "He was commissioned [by Governor Sprague] in June, 1861, surgeon of the Providence Horse Guards. He followed the varying fortunes of the conflict with intense interest." This local militia unit served as a Home Guard.

As of May, Usher apparently still expected to be called to active duty. On the 20th he wrote to Colonel Benjamin Emerson of Pittsfield, New Hampshire, husband of niece Frances Leighton:[5] "The prospect is that I shall not be wanted before autumn. The two R. Island Regts. enlisted for three months will be reduced to one Regt. for three years, and this Regt. will take the surgeons of the first Regt."

The Rhode Island Medical Society, with Charles Parsons in the chair and Usher Parsons present, held its fiftieth annual meeting on June 19, 1861 in the rooms of the Franklin Society of Providence.[6] The Society, actually forty-nine years old, had started counting anniversaries on the year of its birth. Although its members gathered in the shadow of a great war, the only reference to it in the records is an oblique one. Doctor Walter Channing of Boston, a native of Newport and the oldest living honorary fellow, sent a letter in which he paid tribute to the Society "for its prompt, practical and sublime patriotism at the call of a threatened country." After the annual dinner at the Aldrich House and "some remarks elicited from Dr. Usher Parsons . . . the members of the Society separated."

On June 28 Usher wrote to Laura Sanford of Erie, whose *The History of Erie County, Pennsylvania* was nearing completion:[7]

> I yesterday visited the naval school in Newport, on board the *Constitution*, and was delighted to see once more the identical flag, 'Don't give up the Ship', which Perry hoisted on board the *Lawrence* on going into action, and took with him to the *Niagara* when he had fought his own ship to the last. The flag was immediately sent to Washington by Lieutenant Forest, and has ever

since been preserved—of late years in the naval school—and is exhibited only on particular occasions. The sight of it created such emotions and reminiscences of the past that I could not refrain from shedding tears over it.

In the preface of her book Miss Sanford acknowledged the help she had received from Usher. On November 11 Usher wrote to Dobbins,[8] sending along for the benefit of Laura Sanford further details of the battle. Commenting on Bancroft's serialized history of the Battle of Lake Erie carried by the *New York Ledger*, Usher complained of "some errors," but deemed his description of the battle "very graphic." The account of the battle in Bancroft's published work was based largely on this story.

During 1861 another of Usher's numerous avocations bore fruit. "After his principal historical work was published," wrote Charles,[9] "and when he was about seventy years old [about 1857], he began to collate and arrange his notes on Indian localities in Rhode Island. He made new researches on this subject and by examination of various maps, of historical works relating to Rhode Island, and old records, collected many new names, with supposed explanations of some." The pamphlet of thirty-two pages, titled *Indian Names of Places in Rhode Island*,[10] contained over three hundred entries. Several of the names are repeated in different applications, that of Pettaquamscutt, for example, recurring as a river, a tract of land, and a rock. There are a few inadvertent repetitions, sometimes due to unimportant variations in spelling. In his preliminary remarks Usher discusses some interesting etymological sidelights and observes that "differences in the mode of spelling Indian names of places are very apparent in written documents and records, attributable to various dialects, but more to the changes in the language as uttered at different periods of time." The preface contains a charming historical sketch of the Narragansett Indians and a statement of his reasons for undertaking the study:

The Narragansett nation or tribe by whom this vocabulary was used, were in early times the most numerous and powerful of all the eastern Indians. They inhabited nearly all the present State of Rhode Island, including the islands in the bay, Block Island and the east end of Long Island. Their dominion extended northward to the Nipmucks in Providence county, and by conquest, eastward from the Pawcatuck river to the Merrimack. They were the most civilized and commercial tribe in New England, and so numerous, that, at one time, they could bring five thousand warriors into the field, and one could meet a dozen of their towns in the course of twenty miles travel.

The Narragansett language was considered a variety of the Delaware, and extended some hundreds of miles, but varied in its idioms within a comparatively short distance. It has ceased to be a spoken language in the tribe for nearly half a century. The best records of it remaining, are Roger Williams' key to the Indian language, and the Apostle Elliot's Bible and Grammar, and Cotton's Vocabulary.

In 1766, the Narrangasetts were reduced to three hundred and fifteen persons, residing on the Indian reserved lands, in Charlestown. In 1832, the number was precisely the same, but only seven of them were pure blooded. Last year, the number was reduced to two of three-fourths blood, and sixty-eight of less than quarter blood, the total being 122 who claim descent from the original Narragansett tribe, and all of them exhibiting marks of the race.[11]

No attempt is herein made, by the author, to examine Indian names of places as a philologist or grammarian, but merely to gather such as were in existence when civilization commenced, within the State of Rhode Island, according to its present boundary, and to indicate, as near as practicable, their exact locality; and, in a few instances, give the meaning or derivation of the word used.

I was led to this enterprise partly for the amusement it might afford in leisure hours, but more for the purpose of rescuing from oblivion names of places in use among the aborigines, and for the convenience of those who may hereafter wish to apply them to their country villas, factories, or institutions, as has often been done in this and other states.

Another aspect of local Indian lore occupied Usher's attention during the next year or two. Charles wrote:[12]

As early as the year 1841, he visited the Indian burying-ground and old fort [Fort Ninigret] in Charlestown, Rhode Island, and made some examinations of Indian graves. He went there several times in subsequent years, procured various Indian relics, wrote out descriptions of the places, and took part in some attempts at disinterment. In 1860, and again in 1861, he made these entries in his diary:[13]—"Saw the old Indian burying-ground and fort, and the articles lately dug up from Indian graves, as coins, wampum-peag, kitchen utensils, chains, iron and silver." * * * "Six of us went to the place and worked with spade till near midnight. Took up a well preserved skeleton, eight feet deep."

"When some Indian graves were afterwards opened by another party," added Charles, "Dr. Parsons bought many of the bones and articles found with them, and retained some in his possession at his death." Usher was fascinated by the subject and found several opportunities to present papers before various organizations based on this material. On October 7, 1862, at a quarterly meeting of the Rhode Island Historical Society[14] held in its Cabinet on Waterman Street, "after the transaction of the regular business, Dr. Usher Parsons read an interesting paper, interspersed with verbal descriptions, on Indian relics, lately found in Charlestown, in this state, with brief notices of the Nyantic tribe of Indians. . . .[15] The interest of the Doctor's papers was greatly enhanced by an exhibition of a portion of the relics, taken from the graves of Ninigret and his daughter, all in an excellent state of preservation. So large a collection has never before, probably been found in any Indian grave." The first portion of the published sketch is devoted to a description of Indian customs in regard to burial and to a history of the Nar-rangansett tribes, including the Niantics, whose reign started in the 1620s.

The most interesting portions of the account contain descriptions of the grave of Ninigret himself and that of his daughter. In May of 1859 several citizens of Charlestown, Rhode Island, spurred on by curiosity as to whether Indians were buried in a horizontal or sitting posture, repaired to the Sachem's burial ground with spades and crowbars. They began their excavation at the west end of the cemetery, reputedly the site of the earliest interment. Four feet down they encountered a floor or roof of flat stones, which they removed. Excavating another four feet, they struck a metallic object, which proved to be a large iron pot of some five-gallon capacity, filled with a variety of iron, copper, and brass skillets, small kettles, and sauce-pans. A large brass kettle contained glass bottles, pewter porringers, and small kettles. Below these objects they encountered decayed wood in the form of a large log surrounded by a chain and with hinges on one side and a padlock on the other. On breaking the chain, the top half of the log was easily lifted off. The log had been split into two nearly equal halves, each half excavated so that the whole could accommodate an adult body.

The body, when revealed, was elegantly arrayed in a green silk robe. A silk cloth covered the head, and from it descended a silver chain to the soles of a pair of copper moccasins lined with leather. These were of neat workmanship and indicated a slender and delicately formed foot. Around the waist was a belt covered with bead work of wampumpeag (Indian shell money) and studded with silver brooches. The neck was ornamented with both a wampumpeag collar and a copper necklace, while the arms were adorned with wampumpeag bracelets. Two loose coins were found, one an English farthing and the other a French silver half livre, scarcely worn at all, dated 1650 and bearing the legend *Ludovicus XIIII* (Louis XIV), whose reign began in 1643. The brightness of the coins indicated to Usher that the interment could be dated circa 1660.

Inside the sarcophagus was an assortment of tablespoons, a fork, pipes, several thimbles of Dutch plate on copper, and a large amount of wampumpeag equal to ten or twenty dollars in legal tender. There was also a sealed glass flask containing a brandy-like fluid which did not freeze in winter temperatures. The only artifacts of unquestionably Indian manufacture were stone mortars and pestles used for grinding corn. The fine preservation of the objects was attributed by Usher to the manner of excavating the log sarcophagus with heated stones "that charred the whole cavity, giving it an antiseptic quality." The skull was in an excellent state of preservation, with the tooth sockets symmetrical and perfect, indicating a fine set of teeth. The skull was well proportioned, and the hair was abundant and neatly dressed. There was strong evidence that the body was that of the daughter of Sachem Ninigret, as all of his other children had married and lived to advanced age. Her dress and ornaments denoted exalted rank, and she was buried in the first grave in the Sachem's cemetery, indicating that hers was the first death in the family.

The second death, twenty years later, was that of the Sachem himself. Usher was able "with some pains and trouble" to recover a skull and skeleton from the next adjacent grave. The bones conformed to an age of seventy, as did the angle of the lower jaw, as confirmed "by an eminent dentist." The *os femoris* (femur, *i.e.* the thigh bone) indicated a man of large stature, more than six feet tall. This was undoubtedly the skeleton of Ninigret himself, Sachem of the Niantics, and the smaller one with its elaborate array of relics that of his young daughter.

On the following evening at a meeting of the Rhode Island Medical Society in Newport,[16] Usher "exhibited some coins and articles of Jewellry recently removed from the grave of an Indian Princess in the Town of Charlestown in this State. He also stated the name and lineage of the chieftain's daughter and described the very careful and secure manner of interment. As a point of anatomical interest it should be recorded that the Doctor found in the grave a moccasin from whose dainty proportions he inferred a small and comely foot." Usher twice more presented this material to interested audiences. At a meeting of the Massachusetts Historical Society,[17] "Dr. Usher Parsons, Corresponding Member, exhibited a large collection of curious relics of the Indians of Rhode Island, recently exhumed near the seashore, on ground which formerly belonged to the Sachem Ninigret"; and before the New York Historical Society in New York City he read a formal paper on the subject.[18]

There are sidelights to this affair, which were not revealed until many years later. Sidney Smith Rider, the Rhode Island historian, writing a half century after the event, quoted from another account of the same episode in Tucker's *Historical Sketch of the Town of Charlestown*, published in 1877.[19] Although some differences in the accounts were, as Rider expressed it, "material," they were "not fatal." There were details in Tucker's account, however, "which Parsons either did not know, or suppressed." After giving a brief account of the origin of the venture, Rider continued:[20]

Quite a large collection of relics were taken out of the grave and carried to the village of Crows [Cross] Mills, whence a portion of them were sent to Brown University, in Providence, as I have been informed. A suit was brought against these men by Henry Hazard, John Noca and Gideon Ammons of the tribe, for opening the grave and taking therefrom sundry articles, or, in other words for crime and misdemeanor against the laws of the State of Rhode Island. They were arraigned before Joseph H. Griffin, Justice of the Peace, examined, and held to answer therefor before the Supreme Court of Kingston, where they were duly acquitted, and exonerated from blame. . . . Subsequently Dr. Parsons of Providence opened quite a number of graves to obtain a supply of scientific curiosities. Those who saw his collection make the assertion that he did not accumulate one-half as many relics as the party found in the first grave, against whom the prosecution was directed.

Rider also recalled the following:[21]

> On the evening of the 7th of October, 1862, nearly 50 years ago, the Rhode Island Historical Society held a meeting to listen to a paper from Dr. Usher Parsons about the opening of a grave. I was a member, and present; there were about 18 members present. I was the 18th—not one of these members, myself excepted, is now living. I took up the skull and found on the back of it a small bunch of what I took to be earth, but it proved to be filled with short pieces of black hair; with my knife I lifted a bit and carried it home. I brought my microscope to bear upon it.
>
> It was a bit of hair. I mounted it in Canada balsam on a 'slide' for use under my microscope, which I was then much interested in using. I can show that the hair was jet black like that of all Indian women. I can show that it is tubercular. I have the 'slide', and the microscope to this day. All of this came to me when I read . . . Tucker's History, and rushed at once to find the skull. But nobody had ever heard of it. I ran, actually ran, to Rhode Island Hall [at Brown University] to see their skulls. Dr. [Albert Davis] Mead [of the Brown biology department] led me to them, and there I found one beneath which was a card on which was written, "Skull of Sachem Ninigret's Daughter, Charlestown. Prof. C. W. Parsons, M.D., see Historical Magazine, Feb. 1863." It was the skull of Weunquesh, the daughter of Ninigret; she became the Queen of the Niantics upon her father's death in 1676.

Whether the skull belonged to an Indian princess who died twenty years before Sachem Ninigret's departure to an Indian heaven or survived to succeed him as queen of the Niantics is a question for other historians to ponder.

Usher's preoccupation with Indian anthropology did not preempt other interests. On January 21, 1862 he "exhibited a silver hilted sword worn by Gen. Pepperrell in the seige of Louisburg" before a meeting of the Rhode Island Historical Society.[22] Later he gave the sword to the Massachusetts Historical Society, along with a portrait of his late father-in-law, the Reverend Abiel Holmes. The gifts were announced at the annual meeting of April 10, 1862.[23]

At the July 1862 meeting of the Massachusetts Historical Society George Livermore, antiquarian and vigorous proponent of the Union cause, read selections from a scholarly essay of two hundred pages on a timely subject:[24] "Respecting the Opinions of the Founders of the Republic on Negroes as Slaves, as Citizens, and as Soldiers," which Abraham Lincoln consulted in preparing the Emancipation Proclamation. Edward Everett, the distinguished orator and abolitionist, expressed the hope "that Mr. Livermore would extend his researches so as to include the services of colored seamen in the American Navy."[25] In the published paper, Livermore was able to comply, presenting "testimony on this subject of one of our Honorary Members, Usher Parsons, M.D., whose character and experience give authority to his statements." The information was contained in a letter from Usher dated October 18, 1862:[26]

> In reply to your inquiries about the employing of blacks in our navy in the war of 1812, and particularly in the battle of Lake Erie, I refer you to documents in Mackenzie's "Life of Commodore Perry," vol i, pp. 166 and 167. [Captain Perry to Commodore Chauncey: "The men that came by Mr. Champlin are a motley set,—blacks, soldiers, and boys. I cannot think you saw them after they were selected. I am, however, pleased to see anything in the shape of a man." Chauncey in reply to Perry: "I regret that you are not pleased with the men. . . . I have yet to learn that the color of the skin, or the cut and trimmings of the coat, can affect a man's qualifications or usefulness. I have nearly fifty blacks on board of this ship, and many of them are among my best men. . . ."]
> In 1814 our fleet sailed to the Upper Lakes to co-operate with Colonel Croghan at Mackinac. About one in ten or twelve of the crews were black. In 1816 I was surgeon of the *Java* under Commodore Perry. The white and colored seamen messed together. About one in six or eight were colored. In 1819 I was surgeon of the *Guerrière,* under Commodore Macdonough; and the proportion of blacks was about the same in her crew. There seemed to be an entire absense of prejudice against the blacks as messmates among the crew. What I have said applied to the crews of the other ships that sailed in squadrons.

Usher's testimony was very possibly influenced by the climate of the times, but nevertheless appears to have been objective. The subject was very timely at the height of the war. There was prejudice abroad that blacks would make poor combat soldiers. This attitude had Rhode Island ramificatioins as well. The 14th Regiment, Rhode

Island's black Civil War military contingent, had to fight for the privilege of participating in the war, and then, on their return, the black veterans were obliged to agitate further to get the equal pay promised to them.[27] At an earlier period, during the Revolution, some one hundred fifty blacks had joined the existing first Rhode Island regiment and fought valiantly under white officers against the British on Aquidneck Island in the Battle of Rhode Island. Slave recruits received their freedom if they survived. Many other free blacks as well went off to the war. Blacks also had a considerable experience at sea. Ironically, blacks served as crewmen even aboard slave ships in Rhode Island's triangular trade, in the navy after the war, and aboard coasters and other merchantmen, privateers, and whaling vessels.[28] During the years 1803 to 1807, when blacks comprised but seven per cent of the population of Newport, Rhode Island, black seamen made up twenty-one per cent of all Newport crews engaged in the West Indian, European, and African trades.[29]

Despite his advanced years, Usher's participation in medical affairs had not noticeably diminished. His name apeared in the minutes of a spring meeting of the Rhode Island Medical Society on April 22, 1862 in connection with no less than three separate items of business.[30] At the annual meeting on June 4, Charles retired from the presidency, having served two terms. Usher attended the Connecticut Medical Society meeting as a delegate from Rhode Island and "bore warm testimony of the courtesy and ability of that body."[31] At the fall meeting of the Rhode Island Medical Society on October 8 in the Redwood Library in Newport,[32] Usher presented his Indian relics, and a collation and an excellent lunch followed. Despite these gay amenities, echoes of the distant war could be heard on the shores of Narragansett Bay: "The Fellows present at this meeting had the pleasure of making the acquaintance and enjoying the society of two gentlemen attached to the Military Hospital at Portsmouth Grove, [the commanding officer] Dr. [George Miller] Sternberg of the U.S. Army, and Dr. Bernoni [Benoni] Carpenter of Attleborough, Mass." This great Army General Hospital of over two thousand beds in nearby Portsmouth on Aquidneck Island had recently been established amid a welter of confusion and criticism.[33]

Usher continued to see occasional patients during this period. Charles wrote,[34] "For several years before his death, Dr. Parsons was almost wholly withdrawn from active practice, though he

sometimes visited in consultation and even performed some operations. His last amputation was of the fore-arm, performed when
he was seventy-four years old, in Rehoboth"—which would have
been just about this time.

Late in 1862 Usher had completed his "Brief Sketches of the
Officers Who Were in the Battle of Lake Erie," upon which he had
been working for several years. It appeared in the *New England
Historical and Genealogical Register* of January, 1863, together
with a sketch of Usher by the editors. A by-product of his accounts
of the battle, it has proved useful to historians over the years.

While the question of a general hospital in Providence had been
dormant for a number of years, developments at this time warranted
renewed hope. Although Usher had resigned in 1855 from the Providence Medical Association's Committee on a Hospital, his lively
interest in the project had not diminished. Moses Brown Ives, who
had died in 1857, bequeathed $50,000 to be devoted to such objects
of beneficence as his trustees might select. After bequests to various
charities, $40,000 remained. Toward the close of 1862 the trustees—
Robert Hale Ives and Thomas Poynton Ives—determined to devote
the balance to the establishment of a general hospital. In January
1863 a group of twelve Providence physicians petitioned the legislature for a hospital charter. Usher's name headed the list. The
Rhode Island Hospital was chartered in March 1863. Doctor J. W.
C. Ely, a member of the original hospital staff, many years later
recalled these events:[35]

> . . . during the years 1855, 1856, and 1857, Mr. Thomas Poynton
> Ives was a student of medicine in my office, attended lectures at
> the College of Physicians and Surgeons, in New York, completed
> a full course, but did not take the degree [or practice]. . . . His
> father, Moses Brown Ives, died during the summer of 1857. Before
> this the son induced his father to make a bequest in his will to
> a hospital whenever it should be built in Providence. This bequest
> was $40,000. This I know to be true, as he requested the medical
> attendant of his father to urge upon him the great necessity of a
> hospital in the city, and also the duty of those possessed of wealth
> to establish it. . . .
>
> In 1861, upon the breaking out of the war between the North
> and South, Mr. Thomas P. Ives gave to the government his yacht,
> *Hope,* for a gun boat and received a commission as lieutenant
> commander and served through the war. Late in the year 1862,

Charles William Parsons, M.D. (1821–1895). The only child of Mary and Usher Parsons, he became Professor of Physiology at Brown University. Brown University Archives.

Oliver Wendell Holmes, M.D. (1809–1894), brother-in-law of Usher Parsons, as a young man. He and Usher Parsons's son Charles grew up together virtually as brothers. Countway Library, Harvard Medical School.

Sham naval battle at Put-in-Bay Island celebrating on September 10, 1880 the 67th anniversary of Perry's victory on Lake Erie. While Usher Parsons was not there to witness this event, it was strongly reminiscent of the 45th anniversary celebration at Put-in-Bay in 1858, and of the 47th anniversary celebration at Cleveland in 1860 with its sham battle, in both of which Usher participated. Print of engraving from sketches by French Bros., showing a

Romeo Elton, D.D. (1790–1870), Professor of Greek and Latin at Brown University from 1825 to 1843. He was a close friend and correspondent of Usher Parsons. Oil painting from a photograph by James Sullivan Lincoln in the Brown University collections.

High view of the Cove, Providence, 1860. Taken from the steeple of Grace Church by Manchester Brothers. A small portion of the railroad station designed by Thomas A. Tefft can be seen at the far right extremity of the Cove. Usher Parsons described the Cove and station in his letters. Rhode Island Historical Society.

Rhode Island Hospital, Providence. Engraving of architect's rendering (1863–1868 period) of its appearance when completed. Rhode Island Historical Society.

Usher Parsons, as he appeared in his later years. Rhode Island Historical Society.

being at home on a furlough, he called at the office and desired me to get the signatures of the physicians. . . . to the petition for the hospital Charter, which I did.

On June 3, 1863 at the annual meeting of the Rhode Island Medical Society[36] "the members of the Society were invited to attend a meeting of the Corporation of the Rhode Island Hospital, this day." The membership adopted the following resolution: "That this Society view with the deepest interest the successful progress of the movement for the foundation of a Rhode Island Hospital,—a movement which began with the medical profession of the City of Providence . . . and we promise to the corporators of the Hospital all the aid and influence we can furnish."

The Society on December 16, 1863, at the request of the Board of Trustees[37] of the hospital, appointed a committee "with whom the Committee on plans of this board may consult with regard to the construction and arrangements of the Hospital buildings." Charles Parsons was a member of the Committee, but Usher was not mentioned. (He was, however, again named delegate to the American Medical Association.) The hospital committee, headed by Isaac Ray, distinguished superintendant of Butler Hospital, was "favorably impressed by the general plan," which embodied "the most approved results of modern experience." The report, containing certain constructive suggestions regarding ventilation and sanitation, concluded, "In the examination of the plan, the committee were joined by Drs. Usher Parsons, Mauran, L. L. Miller, and N. Miller, and we are allowed to state that these gentlemen all fully concur in the above suggestions." The first three surely qualified as elder statesmen, ranging in age from sixty-four to seventy-seven years. As Ely later recalled, "Dr. Usher Parsons did more than talk; he gave $1,000."

But while Ely gave Usher, whom he referred to as "another noted surgeon," full credit for his part in the founding of the Rhode Island Hospital, he was more reserved in his estimate of Usher's capacities:[38]

Short, stout, of a waddling gait, bald—when his baldness was not concealed by a yellowish brown wig, none of the personal charms of Drs. Miller and Mauran, yet he was more widely known out of the State and in it than any medical man we had.

He was at one time one of the vice presidents of the American

Medical Association. He had taken several of the Boylston and
Fiske fund prizes, had served as surgeon for Perry's flagship, the
Lawrence, and it was not much of a meeting—either medical or
other—that those present did not have a chance to learn that fact.
He was a slovenly operator—no manual dexterity. His surgical
judgement may have been great, but I failed to discover it, yet it
is but simple justice to his memory to state that year after year,
in both this society and the city association, he urged the importance and necessity of a city hospital. At last he brought about
the appointment of a committee to apply to the General Assembly for a charter. Dr. Parsons did much by talk to arouse an
interest in this charity. . . .

From June 7 to 9 Usher and Charles attended the A.M.A. session
of 1864 in New York.[39] Doctor James Anderson of New York cited
one of war's realities in his welcome to the visitors: "Let us trust
[that] the time is not far distant when we may again offer to our
alienated brethren the hand of professional fellowship which it is
our privilege to extend to you this day." Usher was awarded two
signal honors: election to permanent membership in the Association and an invitation to sit on the platform. The illustrious Charles
Édouard Brown-Séquard, who had recently been appointed professor
of neurophysiology at Harvard, was similarly honored.[40] Charles
Parsons was appointed to the Committee on Education.

Concerning the many cultural activities in which Usher was even
now engaged, Charles wrote:[41]

Dr. Parsons's various labors were recognized by his election to
many literary and historical societies. He was a corresponding
member of the historical societies of Maine, Massachusetts, New
York, New Jersey, Georgia and Wisconsin, the American Antiquarian Society, the Academy of Natural Sciences, &c. He was
an active member of the New England Historic Genealogical
Society, and was its Vice-President for Rhode Island from September 1864 till his death.

Usher had planned to travel to Philadelphia in mid-April by Long
Island Sound steamer and rail, but his plans were abruptly changed
by sad news from Washington. President Lincoln was assassinated
on April 14, 1865. Memorial services, which Usher planned to
attend, were held in churches throughout Providence on April 19.
He eventually made good his departure on the 24th and visited his
nephews George and Edwin in New York on the return trip.[42]

The April 1865 issue of the *New England Historical and Genealogical Register*[43] carried another of Usher's genealogical studies, the "Memoir of Honorble James F. Baldwin." Baldwin married Sarah Parsons Pitkin of East Hartford, Connecticut and thus was related to Usher's family through marriage. A native of Massachusetts, he had planned the Middlesex Canal in that state and had made surveys for the Boston and Albany Railroad and of the water resources of the City of Boston. Sarah Pitkin, a distant cousin, and Usher had corresponded many years earlier, as we have noted, regarding mutual genealogical interests.[44]

From June 6 to 9 Usher attended for the last time the meetings of the American Medical Association held, conveniently, in Boston.[45] He and Charles were delegates from Rhode Island. Henry J. Bigelow of the Committee on Arrangements welcomed the delegates gathered in the elegant Bulfinch State House and spoke eloquently of the recent end of the "titantic struggle" between the North and South. On the afternoon of the 8th, the members were taken on a steamboat excursion down Boston harbor "by invitation of the city government."[46]

A few weeks later the annual session of the Rhode Island Medical Society was held in Providence with both Usher and Charles in attendance.[47] Usher "read a very interesting notice of Dr. [William Gorham] Shaw" of Wickford, Rhode Island, who had died in his ninety-sixth year. A charter member of the Rhode Island Medical Society, his long life had spanned the period from colonial times to the Civil War. Unfortunately, the text has not survived. "It was voted, on motion of Dr. Usher Parsons, that a list of Fellows and Honorary Members of the Society be printed with the next volume of its communications." It did not actually appear until 1877. According to a newspaper account,[48] "Drs. Usher Parsons and Hervey Armington, desiring to retire from active membership of the Society, their request was referred to a [special] committee. . . ." It was later voted that a Fellow of the Society upon reaching the age of seventy years "be exempted from taxation, and shall enjoy and possess all the rights and privileges belonging to this Society," a custom that still prevails.

On August 14, 1865 Usher wrote to his nephew George Parsons:[49] "I think you act wisely in going to the springs [Saratoga] and it is not improbable that I shall join you [there next week] if Charles gets better. He has been confined to his bed with fever two days and though not dangerously ill is likely to be kept in for some days. You ... should drink freely of the Empire spring. It has the most iron and will do you [the] most good. . . ."

During November of 1865 Usher traveled to Kennebunk with nephew Edwin, but because of heavy rains visits to his various kin scattered about York County were curtailed. By the 27th he was back in Providence.[50]

Usher's still lively correspondence with his friends in England, the Owens, had spanned a period of more than two decades.[51] Caroline, with a few exceptions, was responsible for keeping up the London end of the exchange, explaining apologetically that Richard worked "incessantly" with little relaxation. Topics discussed were mostly personal, relating to home life and work. Caroline wrote that there were spare rooms waiting for Usher and Charles and Charles's wife Mary on the estate that had been given the Owens by Queen Victoria in recognition of Richard's important work, but it never came to pass that the Parsonses could take advantage of the invitation. "I must say," observed Caroline, "I wish, with you, there was a little family, but that may still, if it please God, arrive." She knew of two separate instances where "a fine healthy child" had materialized after twelve and thirteen years of disappointment. Usher sent the Owens a copy of his *Pepperrell*, volumes of Wendell's poems, and a copy of Wendell's novel *Elsie Venner*, which elicited complimentary appraisals from Caroline. They exchanged photographs of the various family members, a practice apparently initiated by Usher. In the last years of the correspondence they were preoccupied with the American Civil War. The Owens' view of the conflict was colored by Britain's dependence upon Southern cotton for its burgeoning textile mills, which annoyed Usher. In December 1865, however, Caroline sent her "heartfelt congratulations on the [outcome of the] dreadful struggle which has convulsed your noble country."[52]

In January 1866 Usher replied to this letter with news of his small family[53] (these letters proved to be the last of their long correspondence):

Our little family remain in status quo as to numbers. My son was appointed professor of animal and vegetable physiology [at Brown] about a year since. He gives in the spring and summer terms about 80 lectures. The College is within fifty rods of our dwelling, so that it is very convenient and interferes but little with his practice. He was appointed to fill a vacancy that occurred only two weeks before he commenced, which was a brief time to prepare. But by great industry he lectured five times a week. During the last autumn he has been very busy in preparing for the next course, and has a fine opportunity to gain a high reputation. His studies lead him into a better acquaintance with Mr. Owen's writings than he would otherwise have, and to appreciate duly the grounds of his exalted reputation.

I have retired from practice and give much of my time to historical studies, and in writings for our periodicals—and to horticulture, being associated with others. I am also engaged somewhat in perfecting a large and elegant Hospital, now nearly completed, and which will be superior to any in America, and will be opened in the course of the next summer. . . . Although retired I attend the meetings of the Medical Societies—have been President of our State Society and of the National Association, whose meetings comprise as members about all the respectable medical men of the land. Sometimes a thousand are present. . . . My kind regards. . . .

No further letters to or from the Owens survive. After a quarter of a century, in the twilight years of Usher's life, the spirited correspondence came to an end. There is little doubt that Usher was beguiled and deeply flattered by his long and cordial relationship with Caroline and Richard Owen. He considered Owen to be "the greatest naturalist of the age."

During the last years of his life Usher worked on a fifth edition of his *Physician for Ships*,[54] which appears to have reached publication posthumously. His last work published before his death was the carefully prepared "Pepperrell Genealogy," which appeared in the January 1866 issue of the *New England Historical and Genealogical Register*.[55] The study was largely a by-product of Usher's earlier Pepperrell researches, but he was probably also assisted in its preparation by Caroline Owen through her nearby access to British sources. Only one child of the first Sir William, his daughter Elizabeth, survived to produce issue. Elizabeth's son, William Pepperrell Sparhawk at the request of his grandfather changed his name to William Pepperrell, and became in turn the second Sir William. Usher concluded with a fine edge of irony:

> The foregoing sketch of the descendants of the second Sir William Pepperrell presents a striking contrast, compared with the

descendants of his brothers and sister [all of whom supported the
Revolution]. They all number less than a dozen of highly respectable individuals, whilst those that descended from the single
loyalist, who was driven from America at the commencement of
the Revolution, comprise probably a hundred, holding the highest
social position, including dignitaries in church and state, Baron-
ets, Presidents of Colleges, D.D.'s, and Bishops and others of
exalted rank, perhaps more numerous than can be found in any
one family in the British realms.

Charles's *Memoir* describes his father during this period:[56]

His sturdy health of body and mind gradually failed, but with
very little suffering, and with many circumstances fitted to make
old age happy. An increasing forgetfulness in regard to business
matters, and hesitancy in speech and uncertainty in locomotion,
showed that his powerful brain was yielding to the natural
changes in its texture; but he still enjoyed reading, frequented
the Athenaeum [across from his home], called at the houses of a
few familiar friends, kept up a rather extensive correspondence,
visited his near relatives in Maine and New York City, and interested himself in watching the progress of the Rhode Island
Hospital.

His letters, perhaps because of his greater leisure, were clearly written and firm of hand, and his spelling and syntax were almost
perfect. Never had his notes to his friends and relatives been more
carefully composed.

Usher regularly attended meetings of the Massachusetts Historical Society in Boston. He also very likely continued to attend
sessions of the Providence Medical Association and the Rhode Island Medical Society, but his name did not again appear in the
minutes of either. He was occupied less and less with medical
affairs.

Dimming echoes of his long life were still occasionally heard.
Lossing wrote in his history of the War of 1812:[57] "Dr. Parsons is
still (1867) in the enjoyment of perfect physical and mental health,
at the age of seventy-nine years." And on June 10 Usher wrote to
his niece Abigail Lewis Gerrish of South Berwick, Maine:[58]

... I shall probably be in Berwick very soon for I want to see
you. ... I have enjoyed good health as we all have. Two months
since, being in Salem, I called at the Academy to see your nieces,
but found them out. I shall again soon, perhaps in a week from

this. Would you like to accompany me again to Alfred and spend two days there? I thought when I last saw your brother Daniel that his health was much improved. I shall see him again as I go eastward next week. I feel the infirmities of old age coming over me fast, and very much doubt if I shall ever visit the County of York again after my next trip.

Charles is well and doing well enough in his Profession whilst I am left entirely in the lurch. But I still cling to my childhood friends, to none of them more than to yourself. I almost think that I will leave here and take up my abode with yourself, but I have but a short time to pass anywhere. Am now in my 79th year. I visited New York recently and passed two days very pleasantly with George and Charles. They are about to leave there for Kennebunk for the summer. George has a very good wife and a son that is very likely and healthy.

We are in our house opposite the Atheneum [254 Benefit Street], better situated than we ever were before, and [have] a good lodging room for you when you favor us with another visit, which I wish may be soon.

What Usher saw during this last visit to Alfred doubtless saddened him. He wrote that "the town is fast declining and is not to be compared with what it was formerly in respectability. The Bank has burst up, and stockholders and perhaps bill holders are losers."[59] The decline has been well chronicled by a contemporary, Samuel M. Came, a life-long resident of Alfred. He wrote in 1876 at the time of its Centennial Celebration:[60]

Each of the three classes [of settlers—merchants and professional men, mechanics and manufacturers, and farmers] decreased in number from 1845 to 1867. The growth of other places in the County, especially Saco & Biddeford, drew away professional men, which lessened trade. The small demand for lumber for home use and the increased facilities for obtaining it at other places lessened that business, while the Western fever and the war decreased the farming population. This continued till about 1867, when Alfred may be said to have reached the lowest ebb of its prosperity. During the Summer & Fall of 1866 there was but one store in town supplied with a general variety of goods and even this was not overburdened with customers. As if to give a final blow to mercantile business, this store, together with the old Griffin Hotel, so long a pleasing and conspicuous landmark, were burned in Jan. 1867, sadly marring the beauty of our village.

About Usher, Came wrote:

The strength of local associations was a marked trait. It prompted him to revisit often the localities of his youth, and to write the history of his native town [published posthumously in 1872]. Another characteristic was his ready sympathies and strong affections. They made him tenacious in friendship. He would go out of his way to visit the humble roof of an acquaintance in early life, and the honest smile and cordial greeting revealed the delight which the interview afforded him. When with the breadth of his reflective powers, and love of the old he pondered over time honored institutions, his affections clung to them as a living friend. In regard to his social intercourse, one has written: "That his was a genial temperament, kindly heart with much of the jovial spirit of the seas in his hours of relaxation."

In a letter to his brother-in-law Charles Wentworth Upham, Usher took note of the recent publication of Upham's literary classic, *Salem Witchcraft*, (October 22, 1867):[61]

Your favour was duly received the day after I had received a copy of your magnificent work. On the day following (yesterday) I conversed with Revd. Prof. Dimon [Jeremiah Lewis Diman],[62] who writes the choicest articles for the Providence Journal, and found him very willing to write a Review of your work, and he will call today for it, after receiving Genl. Sherman at the College.

As the work is in the Atheneum[63] opposite our house, I can read it there at my leisure and would therefore prefer you not sending me a copy, but let the publishers have the full benefit of *sales*, until they are remunerated for their responsible undertaking. I will write brief notices for other papers and do what I can to help the sale.

During the last year of his life, Usher lived largely in retirement. Yet he retained his faculties and had the great satisfaction of knowing that the goal of his declining years, the opening of the Rhode Island Hospital, had been realized.

It was a handsome structure for its day and the most advanced example of hospital architecture in the world. Chairman of the building committee was Thomas Perkins Shepard,[64] a graduate of Brown University (A.B. and A.M. 1836) and the Harvard Medical School (M.D. 1840), who had studied for four years in Europe and was now a successful industrial chemist in Providence. He had had a large acquaintance with the leading hospitals of Europe and together with his committee had recently visited those of New England, New York, and Pennsylvania. According to Professor William Gammell of Brown University, who gave the principal address at the dedication ceremony,[65] the chairman had concluded "that ours is not surpassed by any other that exists." The architects were A. C. Morse of Providence, who designed the exterior, and Samuel Sloan of Philadelphia, the interior.[66] The new complex conformed well to the high standards set by the trustees and approved by the Medical Society with Usher's concurrence.

The dedication took place at eleven o'clock on the morning of October 1, 1868. Usher was conducted to a seat on the platform as the guest of honor. Professor Gammell's address, an eloquent but lengthy affair, referred to the prominent role played by the Providence Medical Association, which had advocated a hospital as early as 1851. "This was done," said the Professor, "at the instance of their President, Dr. Usher Parsons, our venerable friend, who today beholds the full accomplishment of all his benevolent plans." According to Charles,[67] "He wrote in his diary the next day, with a trembling hand, 'I feel very happy for yesterday's doing'."

The library of the new edifice, already containing some 1350 volumes, owed its riches to the gifts of books from four Rhode Islanders, including 250 volumes from the library of Usher Parsons. The three other donations were bequests from Doctor Ezekial Fowler of Woonsocket and from Doctors Nathaniel Miller and J. Davis Jones, both of Providence—all of whom had died very recently, "two of them in the prime of their career." Fowler, trained by apprenticeship, died at age 76, leaving not only 500 volumes, but a considerable estate to Rhode Island Hospital. Jones, who had studied in the United States and Europe and obtained his M.D. degree at Harvard Medical School, deceased at the untimely age of 28, bequeathed 100 volumes to the hospital. Miller, who had studied for two years in Paris, died at age 42, leaving to the hospital 300 volumes, mostly in French.[68]

Usher was appointed to the staff of Consulting Physicians and Surgeons, and Charles to the Active Staff as Visiting Physician.[69] The first patient, a fifty-nine year old Scotsman, a shoemaker by trade, was admitted on October 6 because of necrosis of the upper jaw. An extensive and ultimately successful maxillary (upper jaw) resection for what proved to be a cancer was carried out under ether on October 10 by a well-trained, handsome young surgeon, George

Edward Mason. A fistula was later closed by plastic surgery, and the patient lived out a normal life. At the annual meeting of the corporation on November 10, it was reported that this striking event had taken place in the "presence of Consulting Surgeons who were present from all parts of the State." We have it on the authority of Charles that Usher was among them. As pointed out by Garland, this case was presented (by this author) ninety years later before a meeting of the New England Cancer Society at the Rhode Island Hospital. It was generally agreed that medical science in 1958 could not have done better.[70] The brilliant success of this first case augured well for the future of the fine institution which Usher had done so much to foster.

Barely a week later Usher contracted what would prove to be his last illness. "On the evening of October 17," wrote Charles, "after exposure to cold, he had a severe acute attack, involving the brain, and followed by persistent nausea, headache and confusion of mind." Yet he rallied sufficiently to leave the house on November 3, characteristically, to vote in the Presidential election.[71] This turn of events offered enough hope that Wendell could write to Charles on November 11, ". . . I had not heard of your father's illness which I am glad to know is in the way of amendment," and added, "I am glad to hear of your new Hospital and that you are engaged in it."[72]

Yet the end was near at hand. Charles described the last few weeks of Usher's life:[73]

> He continued to go out almost every day for a month more, but with feeble and uncertain steps, and a degree of mental disorder that gave his family great anxiety. From December 4, he was again confined to the house and mostly to his chamber, and died on the morning of December 19, 1868, aged eighty years and four months. He was very faithfully attended in his last sickness by his friend Dr. Stephen S. Keene. An autopsy showed chronic degeneration in the arteries and membranes of the brain, and acute inflammatory disease in the cerebellum. This last probably dated from the 17th of October, and was the immediate cause of death. His funeral was kindly attended by Rev. J. G. Vose, of the Beneficent Congregational church. He was buried in Swan Point Cemetery.

In his last will and testament,[74] drawn some two years before his death, Usher left charitable bequests of $100 each to the Rhode Island Medical Society, the American Antiquarian Society, the Shelter for Colored Children in the City of Providence, the Children's Friend Society of Providence, the Old Ladies Home of Providence, and the Rhode Island Hospital. After further bequests to his various nieces and nephews, the bulk of his estate was left in trust to his son Charles.

His obituary,[75] prepared by son Charles and read before the Rhode Island Medical Society, covered in condensed form much of the same ground as Charles's later *Memoir*. It contained these sentences which summarized his life: "He gradually became very prominent in the profession, especially as a consulting and operating surgeon, and had a large practice outside of Providence. He performed repeatedly many of the capital [major] operations. He had more than fifty private medical students, kept up the practice of dissections, and was Professor of Anatomy in Brown University, 1822–1827. . . . Dr. Parsons engaged in many studies outside of medical pursuits— in some branches of natural science, and in some departments of historical and antiquarian inquiry. He was an industrious genealogist."

The notice of his death which appeared in *The Providence Daily Journal*[76] was lengthy, but contained this succinct appraisal: "The members of many classes in college [neighboring Brown University] looked upon him as their physician and friend. . . . As a surgeon, his reputation for a long time after coming to the State, was superior to that of any other in the State, and his opinion as well as his skill as an operator, was often sought in difficult cases, both in the city and in all of the neighboring country." While Usher Parsons was a man of varied accomplishments, this assessment would have given him much satisfaction, since he was, before all else, a physician.

NOTES

1. Usher Parsons to W. W. Dobbins, January 22, 1861, Buffalo Historical Society.

2. Rhode Island Society for the Encouragement of Domestic Industry, *Transactions for the Year 1860* [sic] (Providence, Knowles, Anthony & Co., 1861), p. 11. This volume was actually for the year 1861.

3. *Ibid.*, p. 64–71.

4. C. W. Parsons *Memoir*, p. 39

5. Usher Parsons to Benjamin Emerson, May 20, 1861, Parsons Memorial Library, Alfred, Maine.

6. Rhode Island Medical Society, "Minutes;" also, *Communications of the Rhode Island Medical Society*, v. 1, no. 3. Second Part [Proceedings], pp. 13–18, 1861.

7. Usher Parsons to Laura G. Sanford, June 28, 1861, transcript, published in Laura G. Sanford, *The History of Erie County, Pennsylvania* (Philadelphia, J. B. Lippincott, 1862), p. 266.

8. Usher Parsons to W. W. Dobbins, November 11, 1861, Buffalo Historical Society.

9. C. W. Parsons *Memoir*, p. 45.

10. Usher Parson, *Indian Names of Places in Rhode Island* (Providence, Knowles, Anthony & Co., 1861).

11. The remnants of the Narragansetts have only recently been recognized as a tribal council by the federal government.

12. C. W. Parsons *Memoir*, p. 45.

13. The original manuscript has not been discovered.

14. *Providence Daily Journal*, October 8, 1862. Also, Rhode Island Historical Society, "Minutes."

15. Usher Parsons, "Indian Relics Recently Found in Charlestown, R.I., With Brief Notices of the Nyantic Tribe of Indians," *The Historical Magazine*, 7:41–44, 1863. This was read before the Rhode Island and New York Historical Societies.

16. Rhode Island Medical Society, "Minutes."

17. Massachusetts Historical Society, *Proceedings*, 1862–1863, p. 428.

18. See note 15.

19. William Franklin Tucker, *Historical Sketch of the Town of Charlestown in Rhode Island, from 1836–1876* (Westerly, R. I., G. B. and J. H. Turner, 1877).

20. Sidney S. Rider, "Aborigine Remains in Rhode Island and the Exhumation of Weunquesh Daughter of Ninigret, and Queen of the Niantics, Part 2," *Book Notes: Historical, Literary and Critical*, 29:25–32, 1912.

21. *Ibid.*, Part 1, 29:17–24, 1912.

22. Rhode Island Historical Society, "Minutes." See also p. 340.

23. Massachusets Historical Society, *Proceedings*, 1862–1863, p. 17. Ellis Ames, an alumnus of Brown University, class of 1830, and a lawyer of Canton, Massachusetts wrote in a letter to Charles many years later: "I became acquainted with Dr. Parsons in 1827. I was more unwell while in college than in all the rest of my life; he was my physician. . . . During the last 14 years of his life he & I met at the meetings of the Massachusetts Historical Society in Boston (of which he was a corresponding and I a resident member) so often that I was of opinion that he selected the days to go to Boston when the Society met. The Massachusetts Historical Society regarded him always as a distinguished visitor. He was at one of our meetings a short time before his death. . . . He was one of my most delightful acquaintances and the picture of

him in your book [the *Memoir*] is just like him in the prime of life."
Ellis Ames to Charles W. Parsons, April 22, 1876, collection of the late
Miss Georgia Stearns, Alfred, Maine.

24. Massachusetts Historical Society, *Proceedings*, 1862–1863, p. 78.

25. *Ibid.*, p. 79.

26. *Ibid.*, pp. 239–240. Printed here is a transcript of the letter of Usher
Parsons to George Livermore, Octobeer 18, 1862.

27. Jay Coughtry, *Creative Survival: The Providence Black Community in
the 19th Century* (Providence, The Rhode Island Black Heritage Society, 1984), p. 65. This was a catalog of an exhibit shown at the Rhode
Island Historical Society and elsewhere. Materials also come from some
of the captions in the exhibit.

28. *Ibid.*, pp. 41–43, and caption at the exhibit. Also, Elmo Paul, *The
American Whaleman* (New York, Longmans, Green, 1928), pp. 50–51,
and Charles Boardman Hawes, *Whaling* (Garden City, N.Y., Doubleday,
1924), pp. 156–157.

29. Jay Coughtry, *Creative Survival*, p. 43. Also, *Memoirs of Elleanor Eld-
ridge* (2d ed., Providence, B. T. Albro, 1847), p. 47. The sea also offered
Providence blacks expanding opportunities during the nineteenth century. In fact, in 1805 at least two black seamen from Rhode Island were
impressed by the British. According to Jay Coughtry, a student of black
life in Rhode Island: "The town [of Providence] did not lack for seasoned seamen in the early national period, and, in Providence, 'Jack
Tar' was as likely to be black as white." This very real presence in our
early naval and maritime history has until now been all but invisible.
In fact, as far as the Union Army is concerned, it is worthy of mention
that ultimately nearly ten per cent of the Northern troops were black.
(This last statistic comes from Philip Cash, "Pride, Predjudice, and
Politics," *Harvard Medical Alumni Bulletin*, 54:24–25, 1980). William
M. Fowler, Jr., in *Jack Tars and Commodores*, p. 129, cites Ira Dye
("Early American Merchant Seafarers," *Proceedings of the American
Philosophical Society*, 120:331–360, 1976) as stating that nearly 18 per
cent of seamen out of Philadelphia in the periods 1796–1803 and 1812–
1815 were blacks. Fowler further states, pp. 129–130, that "perhaps as
many as 25 per cent of Oliver Hazard Perry's men on Lake Erie were
black."

30. Rhode Island Medical Society, "Minutes." See also *Communications
of the Rhode Island Medical Society*, v. 1, no. 4, Second Part [Proceed-
ings], pp. 26, 1862.

31. *Ibid.*, pp. 27–29.

32. Rhode Island Medical Society, "Minutes."

33. Seebert J. Goldowsky, "The Hospital at Portsmouth Grove," *Rhode
Island Medical Journal*, 62:733–746, 1959.

34. C. W. Parsons *Memoir*, p. 55.

35. J. W. C. Ely, "Personal Recollections of the Early History of the Rhode Island Hospital," *Providence Medical Journal*, 1:81–83, 1900.

36. *Communications of the Rhode Island Medical Society*, v. 1, no. 5, Second Part [Proceedings], pp. 34–36, 1863–1864.

37. Ibid., p. 36.

38. J. W. C. Ely, "The Rhode Island Medical Society of Fifty Years Ago," *Transactions of the Rhode Island Medical Society*, 5:570–576, 1898.

39. American Medical Association, *Transactions*, 15:9–61, 1864.

40. Charles Édouard Brown-Séquard (1817–1894), born of an American father and a French mother on the island of Mauritius, was Professor of Physiology and Pathology of the Nervous System (then a new chair) at the Harvard Medical School from 1857 to 1864. For details on the Harvard career of the peripatetic Dr. Brown-Séquard see H. Richard Tyler and Kenneth H. Tyler, "Charles Édouard Brown-Séquard: Professor of Physiology and Pathology of the Nervous System at Harvard Medical School," *Neurology*, 34:1231–1236, 1984.

41. C. W. Parsons *Memoir*, p. 47.

42. Usher Parsons to George Parsons, April 17, 1865, and Usher Parsons to George Parsons, April 18, 1865, DPC.

43. Usher Parsons, "Memoir of Honorable James F. Baldwin," *New England Historical and Genealogical Register*, 19:97–100, 1865.

44. In August of 1824, to be exact. See Chapter 9, pp. 200–201.

45. American Medical Association, *Transactions*, 16:9–67, 1865.

46. *Manufacturers & Farmers Journal* (Providence), June 12, 1865.

47. Rhode Island Medical Society, "Minutes." Also, *Communications of the Rhode Island Medical Society*, v. 1, no. 6, Second Part [Proceedings], pp. 43–45, 1865–1872.

48. *Manufacturers & Farmers Journal* (Providence), June 12, 1865.

49. Usher Parsons to George Parsons, August 14, 1865, DPC.

50. Usher Parsons to Abigail Gerrish, November 27, 1865, collection of the late Miss Georgia Stearns, Alfred, Maine. Usher told his niece, who lived in South Berwick: "I was in Kennebunk last week, and but for heavy rain should have called on you. . . . Edwin Parsons was with me. . . ."

51. The majority of these letters are in the Dwight-Parsons Collection, Brown University Library, though a few have strayed to other institutions, such as the American Antiquarian Society.

52. Caroline Owen to Usher Parsons, December 22, 1865, DPC.

53. Usher Parsons to Caroline Owen, January 12, 1866, DPC.

54. See note 25 of Chapter 7.

55. Usher Parsons, "Pepperrell Genealogy," *New England Historical and Genealogical Register*, 20:1–6, 1866.

56. C. W. Parsons *Memoir*, p. 55.

57. Benson John Lossing, *History of the War of 1812.*

58. Usher Parsons to Abigail Gerrish, June 10, 1867, collection of the late Georgia H. Stearns, Alfred, Maine.

59. Usher Parsons to Usher P. Leighton, November 20, 1864, Parsons Memorial Library, Alfred, Maine.

60. Usher Parsons, *A Centennial History of Alfred, York County, Maine. With a Supplement by Samuel M. Came, Esq.*

61. Usher Parsons to Charles Wentworth Upham, October 22, 1867, HUCC.

62. Jeremiah Lewis Diman (1831–1881) was professor of history and political economy at Brown University.

63. A Greek revival gem built in 1838, which still survives.

64. *Brown University Historical Catalogue, 1765–1904,* p. 171.

65. *Proceedings of the Opening of the Rhode Island Hospital, October 1, 1868* (Providence, Providence Press, 1868).

66. The following description derives from the *Proceedings,* cited before. The handsome structure was in the Italian Gothic style, of red brick trimmed with granite and red sandstone, built on an elevated site overlooking upper Narragansett Bay. It was oriented on a north-south axis to permit a maximum of sunlight to enter the wards. It utilized the "pavilion system," two pavilions attached to a main core central building, each two stories high. Each floor of a pavilion was occupied by a ward capaciously accommodating 30 beds—four wards in all. The central section contained the administrative offices and apartment, lecture room, library and museum, apothecary shop, accident room, operating theater, and kitchen. The operating room was on a third floor level to provide sky lighting and had a communicating instrument room, a rarity at the time, and also a small recovery room. The brick walls were extremely thick, in two layers with an air space between for insulation. The walls carried pipes vented to the outside, which entered the wards at three levels to provide ventilation. Heating was by forced steam-heated hot air, with a blower driven by a twenty-four horsepower steam engine. With the germ theory of disease still just over the horizon, "foul air" was believed to be responsible for the transmission of disease. The system of vents provided for circulation of fresh air by convection in the warm weather and by positive pressure in the winter when hot air was introduced by forced draught. There were two great towers, 142 feet tall, each accommodating a four-thousand gallon tank of fresh water pumped from springs on the hospital grounds. An up-to-date laundry and steam generating plant were in a separate building.

67. C. W. Parsons *Memoir,* p. 55.

68. *Proceedings of the Opening of the Rhode Island Hospital,* p. 21; also, Rhode Island Hospital, *Annual Reports,* 1864–1869. The biographical notes were largely extracted from obituary notices in various issues of

the *Communications of the Rhode Island Medical Society*. Within a few weeks of the dedication, two further bequests were received. The first was from Doctor Samuel Boyd Tobey, deceased at age 66, who had graduated with an M.D. from the University of Pennsylvania: The other was from Doctor Henry Wheaton Rivers, who had studied at Harvard Medical School, received his M.D. from the University of Pennsylvania, and served as resident at Pennsylvania Hospital. He died at age 56. He had served as surgeon with various contingents of the Army of the Potomac. His bequest appropriately consisted of a copy of the *United States Army and Medical Museum* and several Surgeon General's office circulars. Finally, Doctor George L. Collins, aged 48, who had received his M.D. degree from New York University, donated 250 volumes and a "cabinet of very choice pathological specimens."

69. Rhode Island Hospital, *Annual Reports*, 1864–1869.

70. Seebert J. Goldowsky, "Some Rhode Island Pioneers in Cancer Surgery," *Rhode Island Medical Journal*, 41:492–497, 512, 1958. The case is reported in full in this paper.

71. C. W. Parsons *Memoir*, p. 56.

72. Oliver Wendell Holmes to Charles W. Parsons, November 11, 1868, Barrett Collection, University of Virginia.

73. C. W. Parsons *Memoir*, p. 56.

74. "Last Will and Testament of Usher Parsons," Will Book no. 22, Probate Records, Providence, Rhode Island. Usher's will was dated July 28, 1866.

75. *Communications of the Rhode Island Medical Society for the Years 1865–72*, v. 1, no. 6, Second Part [Proceedings], pp. 329–330, 1865–1872.

76. *Providence Daily Journal*, December 21, 1868.

INDEX

Abbot, Joel, 165
Abernethy, John, 137, 138, 144n.57
Academy of Natural Sciences, 331
Adams, Jasper, 213n.7
Adams, Jasper, Mrs., 213n.7
Adams, John Quincy, 201, 202, 312
Aldrich, Henry, 282
Alexander, Francis, 188, 196n.66
Alfred, Maine, 1, 2, 267, 268, 277n.71, 423, 424
Algerine cruises, 91, 103
Algiers under the Turks, 115–116n.20. *See also* Dey of Algiers
Alibert, Jean Louis, 135, 142n.57
Allen, Candace, 175, 191–192n.18
Allen, Eliza Harriet Arnold (Mrs. Zachariah), 172, 174, 190n.5, 191n.16
Allen, Zachariah, 190n.5, 191–192n.18
Allen, Zachariah, Jr., 182, 191–192n.18, 200, 264
Almy, Anne, 188, 196n.69
Almy, Thomas C., 380
Almy, William, 188, 196n.69
American Antiquarian Society, 319, 387
American Band, The, 384, 398–399n.22
American Institute of Instruction, 283, 284
American Medical Association, 328, 329, 331–336, 340, 357, 362–366, 367, 395, 396, 417–419
Ames, Ellis, 428
Ames, Jeremiah Fisher, 203, 214n.24
Ames, Samuel, Jr., 240, 248n.46
Ammons, Gideon, 408
Anderson, James, 418
André, John, 20

Angell, Miss, 340
Anthony, Walter E., 282
Appleton, Nathan Dane, 267
Appleton, Thomas, 150
Arcade, The, 305, 321n.4
Armington, Hervey, 419
Armstrong, John, 291
Arnold, Jonathan, 185
Arnold, Richard J., 164, 172, 174, 190n.5, 345n.25
Arnold, Salmon Augustus, 347, 371–372n.37
Arnold, Samuel Greene, 351, 355
Arnold, Welcome, 190n.5
Assilini, Cavaliere Paolo, 127, 128, 140n.18
Athenaeum (Providence), 423
Avery, Ephraim K., 259

Babcock, Joshua, 193–194n.31
Baily, Ben, 24, 67
Bainbridge, William, 13, 113, 125
Baker, Samuel, 158
Baldwin, Dr., 109
Baldwin, Mr., 104
Baldwin, Sarah Parsons Pitkin, 206, 207, 419
Baltimore, 157–159
Bancroft, George, 41, 353, 354, 384, 386, 387, 404
Banks, Sir Joseph, 136, 144n.58
Barbary pirates, 91
Barclay, Robert, 50
Bard, Samuel, 152
Barnes, J., 249n.57

433